T0301335

WOMEN IN BUSINESS, 1700–1850

Women in Business, 1700–1850

Nicola Phillips

THE BOYDELL PRESS

To Sam and my parents

First published 2006
The Boydell Press, Woodbridge

ISBN 1 84383 183 X

The Boydell Press is an imprint of Boydell & Brewer Ltd
PO Box 9, Woodbridge, Suffolk IP12 3DF, UK
and of Boydell & Brewer Inc.
668 Mt Hope Avenue, Rochester, NY 14620, USA
website: www.boydellandbrewer.com

A CiP catalogue record for this book is available
from the British Library

Typeset by Keystroke, Jacaranda Lodge, Wolverhampton

Contents

CONTENTS

Illustrations

Figures

Tables

ILLUSTRATIONS

Acknowledgements

During the years it took to complete this book I have met many people who have contributed to the success of this project. There are some whose help has proved particularly invaluable who I would like to acknowledge here. First, and perhaps above all, I wish to thank Penelope Corfield in the Department of History at Royal Holloway, University of London, for her excellent supervision of the thesis on which this book was based and for her continued support in so many areas that enabled me to finish this book afterwards. I would also like to thank Amanda Vickery, whose teaching and writing provided the initial inspiration for the project, and both she and John Styles supplied useful source references and comments on drafts of chapters. The work of, and discussions with, Pam Sharpe and Deborah Simonton 'on tour' also proved very valuable. A number of people gave much needed technical information and advice on creating and managing databases. Catherine Harbor provided all the technical knowledge to construct and interrogate the database, and Edmund Green gave much-needed assistance with producing the codes and tables necessary for the analysis of data. David Barnett provided a great deal of information about insurance registers and patient discussions about data entry. Leonard Schwarz gave important advice on using historical databases, as did John Black on the design of the tables. The legal research would have been impossible without the guidance of Karen Pearlston, and Margaret Hunt and Amy Lee Erickson provided additional advice and comments. Mary Clayton painstakingly relayed every reference to women in business for two years during her work indexing Chancery pleadings for the Public Record Office, which provided the source material for Chapter 4. Linda Drury proved an invaluable guide to references to women in business in Judith Baker's papers in the Palace Green Section of Durham University Library, and Susan Bennett provided the same for the Royal Society for the Encouragement of Arts, Manufactures and Commerce papers at the RSA in London. Staff at the Guildhall Library were more than helpful in searching for information on women in business in the Sun Fire Insurance records and in their collection of trade cards and satirical prints. Numerous participants in the Long Eighteenth-century Seminar at the Institute for Historical Research have, either openly or inadvertently, aided this research through discussion and by providing references. It is perhaps invidious to single out individuals, but the list should include Michele Cohen, Amanda Goodrich, Tim Hitchcock and Susan Whyman. The research would not have been possible without the financial support provided by various grant-awarding bodies.

ACKNOWLEDGEMENTS

I would therefore like to thank Royal Holloway for the Thomas Holloway Scholarship; the Arts and Humanities Research Board for a two-year studentship; the University of London for a Central Research Fund grant for travel to Durham; the Institute of Historical Research for a Scouloudi Fellowship (2000–2001), and the Isobel Thornley Bequest Fund for supporting the publication of this book. On a more personal note, I would like to thank my parents and my aunt Eileen Moore for their unwavering support and encouragement throughout the project. I must also thank my son Sam, who has had to learn to live with an often distracted mother, for his patience. Lastly, I could not have got through the final stages without the guidance, understanding and considerable editing skills of my husband, Jonathan Phillips.

Abbreviations

BL	British Library
BPP	*British Parliamentary Papers*
ER	*The English Reports* (1220–1867, CD-Rom)
GL	Guildhall Library
LDA	London *Daily Advertiser*
OED	*Oxford English Dictionary*
PRO	Public Record Office
RSA	Archive of the Royal Society for the Encouragement of Arts, Manufacture and Commerce
UDL/PG	University of Durham Library, Palace Green Section

This book is produced with the assistance
of a grant from Isobel Thornley's Bequest to the
University of London

1

Introduction

The business of life or a life in business

We go on talking as if it were still true that every woman is, or ought to be
supported by her father, brother, or husband. . . . We are (probably to a man)
unaware of the amount of the business of life in England done by women; and
if we do not attend to the fact in time, the knowledge will be forced on us in
some disadvantageous or disagreeable way.

                                                       Harriet Martineau (1859)[1]

Business is just life, and we had life long before we had business.
                                                     Edith Mae Cummings (1929)[2]

For women today, the distinction between the business of daily life and business
as an economic activity is probably as relevant a question – particularly
with the advent of 'home-working' and 'the virtual office' – as it was in the
eighteenth and early nineteenth centuries. For Harriet Martineau and Edith
Mae Cummings the two appear to have been inextricably linked. For most
historians of women's work in this period, however, the idea that the business
of life and the business of making a profit could be seen as interlinked activities
for women is rare. Even though, in economic terms, all business depends
on the generation of profit, the pursuit of which is a common goal for men
and women regardless of gender, racial or class differences, it is these very differences that are most often highlighted at the expense of other considerations.
Business has been located primarily within an economic public sphere and
gendered as masculine. By contrast women's daily lives have been described
primarily in terms of a private domestic sphere, which is gendered as feminine.
The success of 'domestic' enterprises run by women from home tends not to
be calculated in the same terms as those of burgeoning corporate ventures,
although the modern emphasis on achieving a better work/life balance may
force a reassessment of the ways it is measured. Since women have remained
largely invisible in histories of economic enterprise, narratives that seek to
redress this gender-blind approach focus chiefly on hierarchies of difference,

---

[1] Harriet Martineau, 'Female Industry', *The Edinburgh Review*, 109 (1859), p. 298.
[2] Edith Mae Cummings, *Pots, Pans and Millions: A Study of Woman's Right to be in Business*
(Washington, 1929), p. 100.

particularly along the lines of gender and class. Yet, while it remains paramount to consider the inequalities of power implicit within social categories of difference, it is also important to examine areas of co-operation and common interaction between men and women, families and friends, and notions of public and private.[3] This book aims to retain this broader focus while analysing the role of women in business from 1700 to 1850 and the impact of changing perceptions of gender on that role.

The term 'business' can have many meanings, and those meanings have also shifted subtly over time. Originally stemming from 'busy', the word still incorporates notions of industrious employment in a 'multiplicity of affairs' not necessarily connected with trade. Daniel Defoe seems to have been one of the first to use the word in terms of 'trade, commercial transactions or engagements' in his famous advice book, *The Complete English Tradesman* (1727). In 1768, however, Dr Johnson listed 'business' and 'employment' as synonymous, but only 'trade' was solely connected with commerce and monetary exchange.[4] Perhaps this was one reason why it was possible for a woman seeking a partnership in a chandlery shop to advertise in 1765 that 'A Sober Woman would be glad to be in business', while another could emphasise that investing in a girls' boarding-school would be far safer 'than to risk it in trade'.[5] In the eighteenth century at least, to be in business suggested a broader and less vulgar enterprise than to be in trade. In this book, the term 'business' has been chosen precisely because it could include the economic enterprises of women from a wide range of social backgrounds. It might equally be applied to the activities of women of very limited means struggling to make ends meet, of middling-sort women aspiring to gentility, and to those of the higher orders who would have disdained to see themselves 'in trade'. Today, entering business is seen chiefly as a means of upward mobility but for many in the earlier period, while money remained a key motivation, it was a final resort intended to prevent a further decline in their social or economic status.

Tracing women in business in the past is a difficult task; they tend to be obscured from the record by law and custom, which gave primacy to the identities of their male relatives, and by the often informal organisation of their enterprises. Defining women in business is equally difficult. The *OED* only quotes usage of the term 'business woman' from 1844. Although this suggests a degree of acceptance of their role rather earlier than might be expected, it does mean that, strictly speaking, reference to businesswomen in

[3] Mary A. Yeager, 'Review of Angel Kwolek-Folland, *Incorporating Women: A History of Women and Business in the United States*', H-Business, H-Net Reviews, April, 1999. URL: http://www.h-net.msu.edu/reviews/showrev.cgi?path=30313927576847, pp. 14–16, presses for a greater focus on the interaction between men and women in business.

[4] *OED* sub: 'Business'; *Samuel Johnson, Dictionary of the English Language* (3rd edn, 1768), sub: 'Business', 'Employment', 'Trade'.

[5] *LDA*, 8 November 1765; 5 August 1765. For an extended discussion of these and other advertisements placed by women in business see below, pp. 203–29.

the eighteenth century could be considered anachronistic, even if the activities they engaged in conform to our expectations of independent economic enterprise. Mary Yeager has pointed out that, 'as an activity business confounds with multiple meanings and definitions': it includes production, trade, agriculture, manufacturing, service and retail; it also encompasses producers, professionals, entrepreneurs, workers, administrators and managers.[6] In this book the definition of business is narrowed somewhat because it does not include those entering it as a form of paid employment. Women in business are thus defined here as any females, whether in partnership or alone, who owned any independent unit of production or service. This definition includes those who were independently self-employed and those who were involved in, sometimes multiple, partnerships with men or other women. The notion of 'ownership' did not necessarily include proof of hands-on daily activity in the business and there was no restriction on size or profitability. Nor did the business need to be the sole, or even the main, source of income. Indeed, in some cases, it included a projected income that may never have materialised. The focus here then is solely upon women running businesses rather than upon the rather different issues relating to women's waged labour; it is, none the less, overwhelmingly towards the latter that debates about changes in women's economic role have focused.

Continuity vs. change: women's economic position, 1700–1850

In an attempt to provide a historical basis for women's current inequality in the workplace the historiography of women's work has ploughed some deep and well-worn theoretical furrows.[7] Most accounts focus chiefly around long-term models of linear change. However, within the commonly argued case for women's declining economic opportunities and an increasing separation of the public sphere of work from the private sphere of home, there are a number of complex and overlapping debates. One issue is the question of whether the advent of capitalistic or industrial modes of production restricted or improved women's position in society. Yet for those who see the persistence of patriarchal power as the chief factor in restricting women's economic opportunities, there is little question of any change at all.[8] Then there are debates over the change in the dominant mode of production from a family-based economy at home

---

[6] Yeager, 'Review of Angel Kwolek-Folland', p. 2.

[7] Amanda Vickery, 'Golden Age to Separate Spheres? A Review of the Categories and Chronology of English Women's History', *Historical Journal*, 36 (1993), pp. 383–414, critiques the two main historical narratives of women's work.

[8] For the uncertainties of definition and chronology of organising categories such as 'capitalism' and 'patriarchy', see below, pp. 6–8.

to more mechanised production outside the home and how far the separation of work and home created specifically gendered separate spheres of activity for men and women. There is also considerable argument over the concepts and chronologies used to link narratives of industrial change and rapid economic growth to a story of class formation. Often, the rise of a powerful middle class with its own distinctive cultural identity is seen as crucial in narratives of how new perceptions of sexual difference were mapped on to the public/private division to create a domestic ideology that confined women to the home.

The two seminal works that still serve as a starting point for many studies are Alice Clark's *Working Life of Women in the Seventeenth Century*,[9] and Ivy Pinchbeck's *Women Workers and the Industrial Revolution*.[10] Both books are chiefly concerned with the effects of capitalism/industrialisation on the lives of working women and consequently the changing position of women in society, but they locate that change in different centuries. Clark argued that women's economic power declined during the seventeenth century with the advent of increasingly capitalistic forms of industry, which removed production from the home. Pinchbeck found that increasing industrial change in the eighteenth century robbed women of economic opportunities but argued that it had beneficial effects in the very long term. More recently historians have divided into those who, like Peter Earle, believe that Clark's model of decline was 'more or less right',[11] and those who, like Bridget Hill and Tilly and Scott, favour Pinchbeck.[12] In the latter case, a U-shaped model is implied, with initial decline followed later by improvement in the twentieth century.

Nevertheless, the central concern of much recent scholarship, divided by Janet Thomas[13] into 'optimists' versus 'pessimists', remains the view that capitalism and/or industrialisation[14] was a watershed for women's experience of work. This approach relies implicitly or explicitly on an assumption about

[9] Alice Clark, *Working Life of Women in the Seventeenth Century* (1919; reprinted London, 1992).

[10] Ivy Pinchbeck, *Women Workers and the Industrial Revolution, 1750–1850* (1930; reprinted London, 1981).

[11] Peter Earle, *The Making of the English Middle Class: Business, Society and Family Life in London, 1660–1730* (London, 1989), p. 166.

[12] Bridget Hill, *Women, Work and Sexual Politics in Eighteenth-century England* (1989; reprinted London, 1994); Louise A. Tilly and Joan W. Scott, *Women, Work and Family* (1978; reprinted London, 1987); Eric Richards, 'Women in the British Economy Since about 1700: An Interpretation', *History*, 59 (1974), pp. 337–57.

[13] Janet Thomas, 'Women and Capitalism: Oppression or Emancipation? A Review Article', *Comparative Studies in Society and History*, 30 (1990), pp. 535–49.

[14] As Thomas points out there is some confusion regarding the use of the terms 'industrialism', 'capitalism', 'modernisation', and 'urbanisation' which requires clarifying, as do the chronologies attached to these concepts which also vary considerably. Amy Erickson also criticises Clark's conflation of 'industrial' and 'capital' in her Introduction to the third edition of Clark, *Working Life* (1992), pp. vii–x.

a medieval 'golden age' of economic opportunity for women which has proved notoriously difficult to locate.[15] It also corresponds with traditional narratives of 'the industrial revolution' as a period of dramatic transformation, although this view too has been seriously undermined by recent scholarship stressing the more gradual nature of change.[16] Yet this 'revisionism' in turn is also coming under attack; and there are now calls to study both the continuities and discontinuities of industrialisation on a regional basis along with the social and cultural impact of such changes.[17] Although this indicates a general lack of consensus, it nevertheless suggests that histories of women's work should no longer be tied to overarching narratives of a nation-wide transformation in methods of manufacturing and production.

One of the most commonly highlighted features of industrial change for women is the belief that there was a transition from a pre- or proto-industrial family or household economy to a waged economy, making home and work increasingly separate.[18] According to this view, women could no longer work with their husbands at home but became increasingly dependent on the male breadwinner's wage.[19] There has, however, been a growing criticism of models based on the conception of an idyllic pre-industrial family unit of production.[20] The notion of universally harmonious family relations of shared domestic

[15] There is a fierce debate between those like Caroline Barron, 'The "Golden Age" of Women in Medieval London', *Reading Medieval Studies*, 15 (1989), pp. 35–58, who argue that women were economically active in the medieval period, and others like Maryanne Kowaleski, 'Women's Work in a Market Town: Exeter in the Late Fourteenth Century', in *Women and Work in Preindustrial Europe*, ed. Barbara Hanawalt (Bloomington, 1986), pp. 145–64, who argue that women's work was always restricted. Others like Martha C. Howell, 'Women, the Family Economy, and the Structures of Market Production in Cities of Northern Europe during the Late Middle Ages', in ibid., pp. 198–222, see a decline beginning in the sixteenth century.

[16] For the view that 'less happened, less dramatically than was once thought', see David Cannadine, 'British History: Past, Present and Future?', *Past and Present*, 116 (1987), pp. 131–72.

[17] For an overview of the changing historiography on the speed and extent of industrial change but arguing for the concept to be retained, see Pat Hudson, *The Industrial Revolution* (London, 1992); and Maxine Berg and Pat Hudson, 'Rehabilitating the Industrial Revolution', *Economic History Review*, 45 (1992), pp. 24–50. See also Katrina Honeyman, *Women, Gender and Industrialisation in England, 1700–1870* (Basingstoke and London, 2000), pp. 9–14.

[18] For a discussion of how the idea of a family economy underpins most writing on women's work and a European-wide perspective, see Deborah Simonton, *A History of European Women's Work, 1700 to the Present* (London, 1998), pp. 17–18, 37–47.

[19] Sara Howell and Jane Humphries, 'Women's Labour Force Participation and the Transition to the Male Breadwinner Family, 1790–1865', *Economic History Review*, 48 (1995), pp. 89–117.

[20] Maxine Berg, 'Women's Work, Mechanisation and the Early Phases of Industrialisation in England', in *The Historical Meanings of Work*, ed. Patrick Joyce (London, 1987), pp. 64–98, argues that the concept of the household economy is a 'myth'.

production has also been revised to allow for a greater degree of family conflict over economic matters.[21] Domestic industry is now thought to have been far more diversely organised than these models allow and not to have followed any one route towards industrial production.[22] Studies have also shown that wives, particularly in towns, frequently worked at separate trades from their husbands, although as Joanne Bailey has shown, there is no clear correlation between spouses' work patterns and the quality of their marital relationship.[23] Nevertheless, the separation of work and home remains the dominant paradigm for analysing women's experience of industrialisation. In socialist feminist accounts, class issues are linked to explanations of how the separation of work and home contributed to an increasingly gendered division of labour outside the home. Women's childbearing activities are held to have formed the 'natural' basis for such a division of labour,[24] and capitalism ensured women's economic dependence on their husbands. This meant that with the ending of an idyllic 'handicraft era' women working outside the home became increasingly marginalised in occupations designated as 'feminine', which were deemed unskilled, and so became low-paid and overcrowded.[25]

If narratives of universal dramatic change are problematic, those which deny any change are equally so. For radical feminists, who argue that society has always been organised around institutions of patriarchal power, women's work has constantly been seen as lower paid, less skilled and of lower status than

[21] Margaret Hunt, *The Middling Sort: Commerce, Gender and the Family in England, 1680–1780* (Berkeley and London, 1996), pp. 134–42. Tilly and Scott, *Women, Work and Family* (revised edn London, 1987), p. 9, also conceded that their earlier model did not allow for conflict between family members.

[22] Hill, *Women, Work and Sexual Politics*, p. 22, has critiqued the separation of work and home by problematising terms like 'household' or 'family economy' but nevertheless retains the basic framework.

[23] Joanne Bailey, *Unquiet Lives: Marriage and Marriage Breakdown in England, 1660–1800* (Cambridge, 2003), pp. 93, 96–7, 197–8, found that twenty-three out of forty-three couples in ecclesiastical records of marital difficulties worked in separate trades. Peter Earle, 'The Female Labour Market in London in the Late Seventeenth and Early Eighteenth Centuries', *Economic History Review*, 2 ser., 42 (1989), pp. 328–53, found that of 256 wives who listed their employment in church court depositions only twenty-six were engaged in the same trade as their husbands. Dorothy George, *London Life in the Eighteenth Century* (1925; reprinted 1966), pp. 425–8, found that of eighty-six married couples whose occupations were listed in Old Bailey sessions papers, only two shared the same trade.

[24] Hunt, *Middling Sort*, p. 134, challenges functional biological arguments for gender-segregated work outside the home, and argues that eighteenth-century women were most likely to work outside the home during their childbearing years because low fertility rates meant few children, and these were usually cared for by servants or female relatives.

[25] Sally Alexander, *Women's Work in Nineteenth Century London: A Study of the Years 1820–50* (London, 1983). For a non-Marxist variant, see also Mary Prior, 'Women and the Urban Economy: Oxford, 1500–1800', *Women in English Society 1500–1800*, ed. M. Prior (London, 1985), p. 113, arguing that the concentration of women in millinery and mantua-making led to their exploitation in the nineteenth century.

men's.[26] They seek to avoid the charge of denying historical change by emphasising the protean nature of patriarchy, arguing that the social and institutional arrangements which reinforce male hegemony can remain dormant for long periods, only to reappear in times of gender conflict.[27] This has given rise to fierce debates over the issues of continuity and change in women's work, which are broadly aligned to whether capitalism (change) or patriarchy (continuity) is considered the dominant factor.[28] Attempts by socialist feminists to consider the effects of both capitalism and patriarchy have resulted in either a dual systems analysis, or an attempt to combine the two as 'patriarchal capitalism'.[29] Another 'solution' has been to envisage the competing interests of capitalism and patriarchy resolved through a concept of paternalism, which also serves to link systems of gender and class.[30] Yet, more recently, models describing the working of patriarchal power in early modern households have been significantly revised. Alexandra Shepard has argued that although patriarchal status theoretically rested on men's economic independence in providing for their families, many men were unable to realise this ideal.[31] The economic survival of households therefore 'required adaptability and the best possible use of resources, rather than adherence to a patriarchal blueprint'. In practice, this meant the engagement of many married women in commercial pursuits. Similarly, Bailey has argued that both spouses' labour and earnings helped to forge a greater interdependence, and although this cannot be said to have necessarily improved the quality of their emotional relationship it did foster a model of marriage based on co-dependency rather than hierarchical patriarchal power.[32] What remains to be seen is whether the practical subversion

[26] See, controversially, Judith Bennett, '"History that Stands Still": Women's Work in the European Past', *Feminist Studies*, 14 (1988), pp. 269–83, and idem, 'Medieval Women, Modern Women: Across the Great Divide', in *Culture and History, 1350–1600: Essays on English Communities, Identities and Writing*, ed. David Aers (London, 1992), pp. 145–75.
[27] Katrina Honeyman and Jordan Goodman, 'Women's Work, Gender Conflict, and Labour Markets in Europe, 1500–1900', *Economic History Review*, 44 (1991), pp. 608–28.
[28] See esp. the debate in which Bridget Hill accuses Judith Bennett of undermining the project of women's history and isolating it from mainstream history. Bridget Hill, 'Women's History: A Study in Change, Continuity or Standing Still', *Women's History Review*, 1 (1993), pp. 5–19; and Judith Bennett, 'Women's History: A Study in Continuity and Change', *Women's History Review*, 2 (1993), pp. 173–84.
[29] See e.g. Sylvia Walby, *Patriarchy at Work: Patriarchal and Capitalist Relations in Employment* (Minneapolis, 1986).
[30] For a comprehensive study based on this approach, see Judy Lown, *Women and Industrialization: Gender at Work in Nineteenth-century England* (Oxford, 1990). By envisaging several interlinking sets of social relations Lown seeks to dissolve the concept of two separate spheres.
[31] Alexandra Shepard, 'Manhood, Credit and Patriarchy in early modern England c. 1580–1640', *Past & Present*, 167 (2000), pp. 75–106.
[32] Bailey, *Unquiet Lives*, esp. pp. 96–7, 193–4, but she remains pessimistic about the extent to which co-dependency meant that wives were able to derive any wider 'institutional, political or legal power'.

of patriarchy in the household could have wider implications for institutionalised patriarchy.

Nevertheless, the preponderance of literature based on feminist categories of analysis linked either to the transformations wrought by capitalism or the persistence of patriarchy has resulted in the widespread assumption that there are only two ways to discuss women's economic opportunities; that is, that they were always limited, or that they became more so after the Industrial Revolution. This was how Leonard Schwarz framed the question when researching women's employment in London by comparing eighteenth-century insurance records with the 1851 census. His findings, which were chiefly for waged employment, showed that women were employed in broadly the same occupations in both periods.[33] By contrast Catherine Hall has argued that women's economic activities narrowed in the nineteenth century. Using trade directories, she found that, although the percentage of women engaged in business rose, the types of business run by women declined in the early nineteenth century.[34] Although the trade directories suggest an increasing concentration of women in 'feminine' trades (as opposed to an outright decline), the assumption is that marginalisation rather than specialisation lies behind the change. In other words these narratives of women's work have been largely determined by the old analytical categories, but while the analytical categories themselves have now been questioned, the boundaries to debates about women's economic opportunities have shifted very little.

In a review of the literature on women's economic roles, Pamela Sharpe has argued convincingly that 'neither change nor continuity is satisfactory as an explanatory or descriptive scheme'.[35] She points out not only the 'nebulous character of the benchmarks' used for making quantitative comparisons but also that uneven economic development could affect groups of women differently, so that specialisation could benefit some but reduce opportunities for others.[36] Retailing, for example, used to be seen as another area in which the advent of new commercial practices in the nineteenth century drove women out of business.[37] Yet recent research suggests that in some areas women

---

[33] Leonard Schwarz, *London in the Age of Industrialisation: Entrepreneurs, Labour Force and Living Conditions, 1700–1850* (Cambridge, 1992), pp. 14–22. Peter Earle, 'The Female Labour Market', pp. 328–53, also stressed broad continuities.

[34] Catherine Hall, 'Gender Divisions and Class Formation in the Birmingham Middle Class, 1780–1850', in idem (ed.), *White, Male and Middle Class: Explorations in Feminism and History* (Cambridge, 1992; reprinted 1995), p. 99.

[35] Pamela Sharpe, 'Continuity and Change: Women's History and Economic History in Britain', *Economic History Review*, 48 (1995), pp. 353–69.

[36] Ibid., pp. 358–9.

[37] Older narratives describing women's increasing marginalisation within retailing were linked to notions of both the industrial revolution and/or a mid-nineteenth-century retailing revolution. See e.g. David Alexander, *Retailing in England During the Industrial Revolution* (Edinburgh, 1970); Catherine Hall, 'The Butcher, the Baker, the Candlestick-maker: The

could benefit from increasing consumer demand for new and luxury goods.[38] Sharpe's study of labouring women in Essex between 1700 and 1850 showed that 'adapting to capitalism was not a unilinear process'.[39] While there was an increasing disparity between male and female wages in trades such as spinning, opportunities for women increased in the Essex fashion trades and in some areas of agriculture.[40]

Throughout all these debates there has been a marked bifurcation of studies, which focus either on working-class women at work or upon the idleness of middle-class women and the growth of domestic ideology.[41] Within this view, an ever-increasing amount of literature prescribed how the ideal wife and mother should best exercise her superior moral influence from within the home where she could provide the necessary support for her husband to run his business. In addition to the assumption that the majority of middle-class women were at home, one of the reasons why so little work has been done on their economic activities is the lack of conceptual space available when class is used as the primary paradigm for relations of power. Most accounts have focused on labouring women as the victims, or at least employees, of middle-class male capitalists. Middle-class women in business do not fit comfortably into either the Marxist category of exploited workers or the feminist category of exploited women. Even more problematic is the need to conceptualise successful businesswomen both as female capitalists and, sometimes in ethical terms, as the oppressors of other women whose labour they exploited. Accounts of poor exploited seamstresses, for example, are numerous,[42] but references to their female employers are negligible.

Shop and the Family in the Industrial Revolution', in idem, *White Male and Middle Class*, pp. 108–123.
[38] For the diversity of eighteenth-century shopkeeping practices see Neil McKendrick, John Brewer and J.H. Plumb (eds), *The Birth of a Consumer Society: The Commercialisation of Eighteenth-century England* (London, 1982) and H.C. and L.H. Mui, *Shops and Shopkeeping in Eighteenth-century England* (London, 1989). For women's trading opportunities, see also Hunt, *Middling Sort*, pp. 132–4; Pamela Sharpe, *Adapting to Capitalism: Working Women in the English Economy, 1700–1850* (London, 1996), pp. 17–18.
[39] Ibid., p. 149.
[40] Ibid., pp. 149–53.
[41] Jane Rendall's synthesis of women's work, *Women in an Industrialising Society: England, 1750–1880* (Oxford, 1990), clearly associates working-class women and work and middle-class women with the growth of domestic ideology.
[42] For work on the image of the poor seamstress, see Beth Harris, '"The Works of Women are Symbolical": The Victorian Seamstress in the 1840s' (Ph.D., City University of New York, 1997), pp. 11–15; for studies of milliners which focus only on the apprentices, see Alexander, *Women's Work*, pp. 34–6; Wanda Fraiken Neff, *Victorian Working Women: An Historical and Literary Study of Women in British Industries and Professions, 1832–50* (1929; reprinted London, 1966), pp. 115–50.

The chronology for the decline of middle-class women from 'stirring activity' to 'the triumph of the useless woman'[43] is vague and contested. One of the reasons for this is the lack of agreement about which period the middle class may actually be said to have 'emerged'.[44] Another is the existence of research that questions just how separate commercial middle-class culture was from that of other landed gentry families.[45] For Peter Earle, 1660 to 1730 are the seminal dates for the making of the middle class, which also witnessed a growth of literature complaining that wives refused to become involved with business.[46] Margaret Hunt follows a similar chronology, placing the middling sort as a distinct section of society between 1680 and 1730.[47] Many literary historians' narratives about eighteenth-century women of the middling sort focus upon the creation of the 'proper lady' in print culture and particularly upon the explosion of didactic literature on the subject.[48] Yet John Tosh has argued that, while women have long been associated with the home, the heyday of the Victorian cult of domesticity, which was equally aimed at men, was dominant for only two generations from 1830 to the 1870s.[49] Wahrman's analysis supports this chronology, by locating a shift in middle-class identity from representing a masculine public opinion to a focus on domestic virtue after 1832.[50] However, for Leonore Davidoff and Catherine Hall, the formation of the middle class and its adoption of a specific oppositional culture, commensurate with its new-found wealth and power, took place between 1780 and 1850.[51]

[43] Ibid., p. 186; Neff follows Alice Clark in seeing the process as completed by the eighteenth century.
[44] See Dror Wahrman, *Imagining the Middle Class: The Political Representation of Class in Britain, c.1780–1840* (Cambridge, 1995), pp. 1–10; David Cannadine, *Class in Britain* (1998; reprinted London, 2000), pp. 8–15.
[45] Amanda Vickery, *The Gentleman's Daughter: Women's Lives in Georgian England* (New Haven and London, 1998), pp. 3, 13–37, critiques the ever-emerging middle class and argues for the existence of greater social interaction between the commercial and landed classes.
[46] Earle, *Making of the English Middle Class*.
[47] Hunt, *Middling Sort*.
[48] Kathryn Shevelow, *Women and Print Culture: The Construction of Femininity in the Early Periodical* (London, 1989); Mary Poovey, *The Proper Lady and the Woman Writer: Ideology as Style in the Works of Mary Wollstonecraft, Mary Shelley and Jane Austen* (London, 1984). Nancy Armstrong, in *Desire and Domestic Fiction: A Political History of the Novel* (Oxford, 1987), pp. 16–17, offers a more balanced view, arguing that idealised representations of women co-existed with misogynous and even proto-feminist writings. See also Ingrid Tague, *Women of Quality: Accepting and Contesting Ideals of Feminity in England, 1690–1760* (Woodbridge, 2002), p. 21, on how conduct books did not represent the only discourse of feminity.
[49] John Tosh, *A Man's Place: Masculinity and the Middle-class Home in Victorian England* (London, 1999), pp. 5–6.
[50] Wahrman, *Imagining the Middle Class*, pp. 377–408.
[51] Leonore Davidoff and Catherine Hall, *Family Fortunes: Men and Women of the English Middle Class, 1780–1850* (London, 1987).

Davidoff and Hall's *Family Fortunes* has arguably become the most classic articulation of the formation of a doctrine of gendered separate spheres based on a Marxist conception of class. Although some distinction is made between the higher and lower middle classes, Evangelicalism and domestic ideology form the central pillars of a unifying and specifically middle-class culture. Within this schema, the majority of middle-class women became the archetypal 'angels in the house' and their only access to the world of economic enterprise was by making a 'hidden investment' in the family business.[52] The legal restrictions on women regarding property are seen as a major impediment to their economic activities, causing women to be considered 'poor credit risks', and preventing them from raising finances through institutional sources as men did. The lack of property as capital is theoretically the chief element in 'social closure'; that is, their 'exclusion from control over one's own life chances'.[53] However, there were a few exceptions. Widows are allowed to have been independent but only 'temporary incumbents' of their husbands' enterprises. Moreover, these women are represented as an extreme case of lack of male support. Women in 'active occupations' are assumed to be widows or spinsters, partly because some sources recorded occupations only for these groups. For Davidoff and Hall, the few women in 'trade' were generally characterised by their confinement to less capitalised, less formal enterprises with quick turnovers and short credit runs, in low-status occupations such as retailing. It is argued that, although married women could start their own small businesses, the loss of status and the enticements of domesticity, coupled with the increased scale and technical advances in manufacturing enterprises, meant that fewer and fewer did so. In sum, for Davidoff and Hall women were increasingly marginalised in the economy from the late eighteenth century onwards.[54]

Some localised case studies have in fact shown that 'genteel' women were in business, although primarily in the 'feminine' trades of millinery and mantua-making, but the most common conclusion is that even this limited form of economic enterprise decreased in the nineteenth century.[55] In a broader study, Margaret Hunt has shown women operating as a matter of course in the eighteenth-century marketplace, but there is an all-too-brief examination

---

[52] See also Catherine Hall, 'Strains in the "Firm of Wife, Children and Friends": Middle-class Women and Employment in Early Nineteenth-century England', in idem, *White, Male and Middle Class*, pp. 172–202.

[53] Davidoff and Hall, *Family Fortunes*, p. 278ff., for women and property; p. 315 for social closure.

[54] Ibid., pp. 301–15.

[55] Shani D'Cruz, '"To Acquaint the Ladies": Women Traders in Colchester, c.1750–c.1800', *Local Historian*, 17, (1986), pp. 158–61; Elizabeth Sanderson, 'The Edinburgh Milliners, 1720–1820', *Costume*, 20 (1986), pp. 18–28, and idem, *Women and Work in Eighteenth-century Edinburgh* (New York, 1996).

of their actual trading activities and greater emphasis on the prescriptive literature aimed at limiting the aspirations of daughters. Hunt's terminal date of 1780 prevents any speculation about nineteenth-century developments.[56] In Deborah Valenze's study of changing representations of working women, eighteenth-century praise of women's productivity vanishes in the nineteenth century, which in her view entirely lacked a vocabulary of praise.[57] Middle-class women are portrayed only as proselytising to the poor, and women in business are not discussed at all. Yet other historians have challenged the very existence of a nineteenth-century idle, middle-class 'angel in the house'. Jeanne Peterson argues that only upper-middle-class women had enough privacy, prosperity and leisure to fulfil the role, and her micro-study of the Paget family shows that these women had too many choices and opportunities to want to join movements for suffrage. For Paget, the 'angel' was an aspirational ideal for lower-middle-class wives rather than a reality.[58]

The whole question of separate spheres has generated extensive debate among academics attempting to dissolve or to reformulate the boundaries, of the public and private.[59] There have, for example, been attempts to end the polarities implicit within such a framework by theorising the existence of a third sphere of public activity or the existence of a grey area between the two.[60] Leonore Davidoff has posited the existence of several public spheres, but argues that these are nevertheless explicitly gendered as masculine. This had material effects upon women, which reached an apogee in the nineteenth century.[61] Jane Rendall also posits the existence of multiple public and private spheres, but does not view gender as the single overriding factor in determining

[56] Hunt, *Middling Sort*, pp 125–6, 145–46, remains on the whole agnostic over the question of women's retreat from trade, identifying factors that could have both encouraged and inhibited their participation.

[57] Deborah Valenze, *The First Industrial Woman* (Oxford, 1995).

[58] M. Jeanne Peterson, 'No Angels in the House: The Victorian Myth and the Paget Women', *American Historical Review*, 89 (1984), pp. 677–708.

[59] Linda Kerber, 'Separate Spheres, Female Worlds, Woman's Place: The Rhetoric of Women's History', *Journal of American History*, 75 (1988), pp. 9–39, and idem *et al.*, 'Beyond Roles, Beyond Spheres: Thinking about Gender in the Early Republic', *William and Mary Quarterly*, 46 (1989), pp. 565–85. For a comprehensive discussion of the literature, see Hannah Barker and Elaine Chalus' 'Introduction' to *Gender in Eighteenth Century England: Roles, Representations and Responsibilities*, ed. H. Barker and E. Chalus (London, 1997), esp. pp. 18–24.

[60] Dena Goodman, 'Public Sphere and Private Life: Toward a Synthesis of Current Historiographical Approaches to the Old Regime', *History and Theory*, 31 (1992), pp. 1–20; John Brewer, 'This, That and the Other: Public, Social and Private in the Seventeenth and Eighteenth Centuries', in *Shifting the Boundaries: The Transformation of the Languages of Public and Private in the Eighteenth Century*, ed. D. Castiglione and L. Sharpe (Exeter, 1995), pp. 1–21.

[61] Leonore Davidoff, 'Regarding Some "Old Husband's Tales": Public and Private in Feminist History', in idem, *Worlds Between: Historical Perspectives on Gender and Class* (London, 1995), pp. 227–76.

these oppositions.[62] Many historians no longer consider the boundaries of public and private to be impervious, or fixed to any specific physical location, and accept that their meanings are relative and historically contingent.[63] Amanda Vickery's critique has perhaps done more than any other to undermine the analytic purchase of this ubiquitous metaphor to account for social and political developments in any particular century or for Victorian class formation. To establish a more credible chronology, she has called for a more integrated approach to studying a range of debates about women's role in society, found in a wide variety of sources, rather than the narrow focus on domestic ideology.[64] More recent syntheses of research in women's history have also come to question the usefulness of the separate spheres model and to call for new conceptual approaches that acknowledge a far wider diversity of experience.[65] Although the right to work is seen as important today, it is also important to acknowledge that the acquisition of greater leisure would have been welcomed by many women. Perhaps even more significantly, some studies are now beginning to revise the sad story of decline and separation, opening the door for a revised assessment of women's economic roles during the period.[66]

To summarise, then, the main picture that emerges from the majority of accounts is one of women in business being increasingly marginalised into low-status, unprofitable feminine trades, or removed from the scene altogether by the impact of domestic ideology. Those few women who could have been left in trade after centuries of marginalisation were severely hampered by a legal system that prevented married women from owning property or making contracts. Some women could claim *feme sole* status, which enabled them to trade as if single, under local borough customs. Yet these customs are also believed to have become increasingly rare so that by the nineteenth century only women in the City of London could claim the privilege.[67] The combination of legal and ideological restraints made it difficult for women to raise credit and capital for their businesses, which therefore relied on short credit runs and were generally under-capitalised. For the majority of women, forays

---

[62] Jane Rendall, 'Women and the Public Sphere', *Gender and History*, 2 (1999), pp. 475–88.

[63] Robert Shoemaker, *Gender in English Society, 1650–1850: The Emergence of Separate Spheres?* (London, 1998), p. 318, concludes that the period witnessed an 'accentuation' rather than emergence of separate spheres that never became watertight. Michele Cohen, *Fashioning Masculinity: National Identity and Language in the Eighteenth-Century* (London, 1996), pp. 66–7, emphasises the shifting meanings of 'public' and 'private'.

[64] Vickery, 'Golden Age to Separate Spheres?', pp. 412–13.

[65] Barker and Chalus, 'Introduction', in idem (eds), *Gender*, p. 24.

[66] Hannah Barker, 'Women, Work and the Industrial Revolution: Female Involvement in the English Printing Trades, c. 1700–1840', and Susan Skedd, 'Women Teachers and the Expansion of Girls' Schooling in England, c. 1760–1820', in *Gender in Eighteenth-century England*, ed. Barker and Chalus. See also Sharpe, *Adapting to Capitalism*, pp. 149–53.

[67] Prior, 'Women and the Urban Economy', p. 103.

into the world of business are therefore generally thought to have been of short duration and limited by marriage and their life cycles to spinsters or widows. Middle-class women in particular apparently avoided business wherever possible by raising enough income from rentals to support their aspirations to leisured gentility, or by ensuring that their husbands earned enough to maintain their social pretensions.[68] One of the key aims of this study is to re-evaluate the rather limited picture painted above in the light of recent research, which has cast so much doubt on the old categories of analysis such as class, industrial revolution, separate spheres and the usefulness of linear narratives to explain complex social and economic change.

Concepts and categories

Class is a notoriously difficult concept to define. Having stressed the broad social range of women who found themselves in business, it is important to note that the vast majority of women featured in this book could nevertheless be broadly defined as the 'middling sort'. In one way this exemplifies one of the major criticisms levelled at the notion of a 'middle class': that it is so vague that it includes anyone below the rank of aristocrat but above the labouring poor. However, the existence of women from a broad range of social backgrounds with widely varying incomes is not a problem in itself, rather it is the mode of representing them that needs examining. The emergence of specifically 'middle-class' women has come to assume great importance because of feminist arguments about the impact of domestic ideology. Yet Nancy Armstrong argues that eighteenth-century conduct books were aimed at readers from all social levels, so that it was the books themselves that gave the impression of a unified middle class when 'other representations of the social world suggest that no such class yet existed'.[69] However, as Dror Wahrman has stressed, many historians have ignored 'the degree of freedom which actually exists in the space between social reality and its representation'.[70] In her polemical article of 1859, Harriet Martineau linked the *increasing* 'need and supply of female industry' to 'the uprising of a middle class', the roots of which she located in an imagined and unspecified late medieval period.[71] Language can thus be both an inadequate and frequently politically determined guide to the many gradations of social status shaped by birth and/or income. Indeed, Penelope Corfield has shown that there were multiple terminologies

[68] See Peter Earle, *A City Full of People: Men and Women of London, 1650–1750* (London, 1994), p. 150, and idem, *Making of the English Middle Class*, pp. 163–6, for middle-class wives' foolish pretensions to idle gentility.
[69] Armstrong, *Desire and Domestic Fiction*, p. 63.
[70] Wahrman, *Imagining the Middle Class*, p. 6.
[71] Martineau, 'Female Industry', p. 298.

of social status or position circulating in the eighteenth century.[72] While 'class' as a socio-economic label was in common usage by 1750, the older categories of 'rank' and 'order' were still preferred as descriptions of social status conferred by birth. Moreover, even where 'class' was the descriptive category employed it was not confined to a tripartite model, but could include five or more classes of society.[73] Conversely, there were occasions when the 'middle' could disappear entirely from social representation, leaving only the picture of a nation divided between rich and poor.[74] Since the gap between social reality and class representation is not only wide but contingent, it is no longer possible to link the grand narratives of industrial revolution with those of class formation on to which gender has so often been grafted in order to explain changes in women's economic activities.

The 'middle-class' woman in business is an elusive figure, one whose appearance or (more commonly) disappearance should not be tied to a preponderance of one kind of representational literature over another. The term 'middle class' also conveys an impression of an essentially stable social group, particularly if it is viewed as sharing common cultural values. This could be equally misleading because economic misfortune could strike at any level and the attitudes and reactions of those born into 'gentility', but who were forced to support themselves through necessity, cannot be understood in the same terms as those of women who viewed themselves as 'bred' into trade. Of course, social mobility could work both ways, so the values and beliefs of those whose social and economic status was improved by the acquisition of profit were also not necessarily uniform. As we shall see, women's attainment of wealth through business (as opposed to through the more traditional route of marriage) could earn them huge public opprobrium. While it is often necessary to refer to a middling sort/class throughout this book for the sake of broad description, this should not be confused with any attempt to elide differences of rank and income, or to link the representation of middle-class women with any precise social referent. It is therefore more useful to refer to the 'middle classes' or 'middling sort' when dealing with social groups and 'middle class' only when this description is used in contemporary literature. Removing *the* middle class as a driving force in the historical process means it is also possible to abandon linear narratives of *its* development, in the same way that the unilinear approach has been dropped from narratives of industrial and economic developments during the period.

The language of 'public' and 'private' conveys an equally elusive range of concepts. Since the language was present in both eighteenth- and nineteenth-

[72] Penelope J. Corfield, 'Class by Name and Number in Eighteenth-century Britain', in idem (ed.) *Language, History and Class* (Oxford, 1991), pp. 101–30.
[73] Ibid., pp. 101, 112–17.
[74] Cannadine, *Class in Britain*, pp. 19–20, argues that there have been three major models of social description: the hierarchical view of ranks and orders, the tripartite model, and the dichotomous picture of patricians and plebeians.

century discourses, its importance cannot be discounted even if the metaphor of separate spheres has lost its analytical power within overarching narratives of women's history. But it can no longer be used to explain 'the rise of the domestic woman', 'the separation of work from home' and 'the sexual division of labour' in several different centuries. For the purposes of this study the categories of public and private are assumed to be always relative and the boundaries highly flexible and entirely historically contingent. Since one term necessarily constructs the other, it is important to consider what is inscribed within each category at any given time or place and how these terms are articulated in terms of one another. This formulation allows for the possibility of issues moving from the private to the public domain and back,[75] as well as for much eighteenth-century usage, which was not at all consistent. It is in the fields of women's and gender history, perhaps above all, that it is essential to pay attention to subtle nuances of language and how these change over time. Given the ubiquitous stress on issues such as the essential nature of women and their association with domesticity, reproduction and motherhood in contemporary debates across most historical periods, it is only by studying how these ideas are articulated, when and why they change partners and in the service of what interests that gives them their historical specificity.

An integrated methodology

This project was conceived with the idea of answering calls for a more inte-grated approach to studying women's economic activities alongside ideological representations of those activities,[76] using a wide range of quantitative and qualitative sources. The time-span from 1700 to 1850 allows for the analysis of the *longue durée*; but the structure of the book has been designed to avoid the pitfalls of simple linear narratives whether of decline, progress or con-tinuity. As a result the book is constructed via a series of case studies in which common themes recur but with different emphases in each period. Although there are obvious disadvantages in terms of continuity with this methodology, cumulatively, it does allow for an analysis of diachronic change. The structure was also determined by the availability or, more accurately, the dearth of sources available to study women's business activities. Two major problems needed to be overcome. First, the difficulty of obtaining commensurable quantitative sources for both the eighteenth and nineteenth centuries and,

[75] For the indeterminacy of the boundary between public and private, see Daniella Gobetti, *Private and Public: Individuals, Households and Body Politic in Locke and Hutcheson* (London, 1991), p. 152.
[76] Sharpe, *Adapting to Capitalism*, p. 10, argues that the impact of ideological factors needs to be considered in conjunction with and not in isolation from women's economic activities. See also Sonya Rose, *Limited Livelihoods: Gender and Class in Nineteenth-century England* (Berkeley, CA, 1992), p. 10, for similar comment.

second, the complexity of reconstructing women's experiences of being in business when so few traces of their voices remain.

The need for a directly comparable source covering both the eighteenth and nineteenth centuries was met by using the information found in the insurance policy registers of the Sun Fire Insurance Company in the years 1735 to 1850. This has meant that the sample was restricted to those women who were not only in business of a sufficient size to be able to afford insurance but who also believed in the very idea of protecting their property in an age when the culture of insurance was in its infancy. However, the policy registers are uniquely suited as a source for providing information about women in business rather than merely about female employment. Each policy recorded not only the name, address and occupation of the policy holder (or holders in partnerships), but also the types of buildings insured, plus their locations and contents, as well as the name and occupation of any tenants if the buildings were let, and their insured value. The policies also recorded the type and value of household goods and stock or merchandise. These records have been profitably used before for counting the numbers and types of female occupations but here they also lend themselves to a more in-depth analysis.[77] As the format of each policy in the registers remained the same over the entire period, it was possible to construct a relational database and all the policies taken out by women in business were recorded for five sample years, at roughly equidistant intervals throughout the period. The resulting database of 1490 policies, predominantly from the London area, forms the quantitative core of this study. This information was further supplemented by the addition of material from 600 advertisements placed by businesswomen in the London *Daily Advertiser* (1731–75). In order to provide a regional contrast the metropolitan economy of London was then compared with a micro-study of businesswomen's networks in the county town of Durham. It was possible to study a network of fifty-six women over a thirty-year period from 1755 to 1784 to discover to what extent women were supplied by female traders, by using the accounts and bundles of receipts belonging to Judith Baker, a wealthy member of the local gentry. Baker's papers not only provided material to reconstruct business dealings between women but they also contained letters from some of the suppliers that provide a rare glimpse of women writing about their business activities.

Further important insights into women's own experience of business were provided by the personal testimonies of litigants in equity cases. This material

---

[77] Earle, *Making of the Middle Class*, pp. 168–71, counted occupations and marital status from 1726 to 1729; Hunt, *Middling Sort*, pp. 132–4, counted women in each trade from 1775 to 1787; Schwarz, *London in the Age of Industrialisation*, pp. 14–22, counted occupations and compared them with census records; Beverley Lemire, *Culture and Commerce: The English Clothing Trade before the Factory, 1660–1800* (Basingstoke, 1997), pp. 104–12, calculated the number of female pawnbrokers and clothes sellers as a percentage of men from 1777 to 1796. The exception is David Barnett, *London, Hub of the Industrial Revolution: A Revisionary History, 1775–1825* (London, 1998), pp. 208–18.

has only very recently come to light as a result of the Public Record Office's indexing project of Chancery pleadings. The project is the first of its kind and has therefore so far only covered the period c. 1660 to 1714, but it nevertheless made it possible to study in great detail thirty cases concerning women in business. The personal nature of the testimonies in the equity cases provides a contrast to the prescriptive literature that purports to describe the workings of the common law and the borough custom of *feme sole* trading. In addition, legal treatises from 1632 to 1884 have been used to assess changing interpretations of the apparently fixed legal fiction of 'coverture', which effectively construed a husband and wife as one person by collapsing the legal personality of the wife into that of her husband. It was possible to make an almost direct comparison with the legal treatises by studying law reports of cases concerning *feme sole* traders in the years 1627 to 1852. The resulting sample of fourteen cases was analysed in detail to examine how and when judges decided to impose common law doctrine over that of borough custom, but also to see how married women used the plurality of the English legal system to defend themselves in cases of debt.

One further category of evidence has been employed. In order to study changing representations of women in business in both eighteenth- and nineteenth-century discourses, two different sets of sources were used. For the eighteenth century, the net was cast very wide to analyse the interaction of several competing discourses surrounding women in trade. The sources studied included contemporary fiction, autobiographies, journals, plays, poems and satirical prints, pamphlets and other writings on trade disputes, trade cards, and the database of newspaper advertisements. Particular attention has been given to the proceedings of the patriotic Society for the Encouragement of Arts, Manufactures and Commerce in the Strand, because it was one of the few eighteenth-century institutions that could be shown to be active in encouraging women in the field of manufactures. For the nineteenth century, the focus has been more selective. One major debate on the condition of milliners and dressmakers in mid-nineteenth-century London has been examined in detail. However, by using a wide range of sources including contemporary art, novels, newspapers, magazines, and the evidence of the 1842 Children's Employment Commission, some wider themes can be analysed to show the range of competing discourses around women and business.

Arguably there are three major factors that are commonly believed either to have always severely limited women's economic enterprise or to have increasingly done so during the eighteenth and nineteenth centuries. These are: the legal system; the difficulty of gaining access to property and capital; and the impact of a restrictive domestic ideology.[78] In broad terms, the three sections of the book address each of these issues in turn and indicate ways in

---

[78] Adapted here for women in business from factors identified by Sharpe, *Adapting to Capitalism*, p. 9.

which the impact of these factors may have been less universal than has been previously thought. The book is therefore divided into three parts: the first examines the legal position of women in business, the second forms a predominantly quantitative study of women's business practices and networks, and the third focuses on representations of women and trade.

Part I addresses legal issues that affected women in business. Chapter 2 examines how far the common law doctrine of coverture affected married women in business and what means there were available for avoiding its consequences. Chapter 3 focuses specifically on the borough custom of *feme sole* trading, which allowed a married woman to trade as if she were single. This chapter considers how women could manipulate the pluralistic legal system and questions to what extent the custom could be seen as a 'privilege' for women. Chapter 4 examines Chancery cases of debt and bankruptcy, as well as disputes over estates and contractual obligations in which businesswomen were involved. It reconstructs the complex de facto trading arrangements between men and women, which often left litigants of *both* sexes remedyless under the universal rigidity of the common law, and highlights the importance of credit networks and extended family relations.

In Part II, trading networks between family and friends is also the central concern of Chapter 5, which examines the relationships between a Durham gentlewoman and her female suppliers. Switching the focus back from a regional to a metropolitan economy, chapters 6 and 7 centre on the database of insurance policies. Chapter 6 looks at the culture of insurance and the women who bought and sold it. It examines the wide variety of businesses in which women were involved and questions whether increasing marginalisation is an adequate description of changes in women's trading practices. Chapter 7 continues to examine women's diverse business practices and insurance strategies. In particular, it addresses questions about what constituted business capital for women, and how property was divided between men and women in marital, mixed and same-sex business partnerships.

Part III deals with representations of women in business. Chapter 8 discusses what 'other languages', apart from that of separate spheres, were available for discussing the activities of women in business in the eighteenth century. The focus here is chiefly on how debates around the nature of profit, luxury trades and patriotism impacted on representations of businesswomen. The discussion of different uses of public and private in the eighteenth century is extended in Chapter 9, which considers the language and strategies employed by businesswomen advertising in a London daily newspaper. Chapter 10 focuses on nineteenth-century debates about the appalling working conditions of milliners' and dressmakers' apprentices in London. It discusses how the often wealthy female proprietors of these businesses were represented according to whether protective legislation, political economy or moral reform was thought to be the solution to the problem. These three chapters are linked to material already discussed in the previous sections, showing that there was no simple relationship between women's actual economic activity and public representations of them.

Overall, this book provides evidence of women in business operating as fully integrated members of local trading networks, exchanging money, credit, property and goods with male traders on a regular basis throughout the period. In addition, a study of a range of debates about women in trade shows that, while the discourse of domesticity was a powerful one, it was by no means the only one within which businesswomen were discussed or could themselves negotiate. There is thus a need to reassess the extent to which patriarchal power, operating through marriage or the common law doctrine of coverture, may be seen to have actually curtailed women's economic enterprises. While patriarchy could disadvantage women in business, its effects were greatly modified by economic imperatives. Finally, while gender remains an important analytical tool for examining the experience of women in business, there were numerous other factors that impacted on the opportunities for and success of women's economic enterprises.

Part I

Law

2

Legal fictions vs. legal facts

Common law, coverture and married women in business[1]

Fiction of use to justice? Exactly as swindling is to trade.

Jeremy Bentham (1748–1832)[2]

Among other disadvantages legal fictions are the greatest obstacles to symmetrical classification. The rule of law remains sticking in the system, but it is a mere shell.

Sir Henry Maine (1822–88)[3]

Perhaps the most powerful and commonly cited impediment to women's economic opportunities is the common law doctrine of coverture based on the legal fiction that a husband and wife were one person, and that person is usually understood to have been the husband.[4] Most accounts detail how, for a married woman in trade, the legal disabilities that proceeded from coverture meant that she could not keep anything she earned from her business, that her husband could shut it down whenever he pleased, that she could not contract on her own account and that she could not sue or be sued alone. Although the borough custom of *feme sole* trading did allow married women to trade as if single in some towns, this medieval privilege is widely believed to have died out as the common law became more powerful and centralised. It was also possible for a wife to retain control of her separate property and to preserve the proceeds of her economic enterprise through the creation of a trust in equity, but this has been seen as an expensive and time-consuming legal procedure of use only to the wealthier ranks. The dominant impression of women's legal position during the period 1700 to 1850 remains one of the disabling effects of coverture produced by the overarching power of the common law

---

[1] This chapter and the one that follows have benefited greatly from discussions with Karen Pearlston, for whose advice and guidance I am deeply indebted.
[2] Jeremy Bentham, 'The Theory of Fictions', Appendix A, in C.K. Ogden, *Bentham's Theory of Fictions* (London, 1932), p. 141.
[3] Henry Maine, *Ancient Law* (London, n.d.), pp. 16–17.
[4] For this version of Blackstone's 'famous dictum' see e.g. Hall, 'Gender Divisions and Class Formation', p. 97.

– and the patriarchal values underlying it – which, in turn, mirrors narratives of women's declining economic position. As this chapter will demonstrate, however, the legal position of women in business was both less restrictive and considerably more complex than most accounts allow.

Coverture was just one of many legal fictions in eighteenth- and nineteenth-century English law, defined by Jeremy Bentham as 'an assumed fact notoriously false, upon which one reasons as if it were true'.[5] Yet the legal fiction of marital unity of person is also one of the longest surviving. It has been in existence at least since the Norman Conquest[6] and has still 'never been abolished outright by legislation', although most of its consequences have now been removed.[7] Its effects were obviously alleviated by the Married Women's Property Acts from 1870, but this longevity and the fact that wives did continue to trade throughout a period of enormous social and economic change still raises questions as to what extent the legal disabilities proceeding from the doctrine of coverture actually impacted upon their ability to trade.

This chapter therefore, examines how far the legal fiction of marital unity of person could theoretically affect married women in trade by studying the changing definitions of coverture given in legal treatises published between 1632 and 1884 and identifying the means suggested for avoiding it. In doing so it suggests new ways of considering long-term linear narratives of women's changing legal position and the nature of the relationship between law, culture and social change. In order to do this it is necessary to separate narratives of women's legal rights from those detailing their ability to trade under the legal system. The question of rights is not an inevitable pre-condition for the practice of trade, despite the desirability of such legal rights in terms of social justice. In terms of the latter criteria of ability to trade, it will be argued that although coverture could be a great disability for married women, for those in trade it was an entirely historically contingent doctrine, the definition, use and means of avoidance of which has varied over time. Moreover, the 'privilege' of *feme sole* status also conferred considerable liabilities against which the 'disability' of coverture was an effective protection.

Narratives of women's legal position

Jeremy Bentham's antipathy to the logical inconsistencies of English juris-prudence was early fuelled by his attendance at lectures given by the Vinerian

---

[5] Bentham, 'Theory of Legislation', cited in Pierre J.J. Olivier, *Legal Fictions in Practice and Legal Science* (Rotterdam, 1975), p. 32.
[6] Maeve E. Doggett, *Marriage, Wife-beating and the Law in Victorian England* (London, 1992), p. 70, traces the earliest references to legal literature produced after 1066 and found in every leading work on English common law since the twelfth century.
[7] J.H. Baker, *An Introduction to English Legal History*, 3rd edn (London, 1990), p. 551, bases his observations on arguments from the 1981 case of *Midland Bank Trust Co vs. Green*.

Professor of Law at Oxford, Sir William Blackstone,[8] whose *Commentaries on The Laws of England* (1765) were widely acknowledged to have been the first, most complete and systematic compilation of English law.[9] It is Blackstone's powerful articulation of the legal fiction of marital unity of person that is most often cited in narratives describing women's legal position during the long eighteenth century, particularly those which stress the legal disabilities under which women suffered.[10] Blackstone's famous passage graphically described how:

> By marriage, the husband and wife are one person in law: that is, the very being or legal existence of the woman is suspended during the marriage, or at least is incorporated and consolidated into that of the husband: under whose wing, protection and *cover*, she performs every thing; and is therefore called in our law-french a *feme-covert, foemina viro co-operata*; is said to be *covert-baron*, or under the protection and influence of her husband, her *baron*, or lord; and her condition during her marriage is called her *coverture*. Upon this principle, of an union of person in husband and wife, depend almost all the legal rights, duties, and disabilities, that either of them acquire by the marriage.[11]

This 'suspension' of a wife's legal identity and the consequent erasure of her rights to individual citizenship has outraged generations of feminists.[12] The 'protection' that coverture offered a wife, which meant *inter alia* that she could not be sued and imprisoned for debt, led some treatise writers, most notably

---

[8] Ogden, *Bentham's Theory of Fictions*, p. xvii.

[9] William Holdsworth, *Sources and Literature of English Law* (Oxford, 1925), p. 158, comments on Blackstone's accurate translations and contemporary acknowledgement of his achievement in an era when belief in systematisation and certainty was paramount, but describes how his reputation declined under Bentham's influence in the early nineteenth century. For an extensive discussion of Blackstone's classic work and his contemporary critics see David Lieberman, *The Province of Legislation Determined: Legal Theory in Eighteenth-century Britain* (Cambridge, 1989).

[10] Hill, *Women, Work and Sexual Politics*, p. 196; Earle, *Making of the English Middle Class*, p. 159; Doggett, *Marriage, Wife-beating and the Law*, p. 35; Lee Holcombe, *Wives and Property: Reform of the Married Women's Property Law in Nineteenth-century England* (Oxford, 1983), p. 18.

[11] William Blackstone, *Commentaries on the Laws of England*, 15th edn (London, 1809), pp. 441–2.

[12] Anon., *The Hardships of the English Laws in Relation to Wives* (1735), rep. in Vivien Jones, *Women in the Eighteenth Century* (London, 1990), pp. 217–25. Barbara Todd, '"To be Some Body": Married Women and *The Hardship's of the English Laws*', *Women Writers and the Early Modern British Political Tradition*, ed. Hilda L. Smith (London, 1998), pp. 343–61, argues, in sympathy with the *Hardships*' author, that 'the rights of married women to "existence" were only achieved in the twentieth century'. Leonore Davidoff, 'Regarding Some "old husbands' tales"', p. 234 also argues that 'upon marriage, women died a kind of civil death, losing legal personality along with potential capacity for active agency in either civil or commercial life'.

Blackstone, to see wives as favoured by the law.[13] But this 'myth' of male protection has also angered those who view it as an abrogation of a wife's right to individual agency and responsibility for her own actions, reducing her to little better than the status of a child. For those who see the law as a reflection of social attitudes, coverture mirrored a patriarchal society's negative perception of women.[14] The law is thus held responsible both for causing women's subordination and being a reflection of the patriarchal attitudes that lay behind it. Hence coverture and its effects have long been a major focus for feminist attacks, not least because of the perceived relationship between women's legal status and their social and economic roles. For many feminists the metaphor of coverture became a highly politicised synecdoche for 'the law', highlighting its worst inequities and providing a basis for calls for social equality and female suffrage. Histories of women's legal 'position' in society, like those of their economic position, frequently replicate a very similar pattern of loosely dated decline, followed by a struggle towards greater freedoms.

As early as 1735, the anonymous female author of *The Hardships of the English Laws in Relation to Wives* appealed to 'the Laws of our Country' as the best way to promote moral equality between husbands and wives.[15] She argued that the law reduced wives to a state 'more disadvantageous than *Slavery* itself', leaving them with no property 'neither in their *own Persons*, Children, or Fortunes'.[16] The claim that the common law reduces women to mere objects of property is, as Greenberg notes, still a common one among modern feminists, despite the fact that in 'no period of English history . . . since the Norman Conquest, have women been given the legal status of chattels'.[17] More recently, Tim Stretton has argued that this tendency to cast the common law as 'the villain of the piece' is misleading.[18] As we shall see, many legal treatises throughout the eighteenth and nineteenth centuries were at pains to explain both the many common law exceptions to coverture and the additional relief provided by equity and borough customs.

Histories of women's allegedly declining legal and civil liberties may be traced back to the suffrage-inspired narratives at the turn of the twentieth

---

[13] For a discussion of how favoured wives were at law see Joanne Bailey, 'Favoured or Oppressed? Married Women, Property and Coverture in England, 1650–1800', *Continuity and Change*, 17 (2002), pp. 351–72.

[14] Janelle Greenberg, 'The Legal Status of the English Woman in Early Eighteenth-century Common Law and Equity', *Studies in Eighteenth-Century Culture*, 4 (1975), pp. 171–81, argues that 'the treatment that the law accords women reflects society's perception of women and of what it means to be a woman'.

[15] Anon., *Hardships of the English Laws*, pp. 217–18.

[16] Ibid., p. 218.

[17] See Greenberg, *Legal Status*, p. 172, esp. footnotes 1–2, for examples of modern feminist arguments based on the proposal that 'women were regarded as chattels' under English common law.

[18] Tim Stretton, *Women Waging Law in Elizabethan England* (Cambridge, 1998), p. 31.

century by authors such as Charlotte Stopes, and Mary and Beatrice Wallis Chapman. Stopes charted the many 'privileges' held by women, until the 'errors of Sir Edward Coke'[19] signalled the beginning of the 'long ebb', which lasted until 1868 when support for the Married Women's Property Acts signalled a sea change. The Chapmans traced a long slow decline from 1066 until 1832 when the 'tide of events . . . made for liberty'.[20] The pace of decline was deemed to have increased from 1485 with the change in relative importance of local and central government, particularly concerning the erosion of borough privileges and their local courts. Alice Clark was equally convinced that 'abrogating customs in favour of common law' effectively deprived married women of their property rights.[21] Quite apart from the questions raised by the common assumption of a pre-conquest legal golden age for women, which is still hotly debated,[22] two legal issues from these early works remain of central concern to historians of women in trade: namely the relative importance of local borough customs in allowing women to trade as *feme sole* merchants on the same terms as men, and the effect of increasing centralisation of the law or the growth of common law jurisdiction.[23] In addition, the ideological work of the law and narratives of increasing patriarchal legal restrictions on women's activities, particularly from *c.* 1800, remain prominent in modern historiography.[24]

Susan Staves has considered how the different frameworks commonly used to explain legal change might be applied to changes in married women's property law between 1660 and 1830. She rejected both a liberal-progressive narrative of increasing 'improvements' to the law, and a sociological story

---

[19] Charlotte Carmichael Stopes, *British Freewomen* (London, 1907), p. 121, referring to Sir Edward Coke's *First Part of the Institutes of the Lawes of England* (London, 1628) which like Blackstone's *Commentaries* also became a target for feminist critics.

[20] Beatrice and Mary Wallis Chapman, *The Status of Women under the English Law* (London, 1909), p. 40.

[21] Clark, *Working Life of Women*, p. 237.

[22] Doggett, *Marriage, Wife-beating and the Law*, p. 72, begins her analysis with the assumption that 'After 1066 things changed'. But see Pauline Stafford, 'Women and the Norman Conquest', *Transactions of the Royal Historical Society*, 6 ser. 4 (1994), pp. 221–49, for a strong critique of the 'Golden Age for women pre 1066' and p. 234, positing a somewhat 'flexible legal situation' afterwards.

[23] Amy Louise Erickson, *Women and Property in Early Modern England* (London, 1993, rep. 1995), pp. 6, 28–30, argues that this 'rationalisation' of the law occurred between 1300 and 1800 and resulted in a deterioration of women's legal and economic position.

[24] Susan Staves, *Married Women's Separate Property in England, 1660–1833* (London, 1990) and Todd, 'To Be Some Body', both trace a decline from 1800. Davidoff and Hall, *Family Fortunes*, p. 276, note that 'in legal and practical terms' women's position had deteriorated from about the seventeenth century but base their analysis primarily on the ending of customary rights of dower and a wife's testamentary incapacity in the nineteenth century.

of 'functional adaptation' to economic and social change,[25] in favour of a radical feminist explanation. Her study of the political choices made by judges in individual cases argued that their decisions were based on patriarchal ideology, which, she admits, is 'the story you might get . . . from Blackstone's sister'.[26] For Staves, this 'patriarchal history is a nightmare' which is not yet over. In a similar vein, Maeve Doggett argues that the patriarchal 'power principle' of women's subordination to men lay behind the fiction of coverture in cases of wife beating.[27] For Doggett, the legal fiction of unity was an ideological structure designed to obscure unequal relations of power within marriage rather than a legal principle per se.[28] Yet the use of patriarchal ideology as an analytical device has been critiqued by legal feminists as a rather blunt instrument.[29] As Shelley Gavigan has argued, feminists need to use sharper analytical tools and to consider how the law could reflect more than one single interest.[30] As in narratives of women's economic position, the radical feminist approach can result in a denial of historical differences and in the reaffirmation of a story of the way things always are.[31]

Instead, historians need to navigate between the pitfalls of a gender-blind versus a gender-specific narrative of legal change, and to avoid a simple linear narrative of decline or liberation. The resulting interpretation is less one of the functional adaptation of the law to social change or to women's rights, but of an extremely imperfect interaction between law, society and economy which cannot be said to have taken any form of linear trajectory. This in effect could leave spaces for married women to continue trading while not actually conferring upon them the same rights as men to do so. Indeed, the argument that coverture was neither so monolithic nor so effective at preventing married women from economic bargaining has recently been endorsed by the work of Margot Finn and Joanne Bailey. Their research highlights the ways wives as consumers evaded the strictures of coverture to contract for far more than the 'necessaries' the common law allowed them as legitimate agents of their husbands.[32]

[25] Staves, *Married Women's Separate Property*, pp. 199–230.

[26] Ibid., p. 230.

[27] Doggett, *Marriage, Wife-beating and the Law*, p. 61.

[28] Ibid., p. 99.

[29] Shelley A. M. Gavigan, 'Law, Gender, and Ideology' in *Legal Theory Meets Legal Practice*, ed. Anne F. Bayefsky, (Edmonton, 1988), pp. 283–95, esp. pp. 292–4.

[30] Ibid., p. 294.

[31] Diane Purkiss, *The Witch in History* (London, 1996), p. 11, argues that the radical feminist approach results in a 'refusal of historicity'; for another critique of 'history that stands still' see Hill, 'Women's History', pp. 5–19.

[32] Margot Finn, 'Women, Consumption and Coverture in England, c. 1760–1860', *The Historical Journal*, 3 (1996), pp. 703–22; Bailey, 'Favoured or Oppressed?', pp. 351–72.

Legal fictions in legal treatises

In addition to Bentham's objections to scientific untruthfulness, legal fictions have been critiqued on numerous grounds. Two of these are of particular concern here. One criticism was that legal fictions created uncertainty, which raised problems of application in individual cases. The second was that their use concealed the fact that judges were effectively able to change the law, when legal theory suggested that they should act only as interpreters of law. Conversely, therefore, it was argued that fictions helped the law evolve in a peaceful and conservative way by enabling new interpretations to be based upon old principles.[33] Studying a legal fiction can therefore prove a useful way of considering the relationship between law and social change. Furthermore, one way of examining the paradox of the 'changeless yet ever changing'[34] common law and the role of legal fictions such as coverture within it is to study legal treatises and commentaries on the subject over a long period of time. In consequence, this section is based on a study of the changing explanations of coverture and married women's separate trading found in legal treatises between 1632 and 1884.

There are several reasons for studying legal treatises separately from the law reports of individual case decisions considered in Chapter 3. First, they provide a glimpse of some of the circuitous routes by which different sections of the law allowed married women to trade in certain circumstances, while the principle of coverture remained unchanged. To do this, treatises had to take account of borough customs but also of equity as a separate but co-existent system of law that did recognise married women's separate property. Although treatises cannot reveal the extent to which equity was actually used, they can give a good indication of when and how equitable principles were both incorporated into the common law and accepted as a necessary alternative.[35] Second, as we shall see below, narratives of legal history based on different sources can appear to proceed in entirely different directions, so that treating them independently can provide a more balanced picture.

Third, treatises provide a distilled version of the law as it stood at any moment in time. The common law was an unwritten set of maxims or principles

---

[33] See Olivier, *Legal Fictions*, pp. 88–92, for an assessment of the advantages and disadvantages of the use of legal fictions. In the nineteenth century, Maine, *Ancient* Law, p. 16, asserted that the expression 'legal fiction' signified 'any assumption which conceals, or effects to conceal, the fact that a rule of law has undergone alteration, its letter remaining unchanged, its operation being modified'.

[34] Roger Cotterell, *The Politics of Jurisprudence* (London, 1989), p. 28.

[35] In England equity and common law had developed as two separate systems but in the classical formulation 'equity represented an essential though distinguishable feature of any judge's authority' and there was considerable debate as to what extent if any this should occur in eighteenth-century common law courts; for an illuminating discussion see Lieberman, *Province of Legislation*, pp. 71–87.

based on ancient customs and the accumulated wisdom of judges, which was both always pre-existent yet also developing, 'with the accumulation, reinterpretation and restatement of precedents and the adjustment of legal doctrine to new circumstances'.[36] Legal treatises therefore are, in effect, historically contingent interpretations of the law based on judges' decisions in important cases and the issue of new statutes. This is particularly important because juridicial change could be made only incrementally, founded on existing legal principles, but legislative change could effectively change the principle itself. Only the latter is now acceptable to feminists rightly seeking 'true equality' in the eyes of the law, but this view tends to leave the impression that legal change in the long eighteenth century was moribund compared to that produced by the zeal for reform in the later nineteenth century. Yet legal historians have shown that, not only was there a great deal of debate over whether legal remedies for new problems were best developed by the courts or by Parliament, but also that the courts did carry out a great deal of reform in a number of areas, including property, contract and commercial law, without resorting to parliamentary statute.[37] As Atiyah points out, however, while a number of eighteenth-century lawyers were 'willing to modify the law to bring it up to date with social and economic changes from time to time . . . they certainly never contemplated the idea of using the law so as to *create* social and economic change'.[38]

Finally, it is important to stress not only the interpretative nature of these treatises but also that many were not written solely for legal scholars. Some were a commercial attempt to bring the law to a wider audience and, as such, served as the version of the law available to literate women,[39] including those who were in business, as well as to men from whom women may have sought legal advice. In the Preface to *The Lawes Resolutions of Women's Rights* (1632), the anonymous author expressly dedicated this collection of 'Statutes and Customes, with the Cases, Opinions, Arguments and points of Learning in the Law as do properly concerne Women' to women themselves. In the Conclusion, he explained that he had attempted to set out useful information:

> in some orderly connexion, which heretofore were smothered, or scattered in corners of an uncouth language, cleane abstruded from their sex. Which

---

[36] Cotterell, *Politics of Jurisprudence*, p. 26.

[37] P.S. Atiyah, *The Rise and Fall of Freedom of Contract* (Oxford, 1979), pp. 91–7; Lieberman, *Province of Legislation, passim*, also notes that while the increase in statutes was vast their reforming impact was minimal: pp. 13–28.

[38] Atiyah, *Rise and Fall*, p. 97; emphasis added.

[39] Beth Swan, *Fictions of the Law: An Investigation of the Law in Eighteenth-century English Fiction* (Frankfurt, 1997), p. 11, argues that contemporaries displayed a detailed knowledge of the law, aspects of which were frequently included even in 'women's' fiction. Erickson, *Women and Property*, pp. 21–3, also shows that 'relatively well-off' women were familiar with legal texts.

concealement, because it seemed to me neither iust, nor conscionable, I have framed this worke.[40]

In this work the author bases his explanation for coverture on the biblical story of Adam and Eve as 'but one flesh' and women's subjection to their husbands on Eve's original sin, because the 'common law here shaketh hands with Divinitie'. Two sections are commonly cited from this work. The first declared that all women are 'understood either married or to be married and their desire be subject to their husband'.[41] The second was the graphic metaphor of how, for women, marriage is like a little stream being carried away by a major river; following the Latin definition of coverture as 'nupra', meaning that she was 'vailed, as it were, clouded, overshadowed &c. she hath lost her streame, she is continually *sub potestate viri*'.[42] It is this image of a woman's personal and legal identity being totally subsumed by male power that has most angered feminists; yet, if it is placed in context, a rather less literal reading of women's lack of agency is possible or, as the author put it, 'some women can shift it well enough'.[43] A passage cited less frequently explains that, although man and wife 'bee by intent and wise fiction of law, one person, yet in nature & in some other cases by the Law of God and man, they remaine divers . . . so in other speciall causes our Law argues them severall persons'.[44] Indeed, this interpretation is supported by Shepard's study of working wives involved in debt litigation in the Cambridge University courts between 1580 and 1640.[45] Most importantly, the author of the *Resolutions* concludes by warning his readers:

> not to take it for so strong and substantiall a peece as London bridge is, whereon you set up great building; but I will say to you. . . . There bee some things in these Bookes which are not Law, yet even those may enable you the better to understand the reasons and argument of Law, and to conferre and enquire what the Law is amongst the sage matters therof.[46]

In other words, the treatise's graphic representations of coverture should not be read as exact statements of the common law *per se*, which, as the book suggests, was by no means consistent on the subject. The *Lawes Resolutions* was one of the earliest attempts to present a systematic summary of the common law and was still cited in the eighteenth century. It was written in English rather than in legal French, and although its complex expositions made it

---

[40] Anon., *The Lawes Resolutions of Womens Rights Or, The Lawes Provisions for Woemen* (London, 1632), p. 403.
[41] Ibid., p. 6.
[42] Ibid., pp. 124–5.
[43] Ibid., p. 6.
[44] Ibid., p. 4.
[45] Shepard, 'Manhood, Credit and Patriarchy', pp. 90–5.
[46] Anon., *Lawes Resolutions*, pp. 403–4.

suitable for law students, it was not only addressed to, but specifically dealt with, women's legal issues in a generally sympathetic and enlightened fashion for public consumption.[47]

The anonymous author of *Baron and Feme* (1700) was equally aware of the difficulty of interpreting contract law for married women. He found that 'the Resolutions of our [law] Books have not been very consistent' and in real actions concerning *femmes coverts* 'the law had been much abridged and altered'.[48] This author's previous book had focused on the law concerning children, which may partially account for an infamous passage in which the position of married women was compared to that of children.[49] Hence a woman's lack of contractual capacity was explained in terms of a coverture in which she was represented as being under her husband's power and lacking in free will, in the same way as a child lacks judgement. After the 1882 Married Women's Property Act, legal commentators were anxious to distance themselves from this analogy when explaining coverture. They emphasised that it was lack of a 'disposing *power*' rather than 'want of a disposing *mind*' that explained a wife's lack of contractual capacity.[50] Nevertheless, *Baron and Feme* did highlight exceptions to coverture 'for Necessity-sake of Commerce, and the like'. Two of these anomalies were important for women in trade.

First, the earlier *Lawes Resolutions* (1632) had explained that 'if sisters make a joint purchase they are jointnants, and not partners', which meant that unlike partners their property could not be divided between them.[51] In *Baron and Feme* this principle was extended to include leases, and it was made explicit that, if one of the sisters married, 'the wife continued sole possessed',[52] even if the other sister died. The married sister's title would also hold good against her husband's executors should he die. In other words, sisters purchasing property or a lease were treated as one person, and this fiction of unity could supersede that of marital unity by virtue of being the 'elder title'. As will be shown below,[53] this could have been of great importance to many women, particularly those in 'feminine' trades such as millinery and dressmaking, a

---

[47] W.R. Prest, 'Law and Women's Rights in Early Modern England', *The Seventeenth Century*, 6 (1991), pp. 169–87.

[48] Anon., *Baron and Feme. A Treatise of the Common Law Concerning Husbands and Wives* (London, 1700; rep. 1719), p. A3.

[49] Ibid., p. 7. That women were reduced to the status of children, idiots and outlaws is another legal 'fact' much lamented by modern historians: see e.g. Hill, *Women, Work and Sexual Politics*, p. 196.

[50] Montague Lush, *The Law of Husband and Wife within the Jurisdiction of the Queen's Bench and Chancery Divisions* (London, 1884), p. 263.

[51] Anon., *Lawes Resolutions*, pp. 24–5, explained in which circumstances sisters were considered jointnants and in which as partners. For example, if inheriting land from a common ancestor, they would have been regarded as partners.

[52] With thanks to Margaret Hunt for pointing out this reference in Anon., *Baron and Feme*, p. 231.

[53] See below, p. 135.

significant proportion of whom were in business partnerships with their sisters and other female relatives.

Second, *Baron and Feme* included an entire section on the borough custom of *feme sole* trader in the city of London. The custom is listed as one of several instances when a wife could sue without her husband, although the action had to be brought in the city courts. However, the author explained that 'every feme which trades in London is not a *Feme sole* Merchant',[54] because the custom stated that it must be proved that the husband had not 'intermeddled' with his wife's trade in any way. If the couple lived together outside London 'and the wife deals separately, her Contracts shall charge the husband'. In other words, wives could trade separately outside London but, as the custom was limited to the city, they could not be held solely liable for their debts. There was therefore no suggestion that coverture prevented married women from trading separately. The point was that, if they did so, their husbands would be liable for any debts they incurred. Other towns did have similar borough customs but this treatise focused solely on London, almost certainly because the law reports on which it was based were confined to London cases.[55]

The cases in *Baron and Feme*, which were chiefly taken from the seventeenth century, are poorly explained, and it is difficult to establish firm principles of law. None the less, they give an indication of what constituted a *feme sole* merchant and of the procedural difficulties that could arise in such cases. This was because, although a woman had to be openly trading separately from her husband to qualify as a *feme sole* merchant, her husband still had to be named in any legal action for the sake of conformity to the doctrine of coverture, even though sentence would only be passed on the wife alone. The first case, *Langham vs. Bluet* (1627), focused on whether Mrs Bluet, who had traded as a vintner while her husband was serving in the army abroad, was liable for her own debts. The author drew the extremely broad conclusion that 'if the Husband be beyond Sea, or becomes bankrupt, or leaves his Trade, and the Wife exercise the same Trade or they both exercise the same trade distinctly by themselves',[56] then she could be described as a *feme sole* merchant. Other cases showed that a husband was not liable for his dead wife's debts if she had been a *feme sole* trader, even if he had previously promised to pay, and that a man sued by a married *feme sole* merchant, who pleaded in bar, could not later reverse this as an error of judgement by citing her coverture. The treatise therefore provided evidence of several cases in which the custom had been upheld over common law and emphasised that liability for payment of debts was of prime concern, even though some confusion remained about its exact terms.[57]

---

[54] Anon., *Baron and Feme*, p. 301.
[55] For borough customs, see below, p. 57.
[56] Anon., *Baron and Feme*, p. 301.
[57] One reason for this was probably because as the Law Report of the Bluet case (*ER*,

In direct contrast, however, the 1732 edition, while mentioning the custom of London and noting that not all trading women fell under it, gave no examples of cases at all. The work had been updated, extended and renamed *A Treatise of Feme Coverts: Or, The Lady's Law*, a guise in which it was blatantly aimed at an almost certainly propertied, female audience and/or their legal advisers. The Preface explained that 'the fair Sex are here inform'd how to preserve their Lands, Goods, and most valuable Effects, from the Incroachments of any one'.[58] The emphasis had changed dramatically from the disabilities of coverture to the 'Privileges of Feme Coverts, and their Power with respect to their Husbands'.[59] There was no graphic description of coverture. Instead, the treatise contained information about how women could protect their separate property and a selection of 'precedents of conveyances', or prewritten settlements and bonds. Amy Erickson has shown that far from being confined to the upper ranks of society, even women of the middling orders could protect their separate property after marriage by using simple bonds;[60] but the sample settlements found in this treatise provided examples involving large sums of money. Nevertheless, a legal treatise, originally based solely on the common law, had now begun to include equitable principles of married women's separate property. Since married women could also trade sole on the basis of their equitable separate property, these sample conveyances provided for establishing separate property may have been equally useful to women in business. The creation of separate property was not linked to any specific locality and thus had a wider appeal, which may be another reason why detailed information about the borough custom of *feme sole* traders was omitted from this edition. This did not signify the end of the borough custom, however, which reappeared in later treatises and was still being cited in law reports as late as 1852.

William Blackstone's section on married women in the *Commentaries*, first published in 1765, contained no mention of the borough custom or equity's provisions for wives. As a paean to the common law inspired by Enlightenment enthusiasm for rationalism, Blackstone's attempt to gloss over the 'little contrarities' of English Law,[61] for the sake of a systematic treatise on the subject, effectively obscured the loopholes that continued to allow women to trade. Much later, Blackstone was savagely attacked in 1946 by the American feminist Mary Beard for his omissions,[62] particularly over women's legal rights

---

Langham vs. Bewett, Croke Car 68, 79, pp. 661–2) shows the judges were divided over the verdict and the case was eventually settled out of court. See below, p. 57, but note variant spellings.

[58] Anon., *A Treatise of Feme Coverts: Or, The Lady's Law* (London, 1732), p. vi.

[59] Ibid., p. 78.

[60] Erickson, *Women and Property*, pp. 129–51, 104–6.

[61] For Blackstone's Enlightenment project, see Staves, *Married Women's Separate Property*, pp. 15–16; Holdsworth, *Sources and Literature*, pp. 158–9.

[62] Mary Beard, *Woman as Force in History: A Study in Traditions and Realities* (New York, 1946), pp. 75–107, saw Blackstone as the most influential proponent of the mistaken idea

in equity; but his work represented the beginning of a new form of authoritative legal treatise which clearly stated the general principles of law. Blackstone himself admitted in his 1765 Preface that he may be 'still mistaken' on some points and in a later edition that he had encountered fierce opposition. By 1809, his editor Edward Christian had added substantial footnotes 'apologising' for Blackstone's position on many facets of married women's law, and in particular for his assertion that women were 'a favourite of the law', because of the many exemptions provided by the 'protection' of coverture. The 1809 edition shows that the legal profession was already well aware of the inequity of the common law's doctrine on women. Christian added two pages of notes disputing Blackstone's position and – most importantly – a further note on a wife's ability to sue as if *feme sole* in equity.[63]

Yet other treatises, somewhat less authoritative than Blackstone's, were available to women in the eighteenth century, which did provide a more comprehensive assessment of coverture and the exceptions to it. Blackstone's work was written 'to give educated gentlemen an introduction to the legal system'.[64] In contrast, *The Laws Respecting Women* (1777) was written to address legal issues concerning women – it consisted of 449 pages compared to the meagre nine Blackstone devoted to the law concerning husband and wife. It seems more plausible that middling-sort women wishing to discover where they stood at law would turn to this type of work rather than to Blackstone. Conversely, those wishing to attack the inequities of the common law could find no better target than Blackstone's compelling and succinct description of coverture.

The author of *The Laws Respecting Women* also wrote within the spirit of the Enlightenment and acknowledged his debt to Blackstone, whose 'elegant pen' had done for English law what Newton did for the laws of nature and Locke for those of human intelligence. The treatise declared that the law had now been 'rescued from perplexity and intricacy' and 'proved to be uniform'. For women in trade, however, the most important rationale behind *The Laws* was its economic imperative and its recognition that a nation:

> whose commerce is extended over the whole circumference of the globe . . . must necessarily furnish continual occasion for the creation of new laws; to ascertain the rights of individuals who were before unattended to, because such situations were unknown; to adjust the nice distinctions with regard to property, occasioned by . . . families . . . the concerns of commerce, the interests of those who compose the legislative part of government, and of those of the body of the people.[65]

---

that the law 'extinguished the married woman's personality', based on the erroneous assumption that the common law took no account of equity.
[63] Blackstone, *Commentaries*, ed. E. Christian (London, 1809), pp. 441–5, esp. Christian's notes, 15 and 21.
[64] Staves, *Married Women's Separate Property*, p. 14.
[65] Anon., *The Laws Respecting Women, As they Regard their Natural Rights, or their Connections and Conduct* (London, 1777), pp. iii–iv.

Hence the law was acknowledged to be adaptable to social change and particularly to the interests of commerce. Moreover, the treatise was addressed to women in all situations of life and had dropped the married/to be married dichotomy present in earlier treatises.[66] Even more importantly, it expressly covered principles of common law, statute law, equity and ecclesiastical law, and thus encompassed legal principles applicable to women in all branches of the tangled legal system. It therefore not only covered the category of *feme sole* trader in great detail but also included examples of women resorting to law as a matter of course during other kinds of commercial transactions.

Several of the cases concerning both married and single women in business, as cited in *The Laws*, had been tried before Lord Mansfield, Chief Justice of the common law court of King's Bench.[67] Mansfield was known for his attempts to import equitable principles into the operation of the common law, particularly in the interests of commerce.[68] His influence during thirty-two years as Chief Justice (1756–88) was considerable and contemporaries regarded his judgeship as a unique period for legal innovation and creativity. Mansfield appealed to principles of natural justice and equity rather than strictly adhering to precedent; he also insisted on the superiority of the common law over legislation as the best means to develop new legal rules in response to altered social conditions.[69] He was a firm believer in the principles of free trade[70] and the justice of equitable separate property for married women. Indeed, Lieberman has argued that Mansfield's series of rulings on a *feme covert*'s powers to contract best demonstrate his belief that, 'as the usages of society alter, the law must adapt itself to the various situations of mankind'.[71] He repeatedly upheld the contractual obligations of married women, particularly when those contracts concerned dealings with merchants.[72] His decisions therefore frequently benefited women in trade. It is unlikely that he intended to contribute to women's emancipation in general, but this should not detract from the effect

---

[66] The frontispiece to *The Laws Respecting Women* listed women's roles as 'daughters, wards, heiresses, spinsters, sisters, wives, widows, mothers, legatees and executrixes &c'.

[67] See ibid., pp. 134–5, *Morisset vs. King*; and pp. 173–7, *Lavie vs. Phillips* (1776).

[68] See William Holdsworth, *Some Makers of the English Law* (Cambridge,1938), pp. 172–4 on Lord Mansfield who, before his appointment as Chief Justice of Kings Bench, had been a leading lawyer in Chancery, and his attempts to fuse the principles of equity and common law.

[69] See Lieberman, *Province of Legislation*, pp. 87, 88–143, for a discussion of Mansfield's reform of the commercial code, and his attitude towards equity and common law principles, precedents and reform.

[70] James Oldham, *The Mansfield Manuscripts and the Growth of English Law in the Eighteenth Century* II (North Carolina, 1992), p. 685, Mansfield's 'ultra-free-trade principles' were criticised by some, and it was argued that he could even furnish a defence for a besieged city to sell gunpowder to its invading army.

[71] Mansfield on *Barwell vs. Brooks* (1784), cited in Lieberman, *Province of Legislation*, pp. 126–7.

[72] Oldham, *Mansfield Manuscripts*, pp. 1245–51.

of his decisions, which were widely reported in legal treatises as evidence of women's legal position long after his retirement from the Bench.

In *The Laws Respecting Women* (1777) the distinction between a *feme covert* and a *feme sole* merchant chiefly revolved around the latter's liability to be declared a bankrupt. The treatise explained that a 'Feme-covert is warranted by law to sell goods in open market, and her husband cannot reclaim any goods so sold, provided such woman is usually accustomed to trade for herself'.[73] Hence married women traders were again presented as a normal occurrence. Moreover, the evidence in Chancery cases shows that wives 'usually accustomed' to trading did indeed continue to do so, even through remarriages.[74] The chief distinction made in this treatise was that a '*feme-covert* in London, being a sole trader, is liable according to the custom to a commission of bankrupt'.[75] This was, of course, unlike the situation outside the London custom where a wife's coverture prevented her from being held personally liable for her contracted debts. The 1776 case cited at great length to illustrate this concerned the assignees of Jane Cox, a bankrupt milliner in London, and the assignees of her husband John, who had also been made bankrupt in spring 1764.[76] The dispute concerned Jane Cox's stock of fans, which were seized by her husband's assignees on the grounds that, as she was a married woman, the stock constituted part of his estate by right. The court had to decide whether a commission of bankruptcy could lie against a married woman and, if a wife was a sole trader, whether her goods could be taken to satisfy her husband's debts before those of her own creditors. The defence argued that a husband's rights took precedence and that a married woman was within the letter of the bankruptcy laws but not the spirit. Mansfield, however, judged that the London custom did not impinge on a husband's marital rights, except those subject to the custom's terms. Hence, as a sole trader, the wife was subject to a bankruptcy commission as far as her separate business assets were concerned. Thus the principle of a married woman's ability to contract and be sued separately under London custom was upheld. But this meant that she could also be declared bankrupt. Mansfield had actually acted 'for the benefit of the creditors, who cannot by reason of this custom come at the husband',[77] but who could now claim directly from the bankrupted wife's estate.

---

[73] Anon., *Laws Respecting Women*, p. 172.

[74] See below, pp. 74–81.

[75] Anon., *Laws Respecting Women*, p. 173. It is not clear whether the author meant just the City of London or a wider definition of the capital; later treatises specified the City but cases reveal that there was still some dispute over whether the defendant had to reside in the city or just be trading there. See *Buckland vs. Burges* (1703) discussed below, pp. 84–5.

[76] Ibid., pp. 174–6, *Lavie vs. Phillips*, 3. Bur. Manf. (1776).

[77] Ibid., p. 176. Mansfield also believed that if a *feme sole* trader had not been subject to a bankruptcy commission she would have been 'liable to perpetual imprisonment' for the unsettled debt, which was worse.

Lack of contractual ability has been seen as a major disability for married women; but the ability to make legal contracts also made them liable for the consequences and unable to claim 'male protection' by using coverture as a defence, which in fact many tried to do.[78] In William Cooke's *The Bankrupt Laws* (1785), *feme sole* traders remained the only women in business definitely liable for bankruptcy. Cooke believed that this implication also had a bearing on the status of women trading on the basis of equitable separate property, but they remained an 'exception of a more doubtful nature'.[79] The case Cooke cited to prove that a married woman who lived apart from her husband and traded as a *feme sole* could be liable to bankruptcy was that of Mrs Ann Fitzgerald, which came before the Lord Chancellor in 1772. Mrs Fitzgerald's husband was a linen draper but, when the couple decided to separate, he assigned all his stock-in-trade, household goods and debts owing to two male trustees for her separate use, keeping £600 for himself. It was also agreed that she would trade 'without any interruption from her husband', pay all the trading debts he then owed, and maintain their children at her own expense. He left for the East Indies and she continued to trade as a linen draper for four years in her own name. In December 1771, a commission of bankruptcy was taken out against Mrs Fitzgerald but the commissioners 'refused to find her a Bankrupt, because she was a *feme covert*, residing in the county of *Middlesex*, and not a *feme sole* merchant trading in the city of London'.[80] However, the Lord Chancellor ordered the commission to proceed immediately and Mrs Fitzgerald was declared bankrupt. The authority for this decision, Cooke argued, was later supported by the case of *Ringstead vs. Lanesborough* (1783), in which Mansfield had found that a married woman with a separate maintenance agreement, living apart from her husband, was liable for her own debts. In that case Mansfield had explained that 'the general principle of law' was that a married woman could not be sued for debt on her own contract, 'but as the times change, you must alter the law to them; and therefore, gradually, exceptions have been allowed to prevent injustice'.[81]

This argument was still being cited in the 1823 edition of Cooke, and Mansfield's decisions were also still being recited in R.S. Donnison Roper's authoritative *Treatise on the Law of Property Arising from the Relation between Husband and Wife* (1820). Mansfield had recognised the growing number of exceptions to the unity of persons doctrine, created chiefly to aid those dealing commercially with married women, and he had therefore attempted

---

[78] See the discussion of *feme sole* trader cases below, pp. 48–68.
[79] William Cooke, *The Bankrupt Laws* (London, 1785), pp. 39–41, lists *feme sole* traders and equitable sole traders under 'Person's who, engaging in Trade, can or cannot be made Bankrupts'.
[80] Ibid., p. 41.
[81] Ibid., p. 45.

to reduce these cases to a single commercial principle.[82] He not only held married women, whether traders or just separated from their husbands, liable for their debts but he also upheld female traders' rights to stock and profits, where these had been held in trust, as separate estate by equity. Thus in *Haslington vs. Gill* (1784), Mansfield protected the original herd of cows that had been assigned to a wife as separate trade stock from her husband's creditors, and also the additional cows she had since bred and the profits she had gained from doing so. He reasoned that, although the common law denied a wife separate property, 'in equity women have for ages been protected from the extravagance of their husbands'[83] by means of a trust. Even more importantly, Mansfield declared that 'wherever such a trust could be supported in equity, the trustee would be intitled in a court of law'.[84]

Thus equitable title to separate property could be upheld in a common law court, which would in effect substantially negate the disabilities of coverture for married women in trade. What this arrangement did not do was give wives legal title to their property, since it could only be claimed, on their behalf and for their sole use, by the trustees of that property. This is one of the feminist objections to the use of equity,[85] as it only conferred upon wives the ability to act *as if* they were individual agents. It did not confer the same legal rights as those held by men and single women. It has also been argued that married women of the middling sort would not have been able to afford the lengthy and expensive process of Chancery proceedings,[86] but, as will be shown below, expenses need not have been very high.[87] Nevertheless, as long as equitable title was recognised in a common law court, and sample agreements to create separate property were available in printed legal treatises, then married women's ability to trade on the basis of equitable separate property was far wider than has previously been thought.

It should be noted, however, that there is a significant problem to be considered when writing any narrative of legal change because that change could be achieved by judge-made decisions or by legislative enactments and, as Douglas Hay has shown, judicial politics could proceed in opposition to both legislative intent and various economic interests.[88] Furthermore, legal treatises

---

[82] Oldham, *Mansfield Manuscripts*, p. 1246.

[83] Cited in ibid., p. 1250.

[84] Cited in R.S. Donnison Roper, A *Treatise of the Law of Property Arising from the Relation between Husband and Wife* (London, 1820), p. 170.

[85] Holcombe, *Wives and Property*, p. 47, argues that 'equity failed to meet the feminist criterion of excellence – that all women should have rights and responsibilities equal to those of men'.

[86] Holcombe, *Wives and Property*, p. 46, and Doggett, *Marriage Wife-beating and the Law*, p. 38.

[87] See below, p. 72.

[88] Douglas Hay, 'The State and the Market in 1800: Lord Kenyon and Mr Waddington', *Past and Present*, 162 (1999), pp. 101–63, esp. p. 103.

did not necessarily keep abreast of these developments, whether by intent or by default.[89] Although early nineteenth-century treatises still cited Mansfield's decisions as proof that women could claim equitable title under the common law, his own attempts to fuse equitable and common law principles were largely rejected by his successors. These men were not only more traditionally conservative in their moral principles and their attitudes towards new commercial practices, but wanted the common law and equity to work as separate tribunals run on separate principles.[90] One of the supporters of the two distinct systems was Mansfield's successor Lord Kenyon, a paternalistic, evangelical Tory landowner, whose decisions effectively reversed Mansfield's attempts to make married women with separate maintenance contracts, liable for their own debts. In particular, Kenyon's decision in *Marshall vs. Rutton* (1800) has been seen as critical[91] in restoring the 'old established law founded generally upon the relation of husband and wife, by which, with certain known exceptions, no married woman was capable of contracting or acting as a *feme sole*, or of suing or being sued as such'.[92] However, although recent research has provided much evidence for a conservative moral backlash against married women's independent action in cases of separate maintenance,[93] the evidence of legal commentaries suggests that commercial imperatives remained important even after 1800 and that for women in trade the 'certain known exceptions' were crucial. In 1820 Roper pointed out the implications of the *Marshall vs. Rutton* case, but was concerned to show in what instances the law did permit the wife 'to contract, to sue, and to be impleaded',[94] and how 'a court of law by circuity changes the character of wife into that of a single woman'.[95]

---

[89] Ibid., p. 110: for example, legal treatises still classified forestalling, regrating and engrossing as market offences as late as 1810 despite the fact that these offences had been repealed in 1772. This conservatism was partly because those judges, who were opponents of *laissez-faire* economics, continued to find ways legally to prosecute offenders. See also Atiyah, *Rise and Fall of Freedom of Contract*, pp. 361–9, who suggests one reason for the conservatism shown by judges c. 1793 to 1830 was that many belonged to an older generation and reflected the opinions of an earlier time, but by the 1830s most had been replaced by men more in favour of political economy and commercial enterprise.

[90] Holdsworth, *Makers of English Law*, pp. 174, 200–10.

[91] Staves, *Married Women's Separate Property*, pp. 180ff.; and Todd, 'To Be Some Body', pp. 358–9.

[92] Roper, *Treatise of the Law of Property*, p. 120.

[93] Staves, *Married Women's Separate Property*, pp. 162–95, focuses on separate maintenance contracts of wealthy couples, and Todd, 'To Be Some Body', pp. 351–61, explores the impact of these cases on the separate legal identity of poor married women.

[94] Roper, *Treatise of the Law of Property*, p. 122.

[95] Ibid., p. 171.

Marriage and legal trading in the nineteenth century

According to Roper's treatise, it seems there were four main ways a married woman could continue to trade and contract with others by 1820. Namely, when coverture was suspended because of the husband's absence; as a *feme sole* trader by the custom of London; with her husband's agreement before marriage, or his permission afterwards; or on the basis of possessing equitable separate property. In the first instance coverture was effectively suspended, leaving a wife free to act as a single woman if her husband had been exiled, transported or had left the country for life, and it was reactivated only if he was pardoned and had physically returned to this country. However, if the husband was a foreigner who had never resided in England or who chose to leave the country, coverture continued. But if he was an 'alien enemy' and thus prevented from living in England, the wife would be acknowledged as a *feme sole*. As will be seen below,[96] hostility towards 'aliens' and confusion about different legal doctrines on the Continent made this one of the more contested categories of separate trading for women. Similarly, although divorce completely negated coverture, women trading under separate maintenance agreements, while living apart from their husbands, remained the most vulnerable category of *feme sole* trader and moral imperatives constantly challenged economic considerations in such cases. While advocates of free trade like Mansfield had insisted that such women were effectively single, the evangelical Lord Kenyon and the deeply conservative Lord Eldon[97] were not prepared to sanction any such challenge to the institution of marriage.

The second way in which married women could trade as if single was by the custom of London, but by 1820 its interpretation had become much stricter. The wife must be trading within the City and be able to prove that her husband had never 'intermeddled' in her business at any time. As the custom was now strictly construed as 'regarding only trade and commerce',[98] the husband could do nothing to injure his wife's creditors but he could possess himself of any 'surplus'. A *feme sole* trader could only sue or be impleaded within the City courts, although she could cite the custom in her defence in the superior courts at Westminster, but on all occasions her husband must be named in the action for the sake of conformity. Thus far, then, the custom had been interpreted as far as possible so as not to conflict with the common law and to give the appearance of a single doctrine on the matter. Nevertheless, in two instances where a stricter interpretation was indicated, Roper immediately provided examples of equitable relief available. While a husband could close down his wife's business and appropriate what remained of her business assets after her

---

[96] See pp. 64–7.
[97] On the 'extreme' conservatism of Kenyon and Eldon, see Atiyah, *Rise and Fall of Freedom of Contract*, pp. 361–7.
[98] Roper, *Treatise on the Law of Property*, p. 127.

creditors had been paid, a court of equity might still consider these assets to be her own separate property, 'she having procured it by her own industry, and with the permission of her husband, and without any risk incurred by him'.[99] Roper also pointed out that, although technically a wife could not enter into a bond (because it might have bound her heirs if she had any real property), again equity would have considered a bond to have good security if it had been made on her separate property.[100]

The situation was clearly intricate. Yet, according to Roper, under the common law a wife did not need either borough custom or equity to be able to trade separately, although the means by which this could be achieved sometimes followed a tortuous logic. In theory, a wife could 'trade on her own separate account, apart from and without the interference of her husband',[101] if this had been expressly agreed before the marriage or if during the marriage he subsequently gave his 'permission'. Roper explained that:

> When the agreement is made *previously* to the marriage since the consideration is valuable, the transaction will not only be obligatory upon the husband, but also binding upon his creditors. When the agreement originates *during* marriage, it will be void against his creditors, but good against himself.[102]

To make this possible, the common law had to accommodate equitable principles without sacrificing its own integrity. As the wife had no separate legal identity under common law, she had to be construed as acting as an *agent* either of her husband or the trustees of her separate estate.

The strongest protection for married women traders was a written premarital agreement that she could trade separately using her own property. Verbal agreements were possible but liable to be construed as fraudulent if used as a defence against creditors.[103] In either case, marriage itself served to validate separate trade agreements and hence it was known as being based on a 'valuable consideration'[104] and would be recognised as such even by the common law. Since the wife's separate property was technically owned by her trustees (for her sole and separate use), it could not then be taken away if her husband

---

[99] Ibid.

[100] Ibid., p. 128. The inability of a wife to make a bond was based on *Jewson vs. Read* (1773) which is discussed in detail below, pp. 59–60.

[101] Roper, *Treatise on the Law of Property*, p. 167.

[102] Ibid.

[103] Ibid., p. 305. The Statute of Frauds stated that nobody could be charged with any agreement contracted before marriage unless it was made in writing.

[104] Atiyah, *Rise and Fall of Freedom of Contract*, pp. 139–42, defines 'consideration' in eighteenth-century contract law as meaning the reason or motive for giving a promise (e.g. some expected benefit), which was stronger if there was some pre-existing moral obligation or duty arising from a transaction, or relationship (including e.g. parenthood or marriage) at the time the promise or contract was made.

became bankrupt, as it was no longer regarded as part of his property. That was because the wife was deemed only an agent of her trustees and not the legal owner. However, this meant that the wife could not use her own name when negotiating contracts or taking securities. Roper explained that this was because the common law vested all her personal estates in her husband and 'the mode by which it is evaded by modern legal decision inconsistent with the rule is by considering the wife as the agent of the trustee. But that construction cannot be made against actual expression to the contrary.'[105] Thus, if a wife signed contracts in her own name, they would be void regardless of any premarital settlement, but the law could support contracts signed in her husband's name because then it was presumed that any transactions were conducted with his explicit or implied permission.[106] Roper cited the case of *Barlow vs. Bishop* (date not stated) to illustrate this convoluted reasoning.[107] A wife trading with her husband's consent had received a promissory note of payment made out to her for business purposes; but Lord Kenyon ruled that she could not recover the money because it technically belonged to her husband. Kenyon added that if the note had been endorsed in her husband's name it would have been valid because then she would have been seen to be acting under her husband's authority. However, under the common law, if the wife traded as a *feme sole* with only her husband's permission after marriage, the agreement was considered good against himself but not against creditors. All her contracts would therefore bind him too, but he was entitled to her profits as there were no trustees to prevent him from acquiring them.[108]

Yet even securities in the wife's name could be held good in equity, if they were in respect of a contract based on her separate property, because equity had the power to offer relief against mistakes and 'mere forms', and therefore greater freedom to dispense with the strict legal forms necessary to establish proceedings in a court of law. A wife with even an informal premarital agreement[109] was therefore effectively able to control her business assets and her

---

[105] Ibid., p. 171.

[106] Ibid., p. 172. Roper supported this reasoning (ibid., p. 110) because a wife could act as 'her husband's agent or attorney. If, therefore, he authorises her to receive and pay money, or if she be *accustomed* so to do with his permission (which is an implied authority), he will be bound by such her acts.'

[107] Ibid., p. 172. The case was listed as 1 East. 432.

[108] Ibid., pp. 305–7. Agreements made after marriage were less authoritative, being based only on a 'voluntary consideration', as opposed to a 'valuable consideration', which was stronger because it was made on the expectation of some benefit from the other party, i.e. usually the financial/property agreements made between both parties and their families to seal the marriage arrangement. See e.g. *Bower vs. Holtrop* (1711) below, pp. 77–8. On portions and other benefits accruing from marriage agreements in trading families see Hunt, *Middling Sort*, pp. 151–2.

[109] Ibid., p. 168, states that such an agreement did not even require a detailed schedule of goods/stock to be kept separately.

profits, which were protected both from her husband and his creditors. In equity, the same principles applied in that a premarital agreement remained stronger than one made during marriage. However, if no trustees had been appointed for the wife, equity could make the husband a trustee of her separate business property for her own use. In addition, if a husband could be shown to have deserted his wife, and friends or family had given her the means to carry on a trade to support herself, he could not reclaim this on his return. Merely living separately, however, was not considered sufficient proof that the husband did not have an interest in the trade. More importantly, equity only held a woman liable for her own debts to the full extent of her separate property or business assets, so she could not personally become bankrupt. Wives trading on the basis of equitable separate property therefore effectively incurred only limited liability, an option that was not available to male traders until the Limited Liability Acts of 1861. However, equity did give a husband greater protection from his wife's debts, even where he was considered liable at law, because he could not be held liable for any contracts his wife made on her separate property. Hence the creditor trusted to her credit only, not his. If the separate property was officially vested in trustees by agreement, the husband was totally absolved from all responsibility even at law because the wife was the trustee's agent, not his. The trustee as the legal owner was responsible for both the wife's profits and her debts; but she was the sole beneficiary of the profits. Equity would therefore limit the debts to those payable out of the separate property, thus ensuring that the trustee would not personally suffer a loss.

Thus equity provided a means for women to trade that also limited their husband's liability for their debts even if he was created a trustee of her separate property. Once created, however, it is less clear how separate a wife's property really remained from her husband even if they were both in trade, and, as Chapter 3 shows, other family members may have been even less keen to formally recognise such property. Hunt has shown that some middling-sort wives made quite formal arrangements with their spouses to loan them the separate property with interest, but others were coerced or bullied into using it to pay off their husband's debts.[110] Restraint on anticipation, which was introduced in the late 1780s, was a legal instrument designed specifically to prevent husbands from 'kissing or kicking' their wives out of their separate property and was in common use by the nineteenth century.[111] It has been

---

[110] Hunt, *Middling Sort*, pp. 159–62, but all these cases were prior to 1780 and none concerned women with separate trades.

[111] Restraint on anticipation was a legal device originally conceived by Lord Chancellor Thurlow after he had been unable to prevent a husband (who had persuaded his wife to pledge her separate property to secure his debts) from taking all that property to pay off his creditors in 1785. This means of protecting a wife's separate property nevertheless effectively removed her power to alienate it during marriage. See Walter G. Hart, 'The Origin of Restraint upon Anticipation', *Law Quarterly Review*, 40 (1924), pp. 221–6.

viewed as yet another restriction on the agency of married women, even though its original intention was protective. However, this measure was unlikely to have been adopted so eagerly by those of the middling orders, who had far less to gain by it, than the relatives of wealthy heiresses attempting to prevent the dissipation of inherited family property. This was particularly so since marriage portions in trading families were frequently intended to be used for business purposes; but in families in which both spouses traded separately, the question was whose business.[112]

Roper's 1820 treatise presented a broader, more balanced picture of the whole English legal system than the earlier works had done and appeared to show how equity and common law could work in partnership without compromising each other. On occasions this may have been achieved by a degree of synthesis beyond what may have been suggested by disparate case results, but probably no more so than in Blackstone's *Commentaries*, which also sacrificed diversity for the sake of elegant clarity. Given the number of exceptions to coverture that Roper highlighted, it is perhaps not surprising that his definition of it was also less disabling to women than that provided by Blackstone. For Roper, coverture was merely a 'policy of law', created to prevent a husband from stripping his wife of all her property during marriage, and to prevent a wife from binding her husband by acts which 'might prove ruinous to both them and their family'.[113] This interpretation still assumed the wife to be the weaker partner, but did not entirely deny her a separate identity. Hence coverture was still under construction, and the legal fiction was concealing the fact that the laws had effectively changed.

Nevertheless, it would be a mistake to view legal treatises on the subject of married women's separate trading as evidence of a slow progress towards the more equitable provisions of the Married Women's Property Act in 1870, which gave every wife the right to the earnings of her own separate business. As the jurist Dicey pointed out, the most obvious way to reform the law would have been to give married women the same rights as single women. Instead, the Act merely gave married women in common law equitable rights to their separate property, leaving the fiction of *coverture* unchanged and conservatives unalarmed.[114] This imperfect fusion, however, confused many lawyers and common law judges who were unfamiliar with equity's principles.[115] It thus led to 'many curious legal rules, many doubtful problems and some injustice'.[116] One such injustice was that wives could still not be sued easily for their debts,

---

[112] See Hunt, *Middling Sort*, p. 152, on the different attitudes of elite and trading families towards marriage portions.

[113] Roper, *Treatise of the Law of Property*, pp. 97–8.

[114] A.V. Dicey, *Lectures on the Relation between Law and Public Opinion in the Nineteenth Century* (London, 1905; rep. 1917), pp. 387–9.

[115] Ibid., p. 388.

[116] W.S. Holdsworth, *A History of the English Law* III (London, 1903; rep. 1923), p. 533.

which as one businesswoman pointed out, meant that suppliers were less keen to provide trade goods since their chances of legally recovering any money owing were minimal.[117] Even after the 1882 Act, which did make wives liable for their debts to the extent of their separate property and made those in trade subject to the bankruptcy laws,[118] legal commentators were still trying to explain the balance between the rights and liabilities of each spouse. In order to retain her earnings a woman in business still had to prove that her trade was indeed separate. Hence the 'line between actual interference by the husband, so as to take the case out of the Statute: and the "reasonable assistance" which he may be expected to render to her: is often a very fine one.'[119] A wife was still technically only able to contract on the basis of her separate property and restraint on anticipation could still be applied.[120] The implicit assumption behind both the 1870 move towards creating separate property for wives and the earlier common law accommodations of wives' separate trading based on equitable principles was a model of family unity and a household economy which defined the liabilities of both parties so as to protect the whole. Yet the law could only imagine and define the family in one form with a nominal male head and with a common economic goal.

Conclusion

It seems clear that graphic descriptions of married women's disabilities under coverture should be treated with caution. Legal commentaries should not be taken as literal statements of women's legal status because such studies only distilled the relevant case law at any given moment in time. Moreover, the constant reinterpretation of coverture and its exceptions provides an insight into processes of legal change which cannot be said to have followed any clear linear trajectory. Adaptation to shifting social and economic conditions could only take place within the very limited possibilities defined by judicial or legislative reform, neither of which necessarily proceeded in the same direction. Nevertheless, for women in business, incremental judicial changes had a greater effect than the lack of legislative reform prior to 1870 suggests. Hence the paradox of the changeless but ever-changing law remains the defining paradigm for this narrative of imperfect adaptation, of incremental change and of constant reinterpretation. The treatises also show that wives

[117] Holcombe, *Wives and Property*, pp. 182–3.
[118] Ibid., p. 203.
[119] Lush, *Law of Husband and Wife* (1884), p. 152, provided an entire chapter, on the continuing difficulties encountered when married women traded separately, pp. 149–63.
[120] Dicey, *Lectures*, p. 389, argued that the Married Women's Property Act adopted the conservative tactic of making married women's property separate by equitable means partly because Parliament did not wish to alienate the wealthy who relied on restraint upon anticipation to protect their daughters' property.

could defend their separate business property, even in a court of common law, more than a century before the Married Women's Property Acts enshrined equitable principles in law. Married women did not acquire the same trading rights as men or single women; but the creation of numerous exceptions and the reinterpretation of existing law left – theoretically – plenty of space for them to continue to trade throughout the period 1700 to 1850.

3

A customary privilege?

Common law, borough custom and the *feme sole* trader

> There is a difference between acts done by a *feme covert* and an infant: the one
> is incapable for want of natural judgement. . . . A *Feme covert* is only incapable
> for want of liberty, being sub potestate viri; but where the custom expressly
> enables her to act, in matters concerning her trade independent of her husband,
> she is exempted from that incapacity, and is under no other. If she can manage
> her trade she may surely borrow money.
>
> *Jewson vs. Read* (1773)[1]

One method by which married women in business could avoid the effects of
coverture was by invoking the borough custom of *feme sole* merchant. In theory,
the custom restored the economic 'liberty' that coverture denied women
on marriage, although, as already noted, that denial was neither absolute nor
clear-cut. Nevertheless, the existence of the custom has been seen as a bastion
against the encroachment of patriarchal values embodied in the common law.
According to this view, the custom was a valuable privilege for women in trade
and the growth of common law jurisdiction is seen as a blow to women's
economic autonomy.[2] The first part of this chapter therefore discusses women's
access to local courts and customary law. It considers to what extent the
existence of a pluralistic legal system could be beneficial to women in business
and whether legal doctrine relating to women in trade may be shown to follow
more than just a single, patriarchal imperative, as Gavigan has argued.[3] Instead,
court judgments may, as Finn has argued, have been more informed by 'multiple
layers of legal, social and economic reasoning'.[4] At the same time, however,
the custom was the only legal way that a woman could be made fully *personally*
liable for all her trading debts and therefore subject to a commission of bankruptcy.[5] From this perspective, the custom offered little protection to married

---

[1] PRO, *The English Reports, 1220–1867*, CD-Rom (subsequently *ER*), Lofft 134, 98, p. 574.

[2] Prior, 'Women and the Urban Economy', p. 103; Erickson, *Women and Property*, p. 6.

[3] Gavigan, 'Law, Gender and Ideology', p. 294; and see above, p. 28.

[4] Margot Finn, 'Debt and Credit in Bath's Court of Requests, 1829–39', *Urban History*, 21
(1994), p. 219.

[5] As discussed above, equitable traders could also be made bankrupt but they remained a

women whose husbands could instead hide behind their wives' liability.[6] The second consideration is therefore to examine to what extent the custom of *feme sole* trader could really be seen as a privilege for women in business.

The main sources for this study are the law reports of cases concerning *feme sole* traders in London. Although this means a very narrow focus on a (relatively) small group of women in trade, based on an even smaller number of legal reports, it does highlight a number of key issues. Only cases that dealt specifically with *feme sole* trader merchants have been analysed,[7] which excluded those cases cited as supporting case law (most of which may be found in the treatises) and resulted in a selection of fourteen cases between 1627 and 1852. In studying a different but directly comparable source to the legal commentaries a different narrative and chronology emerges which further highlights the drawbacks of retaining a single linear narrative in histories of women's legal and/or economic 'position' in society. A comparison of the verdicts in *feme sole* trader cases from 1627 to 1852, which, if taken at face value, appear to show an increasing number of cases in which the common law doctrine of coverture was upheld at the expense of the custom. Of the seven identified cases directly concerning feme sole trading between 1627 and 1776, only one returned a verdict that upheld *coverture*, and even that ruling was given with strict reservations.[8] The end of the Mansfield era and the accession of Kenyon in 1788 could be seen to herald a new era of conservatism or of a return to traditional patriarchal values. In only one of the seven cases reported between 1791 and 1852 was the borough custom upheld. At first glance, then, it would seem that the *feme sole* trader cases show women losing economic agency during the period in direct contrast to the evidence provided by the legal treatises. Yet this type of simple linear analysis not only obscures other aspects of legal, social and economic change but implicitly assumes that the custom was both a privilege and a necessity to enable married women to trade at all.

One of the reasons why the law reports apparently tell a different story from the legal treatises, despite the fact that the treatises were largely based on them, is because the reports were specifically written by lawyers for use by other lawyers.[9] As such, they concentrated on cases that turned on a specific point

---

more doubtful category, probably because their liability was more likely to have been limited to the extent of their separate property, the difficulties of establishing how this had been created (that could effect which creditors it would be held good against) and what exactly it comprised.

[6] Hunt, *Middling Sort*, p. 139; Bennett, 'Medieval Women, Modern Women', pp. 154–5.

[7] From *ER*, a searchable CD-Rom database of the English Law Reports.

[8] See below, p. 59, for discussion of *Jewson vs. Read* (1773), and p. 57 for one further case, *Langham vs. Bewett* (1627) in which the judges could not agree on a verdict.

[9] See Holdsworth, *Sources and Literature of English Law*, pp. 74–5, on how judicial decisions based on precedent necessitated the compilation of law reports from which lawyers could learn the principles of the common law.

of law or procedural question. The broad overview of women's position at law, in equity and in ecclesiastical jurisdiction which was found in some treatises was largely missing from the law reports. Reported cases were also heavily biased towards the untypical. None the less, they represented what were considered to be 'turning points' in judicial decision-making and as such may be used to trace a history of such points. As Staves argues, law reports are also useful for histories of 'legal ideology, or . . . what the profession publicly represented its rules and their rationales to be'.[10] However, historians face a number of problems when using these reports. The early reports, in particular, were privately published collections with no set style and they were often inaccurate. From around 1736, there was a greater degree of standardisation, which emphasised reporting of the judge's decision and the reasons for it rather than the lawyers' arguments; but standards still varied considerably. In the eighteenth and nineteenth centuries, reporters also increasingly stressed the rules of pleading because courts became ever stricter over the presentation and formulation of cases, which made it 'more possible for a skilful pleader to snatch a decision, in spite of a total absence of any substantial merit'.[11] Conversely, a lawyer unaware of proper procedure could lose even the strongest case, a point which was of particular importance for married female traders whose coverture necessitated the presence or naming of her husband for conformity's sake. Law reports are therefore particularly useful for the discussion here, because they highlight both issues of legal doctrine and procedure.

One thing the law reports cannot do is to give any indication of how many women in trade had access to legal systems outside the centralised uniformity of the common law. Nor do they allow historians to assess the probably far greater number of women who never resorted to official adjudication to settle commercial disputes. As H.W. Arthurs has argued, the 'rules' for:

> buying and selling, lending and borrowing, shipping and carrying are generated primarily by regimes of private ordering – the contract, the course of dealing, the ritual of exchange. It is extremely doubtful that more than the tiniest fraction of these transactions is made with conscious reference to formal rules and common or statute law. Nor does such law suddenly take over when disputes arise.[12]

Quite apart from private renegotiation or family intervention to settle disputes, which must have happened very frequently, lawyers could also settle cases out of court. As a result, only a small minority of cases would be likely ever to reach a courtroom, and of those that did many were not concluded there.[13] An even

<hr />

[10] Staves, *Married Women's Separate Property*, p. 13.

[11] Holdsworth, *Sources and Literature*, pp. 97–8.

[12] H.W. Arthurs, *'Without the Law': Administrative Justice and Legal Pluralism in Nineteenth-century England* (London, 1985), p. 51.

[13] See below, p. 71, esp. n. 12 on the high number of Chancery cases that did not continue beyond the pleading stage; see also Finn, 'Debt and Credit', p. 218 and n. 27, on how roughly

smaller minority would have been recorded, perhaps even fewer where women were involved. In a case in 1765, the prosecution pointed out that there was only one record of a bankruptcy commission ever having been taken out against a wife, arguing this to support the view that a married woman was not within the spirit of the bankrupt laws. Lord Mansfield, however, ruled that just because this was the only instance found, it did not 'follow that there was certainly none before it'.[14] The law reports in particular cannot be taken as any indication of the number of women involved in *feme sole* trader cases, because the reports were only intended to be examples of current case law.

Local vs. superior courts

Within the pluralist legal system tradeswomen had access to a number of courts, including many that operated outside the common law, although more research is needed to determine the extent of such access. As late as 1830, the superior courts of Westminster – Common Pleas, King's Bench, Equity and Exchequer – were handling some 90,000 lawsuits. Yet more than 300,000 claims were still being processed in over 300 local and special courts,[15] most of which operated on the basis of local customary law or according to equitable principles.[16] Both of these were principles that could operate to the advantage of female traders. Of particular interest were the local Courts of Requests, which grew increasingly prevalent from the mid-eighteenth century and were processing in the region of 400,000 claims annually by 1840. They were designed to facilitate debt collection, and operated on principles of local communal justice and commercial fairness. These were courts for small claims, often with a limit of just 40 shillings (although this was not an inconsiderable amount even in 1800), used predominantly by the lower-middle orders, and particularly by shopkeepers, a trade in which women were numerous.[17] However, Christine Wiskin's brief exploration of Birmingham businesswomen's use of local courts shows that those seeking legal advice from a local attorney were on a higher

half of all cases in the Bath Court of Requests in 1829 and 1839 were settled out of court. Earle, *Making of the English Middle Class*, p. 124, notes that the main object of issuing a writ was to call the debtors' bluff; less than one-tenth of those issued writs for debt in London in 1791 actually went to prison because the majority paid up or settled out of court; and see Craig Muldrew, 'Credit and the Courts: Debt Litigation in a Seventeenth Century Urban Community', *Economic History Review*, 2nd ser., 46 (1993), p. 27 on how just 4 per cent of cases in the borough court of King's Lynn reached judgment.

[14] *Lavie vs. Phillips* (1765), cited in *The Laws Respecting Women*, pp. 174, 175.
[15] Arthurs, *Without the Law*, p. 17.
[16] W.R. Cornish and G. de N. Clark, *Law and Society in England, 1750–1950* (London, 1989), pp. 30–1.
[17] For a description of the Courts of Requests, their limited jurisdiction, type of litigants and commitment to local communal justice, see Arthurs, *Without the Law*, pp. 26–34.

economic level than that of female suitors described by William Hutton in 1787 as using the Birmingham Court of Request. Since, unlike in London, she also found that businesswomen formed a very small proportion of those appearing in Coventry's Town Court, she suggests that they were reluctant to use court proceedings unless the sums involved were large enough to warrant litigation.[18] This is an area that would greatly repay further research, not only into the extent of tradeswomen's use of local courts, but also to throw light upon regional variations and the role played by the threat of litigation.

The borough custom of *feme sole* trading, however, relied on the existence of borough courts. From the medieval period, certain towns possessed one or more borough courts, usually granted under their original charters, which, *inter alia*, regulated disputes between traders before a court presided over by the Mayor and other officials according to a customary law which varied in different towns. In Lincoln, a trading wife could be imprisoned and her husband was not liable for her debts, and she could plead coverture only if she followed the same trade as her husband. In Fordwich, a plaintiff could implead even a woman with a separate business as a wife (presumably therefore making her husband still liable), and a wife could not bring an action without her husband.[19] In Cambridge, a woman could be charged as sole for anything concerning her craft, as long as her husband had not 'medeleth' in it.[20] Bateson noted long ago that while the common law took 'a short cut to clear doctrine', customs regulating relations between husbands and wives were never systematic. Instead, such customs provide evidence of the long persistence of the 'old family organisation of the household', and the difficulty burgesses had in fitting this into borough arrangements for freedom of trade and division of property.[21]

For historians attempting to assess the impact of the *feme sole* custom on women in trade, the question is: How long did these courts survive and how far could their local customary law resist the efforts to achieve legal unity or centralisation that resulted finally in the Judicature Acts (1873–75)? The Courts of Requests were replaced by county courts in 1846 but there is little consensus over the fate of borough courts. Cornish and Clark argue that, as long as a town itself continued to flourish, so would many of its tribunals, and note that borough courts in Bristol, Liverpool, Salford and Norwich survived until 1971, as did the Mayor's and City of London Court.[22] Many

---

[18] Wiskin, 'Women, Finance and Credit', pp. 172–3. Finn, 'Debt and Credit', p. 22, found that female litigants from a wide social spectrum used the early nineteenth-century Bath Court of Requests, but there is little discussion of their occupational status apart from servants.

[19] Mary Bateson (ed.), *Borough Customs* I (1904), pp. cxii–xiii.

[20] Shephard, 'Manhood, Credit and Patriarchy', p. 91.

[21] Ibid., pp. xix, c–ci.

[22] Cornish and Clark, *Law and Society*, p. 30, and n. 51. Baker, *Introduction to English Legal History* p. 25, n. 32, notes that all these courts were abolished by the 1971 Courts Act, so

more local tribunals had, however, probably become moribund by the mid-eighteenth century when they were largely supplanted by Courts of Requests.[23] The survival of the *feme sole* trader custom is even harder to ascertain. There were at least thirteen boroughs in which the custom was known to exist in the medieval or early modern period,[24] and Erickson suggests that others remain unidentified. Prior, however, argues that by the nineteenth century only the London custom remained.[25] It is therefore not possible to provide a definitive answer to the question of how long the custom might have survived without further detailed research, but it would be equally mistaken to assume that it had vanished. The law reports were still citing the London custom in 1852 and the editor of the 1861 edition of the *Liber Albus* noted that it still held good in the City, which suggests that it may not have fallen completely into abeyance until after the Married Women's Property Acts rendered the distinction unnecessary. Although the law reports cannot show exactly when the custom ended or how widely it spread, they can give an insight into how far the superior courts could overrule the decisions of these inferior courts and to what extent the common law could allow the operation of a custom that clearly operated in opposition to its own principles.

William Bohun, author of *Privilegia Londini* (1702), was convinced that local rights and customs, and London's in particular, were a necessary bulwark against the operation of arbitrary power wielded by monarch and ministers. Whether he regarded the common law per se as an instrument of that power, however, is not so clear.[26] Under the City of London customs, wives could be considered as single women in a number of instances, such as if they were accused of trespass or had been battered. The custom of London, cited in cases concerning wives trading alone, was usually that recorded in the *Liber Albus* (1419), which stated that:

> where a woman *coverte de baron* follows any craft within the said city by herself apart, with which the husband in no way intermeddles, such a woman shall be bound as a single woman as to all that concerns her said craft. And if the husband and wife are impleaded, in such case the wife shall plead as a single woman in a

---

that ironically they survived longer than the superior common law courts of King's Bench and Common Pleas which were abolished in 1876.

[23] Finn, 'Debt and Credit', pp. 212–13.

[24] Cambridge, Chester, Exeter, Fordwich, Hastings, London, Lincoln, Oxford, Rye, Southampton, Torksey, Winchelsea, Worcester.

[25] See Bateson, *Borough Customs*, pp. 227–8; Erickson, *Women and Property*, pp. 30, 246–7, and n. 40; Prior, 'Women and the Urban Economy', p. 103; Kowaleski, 'Women's Work in a Market Town', p. 146.

[26] William Bohun, *Privilegia Londini: Or, The Rights, Liberties, Privileges, Laws and Customs of the City of London* (London, 1702; rep. 1723), p. 5, argued that if the fundamental rights of London were overturned, 'the whole Nation would soon be overspread' by a plague of arbitrary power.

Court of Record, and shall have her law and other advantages by way of plea just as a single woman. And if she is condemned she shall be committed to prison until she shall have made satisfaction; and neither the husband nor his goods shall in such case be charged or interfered with.[27]

The *Liber Albus* thus made it perfectly clear that the custom was a double-edged sword. In the 1861 edition the editor noted that '*coverte de baron*' was 'an old legal term' which simply meant 'protected by a husband'.[28] Thus, just as in the legal commentaries, the fiction had been reinterpreted.

Perhaps just as importantly for women in business the *Liber Albus* also stated that if any wife:

> as though a single woman rents any house *or shop* within the said city, she shall be bound to pay the rent of the said house or shop, and shall be impleaded and sued as a single woman, by way of debt if necessary, notwithstanding that she was coverte de baron at the time of such letting, supposing that the lessor did not know thereof.[29]

Under London custom, married women acting as if single were therefore also personally liable for the rent on their premises, regardless of whether they were for commercial or domestic purposes. The important factor, which was also commonly cited in Chancery cases, was that the wife was *known* to have been acting for herself regardless of her marital status.[30] In the Mayor's Court case of *Fabian vs. Plant* (1691), Hannah Plant was described by the defence as living and trading as a lace-maker in a house, apart from her husband, on which she paid the rent. Fabian had sold trade goods to Mrs Plant for which she still owed £57 at the time of her death. Despite the prosecution's assertion that Mrs Plant was trading in a house rather than a shop and that her husband had retired from the Company of Hatbandmakers to preach as a dissenting minister, the custom was upheld. Fabian was held to have known 'her and her trade' and to have therefore traded with a *feme sole* merchant at his own peril, so her husband was not liable to pay her debts after her death.[31]

City wives could therefore trade alone and rent out the premises necessary to do so, but in both cases had to make it clear to other people that they were acting as if single. The consequence of this agency, should they fall into debt, was imprisonment. In the medieval period, trading wives had had to register

---

[27] Henry Thomas Riley (trans.), *Liber Albus: The White Book of the City of London* compiled in 1419 by John Carpenter and Richard Whittington (London, 1861), p. 181. For trespass and battery see p. 182; in addition, a husband could claim 'the aid of his wife' and take an extra day to consult with her if he was accused of debt over a contract that she had signed for him.

[28] Ibid.

[29] Ibid., pp. 181–2; emphasis added.

[30] See below, pp. 79–81.

[31] ER, *Fabian vs. Plant* (1691), 1 Shower KB 183, 89, p. 525.

their right to trade with the local authorities or at least publicly declare their intention to trade sole.[32] This seems to have died out, because even the seventeenth-century case reports state only that a wife's sole trading status should be commonly known. It seems likely that the main reason for reliance upon public reputation was the importance of credit as a facilitator of trade. Other traders had to know with whom they were dealing, and what recourse they would have in case of debt. In 1798, counsel in *De Gaillon vs. L'Aigle* argued that it was 'for the benefit of the *feme covert* that she should be liable to an action . . . otherwise she could obtain no credit, and would have no means of gaining her livelihood'.[33] In other words, it was thought that unless a woman could be held personally liable, other traders would be reluctant to extend her the necessary credit on which so many business transactions relied. This was an argument which, as we have already seen, was still being used in the nineteenth century when the first Married Women's Property Act failed to make wives easily accountable for their debts at law. The evidence thus suggests that the label of *feme sole* trader was far more relevant in law as a category of debt recovery than as a means of conveying the right to trade. However, since *feme sole* trading did confer full liability for debts owing, in order to reclaim the 'protection' of coverture, indebted trading wives sued under the borough custom in a local court had to appeal to the common law in a superior court. In more than half of the cases studied this is precisely what *feme sole* trader wives appear to have been doing, often with their husbands' assistance.

London had at least ten city courts, including numerous Courts of Requests, which by the early nineteenth century were handling an enormous case-load.[34] The court in which *feme sole* trader cases were initially tried was the Lord Mayor's Court held in the Guildhall. It was a court of record, which could try any matter arising within the liberty of the City of London including debt to any value. The Recorder of the City of London was the official judge but the Lord Mayor and aldermen could sit with him and trial was by jury. Moreover, like the Exchequer, it was a court of both common law and equity. It was also relatively simple, quick and cheap to bring an action before this court. A plaintiff had to go to one of the four court attorneys who would empower a sergeant to arrest the defendant, who had to find bail immediately or be imprisoned in one of the compters. Bohun noted in his 1723 edition that it would cost 30 shillings to bring an action to trial within fourteen days and,

---

[32] Bateson, *Borough Customs*, p. cxii; Kay E. Lacey, 'Women and Work in Fourteenth- and Fifteenth-century London', in *Women and Work in Pre-Industrial England*, ed. L. Charles and L. Duffin (1985), p. 44.
[33] *ER, De Gaillon vs. L'Aigle* (1798), 1 Bosanquet & Puller 359, 126, p. 951.
[34] Bohun, *Privilegia Londini*, pp. 290–472, gives detailed accounts of ten City courts and their proceedings. Arthurs, *Without the Law*, p. 26, found that by 1830 a single Court of Requests in Tower Hamlets was handling almost 30,000 claims a year.

if a defendant took more than six weeks between finding bail and entering a plea, he would be unable to remove the case to another court. The equity division was usually held before the Mayor and Alderman but again the Recorder sat as judge and an action was brought by bill of complaint, costing approximately 10 shillings.[35] A defendant in a common law case could issue a bill of complaint in the equity section to act as an injunction to stop the case at law. As will be shown subsequently,[36] this was not an uncommon procedure in Chancery, and there is nothing to suggest that women did not take advantage of it in the City Court. If there was no action pending at law a defendant had only eight days to answer the bill in equity. In theory, therefore, businesswomen in London could have relatively fast and inexpensive access to both customary and equitable law, which gave them the ability to sue and be sued.

Craig Muldrew has argued that local courts were very accessible institutions, and his research on the Palace Court of Westminster supports the view that women were frequent litigants there.[37] Muldrew found that by 1686 the Palace Court was handling some 20,000 cases per annum, and had effectively become a borough court for urban areas of London west of the city. Of 413 cases Muldrew sampled for June 1686, 36 per cent involved women, and in 15 per cent of the total sample the plaintiffs were women. For Muldrew, this constitutes 'evidence that women played a crucial role in the business of the capital'.[38] Combined with the evidence of the accessibility of the Mayor's Court discussed above, it also provides a possible explanation for the fact that all of the reported *feme sole* trader cases were tried in the superior courts but only one law report dealt with a case of a wife suing to recover debts rather than being sued. It would appear, in other words, that women wanting to sue as *feme sole* traders may have done so in a local court of record, while those seeking a defence against being sued would try to have the case removed to a superior common law court in order to plead coverture in their defence.

In the single case where a wife did attempt to sue in a superior court, *Caudell vs. Shaw* (1791), she had been widowed before the case came to court. The widow sued for goods sold and delivered by her while she had been married but trading separately from her husband in Cheapside, although they had lived in the same house. She had obtained a verdict in her favour but the defence managed to obtain a retrial at Westminster. Despite being widowed, she was

---

[35] Bohun, *Privilegia Londini*, pp. 250–3. A bill of complaint had to be signed by one of four city councillors which cost 6s 8d, 4d a sheet to draw, 6d a sheet to engross, 2s to enter in court and 3s 4d to pay the attorneys.

[36] See below, pp. 73, 75, 85–6.

[37] Craig Muldrew, *The Economy of Obligation: The Culture of Credit and Social Relations in Early Modern England* (Basingstoke, 1998), p. 271, also argues that legal accessibility was very 'necessary in a society where credit relations were so intertwined'.

[38] Ibid., pp. 233–4. However, Muldrew could not find enough surviving records for the Mayor's Court and other London courts to assess women's participation further.

claiming her prior right to have traded as a married woman on the basis of the *feme sole* custom of London. The court insisted that she should either have sued the case as a *feme sole* in the city courts or have sued at common law through representatives of her dead husband, because she had still been a *feme covert* while she was trading.[39] The case was tried before the conservative Kenyon, and was only the second report in which coverture was upheld at the expense of the custom. It is quite possible that these procedural abnormalities were used to support both Kenyon's belief in the dominance of the common law and the morality of coverture. As Cornish and Clark point out, law reports give a useful impression of the 'technical objections and procedural stratagems', fostered by the adversarial nature of the eighteenth-century legal system.[40] However, far more frequently the law reports show that *feme sole* traders used procedural stratagems to their own advantage. Eight of the selected fourteen reported cases show evidence of some form of legal manipulation, most commonly in the form of appeals to a 'higher' court to review an inferior court's decision by a prerogative writ.

A *feme covert* sole trader who had been imprisoned by the city court under the custom of London could apply for relief on a writ of habeas corpus, which could remove a defendant imprisoned for debt by an inferior court to the court above. It had been a common remedy against the 'misuse' of borough jurisdiction since the fourteenth century.[41] In a report dated 1627, Mrs Bewett, whose case was cited in both *Baron and Feme* (1719) and *The Laws Respecting Women* (1777)[42] as evidence of the principles of *feme sole* trading, had used this method to attempt to obtain her release. Her defence argued that she should be discharged because she followed the same trade as her husband and was 'but servant to her husband, and the wares coming to his use, he, by intendment, is to be sued: and this case is out of the custom'.[43] Her husband, John Bewett, had been serving in the army overseas while she was trading, and he had since returned 'bare and needy'. As Mrs Bewett would have had to cite him in order to bring the case at all, he was in all probability supporting this attempt to regain his wife's economic assistance. Three of the five judges upheld the principle of the *feme sole* trader and declared that they ought 'not to meddle' in the business of the City Court, 'for in London they are judges of their own customs, and not otherwise; and therefore we ought not to take away their privileges'.[44] Here the common law judges seem to have viewed the borough custom as a local authority 'privilege' above that of a wife but

---

[39] ER, *Caudell vs. Shaw*, 4 Term Reports 364, 100, p. 1066.
[40] Cornish and Clark, *Law and Society*, p. 25. Lord Mansfield had tried to 'free the main branches of process but under his successors, the parasitic growths crept back'.
[41] Baker, *Introduction to Legal History*, pp. 126–8.
[42] Anon., *Baron and Feme*, p. 301; Anon., *Lawes Respecting Women*, p. 177, but note variant spellings. See also above, p. 33.
[43] ER, *Langham vs. Bewett* (1627), Croke Car 68, 79, p. 661.
[44] Ibid., p. 662.

this would have left her liable for the debt. The other two judges thought that because Mrs Bewett had followed the same trade as her husband she was acting as his servant so that the goods were provided for his use and he should be sued, thus discharging her. In the event, neither side prevailed and no action was taken because Mrs Bewett came to an agreement with her creditor, so the case was settled out of court.

In *Moreton vs. Packman* (1669),[45] which was also cited in *Baron and Feme* (1719), another attempt at using habeas corpus was blocked by the superior court even though there was some doubt about whether the trade of victualler fell within the custom. Again the superior court held that the case and the decision over whether victualling could be warranted by the custom could only be decided by the City Court. In *Pope vs. Vaux* (1776),[46] the superior court again decided that there were insufficient grounds to remove the case from the Mayor's Court. After this date there are no more reports of attempts to remove cases from the City courts in this manner, so it seems probable that defence lawyers abandoned this method of directly challenging the jurisdiction of the borough courts, relying instead on challenges to substantive points of law.

Custom vs. common law

Although later cases still show strong evidence of procedural stratagems, the grounds for argument shifted more towards the relative power and morality of the principle of coverture over custom and an attempt to balance the 'rights' of debtors and creditors. The boundaries of economic and moral imperatives thus became highly contested areas, particularly as judicial decisions seem to have partly reflected swings between 'progressive' and conservative attitudes. Atiyah has divided the period into three phases. The first, a period of modest reform and increasing acceptance of economic liberalism, was dominated by Mansfield and continued through to around 1793. The second, which ran from 1793 to 1830, Atiyah has characterised as a 'disastrous period for the law and legal institutions'. It was dominated by the conservative Chief Justices Kenyon and Ellenborough and the Lord Chancellor Lord Eldon, who between them opposed 'practically all legal reform for nearly thirty years'.[47] From 1830 to 1870, judges more in sympathy with political economy, Benthamite legal reform and commercial enterprise rose to prominence.[48] It is a necessarily sweeping generalisation but nevertheless provides a broad framework within which to discuss the role of gender in relation to other issues in *feme sole* trader cases. Discourses around gender did not exist in isolation but always within a

---

[45]   ER, *Moreton vs. Packman* (1669), 1 Modern 26, 86, p. 705.
[46]   ER, *Pope vs. Vaux* (1776), 2 Blackstone W 1060, 96, p. 624.
[47]   Atiyah, *Rise and Fall of Freedom of Contract*, pp. 360–9.
[48]   Ibid., pp. 369–74.

dynamic relationship with debates about other related legal, social and economic concerns. On the legal and social front one of these issues was separate maintenance contracts, cases concerning which could involve wives in trade.[49] But more importantly the judicial decisions and moral concerns involved in separate maintenance cases could, as discussed earlier, also impact on decisions in *feme sole* trader cases. Staves describes the period 1675 to 1778 as one in which equity courts were increasingly favourable towards separate maintenance contracts and contract logic, but from 1778 to 1800 there was a struggle over whether common-law courts would accept equitable principles and fears that the application of contract logic to marriage produced socially disruptive consequences. After 1800 the courts reaffirmed the legitimacy of separate maintenance contracts but imposed stricter controls over contracting parties, which Staves interprets as a revival of deeper patriarchal structures.[50] However, although in later reports of *feme sole* cases, coverture and the patriarchal values it embodied does seem to have become the dominant doctrinal position, in most of these cases there were other points to be considered, and fact-based exceptions did not disappear.

As early as 1765, the extent to which the custom could challenge the common law doctrine of coverture in the interests of trade was questioned. In *Lavie vs. Phillips* (1765), the defence argued that it was 'convenient to trade that the wife should sue and be sued; but no reason, that (subject to this control) the husband should not have the ultimate property'.[51] In this case, cited in *The Laws Respecting Women* (1777), Lord Mansfield held that the custom 'as a good one, use may be made of it in any Court in the kingdom',[52] particularly as a defence by the husband. Hence, as discussed earlier, Mansfield supported the use of the custom as an aid to free trade.[53] However, in 1773 even Mansfield was effectively forced to reverse his decision in a blatant case of legal manipulation. *Jewson vs. Read* is one of the least clear reports but the facts of the case appear to have been as follows.[54] Mrs Jewson was a wealthy milliner, 'dealing on paper-currency' up to £70,000. She borrowed £9,000 on a bond from Mr Read, an apothecary, and entered into a warrant of attorney to confess a judgment[55] on her own account without her husband's apparent knowledge. She subsequently went bankrupt and was

---

[49] See e.g. *Cecil vs. Juxon* (1737), an equity case often noted as supporting case law in legal treatises, in which the judge upheld the wife's right to her stock in trade as a milliner, when her husband had returned after fourteen years' absence and tried to claim it as his own. See Staves, *Married Women's Separate Property*, p. 176.
[50] Ibid., pp. 175–95.
[51] ER, *Lavie vs. Phillips*, 1 Blackstone W 570, 96, p. 330. See also above, p. 37.
[52] Ibid.
[53] See above, p. 36.
[54] ER, *Jewson vs. Read* (1773), Lofft 134, 98, p. 573. See also a summary of the case in ER, *Caudell vs. Shaw*, 4 Term Reports 364, 100, p. 1066.
[55] A way of acknowledging or registering the existence of a loan or bond.

represented in court by her assignees. Read wanted to be included among her creditors but she applied to have the judgment set aside on the grounds of irregularity; this was because she had been declared a *feme sole* whereas now she claimed to be a *feme covert* in joint trade with her husband. There was a strong suspicion of fraud in the case, particularly since Mr Jewson had used part of the money borrowed for his wife's business to build a house and, if Mrs Jewson was declared a *feme covert*, she could evade repaying Read.

The court had to decide whether the bond was void because it had been taken out by a married woman on her own and therefore the confession of judgment on it was an error, or whether the custom could be extended from simple contracts to include bonds. It was also questioned whether the custom was valid at all in a superior court. Lord Mansfield wanted to 'give the creditor a chance' to recover his money and to acknowledge the custom, but he was not prepared to allow that a married woman could give a bond, which was void under common law and could serve to bind her heirs and was an action not covered specifically by the custom. This is one of very few cases in which Mansfield was not willing to hold a *feme sole* trader liable for her debts in the interests of commerce. Perhaps the sums of money involved, and particularly the £70,000, which he felt 'would have startled the City at the time of making the custom',[56] seem to have convinced him that the custom was not meant to cover such eventualities. However, despite the verdict supporting coverture, Mrs Jewson's agency is paramount in this case. She seems to have dealt regularly in huge sums of money, and managed to borrow a large sum and get it officially sanctioned with no apparent difficulty, all on her own behalf. It was only when she went bankrupt that she attempted to reverse this by successfully pleading her coverture.

During the trial, Mr Jewson had been urged to bring a writ of error, a method of questioning substantive points of law. In 1776, during *Hatchett vs. Baddeley*, a case frequently cited in later *feme sole* trader cases, defence counsel had argued that the 'very admission of the fact of *coverture* destroys the action. If a *feme covert* appears as a *feme sole* and has judgement against her, she and her husband may set it aside by writ of error, alleging the *coverture*.'[57] In summing up, the judge argued that to allow a wife to contract or be sued alone would overturn 'the first principles of the English law' and the consequences would result in numerous 'legal absurdities.'[58] This was thus a restatement of the necessity of maintaining the principle behind the legal fiction of marital unity of persons upon which so much law relating to marriage rested. It could indeed be seen as evidence of a resurgence in the subordination of women to the bonds of coverture but the moral (as opposed to economic) considerations in the case were considerable. The woman in question had eloped from her husband and

---

[56] ER, *Jewson vs. Read* (1773), Lofft 144, 98, p. 578.
[57] ER, *Hatchett vs. Baddeley* (1776), 2 Blackstone W 1079, 96, p. 363.
[58] Ibid., p. 367.

was not living separately with his permission. Even though the decision was later cited in *feme sole* cases to support stricter readings of coverture it did not necessarily adversely affect *feme sole* traders because, as in the case of Mrs Jewson, coverture was precisely the verdict many women hoped for.

One such similar case was that of *Beard vs. Webb* (1800), in which the Tory Lord Eldon upheld coverture, but again there are a number of considerations that prevent the case from being read as simply another reassertion of patriarchy. Arabella Beard, a married upholsterer, was sued for debt as a *feme sole* trader by the custom of London in the court of King's Bench and appeared in court on her own account with her attorney. She lost the case and brought a writ of error with her husband Henry, on the grounds that under common law she could not have used an attorney in the court without her husband who should also have been named in the suit for conformity's sake. Lord Eldon made it clear that the custom of London should be seen as executory only; that is, it attached only to the City courts and could not support an action in the superior courts. He argued that even in the City Court the husband should have been named for conformity. Hence his first objection on procedural grounds was upholding the centrality and dominance of the common law. Furthermore, Lord Eldon pointed out that there were a number of difficult cases concerning a married woman's separate property currently undecided, which questioned her position in equity and the ecclesiastical courts, and how far the common law should provide remedies beyond these. He was equally resistant to any suggestion that the common law should bend to commercial necessity. He declared that:

> if the law has decided that a feme-sole trader in London cannot be sued elsewhere than in the city courts, those who deal with her must take their remedy as the law has given it to them. Whatever may be the effect of the prevailing fashions of the times, I do not think that the argument of inconvenience, arising out of those fashions, can at any time be relied upon against a current of decisions: and I am ready to say, that if the policy of the law has withheld from married women certain powers and faculties, the courts of law must continue to treat them as deprived of those powers and faculties, until the legislature directs those courts to do otherwise.[59]

Hence Eldon was greatly concerned with maintaining the status quo between the plurality of legal systems and of upholding the authority of the common law against prevailing commercial 'fashions'.[60] Unlike Mansfield, Eldon was therefore unwilling to import equitable principles into the common law, or to accept that it could be changed except by statutory legislation, even

---

[59] *ER, Beard vs. Webb* (1800), 2 Bosanquet & Puller 108, 126, pp. 1183–4.
[60] At this point Eldon was still a common law judge but he became Lord Chancellor from 1801 to 1827 and in Chancery his conservatism was evident in attempts to reverse earlier decisions on the legality of separate maintenance contracts. Staves, *Married Women's Separate Property*, pp. 184–6, 189, notes that Eldon was anti any form of marital separation

if some legal treatises still suggested that a more flexible situation existed. However, Eldon's argument also made it clear that married women were *de facto* acting as traders, if at some potential risk to all concerned. He upheld coverture in the common-law court, but stressed that there were other 'remedies' against married women available in other courts. Eldon was also concerned to maintain the relationship between the law and 'private families, constituting together that great family called the public'.[61] It has been argued earlier that legal doctrine as reproduced in treatises became increasingly concerned with balancing family members' liability and, under London borough custom, even children could be held liable for debt if they kept a shop or traded goods.[62] Although the family model implicit within contemporary legal doctrine always figures a male head suggesting the persistence of patriarchal ideology, Gavigan has argued that feminists need to study how legal procedures reproduce 'familial' ideology rather 'male' ideology per se.[63] Using this reading, Mrs Beard appears not to have been a victim of patriarchal ideology but acting with her husband to manipulate the legal concept of family within which an appeal to coverture could result in restoring her contribution to the family economy.

In some cases, upholding the doctrine of coverture prevented husbands from evading debts by claiming that their wives were *feme sole* traders. In 1825 Mr Anderson, a baker and confectioner, was sued for debts owing by two grocers, who had gone to his premises to demand payment where they found him 'in working dress'.[64] Anderson told them to speak to his wife, who said she could not pay; but the couple later sent their son with some money. In court, Anderson claimed that his wife employed him but that he received no wages and that they lived in the same house but did not cohabit. As he had told the grocers that they would get no more than 4 shillings in the pound if they sued him, the court was of the opinion that he was well aware of the extent of his liability by maintaining such an arrangement. Witnesses agreed that Mrs Anderson paid the rent and rates, so her name was on the rate books, and that she was employed by the parish to make bread and had been given credit in her own right by other tradesmen. It was revealed that Mr Anderson had been a baker in the same house but had been sent to prison, during which time his goods had been sold under a distress but were bought back by a friend for Mrs Anderson, who carried on in business. After Mr Anderson's discharge

---

except for cruelty and determined to leave any matters concerning it to the ecclesiastical courts. With regard to new commercial enterprise, Atiyah, *Rise and Fall of Freedom of Contract*, pp. 366–7 notes that Eldon made 'a thorough nuisance of himself' on the subject of new companies which he treated as illegal monopolies.

[61] Ibid., p. 1182.
[62] Riley, *Liber Albus*, p. 193; Lacey, *Women and Work*, p. 45: girls from age 15 and boys from age 14 were liable for any debts concerning their craft or trade.
[63] Gavigan, 'Law, Gender and Ideology', pp. 293–4.
[64] ER, *Petty & Another vs. Anderson* (1825), 2 Carrington and Payne 38, 172, p. 18.

under the Insolvency Act, he returned to live with his family again. The court found for the plaintiffs on the grounds that, even if Mrs Anderson was running the business, she must have been acting as her husband's agent and with his knowledge and consent, and therefore under coverture he was still liable for 'her' debts. At a retrial, the review judges refused to change the verdict and commented that 'the granting of new trials, of late, has been too much a matter of course'.[65] Hence husbands were equally able and willing to manipulate both the concept of coverture and the legal system itself, in the interests of maintaining a viable household economy.

The problem with the household economy, as Margaret Hunt has pointed out, is that it presumes a model of family harmony that was far from present in all households.[66] The *feme sole* trader custom could function to protect a husband from his wife's debts, which was definitely to his advantage. But it also protected trading families, probably in much the same way as transferring property into a wife's name today can help to protect a bankrupt husband's assets from his business creditors. This would have been especially valuable prior to the advent of limited liability for families that were not sites of marital discord, because to assume that most were inharmonious would be as erroneous as assuming a state of universal marital harmony. Even J.S. Mill's polemical work *The Subjection of Women* (1869) argued that 'men do not inflict, nor women suffer, all the misery which could be inflicted and suffered if the full power of tyranny with which the man is legally invested were acted on'.[67] Cases like those of Mrs Anderson and Mrs Bewett also suggest that it was not only widowhood that propelled wives into taking over family businesses. Women whose husbands had gone bankrupt, been imprisoned, or who suffered some other financial or physical misfortune had to operate as *feme sole* traders. Margaret Hunt found numerous instances of wives and even sisters or daughters running the businesses of male relatives gaoled for their involvement in radical or illegal publishing.[68] As Defoe put it when commenting on the many disasters that could befall trading families, women 'are not so helpless and shiftless creatures as some would make them appear in the world; and we see whole families in trade frequently recover'd by their industry'.[69] Indeed, it seems that legal problems arose more often when the husbands returned but did not take back the business than when their wives were operating alone.

---

[65] Ibid., p. 19.

[66] Hunt, *Middling Sort*, pp. 134–42.

[67] J.S. Mill, *The Subjection of Women* (London, 1869; rep. 1974), p. 34.

[68] Margaret Hunt, 'Hawkers, Bawlers, and Mercuries: Women and the London Press in the Early Enlightenment', in *Women and the Enlightenment*, ed. M. Hunt (New York, 1984), pp. 53–4.

[69] Daniel Defoe, *The Complete English Tradesman*, I and II (London, 1738), p. 296, also urged wives either to save their husbands from ruin or to take over completely 'if he is forced to fail and fly', p. 288.

Privilege vs. liability

The question of how far the custom of *feme sole* trading could be considered an advantage or a hindrance to married women in trade is therefore a complex issue in which the liabilities of other family members also have to be considered. The advantages or disadvantages the custom could actually confer also need to be separated from the courts' views of this ancient custom. It is possible to consider the latter question from a different angle by looking at cases in which the 'rights' of English women in trade were compared to those of women from European countries whose laws recognised a form of community of ownership between married couples. In parts of France, Germany and Spain, and in areas of European North America, legal systems recognised a co-ownership of acquisitions and/or movables between husband and wife.[70] English law had remained undecided about the position of married women under systems of community of property until the end of the thirteenth century. Once the common law had lost its jurisdiction over testamentary matters to the ecclesiastical courts, it ceased to consider the ownership of property after death and vested the wife's chattels in her husband during their lifetime.[71] Holdsworth argues that the common law thus effectively made the law of the nobles applicable to all classes. Among the lower orders, a system of community of ownership had prevailed because most owned only movables and distinguishing who owned what was difficult. In England, this 'law of the smaller folk' effectively disappeared *except* in some of the borough customs.[72] It is possible to compare how the common lawcourts viewed the concept of the borough custom and the common law doctrine of coverture against European models of community of property in three cases covered by the law reports.

In 1792 a Frenchwoman and her husband emigrated to England, but in 1795 he gave her power of attorney to transact his business while he went to Hamburg. Once alone however, Victoire Harel L'Aigle cohabited with a M. Montelun 'while carrying on trade with him' and bore his child. A client, M. De Gaillon, asked Madame L'Aigle to procure £700 of merchandise for which he paid her £300 on account and sent £600 of goods to her husband in Hamburg for which the client expected brandy or Hollands to that value in return. Madame L'Aigle gave De Gaillon a receipt for the £300 in her own name but no goods arrived from Hamburg, so she gave him £100-worth of

---

[70] For Europe, see Holdsworth, *History of English Law*, pp. 521–2; for America, see Angel Kwolek Folland, *Incorporating Women: A History of Women and Business in the United States* (New York, 1998), pp. 22–4.

[71] Holdsworth, *History of English Law*, p. 524, notes that if, as with property, the common law had been obliged to consider a husband and wife's rights to each other's chattels after death then it may not have given the wife's chattels absolutely to her husband during marriage. Although a husband retained control over real property during marriage the land returned to her or her heirs after his death.

[72] Ibid., pp. 524–5.

goods and four bills for £50 each in her husband's name. However, although John Harel L'Aigle accepted the bills, he refused to pay them when they became due, so De Gaillon had Madame L'Aigle arrested. The case was tried in 1797 and Madame L'Aigle pleaded coverture in her defence, to which De Gaillon replied that her conduct (with Montelun) had been such that he no longer believed her to be married. This was a blatant attempt to get the court to focus on Madame L'Aigle's immorality because in the letter requesting her to set up the deal he had told her that he wanted to trade with 'your husband'.

The court did not want to decide whether her marriage was valid, only whether Madam L'Aigle had used the £300 advance herself for her own separate trade. However, in deciding to allow Madame L'Aigle's coverture to be put on record, Justice Buller noted that the question of the parties' nationality was of great importance. He argued that:

> In France married women have many rights, which are allowed to none but single women in this country. If she received the £300 on her own account, she is entitled to no favour. A discharge is a favour; and the question now is, whether we are to grant a favour or not?[73]

This clearly illustrates the paradox of the *feme sole* trader custom. Buller believed that French law conferred 'rights' that English married women could not claim, but in order to grant the 'favour' of a discharge she would have to claim the protection of the English system of coverture. Madame L'Aigle was discharged on common bail but the case was presented again in 1798,[74] by which time John L'Aigle had returned and was living in Westminster, although it is unclear whether he and Victoire had resolved their marital difficulties enough to cohabit. Madame L'Aigle's defence argued that she was a married woman and could only be sued as a *feme sole* under the custom of London, in which case her husband should have been named for conformity, but that had not happened. Buller stated that in cases where a husband was abroad, 'the disability of the wife was suspended' and the other review judges concurred with him. Justice Heath added that it was 'for the benefit of the *feme covert* that she should be liable to an action in such a case as this, otherwise she could obtain no credit, and would have no means of obtaining her livelihood'. In the reviewed case, then, the judges appeared to view coverture as a 'disability' and the custom as a favour, not because it conferred contractual rights but because a woman's personal liability facilitated the acquisition of credit. However, although the court upheld the right of the *feme sole* trader, it meant that Madam L'Aigle was not granted the 'favour' of a discharge and so lost her case.

By contrast, in *Williamson vs. Dawes* (1832), the English wife of a bankrupt husband (who had absconded abroad) had traded as a *feme sole* but successfully

---

[73] ER, *De Gaillon vs. L'Aigle* (1797), 1 Bosanquet & Puller 8, 126, p. 749.
[74] ER, *De Gaillon vs. L'Aigle* (1798), 1 Bosanquet & Puller 357, 126, p. 950.

pleaded coverture to avoid paying her debts. Again, given the later date, this could be seen as evidence of an increasingly strict application of coverture, but there were other considerations. It was established in both cases that the women in question had traded openly as *femmes soles* and had been recognised as such by other traders for a substantial period of time. However, in Mrs Dawes' case there was no hint of sexual impropriety on her part and she was clearly the victim of a man who had escaped to France after being served with a bankruptcy commission. As this case appeared after Kenyon's famous *Marshall vs. Rutton* (1800) decision, it was held that nothing short of the husband's civil death could leave a married woman 'subject to the liabilities of a *feme sole*'. And because Mr Dawes' absence was voluntary, it could not confer to 'the wife the privileges or affect her with the liabilities of a *feme sole*'.[75] Mrs Dawes was therefore 'protected' from her creditors. Perhaps even more pertinently, the judges' decision also reflected a degree of hostility towards the French engendered by long years of military and commercial conflict. Justice Bosanquet stated that, in the earlier case of *De Gaillon vs. L'Aigle*, 'the husband was a foreigner, which makes an essential difference in the case'.[76] Some legal treatises point out that the law could be applied differently if one of the parties was an alien enemy,[77] but it is possible that there was also a degree of rivalry between the two legal systems.

A similar conflict between English common law and European systems of community ownership was also visible in the 1824 case of *Cosio and Pineyro vs. De Bernales*. A husband and wife who traded as partners in Spain attempted to sue De Bernales in the Court of Common Pleas for *assumpsit*, which in this case was probably a breach of contract, since it appears that the defendant had already received the money. The defence objected that under English law the wife should not have 'joined in the action, as she, as a *feme covert*, could have no property'.[78] The judge held that the plaintiffs must provide proof that a *feme covert* in Spain could engage in trade on her own account so that they could 'put a proper plaintiff on the record', before he would even consider whether under Spanish law a husband and wife who traded as partners could sue jointly in an English court. Furthermore, if the wife chose to sue as a *feme sole*, she could do so only by the custom in the City courts and not in the superior courts. Thus, even if Mrs Pineyro could have proved her right to trade as a married woman in Spain, the judge implied that her case could be heard only in the City courts where a similar customary right existed for English women and not under the auspices of the common law. The defence could not provide such proof at that time and the case was effectively lost over a

---

[75] ER, *Williamson vs. Dawes* (1832), 9 Bingham 292, 131, p. 624.

[76] Ibid., p. 626.

[77] For a particularly partisan approach see Anon., *A Treatise of Feme Coverts* (1732), p. 104. See also above, p. 41.

[78] ER, *Cosio and Pineyro vs. De Bernales* (1824), 1 Carrington and Payne 266, 171, p. 1189.

technicality of pleading. A note on the text adds that in all probability the plaintiffs' attorney was unaware that they were husband and wife, one called Cosio and the other Pineyro, because it was common on the Continent for a wife to continue to use her first surname or simply to add the husband's surname after both of hers. Whatever the reason, at this time the common-law court seems to have been extremely reluctant to accommodate foreign customs, the 'privileges' conferred by which, perhaps not surprisingly, were viewed as even more alien to the system of English common law than were local borough customs.

Fifty years earlier, Lord Mansfield had also compared the use of borough custom within a common lawcourt with that of foreign laws. In *Jewson vs. Read* (1773), on the question of whether an action on the custom of London could be maintained in a common lawcourt, it was argued that the customs of London were not the only ones to have been proceeded upon. Mansfield declared that 'when a right is established by the law of France and the party comes here, the debt must be recovered here, according to the law of France; of which the court will take notice on information upon evidence'.[79] The degree to which common lawcourts were willing to recognise 'foreign' systems of law there-fore varied over time. This is a topic that will repay further examination by legal historians. Nevertheless, it seems that the problems around delineat-ing the appropriate jurisdictions in separate courts with different systems of law, whether local or foreign, was an important factor in deciding the legitimacy or otherwise of *feme sole* traders. Therefore the question of the rights and privileges of *feme sole* trading was also inextricably bound up within the administration of a pluralistic legal system. What seems to have been under consideration was not only the rights or privileges conferred to married women in trade by customary law, but also the extent to which local customs per se should be recognised by the common law, both as a privilege which chal-lenged the internal logic of its own system and as the product of an external jurisdiction.

Conclusion

The paradox of the custom of *feme sole* trading meant that, while it did confer a right theoretically denied to married women by the common law, it also left those in trade far more vulnerable to actions for debt, for which the protection of coverture was the best remedy. In practical terms, the custom seems to have been concerned primarily with debt recovery and personal liability rather than conferring the 'right' to trade in itself, but that still made borough custom relevant to the practice of trade. This was because contemporaries believed that a clear supposition of liability was necessary for the acquisition of credit

---

[79] ER, *Jewson vs. Read* (1773), Lofft 138, 98, p. 575.

on which so much trade was based. Judges had to constantly weigh up the competing demands of creditors against those of married women and their families. The commercial interests of a custom designed to facilitate trade in the City were juxtaposed against the traditional concern of the common law to maintain a particular form of the family with a male head. Moreover, common law judges sought to maintain the integrity and dominance of their own system of law while being forced to recognise the limits of their own jurisdiction and the need for litigants to seek 'remedies' for its often outdated harshness in the legal systems of other courts. There is still much research that needs to be done on this topic, but on this evidence, legal doctrine and judicial decisions appear to have been concerned with upholding far more than a single patriarchal interest in cases concerning women in business.

Married female litigants, and their husbands, seem to have been well aware of the pluralistic nature of the legal system and to have manipulated the relevant systems of law in their own interests whenever possible. For example, the infamous married coffee-woman, Moll King's, increasingly drunken behaviour resulted in frequent court appearances. She displayed an admirable knowledge of how to manipulate the legal system by getting her case removed 'into the Court of Kings bench by Certiorari, thinking . . . that her Prosecutor would not follow her, on account of the great expence'.[80] The existence of jurisdictional competition and an adversarial legal system seems to have greatly facilitated this. The evidence suggests that married women in business were most likely to sue and be sued in local courts where they could gain fast and inexpensive access to customary and equitable law. The superior common-law courts were most often appealed to when a case had been lost and it became necessary to plead coverture as a defence. If the law reports appear to show an increase in the number of decisions which upheld the common law in the later period, this could indeed be seen as evidence of the common law's attempts to impose uniformity, but it did not necessarily mean that this was wholly detrimental to wives in trade because, in most of the cases reported, that was precisely the result desired by the female defendants (and often also by their husbands) in order for the wife's trade to continue to contribute to the household economy. There was still plenty of scope for husbands to exercise an abuse of power within unhappy marriages but in such cases married women could turn to equity as 'the guardian of the weak and unprotected'.[81]

---

[80] Anon., *The Life and Character of Moll King, Late Mistress of King's Coffee House in Covent Garden* (London, 1747), p. 15; and see below, p. 192.
[81] Holcombe, *Wives and Property*, p. 37.

4

Trading 'according to equity and good conscience'

Businesswomen in Chancery

> Having the profitt & benefitt of her trade to her selfe & having greater parte of yr orator's goods by her in her shop at the time of her husband's decease, she . . . ought in Equity and good Conscience . . . to answer and pay to yr orator the said debt contracted during the coverture out of her own estate.
>
> Bill of complaint by John Benney, haberdasher,
> against Jane Long, milliner (1700)[1]

Courts of equity can perhaps best be described as a means of adjudicating disputes according to conscience. In practice this often meant abandoning the application of strict legal rules and resorting to concepts of natural justice by 'introducing an exception from consideration of what is equitable in particular circumstances, to avoid the hardship which would otherwise fall upon individuals'.[2] Chancery has thus long been viewed as providing the necessary correction to the universal strictness of the common law, particularly in the case of married women. In 1905 the legal scholar Dicey even went so far as to argue that equity lawyers viewed husbands as 'the "enemy" against whose exorbitant common-law rights the Court of Chancery waged constant war'.[3] As Chapters 2 and 3 have shown, this opposition is too stark, but echoes of Dicey's comment may be found in narratives of women's legal and economic position that focus on the operation of patriarchy and power relations between husband and wife, which tend to obscure wider family relationships. Yet both male and female plaintiffs in Chancery often justified their appeal to this court by claiming that they had been left 'remidiless by the strictness of the common law',[4] and it was not uncommon for women to sue each other. Furthermore, as we have seen, both the common law and borough custom did, even if some-

---

[1] PRO, C6/380/51, and see below, p. 80.
[2] John Millar, *An Historical View of English Government* (1803), cited in Lieberman, *Province of Legislation*, p. 75, and for a discussion of the development of concepts of equity see ibid., pp 73–87.
[3] Dicey, *Lectures*, p. 376.
[4] See e.g. PRO, C6/399/23, *Collins vs. Allen* (1684).

what imperfectly, attempt to balance the rights and liabilities of members of trading families and, where it could not do so, judges and legal treatises were often quick to point out that alternative remedies were available in other courts. This chapter therefore adopts a broader approach towards analysing relationships between women in business, their families and community networks during disputes over who in 'good conscience' should keep the 'profitt and benefitt' of their trade.

Equitable justice was not only an important recourse for married women. The growth of equitable jurisdiction to cover new forms of property and increasingly complex forms of trusts and contracts[5] meant that its remedial and protective functions were relevant to many women in business regardless of their marital status. By the eighteenth century there were a number of established principles for equitable intervention in cases concerning, for example, mortgages, contracts, trusts, partnerships, disclosure of accounts, debt, bankruptcy and leases on commercial property, as well as cases of fraud, forgery or duress. Litigants were attracted to Chancery precisely because it could facilitate their particular aims in a dispute. While the common law could only provide retributive damages after the event, equity could provide specific immediate relief, compel performance of contracts, and issue injunctions to prevent a future injustice from being committed. As in other courts, many cases were brought merely to put pressure on an opponent to settle a dispute rather than face expensive costs and delays, or to compel a rival to disclose his or her financial position. It could also be used to block an opponent's action in another court, or as a collusive procedure to gain formal legal recognition of an action upon which both parties were already agreed.[6] Something of this nature was probably occurring in 1710 when Blanch Pope, a widow and bankrupt mercer, was sued by her son who wished to gain a portion of his father's estate before Mrs Pope's other creditors took all the family's assets. The same lawyer acted for both mother and son, which strongly suggests a collusive suit, and the hapless lawyer later sued both Popes for non-payment of fees.[7]

Chancery was thus important for women, whose legal status under the common law was limited, but also central to the regulation of many business practices. The highly detailed accounts of each dispute in Chancery bills and answers, written from several different perspectives, provide an extraordinarily rich source for studying how women in business conducted their trade on a daily basis, for examining complex relations of credit, and for tracing how breakdowns in these relations affected both their families and neighbours. As Craig Muldrew has shown, concepts of equity and equality were very important to the social practice of economic bargaining and making contracts in early

---

[5] Holdsworth, *History of English Law*, pp. 446–69.

[6] Henry Horwitz, *Chancery Equity Records and Proceedings, 1600–1800* (London, 1995; rep. 1998), p. 8.

[7] PRO, C6/362/42, *Pope vs. Pope* (1710), and C6/400/61, *Dottin vs. Pope* (1713).

modern society. Moreover, he argues that 'contracting parties, whatever their position on the social scale in other spheres of activity, became morally equal in their responsibility to honour their bargains because everyone in the community had a stake in obliging others to pay their debts'.[8] Litigants in Chancery often appealed to 'equity and good conscience' which, despite its formulaic usage, also seems to have embodied an ideal of fair trading that clearly included holding tradeswomen morally accountable for their debts, an accountability that was all too frequently missing from common law. Since feminists have long argued that contract ideology masks the social and economic inequalities of contracting parties, particularly in the case of women, one of the aims of this chapter is to examine how far the process of economic bargaining within a culture of credit could mitigate this gendered inequality; although the overall focus remains on women's relationships within family and community networks.

Procedure and access

The flexibility of legal action possible in equity was achieved largely through procedural differences. In common law, an action could only be started by a particular type of writ in Latin, but in Chancery the suitor would submit a bill of complaint written in English detailing all her grievances against the other party and praying for suitable relief. The defendant(s) would then have to submit a written answer, which unlike the bill had to be made under oath. The complainant could in theory reply to this answer (replication) and the defendants could also reply again (rejoinder).[9] Occasionally this could continue for some time. In 1691 Mary Richardson and her son Peter Thorn refused to write any more answers when the bills of complaint brought by Isabella Firmin and her husband had reached forty-four pages.[10] Defendants could also file a cross-bill in order to make the complainant a defendant in a second but related case,[11] and both strategies no doubt contributed to Chancery's reputation for lengthy delays. However, the majority of cases never proceeded past the pleading stage, and a substantial minority of bills never even received an answer.[12] Many cases were settled out of court, the threat of litigation being enough to prompt both parties to resolve their differences and some

---

[8] Muldrew, *Economy of Obligation*, p. 318.

[9] For a comprehensive summary of procedure, see Horwitz, *Chancery Equity Records*, pp. 12–24.

[10] PRO, C6/411/58, *Firmin vs. Carter* (1691), and see below, pp. 75–7.

[11] PRO, C6/375/44, *Bower vs. Holtrop* (1711) and C33/317, p. 276, for the judge's decree which details the cross-bill. See also below, pp. 77–8.

[12] Horwitz, *Chancery Equity Records*, p. 26, estimates that as many as one in five bills were not answered and, in a sample of 146 suits in 1685, 75.3 per cent proceeded no further. In a sample of 140 suits in 1785, 65.7 per cent did not proceed beyond the pleading stage.

complainants may have run out of energy or funds before they had managed to compel the defendant to answer. The original bill of complaint and the answer(s), which could be written as a joint statement or as individual replies if there was more than one defendant, plus any schedules of accounts accompanying the answers, are known as Chancery pleadings. This chapter is based on a detailed study of the pleadings for thirty cases in which women in business were involved between 1684 and 1714.[13] The comments made here can therefore only apply to the early eighteenth century, because much needed research on cases in the later period, when the processes of Chancery had become infamously slow and tortuous, has yet to be conducted.[14]

There have been a number of objections as to why women would not have had wide access to Chancery or might have been put off from using it; either because of the expense, the delays or due to ideological pressures.[15] It is not possible to give definitive answers to all these objections, but there are a number of considerations that should be noted which suggest that women's use of the court may not have been so narrowly circumscribed. First, although nineteenth-century feminists argued that equity was only available to wealthy married women,[16] it was, as Margaret Hunt has shown, possible for impoverished litigants in Chancery to plead in forma pauperis, which exempted them from most court costs.[17] Even issuing a bill of complaint cost very little, and heavy expenses only began to be incurred once the case had proceeded to the point of going to court and filing continuations which happened in only a minority of cases,[18] especially given the efficacy of merely threatening to sue. Horwitz's research into Chancery litigants shows that in the period 1627 to 1819 the numbers of those ranked gentlemen or above actually fell, and by contrast, commercial and artisanal plaintiffs rose slightly over the same

---

[13] These cases have only come to light because of a recent indexing project carried out by the Public Record Office, and further research on later cases is hampered because the project ended at 1714. I am greatly indebted to Mary Clayton for alerting me to the existence of these cases and passing on references to those concerning women in business during her work on the project.

[14] The huge volume of cases and the lack of comprehensive indexing have so far proved effective deterrents to historians working in this field.

[15] Greenberg, 'Legal Status of the English Woman', pp. 178–9, argues that women's internalisation of patriarchal ideology would have prevented them from being aware that a wrong had been done, and hence from seeking redress. Dicey, Lectures, p. 383, argues that the creation of separate property only benefited wealthy women, so equity effectively created one rule for the rich and another for the poor.

[16] Holcombe, Wives and Property, p. 47; but note: Dicey and Holcombe are both writing from the perspective of late nineteenth-century reform.

[17] Margaret Hunt, 'Women and Money: Female Litigants in Equity in Eighteenth-century England' (unpub. paper given at the PRO, 1999), p. 12. In order to gain exemption a petitioner had to swear before a court clerk that she had no more than £5 in total assets.

[18] Ibid., pp. 11–12.

period.[19] Furthermore, because the bills and answers were written, litigants did not have to live in the capital to pursue their cases. In a separate survey, Horwitz found that more than 70 per cent of first-named parties lived outside London, and although this figure had fallen to just over half by 1785, it still shows that a substantial proportion of litigants lived in the provinces.[20]

Perhaps more importantly, Horwitz's survey of Chancery bills shows that the proportion of female plaintiffs among his survey of several hundred cases rose from around 14 per cent in 1627 to just over 21 per cent in 1819. Indeed, Horwitz argues that if minors and men who do not fit an occupational/status category (e.g. cases brought by corporate bodies) were removed from the sample, by 1818 to 1819 women formed 'no less than 30.6 per cent of all-named plaintiffs'.[21] It is not possible to estimate how many of these women may have been in business because they are only categorised by marital status. Horwitz suggests that most married women would have been involved in estate or land suits but cases are often very difficult to categorise and disputes over estate did not exclude the possibility that they involved women in business. In the thirty cases analysed here for information about women in business, 46 per cent involved disputes over estates.[22] Furthermore, Horwitz only counted plaintiffs, whereas just over half of the women in this study were defendants,[23] which would suggest an even higher level of participation of women in Chancery proceedings. Since Chancery could be used to block an opponent's action in another court, a woman suing a common law case could become a defendant in a separate but related case in Chancery in order to stop her proceeding at law. Hence, in Chancery, the distinction between plaintiff and defendant did not necessarily imply a distinction of agency between the parties that could be mapped on to gender inequalities. Finally, it has also been well documented that the process of Chancery cases was notoriously slow and that this put many people off, but not only was the delay considerably less in the early eighteenth century than in the nineteenth,[24] but the threat of potentially expensive delays was often an effective way of forcing a settlement.

---

[19] Horwitz, *Chancery Equity Records*, p. 42. A comparison of 446 plaintiffs in 1627 with 269 plaintiffs in 1818–19 showed that those ranked gentleman or above fell from just over 30 per cent to just over 18 per cent.

[20] Ibid., p. 46. In 1685 71.3 per cent of 237 first-named parties lived outside London; this proportion had fallen to 47.1 per cent among 240 cases in 1785.

[21] Ibid.

[22] It is difficult to categorise cases into single subject issues, since many plaintiffs had multiple grievances, but fourteen chiefly concerned disputes over estate, seven were about debt, three were about bankruptcy and six concerned disagreements over contractual issues.

[23] Of thirty cases studied six had female plaintiffs, one had a female plaintiff and defendant, seventeen had female defendants, and six concerned the estates of women in business who had died.

[24] Ibid., p. 28. In Horwitz's 1685 data, 77 per cent of cases were resolved in under one year but by 1818 just 45 per cent were resolved.

The remainder of this chapter is divided into three sections. The first examines cases concerning disputes over estate; the second considers cases of debt and bankruptcy, and the last looks at issues of contractual obligation in partnership and property agreements. The very nature of court documents always produces an undue emphasis on conflict, and each testimony would have been carefully framed to support each litigant's case but there are common themes which constantly recur in the discourses used to describe women's trading activities. First, the penetration of market relations into family life was very evident, particularly in the case of remarriages complicated by the presence of children from an earlier union. Second, married women's status as separate traders seems to have varied more according to the trading relationship established with their creditors and debtors than according to their legal marital status. Third, extended networks of credit feature in many cases, and complex monetary agreements reveal women to have been deeply enmeshed in these networks in which community relations played an important role. In some cases communities seem to have provided their own sanctions against suspect or dishonest behaviour, again regardless of marital or legal status.

Estate

Perhaps one of the most obvious areas for potential family conflicts was a dispute over the estate of a dead parent, particularly if that parent had remarried. Of fourteen cases categorised as disputes chiefly about the division of a deceased's estate, four involved daughters suing to gain a better portion of their father's estate, including one who was suing her paternal grandmother, and four involved second families or other issues around remarriage. The division and paying out of legacies was not only complicated by remarriages but by the deaths of other married children and the claims of their executors/trixes. The formation and dissolution of business partnerships between family members such as sisters, or mothers and sons-in-law, served only to exacerbate family tensions. In fact, the issue of separate trading was not necessarily a gendered one, confined only to disputes between husbands and wives. A dispute in 1713 over the estate of two dead sisters who had traded together showed that even in same-sex partnerships the issue of separate trading, when it came to a division of assets, was just as contentious.[25] Equally contentious was the settlement of debts owed and owing to the estate from other family members, who may have had goods 'in kind' or taken out 'loans' from parents in the expectation that ties of blood would prove strong enough to ensure their eventual cancellation. These expectations were heavily jeopardised should the

---

[25] PRO, C6/364/69, *Alsopp vs. Kelson* (1713): a grandfather sued the relatives of the deceased unmarried sister in the partnership to gain his granddaughter's share of her dead mother's assets in their millinery business.

parent remarry and the surviving spouse be left to call in the 'debt' to the estate. If the myth of the callous stepmother had gained considerable cultural purchase, it could only be heightened further if that stepmother had succeeded in a business of her own.

One example serves to illustrate the complexity of inter-family conflicts when women in business remarried. In 1691 Mary Carter, tallow chandler and widow of John Carter from Colchester, was sued by his daughter Isabella Firmin and her husband Josiah, a linen draper.[26] Mary had previously been married to Thomas Thorne, a tallow chandler with whom she had five children, including Peter Thorne, who helped her run the business, and Mary Richardson who was a baker. Thomas Thorne had left his wife the tallow business and all the household goods. The case hinged chiefly on whether the tallow business remained Mary Carter's separate property on her remarriage to John Carter in 1668. However, the existence of children from previous marriages who were involved in the same or allied trades complicated matters further.

John Carter's daughter from his first marriage, Isabella Firmin, argued that under the common-law doctrine of coverture the business technically became her father's, and in return for this he had paid each of the Thorne children £100. To prove Carter's ownership of the business his daughter argued that he took up the trade of tallow chandler but left Mary Carter to 'manage' it on a daily basis with the help of her son Peter, because John Carter was too busy running several farms. To emphasise the point Firmin insisted that her father had paid for all the tallow stock, utensils and servants' wages. Yet the reciprocal trading relations between the two families while they were reconstituted as one caused further tensions. The Firmins had accused Mary Carter and her son Peter of delivering too much stock on credit, which had remained unpaid for when Carter died in 1690. This alleged mismanagement was compounded by the accusation that Mrs Carter's daughter Mary Richardson (née Thorne) had failed to pay for wheat which she had bought from her stepfather, John Carter, to use in her bakery. Mrs Carter's son, Peter Thorne, was accused of misappropriating money from the business because the Firmins believed that as an apprentice he should not have been able to afford good-quality furniture. Furthermore, he had borrowed £200 from his stepfather and failed to repay it before Carter's death. This was a typically complex saga of inter-family borrowing and trading, of the sort that came before Chancery.

All the Firmins' accusations actually formed part of an attempt to stop Mary Carter suing them at common law for the return of her first husband's goods.

[26] PRO, C6/411/58, *Firmin vs. Carter* (1691): Josiah Firmin was the first-named plaintiff but, as discussed in Chapter 3, all married women had to sue with their husbands for form's sake. The testimony was from both Isabella and Josiah but the claim on the Will was primarily Isabella's. All bills and answers are tied together in one bundle and not all have page numbers to aid reference.

As a widow, Mrs Carter had therefore taken the initiative to sue her step-daughter first and this action in equity was a defensive measure by the Firmins. Part of the problem seems to have been caused by the fact that John Carter had made his second wife and his daughter by his first marriage joint execu-trixes of his estate, perhaps in an effort to promote goodwill between them. The result was that both women were therefore technically liable for his debts before they could claim their share. Mary Carter's loyalties however seem to have lain with her first family and she resolutely refused to allow the Firmins any of her first husband's goods, saying that even 'if she had any she would not give the sd complts any account of such'. She argued that John Carter had agreed not 'to have any interest or any waies to intermeddle with the trade of tallow chandler or in the profit or loss of the sd trade or of the goods belonging to the sd trade'. She refused to present any accounts from the business and argued that the Firmins could not 'in equity have any colour thereunto or unto any greater part of the estate of the sd Thomas than according to the marriage agreement' between Carter and herself.[27] However, Mary Carter also wanted to retain her right as a widow to one-third of John Carter's lands in Colchester, which had been left to her stepdaughter Isabella Firmin, on the condition that she paid her stepmother £20 per annum from the rents and profits. Firmin insisted that her stepmother should give up the claim entirely; Mrs Carter would only agree to a reduction. Not surprisingly, Peter Thorne supported his mother's version of events, claiming that he had only ever worked for her benefit and that neither of them had ever charged anything concerning the trade to Carter. Thorne also claimed to have bought the furniture with his own money, but he admitted having borrowed money from Carter on a bond. However, his mother testified that the bond had been surrendered to her before her second husband's death.

Although the case was ostensibly about the ownership of separate property under a premarital agreement, informal borrowing and trading between members had strained relations in the reconstituted family. On John Carter's death, old loyalties reasserted themselves. Mrs Carter had done everything in her power to retain her separate business for herself and her son. She had insisted on the validity of the premarital agreement, suing the Firmins at law to recover her goods and only agreeing to negotiate over her widow's third share of her second husband's estate. Mrs Carter was therefore not only aware of but actively insisting on all that could be considered legally her property. However, at no point did she claim that the property was directly hers; her 'right' to it was held only by virtue of her first husband and on the strength of a premarital agreement. As was discussed above,[28] women could legally retain their separate property but the tortuous legal technicalities necessary to do so

[27] The reasons for this and the terms of the marriage agreement were apparently set out in one of Mary Carter's earlier answers, which is missing.
[28] See above, pp. 41–6.

meant they could never claim the right to own it personally. Mrs Carter's testimony seems to have been carefully framed to fit this situation. Isabella Firmin, on the other hand, was assuming that her 'right' to a larger portion of her father's estate rested on proving her stepmother's coverture on marriage to her father was total and superseded all previous arrangements. Hence Firmin tried to prove that Mrs Carter had merely managed the business after she was married.[29]

There is only one case, dating from 1711, which gives an indication of how equity upheld the status of wives as sole traders based on separate property while recognising the competing claims of other family members.[30] In this case, a fair division of assets rather than clarification of sole trader status seems to have been the main issue. Lydia Bower (née Lillie)[31] had kept the Log Tavern in St Olave for some years before she met London citizen and carpenter Jeremiah Bower, who was a widower with three children. Widowed herself and concerned that his children might have too great a claim on her estate, Lydia Bower persuaded her brother to draw up a premarital agreement, guaranteeing her £500 if Jeremiah died before her and the ability to make her own Will if he did not. In consideration of this Jeremiah Bower promised to pay £800 on a penalty bond and she paid £400 as a marriage portion.[32] Lydia claimed that, after the marriage, she discovered that Jeremiah was deeply in debt. However, she continued to manage The Log 'as though she was single' and persuaded her husband to buy another, The Kings Head in Southwark, which she also ran and profited by so much that she managed to clear his debts and increase his personal wealth to £2,000. When Jeremiah died in March 1710 he left one-third of his estate to his wife according to London custom, one-third to his only surviving daughter Ruth Wine, and one-third to his friend and executor John Holtrop. He also left £500 to his grandchildren by Ruth, but stipulated that they could not claim that money until they reached 18 years of age. In the meantime Lydia was to have full use of it for five years after his death, provided that she gave Holtrop sufficient security for it.

Jeremiah Bower's daughter and his second wife could not agree on any detail of the settlement which, as in the case of Mary Carter, was complicated by trading relations and inter-family loans. Even Bower's executor, Holtrop, was personally indebted to his estate. Holtrop broadly supported Ruth Wine and her family, and sued Lydia Bower at law over the valuation of the tavern, from

---

[29] In trying to prove coverture the claim that a married woman had merely 'managed' the business was a common one; see e.g. PRO, C6/418/48, *Gwynne vs. Sheppard* (1706).

[30] In addition to the large numbers of cases that did not reach the decree stage, the lack of indexing and the method of filing each stage of every case separately means that tracing the outcome of any one case is extremely difficult.

[31] PRO, C6/375/44, /47, *Bower vs. Holtrop* (1711).

[32] This meant that the agreement was the strongest that could be made, as it was written before the marriage and thus based on a 'valuable consideration', which rendered it a legally binding contract. For a discussion of this, see above, p. 42, and n. 104.

which he was trying to evict her. Part of Mrs Bower's bill was a request for an injunction to stop his action, yet much of the argument was over Jeremiah Bower's attempts to set up his daughter and son-in-law in business as part of Ruth's marriage settlement. The Wines had tried unsuccessfully to run an inn and when that had failed turned to retailing, at which they were also largely unsuccessful. They borrowed money from Jeremiah on bonds and he paid at least part of their shop rent. The Wines, however, blamed their misfortunes on Ruth's stepmother. They claimed it was Lydia Bower's 'declared intention to ruin both' of them. Ruth's father, they said, had 'freely given' them financial help when needed, and he had 'often in his lifetime promised' to release his son-in-law from his debts.[33] If the Wines did not pay back their debts, Lydia Bowers' share of the estate would be considerably reduced, so she argued that Holtrop had tried to trick her husband into signing a general release of all the Wine family's debts on his deathbed. She also claimed that John Wine had written to his father-in-law apologising for being such a burden on him.

The Wines tried to indict Lydia Bower by filing a cross-bill against her. They accused Lydia of trying to claim her share of the estate on three separate grounds: through the terms of the premarital agreement, from the one-third she was allowed by London custom, and under the terms of the Will. It seems likely that the estate was not actually large enough to support all three. The judge's decree went largely in Lydia Bower's favour, while still trying to accommodate the other claimants. She was ordered to make a claim under one of the three grounds, but allowed to wait to decide which until the debts to the estate had been settled. The Wines were ordered to 'clarify' exactly what they had borrowed and all accounts relating to the estate were to be submitted to the court to determine its exact value. Lydia Bower was also granted an injunction to prevent Holtrop from proceeding against her at law, which meant that she could continue to live and trade in her tavern.[34] Thus in providing equitable justice the court seems to have been far more concerned with ensuring a practical remedy for all than determining Lydia Bower's status as a separate trader.

Both Mary Carter and Lydia Bower had to deal with money and relationship problems exacerbated by remarriages. Indeed, even without the added tensions caused by inter-family trading and borrowing, hostility towards stepmothers could be inexplicably strong. Mary Saxby, a silkweaver's daughter born in 1738, admitted that her father's new wife was very fond of her but explained that the 'very name of stepmother gave me such disgust, that I could not endure it; and therefore I was not very careful to please her'.[35] Yet 'natural' mothers were also not immune from the consequences of children made resentful by

---

[33] The schedule of accounts attached to the bill suggests that Jeremiah Bower frequently paid trade and household bills for the Wines.

[34] PRO, C33/317, pp. 276–7.

[35] Mary Saxby, *Memoirs of a Female Vagrant* (London, 1806), pp. 4–5.

the accumulation of profit from trade. Ann Symonds[36] was widowed in 1699 and took over her husband's wine business. As executrix of his estate, however, she was sued by the executors of two of her late husband's creditors in 1710. Of her six children, three had died as young adults, but two of her surviving daughters testified against her. Mary Meakins explained that she did not want to suffer for her mother's 'mismanagement'. Her husband, Edward Meakins, had joined his mother-in-law in a business partnership two years after her father's death. Meakins testified that Ann had 'made great profit' from the business before he joined it, but the partnership had been dissolved in May 1708, so possibly there was some residual bitterness over its termination. Mrs Symond's other daughter, Elizabeth Honblon, had sued her mother in Chancery many years earlier because she had not been paid her legacy. There is no surviving answer from Mrs Symonds herself to explain her version of events.

The ideal widow of didactic literature was only supposed to act as caretaker of the family business in order to maximise the benefits for her children before happily passing it on, preferably to her son.[37] In this case Mrs Symonds had apparently tried to benefit at least one daughter by going into trade with her husband, but the partnership had failed, causing resentment all round. This resentment was exacerbated because Mrs Symonds appears to have continued to enjoy the profits from her business, while her daughters felt that they had not received a fair share of their father's legacy over which she had control. It is not really surprising that the prospect of large legacies could cause great tensions within families, but even relatively poor families exhibited a high degree of mercenary behaviour. Eighteenth-century Exchequer court cases show women repeatedly put monetary values on personal and domestic services to other family members. Moreover, the courts were willing to uphold payments between close family members for lodging, interest on loans and medical expenses.[38] Thus financial and emotional exchange within families seems to have been as closely related as social and economic exchange was in the wider trading community.

If widowhood and remarriage caused inter-generational conflict within trading families, the changing legal status of these women could also prove problematic for creditors. This was particularly true for those who had traded with a woman over long periods during which her marital status may have altered more than once. In 1705, Cornelia Bateman's executor[39] had trouble defending her estate against creditors claiming against both her and her husband, who had died before her. Henry Wood had dealt with the Batemans only as a supplier of beer for domestic use but Thomas Cooper had done

---

[36] PRO, C6/362/9, *Johnson vs. Symonds* (1710).
[37] See Hunt, *Middling Sort*, p. 137, for the role of the idealised widow in trade.
[38] Hunt, 'Women and Money', p. 27.
[39] PRO, C6/393/29, *Crawley vs. Cooper* (1705).

business with Cornelia before she married Bateman. She was then the widow of Harris Vanacker, a wealthy property owner in one of whose houses Cooper had lived and traded as a grocer for twenty years. He claimed that Cornelia had traded with him frequently on her own and had paid in full until 1695 when she remarried.[40] During her second marriage, she began trading with Cooper again, and continued to do so after Bateman's death in 1698. The trading relationship only ended when Cornelia Bateman died in 1702. Cooper claimed that William Bateman had never contracted or paid for any goods during the marriage and that Cornelia had personally acknowledged her debts to him. Cooper had traded with Cornelia for at least seven years, through two widowhoods and definitely one if not two marriages. To Cooper, therefore, she had been a sole trader, but Wood believed she was covert, presumably because to him she was merely a domestic consumer.

In a similar case for debt in 1700, John Benney,[41] a London haberdasher, appealed to 'equity & good conscience' to make Jane Long, a milliner, pay her debts either as a married woman from her dead husband's estate or as a sole trader because she had 'the profitt & benefitt of her trade to herself'. Like Cornelia Bateman, Jane Long's case was complicated because she had traded with Benney both before, during and after her marriage to Reuben Long, a mariner. Benney explained that he had brought the case before equity because Mrs Long would simply claim coverture under the common law and he would be nonsuited. In fact Jane Long used precisely that defence, claiming she was not a milliner but had only made stockings together with her husband 'in his name and to his sole use'. Benney was therefore less concerned with Jane Long's actual status as a *feme sole* or covert trader; instead he was appealing to both principles in the hope of gaining an equitable settlement of the debt. Given the court's decision in Lydia Bower's case, it seems likely that Benney could have received at least some of his money by appealing to equity or at the very least pushed Jane Long towards making some sort of out-of-court settlement. Hence equity may have protected married women but it also provided one of the few ways of making them responsible for their debts.

In the context of an appeal to equity, all these testimonies were framed within a particular legal discourse in which a concept of 'fair' trading would have been paramount and the considerations of the common law minimised. Both Mrs Bateman's creditors would have argued for the status that they considered most likely to guarantee repayment and John Benney argued for both at once. But these cases do show that a married woman could have more than one identity and that this depended largely on the relationship she had with those she dealt with. Indeed, Hunt has argued that 'for some women *coverture* was less *the* normative state than a hiatus in a larger pattern of

---

[40] There is no record of what Mrs Bateman dealt in; Cooper claimed only that she 'had diverse dealings in the way of trade' with him.

[41] PRO, C6/380/51, *Benney vs. Long* (1700), and above, p. 69.

monetary exchange transactions'.[42] England's high mortality rate in the late seventeenth and early eighteenth centuries meant that widowhood could repeatedly end periods of legal coverture; but neither widowhood nor remarriage necessarily disrupted long-standing trading relations.[43] In the following section, an examination of wider monetary exchanges within local trading communities reveals similar patterns of continued exchange with married women until credit relations broke down beyond repair, when the need to use harsher legal sanctions overrode personal relationships.

Debt and bankruptcy

While disputes over the settling of estates chiefly concerned women in the latter stages of the life cycle, problems of debt or bankruptcy could strike at any age and were also likely to involve a wider section of the community. Nevertheless, of the seven cases which were concerned with debt collection, one-third still involved problems caused by remarriage. There were only three cases of bankruptcy, two of which concerned the same family,[44] but there are a number of possible reasons why there were comparatively few female bankrupts.[45] First, particularly before the law of 1706 mitigated its harshness, creditors were reluctant to bring such drastic charges.[46] Second, a charge of bankruptcy could only be brought against a trader owing £100 or more to a single creditor, which would have excluded many women in smaller businesses. Third, the 'trading distinction' meant certain trades were exempt from the bankruptcy laws and these included victualling and innkeeping, both trades

---

[42] Hunt, 'Women and Money', p. 27.

[43] On high mortality rates see Alex Mercer, *Disease, Mortality and Population in Transition* (London, 1990), pp. 28–45, and fig. 3.8, p. 64, but from the mid-eighteenth century the death rate declined. On remarriage see Vivian Brodsky, 'Widows in Late Elizabethan London: Remarriage, Economic Opportunity and Family Orientations', in *The World We Have Gained: Histories of Population and Social Structure*, ed. Lloyd Bonfield, Richard M. Smith and Keith Wrightson (Oxford, 1986), p. 123, who points to a particularly active remarriage market for widows of London craftsmen; but as the eighteenth century progressed overall rates of remarriage for widows fell; see Olwen Hufton, 'Women without Men: Widows and Spinsters in Britain and France in the Eighteenth Century', *Journal of Family History* (1984), pp. 356–7. For a discussion of class, age and regional effects on widows' rates of remarriage see Hill, *Women, Work and Sexual Politics*, pp. 240–2.

[44] *Pope vs. Pope* and *Dottin vs. Pope* (discussed above, p. 70).

[45] Earle, *Making of the English Middle Class*, pp. 167–8, found that between 1711 and 1714 only 2.8 per cent of metropolitan bankrupts were women, and they were more than twice as likely to be creditors as bankrupts.

[46] Julian Hoppit, *Risk and Failure in English Business, 1700–1850* (Cambridge, 1987), p. 23; see also pp. 29–34 for alternative ways of dealing with indebtedness and insolvency outside the law.

in which women were numerous.[47] Finally, as we have seen, the legal difficulty of ascertaining a married woman's liability in such cases probably put many creditors off laying out a £200 bond to bring such charges. Bankruptcy records are therefore a highly unreliable guide to the numbers of women in business.[48]

Central to all economic transactions, whether involving money or goods in kind, was the existence of credit based on mutual trust, and usually guaranteed by local knowledge of the parties involved. Muldrew has defined these relationships as a 'culture of credit', which was 'generated through a process whereby the nature of the community was redefined as a conglomeration of competing but interdependent households which had to trust one another'.[49] Because each household or 'unit of creditworthiness' was serially linked with others in complicated networks of credit and obligation, defaulting on debts owed by one household could cause a domino effect involving the collapse of several others. Moreover, the lack of formal accounting procedures, and high levels of illiteracy among poorer traders, meant that neighbours often acted as witnesses to oral agreements. As such it seems likely that it was in their and the community's interests to police these agreements effectively. For example, John Holtrop had insisted that Lydia Bower should name ten neighbours to agree the valuation of the lease on her inn, but he refused to accept any of her fellow vintners as witnesses.[50] Muldrew has also stressed that the nature of trust required in economic transactions meant that a form of 'equality in exchange was necessary for contracts to be just' but that this was an equality of 'potential to be trusted and certainly not an equality of opportunity or wealth'.[51] The Chancery bills show that on these grounds even married women could *de facto* participate in economic exchanges and contracts, and that their legal or marital status was of less importance than whether they could be *trusted* to be trading 'as if sole'. In fact the degree of trust required to trade with a married woman was probably far higher than any other category of trader, but as the case of *Grey vs. Hawks* (1711)[52] shows, the community could act to regulate the disabilities incurred by a 'bad' marriage, which in this case was very much a May and December union.

In November 1710 John Grey, who described himself as a 'linen-draper', married the widowed shopkeeper Thomasin Moor in Milbrook, a small village two miles from Southampton. Grey claimed that he took over her thriving chandlery and grocery business worth £50 per annum which he became 'lawfully possessed of & intitled to' by virtue of their marriage. Thomasin's

---

[47] For a discussion of the trading distinction, see ibid., pp. 24–5. For exempt trades, see Cooke, *Bankrupt Laws*, pp. 67–70.

[48] Mui and Mui, *Shops and Shopkeeping*, p. 58, found that female milliners formed a 'very insignificant proportion' of retail clothiers on the basis of bankruptcy records.

[49] Muldrew, *Economy of Obligation*, p. 4.

[50] PRO, C6/375/47, *Bower vs. Holtrop* (1711), and above, pp. 77–8.

[51] Muldrew, *Economy of Obligation*, p. 146.

[52] PRO, C6/415/4, *Grey vs. Hawks* (1711).

daughter, Elizabeth Hawks, and her husband William, a tanner, lived next door to her mother, whose remarriage immediately caused tensions between the two families. Grey felt that the Hawks resented his presence because it would lessen their inheritance. Elizabeth Hawks discovered that Grey had lied about his past and was really a 'common soldier'. She feared Grey would sell off her elderly mother's stock and desert her to serve overseas.

In December 1710, Grey claimed that he ordered £19-worth of goods from Thomasin's regular supplier, John Bradburne in Winchester, but as Bradburne was away he made an agreement with Bradburne's servant to pay for the goods over six months. Bradburne claimed that Grey had ordered £80-worth of goods, but that he had received a letter from Thomasin changing the order to £20-worth of goods just a few days later. Bradburne had only received 40 shillings in payment when he heard a rumour that Grey had been trying to sell up. Fearing Grey was about to default, Bradburne had him arrested for debt in February 1711 and held in gaol for several days. At this point, Bradburne went to see Thomasin personally and he also seems to have consulted with her daughter and son-in-law about how best to manage the situation. The Hawks offered to lend Thomasin money to pay off the debt but she refused and returned all Bradburne's unsold goods to him plus other goods as security for the rest. The Hawks loaned Bradburne a cart to carry away the disputed shop stock and then stored it in their own home until May, when the debt was settled and Thomasin's household goods were returned to her. John Grey had disappeared for months after his release from jail but on his return he found the shop shut. The Hawks believed that the locals had been unwilling to trade with Grey, but that, if he was called away on service, Thomasin would soon have just as many customers as before. John Bradburne also testified that Thomasin had 'lost a great deal of trade' by marrying Grey.

Thomasin Moor's unsuitable marriage seems to have raised concerns among her family who were willing to collaborate in removing her household goods, a large section of the village community who stopped buying from her shop, and her supplier from Winchester who was willing to co-operate with the family to settle the debt fairly.[53] All seem to have co-operated to prevent a more serious failure. The rumour that Grey was selling up, which had travelled from near Southampton to Winchester, was enough to start the domino effect by precipitating Bradburne into taking action to reclaim his debt. Despite the fact that he should by law have dealt with Grey, because there is no suggestion that Thomasin had any separate trade agreement with her husband, Bradburne chose to obey Thomasin's instructions to cancel her husband's order and to deal with her and her family as he had always done. This may have been

---

[53] Similarly, Margaret Hunt, 'Wife Beating, Domesticity and Women's Independence in Eighteenth-Century London', *Gender and History*, 4 (1992), pp. 10–33, found that a wife's 'embeddedness in a community of friends, neighbours, relatives and work-mates' was the best way to escape male abuse.

the best way to regain his money if Grey could really dispute liability for the debt, but it also ensured that Bradburne retained his reputation for fair dealing with debtors.[54] Hence the joint actions of himself and the Hawks prevented a more severe break in the chains of credit stretching from Millbrook to Winchester.

Once a credit relationship based on trust had broken down, creditors had a number of legal options for retrieving their money, the most severe of which was to institute a commission of bankruptcy.[55] In the case of *Buckland vs. Burges* (1703),[56] the creditor hedged his bets by causing two bankruptcy commissions to be issued separately against husband and wife. Thomas Burges was a London druggist who was being jointly sued by John and Elizabeth Buckland to stop him taking their household goods in payment of debts, but Burges had already instigated bankruptcy proceedings against both of them. Burges had traded with Elizabeth Buckland, a pork butcher, for two years and he believed her to be a sole trader, as her husband was a ropemaker and she had always paid for goods personally and signed notes in her own name. Apparently she had often declared that her husband's 'weakness and infirmity of understanding' meant that he was incapable of supporting his family. Burges had also heard that her friends and relations had given her the money to set up in business. From May 1701 until January 1702, Burges kept a record of all his dealings with Mrs Buckland. They met occasionally to reckon up the state of the account, and by October 1701 she owed him £80 which, during a meeting at the Bucklands' house in Camberwell, she promised to settle by note. In December 1701, they met again and she gave him two more notes for another £33.

In January 1702, Burges heard that the Bucklands were intending to defraud their creditors by making a fraudulent bill of sale of all their goods to their friends. He therefore caused a commission of bankruptcy to be issued against Mrs Buckland because by this time she owed him £113. The commission found her bankrupt,[57] and issued a warrant to seize her goods from the Camberwell house. A group of the Bucklands' friends tried to prevent the goods from being removed but a constable and watchmen dispersed the crowd. Burges

---

[54] Muldrew, *Economy of Obligation*, p. 181, argues that a creditor's decision of when to press for payment had to be based on careful consideration of the debtor's situation, because should the creditor find himself in the same situation, leniency might be denied if he had a reputation for hardness.

[55] A creditor could pursue small debts through the Courts of Requests, or have the debtor arrested, or regulate the debtor's business via a deed of inspection, and in event of failure close it down, sell off the proceeds and divide them among all creditors informally, which was known as a composition.

[56] PRO, C6/381/24, *Buckland vs. Burges* (1703), answer of Thomas Burges only.

[57] See Hoppit, *Risk and Failure*, p. 36, for the legal definition of a bankrupt. In addition to debts over £100, Mrs Buckland would have had to have committed an act of bankruptcy, which in this case was probably fraudulent conveyance.

was not satisfied, because Mrs Buckland only paid him a further £3, so he caused another commission of bankruptcy to be issued, this time against John Buckland. Burges continued to insist that Mrs Buckland was a sole trader, but he testified that John Buckland was found bankrupt because, 'tho he did not intermeddle with his said wife's dealings', he nevertheless 'permitted her to trade separately'. Thus Mrs Buckland was construed as having acted as his agent with his knowledge and consent, so when the bankruptcy commission was sued Mr Buckland 'became lyable to pay'. In February 1702 the Bucklands formally assigned all their goods over to Burges to relieve both him and their other creditors, but then issued a bill against Burges in Chancery to try to prevent their household goods from being taken.

Thomas Burges seems to have been content to trade with Mrs Buckland in the normal fashion of exchanging goods and money for long periods and then settling the difference of the account every few months. He knew that she lived in Camberwell but hinted that she could have been taken for a *feme sole* trader by the custom of London, because most of the sales of pigs took place in Leadenhall Market. The rumour of the Bucklands' defaulting on their other creditors was enough to persuade Burges to start proceedings, yet the Bucklands obviously had loyal friends and family willing both to collude in the deception and to try to prevent their goods from being taken. Burges was happy to treat Elizabeth as a sole trader until his action against her failed to settle the debt, when a legal technicality allowed him to sue her husband as well. It seems the Bucklands did not have a premarital agreement based on a valuable consideration. They may have had a voluntary agreement between themselves which, while it would be seen as good between each other in law, was not strong enough to withstand the claims of creditors.[58] If there had been no agreement at all, then in equity a husband had only to acquiesce to his wife treating some property as her own for it to be considered as hers; but he remained liable because he was thereby constituted as the trustee of that property.[59]

In cases of debt, legal action was both an effective threat to prompt the debtor to settle, but also, if seen through to its final end, a last resort to regain money when credit relations had broken down. Both men and women seem to have resorted to legal action or the threat of it as part of 'normative business practice',[60] and misunderstandings over the often complicated but informal reckoning of accounts could not but exacerbate the problem. In 1693 Isabel Lambert,[61] a linen draper in Leeds, sued Robert Browne, a dealer in Scotch

---

[58] See above, p. 43, on how trading with a husband's permission meant that the agreement was good against the husband but not against creditors.

[59] Holcombe, *Wives and Property*, p. 40.

[60] Muldrew, *Economy of Obligation*, p. 275. See also Earle, *Making of the English Middle Class*, p. 124, on the efficacy of initiating legal proceedings to force a debtor to settle and the high proportion of litigants who settled out of court.

[61] PRO, C6/367/37, *Browne vs. Lambert* (1693).

linen cloth, over a deficit in a reckoned account amounting to less than £10. For some years she had got her Scotch cloth from Browne and paid him in kind with linen goods as was 'customary', but they disagreed over the value of cloth exchanged in one transaction, so she had him arrested and started an action for debt in Kings Bench. When he refused to pay the £9 7s 1d, Lambert instructed her attorney to press for the full value of the cloth, some £136. Browne failed to appear, so Lambert pressed for judgement by default, but she must have failed, because at a special inquiry in York she agreed to accept the smaller sum. Lambert explained that, because Browne had not shown her 'just and equitable dealings', when she first had him arrested and he had tried to delay her by issuing this suit in Chancery, she was determined to pursue her case in King's Bench.

Initiating litigation by instructing a lawyer to write a letter was normal practice at this time, and even an attachment of person or goods was not too damaging. Making an arrest, however, was a sign that the creditor considered the debtor to be seriously unreliable and could lead to a potentially fatal loss of credit. These cases reveal that there was a very fine line between acceptable pressure, in which even other members of the community would collude, and escalation into adversarial tactics invoking the full spectrum of legal sanctions. Moreover, the power of rumour could be enough to tip the balance from negotiated credit arrangements to legal prosecution. However, it seems clear that women in trade were equally involved in both processes, and also that they could generally rely on the support of family and friends, and even other members of the community while trading.

Contracts

There has been heated debate among feminists over the degree of disadvantage suffered by women despite the ideal of equality between contracting parties.[62] Married women were the most obviously disadvantaged category because of their theoretical inability to contract under the common law. Yet, as we have seen, coverture was by no means a universal block to married women's trading activities and within equity married women could contract on the basis of their separate property. Indeed, as the cases of Thomasin Moor and Elizabeth Buckland show, contracts were sometimes made on the most informal basis but this could leave both spouses and the other party vulnerable. The question that naturally follows from this is whether the situation was any different for single women, or the extent to which gender inequality affected the ability of unmarried women to contract. As a *feme sole* trader an unmarried woman

---

[62] For a radical feminist analysis, see Carol Pateman, *The Sexual Contract* (Oxford, 1988; rep. 1989); for a critique of Pateman, see Susan Moller Okin, 'Feminism, the Individual and Contract Theory', *Ethics*, 100 (1990), pp. 658–99.

was held to be just as fully personally liable for her debts and contracts as was a male trader which, in contemporary thought, meant that other traders should have been more willing to make contracts since they had every chance of recovering the debt should the need arise. If, as Muldrew has argued, all that was required for a fair exchange of contracts was an equality of 'potential to be trusted', then the gender inequalities in operation in most other social situations had the potential to be suspended or ignored in economic transactions concerning single women.

This final section refers to a set of cases that have been categorised as chiefly contractual in nature, concerning disputes over specific non-performance of contracts, either to supply goods or to fulfil the terms of a partnership agreement, or involving property disputes over the terms of leasehold agreements. Of the six cases in this category, half concerned non-performance of an agreement and half were property disputes. None of the women in these cases were married (or at least not at the time the dispute occurred), so the issue of separate trading does not arise here. However, complex arrangements over exchanges of money and credit were still critical,[63] and the role of other members of the community also remained vital to the regulation of many of these agreements. Just two cases will serve to illustrate the extent of single women's contractual abilities and their embeddedness in local networks.

The first was an action for ejectment, which could be served against tenants in commercial properties who had failed to pay the rent.[64] An appeal to Chancery for an injunction could halt proceedings at law and also gave tenants some chance to claim that they had been unfairly treated. Abigail Barber,[65] a chapwoman in Westminster, had to appeal to equity for just that reason when her landlord tried to evict her from her shop. She had sublet a house and shop from Elizabeth Brockhurst, who in turn held the property from William Davis. Mrs Brockhurst proposed that Abigail should pay £12 for one year's occupancy and buy a door, a bed, paper hangings, a counter and shelving from her for £11. They both consulted Davis who agreed to the arrangement. A year later Davis offered Barber the chance to extend her lease for another three years, which is when his own lease would expire. Abigail claimed that she had traded profitably and earned herself a good reputation in the neighbourhood. However, she became ill and went to convalesce in the country, leaving a male friend to look after the business for her. During her absence Davis and his wife seized the property, evicted her friend and took away all her belongings.

[63] In PRO, C6/410/73, *Farncourt vs. Lee* (1706), for example, an eviction case, revealed a web of interconnected personal and business borrowing between four people, which had collapsed when the businesswoman in question had remarried and left the locality.
[64] This was an action, based on a legal fiction, by which a leaseholder could recover possession of a property, and it had become a common way of trying titles to land. See Staves, *Married Women's Separate Property*, p. 235.
[65] PRO, C6/379/78, *Barber vs. Davis* (1712).

From his reply, it seems Davis was angry with Barber for not paying her rent on time but he was also concerned about the affect Barber's reputation would have on renewing his own lease, which he held from another widow. He claimed that Barber's neighbours had complained about 'frequent disorders' for which the Middlesex JPs had issued more than one warrant. Barber, he said, had absconded and then threatened to return with friends to seize the property, so Davis and his wife had gone there to lock her out. Both sides were therefore relying on local opinion to support their case. Although there is no indication of the outcome, it is clear that Abigail Barber was nevertheless sufficiently established in trade to be able to call on friends of both sexes to provide physical assistance in the same way that the Bucklands had, before resorting to law to settle the dispute. It is also evident that loss of credit through loss of reputation was a major factor in prompting Davis to take action, in case the domino effect should cause his own landlady in the chain of subletting to refuse to renew his lease.

Abigail Barber may have been held fully accountable for her rent and reputation as well as being able to call on friends to support her dispute, but she could hardly be classified as a successful businesswoman. Mary Jevon, on the other hand, was. Her case provides perhaps the clearest insight into how issues of gender may have affected women's contractual capacity. The case was a dispute in 1711 between Jevon and her previous partners in a mercery business, Edward Bee and Thomas Bond, whom she was suing at law for non-payment of debt.[66] Bee and Bond had issued a bill in Chancery to stop Mary Jevon proceeding at law, on the grounds that she had broken the terms of their partnership agreement. Although Jevon had started out as the weaker partner in the business, the balance of power gradually shifted over the six years they traded together, and she seems to have held the upper hand in contractual terms once the relationship between the three began to deteriorate.

In 1704 Mary Jevon had joined Bee and Bond at their mercer's shop in London. They claimed that she was taken on as a journeywoman; but she said that she had known Edward Bee previously and that, as she already had a knowledge of the trade, he had asked her to join them in a partnership. She brought £300 of stock into the business and, after many meetings, Bee and Bond agreed to pay her £45 per annum plus dinner. After two years Jevon threatened to leave because she was unhappy with the terms of the first agreement. She further stated that she had heard rumours that they referred to her as their 'journeywoman' to others. Bee asked her to stay and offered to pay her another £15 per annum, and to have her name printed as a partner on their shop billheads. This new agreement lasted for another two years, after which Bee and Bond asked her to become an equal partner with them. A partnership agreement was drawn up on 4 December 1707 stating that all three agreed to trade as equal partners for a term of seven years. Each partner

---

[66] PRO, C6/374/38, *Bee vs. Jevon* (1711).

had to provide £1,000 stock and to give six months' notice of any intention to quit, if this was before the seven years had expired. In this new agreement then, Jevon became the financial equal of her male partners. Then Jevon claimed that Edward Bee came to see her privately on 15 December 1707 and asked her to make a separate agreement with him because he feared Thomas Bond was behaving irresponsibly and was running short of money. Jevon agreed with Bee that, if the first partnership dissolved, the two of them would immediately form a new partnership with a joint stock of £2,000 and would continue to trade together for the rest of the seven-year period.

In 1709, Bee gave Mary Jevon written notice that the partnership was going to be dissolved and on 15 July 1709 an account of all their joint stock was taken on the understanding that if any errors were discovered they should be rectified at a later date. Jevon's share was estimated at £1,010 6s 6d for which sum Bond and Bee entered into a penalty bond of £2,000 plus interest at 5 per cent, which was due by 25 January 1710. However, there was a dispute over debts still owed by the partnership. Bee and Bond claimed that Jevon had refused to pay her share of these debts despite the agreement to adjust the account. Jevon counter-claimed that she had asked her partners simply to deduct her share from the bond. Finally, Jevon left the partnership and began an action at law to recover the money due on the bond. Edward Bee refused to go into partnership with her, so she then began an action for non-performance against him. Meanwhile, she had moved to a shop in Ludgate Hill and had begun trading there, an action which Bee and Bond interpreted as a deliberate attempt to steal their customers.

Mary Jevon seems to have been at some contractual disadvantage when she first joined the partnership and had to negotiate hard for a position in the business. She felt initially that her position was undermined by her male partners' references to her as a 'journeywoman'. Gender may well have played a determining role in her initially disadvantaged position, but it seems likely that, as Thomas Bond's fortunes apparently declined, the need for Jevon's money in the partnership had overcome this. After four years' trading she had also sufficiently proved her ability within the business to make Bee prefer to be in partnership with her, rather than with his male colleague. Contractually, then, by 1707 she was in an equal position with the two men and once Bee had approached her privately she had begun to gain the upper hand. Moreover, after the partnership had broken down, it was she who first began legal proceedings, and she who had gone on to set up another business alone of sufficient size to make her previous partners feel threatened. They felt that 'in equity and good conscience' she should not be allowed to take their customers with her and that she should surrender the private articles of agreement to Edward Bee, and agree to be bound only by the first two. They also argued that she should cease her legal actions and pay her share of the debts discovered after the partnership had ceased. Since the common law would have been unable to provide any of these remedies, Mary Jevon clearly had the upper hand, and a suit in equity was Bee and Bond's only hope of gaining a 'fairer' settlement from her. Although the outcome of this case is unknown, it demonstrates that gender did not necessarily leave businesswomen in a contractually disadvantaged position with their male colleagues, and that the possession of capital and commercial ability could do much to level the field.

Conclusion

The cases studied here in detail provide an intricate 'snapshot' of trading relations for women in the early eighteenth century, albeit one tightly framed within a legalistic discourse of dispute. It is more difficult to speculate for how long and in what ways these conditions continued for women once an increasing number of banks and paper money, better communications and expanding markets made the culture of credit less central to business transactions. Muldrew's study of credit relations only covered the period to 1720 when changes in the volume of litigation and the structure of credit networks began to alter conceptions about the nature of trust, even though the amount of credit and its importance remained high throughout the eighteenth century. Nevertheless, these cases collectively suggest some more general conclusions about tradeswomen's relationships with their families and other members of their immediate community, and about how practical arrangements may have circumvented legal restrictions on married women's business activities.

First, the model of a household economy based on a nuclear family needs to be expanded to take account of the needs and actions of adult children, and to incorporate the tensions caused by second families. The impact of divorce may have been minimal in early eighteenth-century society, but the incidence of remarriage through death meant that second families and their attendant problems must have been a reality for many women in business. Indeed, even 'natural' children could prove problematic when a division of profits was at stake. A wife's patriarchal subordination to her husband, therefore, was not necessarily the chief cause of family conflict for women. Cases of husbands defrauding their wives certainly did exist,[67] but, in this survey, six cases involved remarriage, whereas only one concerned a hostile husband. In that one case, which was also a second marriage, family and friends mitigated the effects of the husband's potentially damaging actions.

The issue of married women's separate trading also needs to be re-examined because of the impact of multiple marriages on trading relationships. For many women in trade, coverture may have been merely an interruption to their usual long-standing credit arrangements with other traders. As long as credit relations between both parties remained mutually beneficial, that interruption may have been barely noticed. The impact of coverture seems to have been

[67] Hunt, *Middling Sort*, pp. 138–42.

greatest when credit relationships broke down. Then it became a convenient defence for married women, or a means for children to sue their stepmothers (and their own widowed mothers) to gain a greater share of their fathers' estates. Creditors chose to argue for either coverture or *feme sole* status depending on which was most likely to result in the retrieval of their money. Some even appealed to both principles in the same case. Thus, despite the common law definition of married women's legal status, both *feme covert* and *feme sole* traders were highly contingent categories rather than concrete determinants of women's trading status.

Married women's contractual capacity may have been theoretically constricted but, in equity, the existence of separate property seems to have rested on even the most informal of agreements. Such agreements, however, left both husband and wife vulnerable to creditors. For single women, gender disabilities could also be overcome by economic considerations in contractual negotiations. Whatever the respective social positions of borrower and lender, once in debt to another the borrower became 'servant to the lender',[68] even if that lender was female. Thus this research supports Muldrew's findings, in that equitable concepts of trading could do much to level the playing field in economic transactions concerning both married and single women in this period. Just as importantly, women in business were deeply embedded within highly complex networks of credit, and they were also able to call on other members of the trading community for assistance in maintaining those networks. As Chapter 5 shows, women remained active participants in mixed-gender business networks throughout the eighteenth century. Wiskin's research has demonstrated that this remained the case for the first three decades of the nineteenth century and, as the mixed-sex partnerships and property sharing discussed in chapters 6 and 7 will show, networking remained important for businesswomen at least until 1845.[69]

[68] A common seventeenth-century phrase, cited in Muldrew, *Economy of Obligation*, p. 98.
[69] Wiskin, 'Women, Finance and Credit', pp. 147–91.

Part II

Business

5

'The friendship of the world'

Female business networks in eighteenth-century Durham

> The whole neighbourhood have quite recovered the death of Mrs Ryder – so much so, that I think they are rejoiced at it now; her things were so very dear! ... Not even death itself can fix the friendship of the World.
>
> Jane Austen (1801)[1]

Thus far, women in business have been shown to be deeply embedded in horizontal networks of credit with fellow traders, but it is also possible to examine these in conjunction with vertical ties of credit and patronage in relation to questions of supply and demand. In this chapter, networks of credit and supply between Judith Baker, a Durham gentlewoman, and her female suppliers have been studied in order to discuss the extent to which female demand might have required goods produced and vended by women, and how this business was conducted. The peerage and gentry were also dependent on credit networks and the expense of maintaining status through an opulent lifestyle required huge amounts of credit that was often provided by those who were not necessarily their social equals.[2] Hence, this chapter examines how women were involved in the process of providing the funds for, as well as the goods necessary, to support high levels of conspicuous consumption. It also continues the discussion of businesswomen's involvement in trading networks begun in Chapter 4, although here the focus is on the later eighteenth century. Although there has been much work done on the trading networks of men in business, there has been very little on those of female traders. In part this has been due to the fact that women have been omitted from narratives describing the role of networks in histories of business development. However, this impression is reinforced by narratives describing women's increasing marginalisation from the public sphere of business, in which it is argued that women were excluded from the formal trade organisations used by businessmen and

---

[1] Jane Austen writing on the death of the local village shopkeeper, cited in Alison Adburgham, *Shops and Shopping, 1800–1914* (1964; rep. 1981), p. 3.
[2] Muldrew, *Economy of Obligation*, pp. 96–7; B.A. Holderness, 'Credit in a Rural Community, 1660–1800', *Midland History*, 3 (1975), pp. 94–115.

hence failed to benefit from the business information, finance and connections these institutions could provide. Instead, despite the lack of detailed research into the matter, the argument is that from around 1780 women were increasingly restricted to the use of mixed-gender kinship networks, which contributed to their lack of 'commercial credibility' and limited the scale of their business enterprises.[3] In the few instances where female economic networks have been studied, as Christine Wiskin has pointed out, they have generally been presented as models of exclusively feminine solidarity among poor women.[4]

The chronological scope of this chapter is limited by the focus on Judith Baker's accounts to the period 1755 to 1784, but evidence that businesswomen continued to operate as fully integrated members of trading networks well into the nineteenth century is discussed further in Chapter 7. The chapter begins by situating Mrs Baker and her family within the context of an expanding consumer economy in the county capital of Durham, and examines the extent of her use of women to supply money and goods. The following section uses the early modern concept of 'friendship' to explain the relationship between Mrs Baker and the women she used as moneylenders, as agents to purchase goods and as traders she patronised. The final two sections focus on local and regional networks of friends, family and traders employed in the business of buying and selling goods. Predominantly but certainly not exclusively female, these networks ensured that Mrs Baker could buy goods from women in and around Durham, but also from Newcastle, Darlington, Richmond, London and Bath. Conversely, it meant that women in business could increase their commercial credibility by providing goods and services to the distant elite as well as to local customers, a practice that was also greatly facilitated by the efforts of their male and female friends, family and fellow traders.

---

[3] Hall, 'Gender Divisions and Class Formation', pp. 101–2; Davidoff and Hall, *Family Fortunes*, pp. 278–9; Hunt, *Middling Sort*, pp. 131–2, argues that women were missing from male civic associations in late eighteenth-century trade directories, which spelt the end for the small-scale local networks based on oral transactions in which women were most commonly found. However, the argument that women were swept out of all public associative life after about 1780 has been substantially challenged in Vickery, *Gentleman's Daughter*, pp. 277–9.

[4] For eighteenth and early nineteenth-century networks see Earle, *Making of the Middle Class*, pp. 112–37; David A. Kent, 'Small Businessmen and their Credit Transactions in Early Nineteenth-Century Britain', *Business History*, 36 (1994), pp. 47–64; Penelope Lane, 'An Industrialising Town: Social and Business Networks in Hinckley, Leicestershire, c.1750–1839', in *Urban and Industrial Change in the Midlands, 1700–1840*, ed. P. Lane and J. Stobart (Leicester, 2000), pp. 139–66. For a detailed discussion of the trends in business history and studies of exclusively female networks, see Wiskin, 'Women, Finance and Credit', pp. 147–50.

The Bakers of Durham

By the eighteenth century the City of Durham had become an elegant and sophisticated county town, whose cultural revival could be seen as a prime example of 'urban renaissance'.[5] It boasted a racecourse, theatres that attracted London actors and assembly rooms. Social events included public assemblies, subscription concerts, card parties and splendid dinner parties thrown by the wealthy canons. During race and assize weeks, when the country gentry occupied their town houses, there were cockfights, raffles and balls. Durham was also an important post town on the Great North Road for many London to Edinburgh stage-coaches and so had regular connections with the capital. In short, Durham was a 'leisure town' in which a provincial economy was stimulated by the new patterns of sociability and consumption of its resident and visiting elite.[6] The Bakers of Elemore Hall, which stood about seven miles east of Durham, were prominent members of the local landed gentry and active participants in the culture, politics and entertainment of their county town.[7] They were also enthusiastic consumers.

Judith Baker, née Routh (1725–1810), was both a meticulous keeper of accounts and an avid consumer with a passion for politics, fashion, food and satirical prints.[8] In 1749 she married George Baker, the son of an MP, with whom she had two children, George and Elizabeth. Her daughter was sent to a boarding-school for young ladies run by Mrs Chewe, who charged over £6 a quarter but was promptly paid.[9] George Baker was elected deputy Lieutenant of County Durham three times, but the family income derived chiefly from their landed estate and the mining of lead, alum and coal.[10] Both Mr and Mrs Baker were active in local politics and their involvement in the 1761 Durham

---

[5] Peter Borsay, *The English Urban Renaissance: Culture and Society in the Provincial Town, 1660–1770* (Oxford, 1989; rep. 1991), p. 199.

[6] Leonard Schwarz, 'Residential Leisure Towns in England towards the End of the Eighteenth Century', *Urban History*, 27 (2000), pp. 51–61, identified Durham as one of fifty-three residential leisure towns outside the London area, with more than thirty families employing manservants in a population of under 10,000. See also P.J. Corfield, *The Impact of English Towns, 1700–1800* (Oxford, 1982; rep. 1989), pp. 51–2, on Durham as a resort town and county capital, and the 'conspicuous consumption' of leisure.

[7] With thanks to Peter Barton for suggesting the Baker Baker papers as a source.

[8] Helen Berry, 'The Metropolitan Tastes of Judith Baker, Durham Gentlewoman', in *On the Town: Women and Urban Life in Eighteenth-century Britain*, ed. P. Lane and R. Sweet (Aldershot, 2003), pp. 131–55; J. Linda Drury, 'The Baker Baker Portfolio of Prints: Its Content and Acquisition', *Durham County Local History Society Bulletin*, 56 (1996), pp. 3–20.

[9] UDL/PG, BB/75/5l/4, bill from Mrs Chewe for £6:6:3 due on 10 December 1755 and paid on 16 December.

[10] Paul Langford, *Public Life and the Propertied Englishman, 1689–1798* (Oxford, 1991), p. 62, on how mining was a crucial part of the 'genteel economy' in Durham and Northumberland.

City election resulted in proceedings in the House of Commons.[11] Mrs Baker kept in touch with national politics through letters from her female friends but she was also consulted in her own right about town council business. Indeed, the evidence of notes that she made indicate that she sat in on Council meetings.[12] She was also involved with the Common Council elections of a mayor and alderman and was consulted by the local trade guilds when they elected wardens.[13] Mrs Baker therefore enjoyed a degree of political leverage more usually associated with male property owners.[14] The Bakers also enjoyed a busy social life, attending race meetings, plays, assemblies, concerts and dinner parties. They also travelled to London and Bath, the receipts from which testify to their enthusiasm for material consumption. George died in 1774, leaving Judith as his executor, legatee and trustee,[15] with debts of at least £6,000.[16] Mrs Baker continued to keep the estate accounts, as she had when married, but she now took on the family lead, alum and coal business which she ran for thirteen years,[17] continuing long after her son had reached his majority in 1775. When her son married in 1787, Mrs Baker retired to Tynemouth at the age of 64. She continued to write her accounts in her own hand until her death in 1810 aged 84.

Mrs Baker's accounts, particularly the bundles of receipts sampled from 1755 to 1775 and studied in detail for the period after her husband's death from 1775 to 1784, provide vital information about how a wealthy gentlewoman used female traders to supply her with material goods. However, this is not to say

---

[11] Drury, 'Baker Baker', p. 5, on the Bakers' involvement March–April 1761 when extra freemen of the city were created to influence the vote. Mrs Baker campaigned actively for Major General Lambton who was eventually declared the winner, and she received not only numerous letters of congratulation but also a ballad entitled 'The London Voters Ditty Humbly Inscribed to Mrs. B-a-k-r' (UDL/PG, BB/11/78/8).

[12] UDL/PG, BB/12/78 (1766), letter from Robert Robinson requesting Mrs Baker to be present when he had some of the newly elected Common Council with him to render his advice to them more effective.

[13] UDL/PG, BB/12/91 and 12/90, letters to Mrs Baker about choosing candidates for wardens of two different livery companies.

[14] Jill Liddington, *Female Fortune: Land, Gender and Authority. The Anne Lister Diaries and Other Writings, 1833–6* (1998), pp. xvii, 44–8, found that Ann Lister (1791–1840) shared a similar interest in politics and used her position to exert a high degree of political influence over Yorkshire tenants.

[15] She had been appointed joint executor with John Bowes, Earl of Strathmore, but he died in March 1776.

[16] Drury, 'Baker Baker', p. 6, and UDL/PG, BB/14/65–7. George had also not finished paying for his daughter's marriage portion, although Elizabeth had married Christopher Tower in 1773.

[17] Mrs Baker was not alone in managing a mining business; UDL/PG, BB/124/51 details the lease of a coalmine from the two Misses Grey in 1703, with the condition that they may continue to inspect the workings in person. Ann Lister also successfully developed her family's coalmines in Yorkshire: Liddington, *Female Fortune*, pp. 53–5.

that Mrs Baker preferred to use female suppliers. The majority of trade bills both before and after she was widowed, when the number of female suppliers rose, were from men. It is only the sheer volume of receipts and the fact that the focus of research was aimed exclusively at determining the role of female suppliers in elite women's patterns of consumption that has prevented a closer examination of male traders. In fact many receipts, and printed ones in particular, had only a supplier's initial on them which prevented determination of their sex. Only those receipts where there was no doubt that the supplier was female were counted, so the numbers of women in trade are likely to be on the conservative side. The evidence was also problematic because of the lack of diaries or comprehensive personal correspondence to help to identify suppliers, although there were fragments of many letters and short notes that had been used as receipts. Account book entries and receipts did not necessarily tally exactly, but it is possible that some suppliers did not provide written receipts or that they have been lost. Of those suppliers who did provide bills, the majority used handwritten notes, sometimes only tiny fragments, but on occasions balanced statements of credits and debits. Printed trade cards were rare, and generally used only by the larger traders in London and Bath.

Consumption has long been considered an essentially feminine occupation and, with the dramatic expansion of new forms of consumption from the early eighteenth century, women of the 'leisured classes' in particular were correspondingly increasingly berated for their over-indulgence.[18] More recently women's role as consumers has been re-evaluated in the light of theories that the Industrial Revolution must have required a demand side to stimulate production.[19] The cynical motives commonly ascribed to women's consumerism – excessive leisure time, vanity and social emulation – are highly problematic, but they should not obscure the effect of women's purchasing power. Indeed, in the 'Remarks' attached to his *Fable of the Bees* (1714), Bernard Mandeville infamously claimed that it was the 'vile Stratagems of Women' that supported 'a considerable portion of . . . the Prosperity of London and Trade in general'.[20] The main issue here, however, is to discover to what extent female demand relied on goods made or supplied by other women, particularly those in the

---

[18] On debates about women and consumption see Vickery, *Gentleman's Daughter*, pp. 161–4 and idem, 'Women and the World of Goods: A Lancashire Consumer and Her Possessions, 1751–81', *Consumption and the World of Goods*, ed. J. Brewer and R. Porter (London, 1993), pp. 274–8; Tague, *Women of Quality*, pp. 133–61.

[19] For the demand side of the Industrial Revolution, see McKendrick *et al.*, *Birth of a Consumer Society*, pp. 9–34. For women's role as consumers, see idem, 'Home Demand and Economic Growth: A New View of the Role of Women and Children in the Industrial Revolution', ed. idem, *Historical Perspectives: Studies in English Thought and Society* (Cambridge, 1975), pp. 152–210.

[20] For an illuminating discussion of this quotation and Mandeville's misogynistic use of women to personify the evils of capitalist desire see Laura Mandell, *Misogynous Economies: The Business of Literature in Eighteenth-century Britain* (Lexington, 1999), pp. 64–83.

fashionable or 'feminine' trades. While there is some debate over the extent to which male and female patterns of consumption differed,[21] it is nevertheless broadly fair to say that women were particularly involved in purchasing food, fashion and luxury items such as chinaware, which involved trades where significant numbers of women could be found. Susan Wright found that the visiting elite in eighteenth-century Ludlow stimulated crafts in which women played a vital role, such as dressmaking and millinery.[22] Judith Baker was a gentlewoman with land and commercial interests, so hardly 'leisured', but her accounts show that she relied on a small but significant number of women in trade to supply her not only with 'feminine' luxuries, but also with some of her more mundane household goods.

In total over the thirty-year period, but predominantly in the nine-year period after her widowhood, Judith did business with at least fifty-six women.[23] Of these, nine were acting as moneylenders and five were 'employed' to act as agents or to acquire goods for her. Seventeen were regular local suppliers and ten were occasional suppliers, based in and around Durham. A further five were regular London suppliers, and five more provided apparently one-off or occasional services. Finally, during a month-long trip to Bath with George in 1768, the Bakers were regularly supplied by three women and bought goods from three others. The number of women Mrs Baker dealt with each year varied but seems to have increased from an average of eight to an average of sixteen after her husband's death (Table 5.1). It seems likely that this was due not only to Mrs Baker's increased reliance upon her female friends and family to acquire goods for her rather than upon her husband's stewards, but also a greater freedom to indulge her own interests, particularly in fashion. Linda Drury suggests that Mrs Baker experienced a new freedom as a widow after years of caring for an ailing husband and two children.[24] As Table 5.1 shows, the circle of women with whom Mrs Baker did business contracted to just four in the year following George Baker's death when the family lived quite frugally, but then rose to ten in 1776 and to eighteen in 1777.

With the probable exception of her regular London suppliers, the majority of tradeswomen would have been in a relatively modest way of business,

---

[21] See Vickery, 'Women and the World of Goods', pp. 279–81; Lorna Weatherill, 'A Possession of One's Own: Women and Consumer Behaviour in England, 1660–1740', *Journal of British Studies*, 25 (1986), pp. 131–56; Margot Finn, 'Men's Things: Masculine Possession in the Consumer Revolution', *Social History*, 25 (2000), pp. 133–55; Tague, *Women of Quality*, 133–61.

[22] Susan Wright, 'Holding Up Half the Sky: Women and their Occupations in Eighteenth-century Ludlow', *Midland History*, 14 (1989), pp. 53–74.

[23] See Appendix 1 for a full list of names and occupations.

[24] Drury, 'Baker Baker Portfolio', p. 8: from 1776 Mrs Baker dramatically expanded the print collection. Weatherill, 'A Possession of One's Own', pp. 131–56, found that women in female-headed households acquired a different range of goods from those in male-headed households.

Table 5.1 Number of women doing business with Judith Baker in selected years

Year	No. of female traders per annum	Year	No. of female traders per annum
1755	11	1778	11
1764	5	1779	17
1774	Mrs Baker widowed	1780	18
1775	4	1781	16
1776	10	1782	13
1777	18	1783	16
		1784	15

Source: Extracted from Baker Baker papers

although it is not possible to gauge size and success with any accuracy on the basis of bills for just one customer. Success, however, is also a relative term. Elizabeth Sanderson, for example, found that, in eighteenth-century Edinburgh, the 'status of women in business depended more on the status of their customers than the size of the business itself'.[25] Mrs Baker's status among the landed gentry was considerable, and she patronised both large and small traders. Most of Mrs Baker's expenditure with them was small but regular, with the exception of George Baker's wine merchant Jane Robson, who was owed hundreds of pounds. Mrs Robson was a widow, as was the ironmonger Mercy Ashworth and the chimney-sweep Isabella Salvin, who worked in 'masculine' trades. The majority, however, provided goods in the traditionally 'feminine' sectors of clothing and textiles. Mrs Baker's expenditure on clothing and material for herself, family, friends and servants was prodigious and her patronage was generous. There are receipts which show that Judith Baker remained a loyal customer to many of these women for over ten years and in one case for nearly thirty years. Moreover, the receipts show that her suppliers were literate, numerate, socially adept, self-supporting, and engaged in businesses that occupied them for long periods of their lives.

Friends

If a case study of just one female consumer can provide only limited answers to the question of to what extent female demand required goods produced by women, the question of how business was conducted can be answered much more fully. For Mrs Baker, the business of shopping involved social as well as economic exchange. She used family and friends to borrow money and acquire goods. Receipts from them and from her suppliers were often just fragments of letters full of other news, with a note of money owed fitted into the text or

[25] Sanderson, *Women and Work*, p. 101.

added afterwards. Indeed, combining personal and business matters was not uncommon in eighteenth-century letters and diaries. Letters requesting charity from Lady Spencer frequently mixed personal thoughts and experiences with more instrumental, businesslike negotiation.[26] Craig Muldrew found that many people recorded 'business' transactions in personal diaries, combining gift-giving and receiving, debts, financial agreements, hospitality and sales transactions. He therefore characterised all these economic and personal transactions as 'social exchanges'.[27] The diary and letters of eighteenth-century shopkeeper Thomas Turner show that he routinely recorded business dealings with and for his mother, who was also a shopkeeper, alongside other family matters. Naomi Tadmor has argued that since Turner regarded his mother as one of his 'related friends', who included close family and wider kin, his 'affective friendship relationships were increasingly tied with instrumental and occupational relationships'.[28] The women with whom Mrs Baker traded certainly relied heavily on informal networks of family and 'friends' to conduct their business. Eighteenth-century male traders also maintained correspondence networks, often based on extended kin networks, to provide commercial intelligence and to assist in sales and purchases, particularly when money had to be remitted over long distances.[29] However, Peter Earle found that the letters of male traders usually pressed for information on prices and customers, 'with just the occasional polite enquiry after a correspondent's health or a little bit of home news'.[30] This suggests that any difference between male and female traders was one of degree rather than essential practice.

Eighteenth-century traders and shopkeepers relied heavily on custom derived from interpersonal links, such as through kinship or friendship, and in particular on cultivating aristocratic patronage. Both male and female traders advertising their goods in newspapers addressed their advertisements to 'Friends and Customers',[31] which reflected the highly personal nature of exchange between people who were most often known to each other. 'Friend' had many connotations in the eighteenth century, which implied a far wider range of relationships than those based purely on mutual affection. Samuel Johnson listed six meanings, of which the fifth was 'favourer; one propitious', a definition that clearly introduces an element of expectation or benefit into the meaning of friendship.[32] Naomi Tadmor's study of Richardson's *Pamela* (1740) reveals

---

[26] Donna T. Andrew, '*Noblesse Oblige*: Female Charity in an age of sentiment', ed. J. Brewer and S. Staves, *Early Modern Conceptions of Property* (London, 1996), p. 278.

[27] Muldrew, *Economy of Obligation*, p. 64.

[28] Naomi Tadmor, *Family & Friends in Eighteenth-Century England: Household, Kinship and Patronage* (Cambridge, 2001), pp. 175–8, and see n.40 for business and family exchanges with his mother, brother and wife.

[29] Earle, *Making of the Middle Class*, pp. 134–7.

[30] Ibid., p. 135.

[31] See below, pp. 215–16.

[32] Johnson, *Dictionary* (1755), *sub* 'Friend'.

three common usages of the term 'friend', the third of which is particularly relevant. In this category Tadmor includes guardians, protectors and supporters who could be parents, siblings, kin related by marriage or consanguinity, or non-related acquaintances acting as patrons, trustees or guardians.[33] In studying Turner's diary Tadmor widened the category of friendship to include trusted tradesmen with whom he had 'special business contacts'.[34] The common denominator with all these groups was their willingness to provide assistance or support, but in 'many of these ties the "friendship" is one-sided, senior is "friend" to junior, rich to poor, man to woman'.[35] Hence social equality was not a pre-condition of friendship, which could be maintained without breaching any social hierarchies. When Mrs Baker sent a letter to one of her husband's agents in 1764 asking him to order more huggaback cloth from Jane Robinson, she sent her compliments to his family and signed it 'believe me yr friend'.[36] This encompassed both the inequality of the relationship and the element of assistance involved. Tadmor found that 'relatives as a whole serve as a body of "friends" mainly for the purpose of certain functions, such as transfer of property, protection or arrangement of marriages'.[37] The Baker evidence shows that the transfer of money and goods may be added to this list and that wider friendship networks which supported trade links were not confined to men.

Gentry families had numerous social links with those in land, trade and the professions.[38] The diaries of Lancashire gentlewoman Elizabeth Shackleton reveal that more than one-third of her social encounters with non-kin acquaintances were with people in trade and that tradespeople, including milliners and mantua makers, were often treated to hospitality at her home. Mrs Shackleton met the retailer Betty Hartley twenty-two times in two years and recorded how she gave Betty and Molly Hartley tea or supper, and then gave them another order or settled her account with them. Yet, as Vickery points out, Elizabeth Shackleton also maintained her sense of social superiority and referred to Betty somewhat disparagingly as 'Betty Hartley Shopkeeper'.[39] No diary survives for Judith Baker but she seems to have been on familiar terms with her milliner Dorothy Verty, whose bills she often labelled simply 'Miss

[33] Naomi Tadmor, '"Family" and "Friend" in *Pamela*: A Case-Study in the History of Family in Eighteenth-Century England', *Social History*, 14 (1989), pp. 289–306.
[34] Tadmor, *Family & Friends*, p. 174. And for a detailed discussion of different types of friendship and how the language of friendship was used to express obligation, see pp. 167–215, 272–3.
[35] Tadmor, '"Family" and "Friend" in *Pamela*', p. 300.
[36] UDL/PG, BB/75/8/5.
[37] Tadmor, '"Family" and "Friend" in *Pamela*', p. 301.
[38] Vickery, *Gentleman's Daughter*, p. 14.
[39] Ibid. pp. 27, 208. See also p. 394, Table 1, for Shackleton's diaries for 1773 and 1780, which shows that 36 per cent of her daily interactions were with those engaged in 'upper' or 'lesser' trades.

Dorty's', although this did not prevent her from writing Dorothy Verty curt notes demanding more pins or returning unsatisfactory goods.

These close social links were further augmented by the fact that, in some lesser gentry families, daughters were not unlikely to find themselves having to earn a living in trade. Sanderson found that in eighteenth-century Edinburgh the majority of milliners came from gentry or professional families.[40] In 1744 the novelist Laurence Sterne hoped to persuade his sister Catherine to become a mantua maker or milliner so that he would not have to support her. She was far from happy with this plan and declared that as she was 'the Daughter of a Gentleman, *she would not Disgrace* herself, but would Live as Such'.[41] But even women born into the highest levels of society could be forced to try millinery when no other funds were available. Lady Jane Flack, daughter of the late Earl of Wigtoun, solicited 'the countenance of the Countess Spencer in prosecuting the Millinery Business' in order to support her large family, while at the same time 'not wishing to make a public shew of business, but to continue her attendance to the Nobility only – at her house'. Sadly, Lady Flack died before Countess Spencer could help.[42] Under rather less dramatic circumstances, Mrs Baker was asked by a relative on her husband's side, Captain William Conyers, to find an apprenticeship for his niece in 1783. Mrs Baker approached Mrs Elizabeth Goodrick who had been her local mantua maker for six years. Mrs Goodrick charged the Captain £21 for 'teaching Miss Conyers Mantua Making & Board for one year', which Mrs Baker paid.[43] In June 1783 Captain Conyers wrote thanking her for paying Mrs Goodrick and further requesting that she use her influence to 'get my Niece a little work amongst your Acquaintances to make a beginning'. He emphasised this point by going on to name several of their joint acquaintances to whom he sent his regards.[44] Conyers also asked Mrs Baker to give his niece five guineas, which he would repay through her sister Elizabeth Bland. In December 1783 he wrote again, in reply to a chatty letter from Judith:

> glad to hear that my friends are chearfull and well. Respecting my Niece she Complains that she cannot get work to do, I will be much Obliged to you if you will let my Niece have three guineas and I will order it to be paid to your sister in town.[45]

---

[40] Sanderson, 'Edinburgh Milliners', p. 20.

[41] Lewis P. Curtis (ed.), *The Letters of Laurence Sterne* (Oxford, 1935), pp. 37–8.

[42] See Andrew, 'Female Charity', p. 288, on how Lady Spencer continued to support Lady Flack's children after her death. Quotation taken from figs 14.2 and 14.3, a handwritten card to Lady Spencer found among her papers. On the reverse the countess noted that Lady Flack had died soon after of want.

[43] UDL/PG, BB/85/50c/7 and 50e/44.

[44] UDL/PG, BB/85/50f/29.

[45] UDL/PG, BB/86/51a/6.

Well-connected friends and relations were vital to success in the genteel business of mantua making, but there is no further record of whether Mrs Baker's influence was sufficient to help Miss Conyer's enterprise.

A language of politeness further blurred distinctions between the business of trade and the business of family and friends. Both Mrs Baker's tradeswomen and her higher ranking friends thanked her for the 'favours' she sent them, which sometimes referred to a letter, but also to goods commissioned, or to an actual order or command. Hence 'favour' could convey gratitude at being asked to be of service to a friend or convey a financial obligation. Indeed, Vickery argues that the exchange of consumer services was basic to female relationships.[46] Yet she also suggests that, for genteel women, shopping was a 'form of employment'.[47] Judith Baker may be seen to have 'employed' both family and friends to conduct business with her suppliers, a practice which would almost certainly have widened the circle of customers for each tradeswoman. For London Mrs Baker relied particularly heavily on the services of her sister Mrs Elizabeth Bland, and less often on her other sister Mrs Hester Chapeau. For goods from Newcastle she used Mrs Perrot, and in Durham Mrs Potts. In addition, a Mrs Tunstall dealt regularly with Mrs Baker's cloth dealer, Jane Robinson, in Darlington. All these women frequently combined local news and gossip when writing about commissions which Judith Baker had sent them and all were filed in her 'accounts' as technical receipts for money owed and paid. Mrs Perrot supplied Mrs Baker with groceries, household goods, the occasional gown, and copious news about people and events in Newcastle. In 1777 she wrote:

Dear Madm,
On Recpt of your last favour set out upon the enquiries for the Countess . . . I live in hope of seeing you this winter tho from what you say not quite so soon as my wishes. The gown was £1-4-0 the fringe 3 shillings, shall take care & bespeak a still when the old one comes, the loss of the shipping falls very heavy on severall of this town, & they begin to doubt the Scotch news vastly. . . . The Bells has Rung today for CB & his bride.[48]

Mrs Baker recorded on the back of the letter that she had sent Mrs Perrot £1 7s, while on the reverse of another she added 'Newcastle News' to the amount paid.[49]

Mrs Baker's female friends provided the means of purchasing goods, but she was also very reliant on women to supply the money to afford these

---

[46] Vickery, *Gentleman's Daughter*, p. 183: Elizabeth Shackleton's female friends were pleased to be asked to acquire goods for her.
[47] Ibid., p. 164.
[48] UDL/PG, BB/81/44/355.
[49] UDL/PG, BB/82/46f/35.

purchases, and thereby completing the demand side of the equation. Research has shown that women at every level of society used moneylending as either a prime or additional source of income, but it is held to have been most common among widows and spinsters.[50] Gentry families seem to have preferred dealing with kinsfolk and friends, but it was not unusual for shopkeepers and local merchants to become creditors, especially if a family had become known as a bad risk and been refused by its social equals.[51]

Mrs Baker borrowed money from at least eight women, including her own mother. The original bonds were taken out in the name of George Baker (senior and later junior), but it was Mrs Baker who managed the payment of these loans. The largest loan of £6,500 was from Mrs Peard in London who could afford to employ an agent, Mr Lloyd, to manage her affairs. The Bakers had to pay £130 interest on the loan every six months, but they sometimes had difficulty in paying such a large sum, and in 1779 Mrs Peard threatened to foreclose on the loan.[52] Some, but not all, of these female moneylenders were linked socially with both Mrs Baker and her sisters, and in several cases mutual exchanges of goods became part of the lending process. Priscilla Atlee was a widow in Newcastle with whom the Bakers had taken out a loan of £500 in August 1774, not long after George Baker's death.[53] Mrs Atlee seems to have been a family friend of equal or higher status who also exchanged goods with Mrs Baker and her sisters.[54] In February 1779, in addition to the interest due, Mrs Atlee received money for goods purchased for Mrs Baker, and for paying Mrs Lyon for linen and glass.[55] The Bakers also took out a loan for £100 in 1776 with Eleanor Nelson, whose sister Mary lived in Chester, and who was sufficiently friendly with Judith Baker to invite her to her son's christening.[56] Mrs Baker used the invitation as a receipt for £3 3s, which was more than the

---

[50] Penelope Lane, 'Women, Property and Inheritance: Wealth Creation and Income Generation in Small English Towns, 1750–1835', in *Urban Fortunes: Property and Inheritance in the Town, 1700–1900* ed. J. Stobart and A. Owen, (Aldershot, 2000), pp. 172–94; Holderness, 'Credit in a Rural Community', pp. 100–1.

[51] Ibid., p. 100.

[52] UDL/PG, BB/14/31.

[53] UDL/PG, BB/80/43a/18 and 43h/2. My thanks to Helen Berry for pointing out that Priscilla Atlee also subscribed to the building of the Newcastle Assembly Rooms in 1776 and was a benefactress of the city's All Saints Church.

[54] UDL/PG, BB/81/44/301: Elizabeth Bland mentions two caps bought for 'Mrs Baker & Mrs Atlee'. An account book entry for 1781 (UDL/PG, BB/45/28) details payments to Mrs Chapeau for numerous articles including a cap for Mrs Atlee.

[55] UDL/PG, BB/82/46b/19: Mrs Lyon was also an acquaintance shared with Captain Conyers, another relative of Mrs Baker. An interest receipt for 1780 also included payment of £3 19s 3d for caps and other items for Mrs Baker: UDL/PG BB/83/47j/19.

[56] UDL/PG, BB/83/47k/33 and BB51c/49: the original bond with Eleanor Nelson was drawn up in October 1776 for £100 at 4.5 per cent interest to be paid every six months. The loan was paid off in March 1784. See UDL/PG,BB86/51a/5 for the invitation to the christening.

£2 10s interest due on the loan and probably indicates more goods commissioned. However, not all the women who lent money to the Bakers were of their social standing. Grace Baites, who loaned £60, and Elizabeth Pickering, who loaned £80, were both unable to write, and signed their receipts only with a cross.[57] As Elizabeth Pickering's interest remained unpaid from 1773 to 1776, it is possible she did not have the social standing or contacts to enforce regular repayments, or the means to employ an agent to do it for her, as could the wealthy Mrs Peard in London.

Regional networks: London, Bath and Richmond

In 1786 a contemporary commenting on the shop tax explained that 'many families who live in the neighbourhood of small towns purchase half-yearly from London many articles they want'.[58] This was often the most economical way of obtaining supplies. Many provincial gentry families maintained an agent in London to conduct business for them, but they also relied on friends and acquaintances, which was Mrs Baker's preferred strategy.[59] One of her chief London agents was her sister, Mrs Bland, although the scale of her shopping could hardly be described as economical. 'Mrs Bland's account' was a regular feature in the Elemore account books every three or four months. Her account from 12 October 1780 to May 1781 alone came to £838 7s 3½d, although many of her accounts were for more modest amounts. She bought goods for Mrs Baker and her friends in London, booked theatre tickets and paid bills for her. She paid the interest due on loans and acted as a conduit for any other payments due to Mrs Baker from people in or passing through the city. Since Mrs Bland was not only commissioned to purchase goods for her sister but also for other female friends, this system of shopping again promoted a wider customer base for London women in the luxury and 'feminine' trades.[60]

Elizabeth Bland was Mrs Baker's chief contact with her regular London suppliers, although she must have met some face to face on her trips to the city. The smartest and probably the largest of the London suppliers were Mrs Leach, a milliner at 154 New Bond Street, and Mary Oliver, a French trimming and flounce maker at 112 New Bond Street, who between them supplied

---

[57] UDL/PG, BB/81/44/106: Grace Baites' receipt for annual interest of £2 12s on the loan, and UDL/PG, BB/80/43L/20 for Elizabeth Pickering's receipt for £3 12s interest. The original bond for £80 was taken out in December 1759 with Elizabeth and her sister Mary Pickering of Sherburn in Co. Durham. The interest was not paid in full until 1801.
[58] Anon., *Policy of the Tax upon Retailing Considered* (London, 1786), cited in Davis, *History of Shopping*, p. 224.
[59] Ibid., p. 225; Ann Buck, *Dress in Eighteenth-century England* (London, 1979), p. 68.
[60] For example, UDL/PG, BB/83/47a/24: in January 1780 Mrs Bland was paid *inter alia* for getting a gown dyed for Mrs Potts and finding a bracelet for Miss Robinson to give as a gift to Mr Ragdale.

Judith, both her sisters and Mrs Atlee. Both these London suppliers had printed bill heads and were in partnership with female relatives, although the bills were still relatively small. This was partly due to the practice of buying material, often the most expensive part of an outfit, separately, and then having it made up by a mantua maker who passed it on to a milliner to finish it off with trimmings. In the second half of the century, however, the costliness of the trimmings, and hence the milliner's art, became a more important part of the overall outfit.[61] Elizabeth Bland paid £2 14s 9d for caps for Judith and Mrs Atlee in 1779, and Mrs Bland and Hester Chapeau paid less for fringes from Mary Oliver in 1782.[62] It seems likely that Mrs Leach and her partner (probably her sister)[63] had been personally recommended to Mrs Baker. This recommendation could have come from friends but it could also have come from a previous supplier attempting to keep the business within her own circle. In 1755 Mrs Catherine Connor wrote to Judith to explain why she was retiring from business and to nominate her successor as follows:

> Madam,
> That you have not Rec'd My Thankfull acknowledgement for your last Bill, and all other favours, was owing to my being oblidg'd to Goe in ye Country for a Little air, after a very Bad fit of illness that Confind me ten weeks to my Room. I am now thank God Greatly Recover'd, but not able to Bear the fatigues of Busness, which was the only Reason for my Quiting it.
> You have ben very oblidgeing to me madam in Desiring me to Recomend a milliner; A favour I intend to ask of you, for two of my People that are sett upe together, and have Enclosed thair Bill of thair shop, thay are Clever in Busness and honest in thair Dealing & I hope will Please you or thay shou'd not have the Recomendation of Madam Your Oblidged and Obedient Servant
>
> Catherine Connor[64]

Another regular supplier was Mary Mackenzie & Co, the London mantua-making business that was used by Mrs Baker and Mrs Bland for at least five years (1775–80). The company consisted of Mary, her sister Sarah Waylin, and possibly Elizabeth Golding as an additional partner, although Sarah usually received any money for just 'sister & self'. In October 1775 Judith paid £6 17s 5d for three items made between January and June,[65] but Mrs Bland complained that Mrs Mackenzie was too slow to bill her, and in January 1777 she wrote:

---

[61] Buck, *Dress in Eighteenth-century England*, p. 160.
[62] UDL/PG, BB/82/46i/19; BB/85/49e/29, 85/49l/29.
[63] UDL/PG, BB/81/44/96: bills were directed to E. and L. Leach.
[64] UDL/PG, BB/75/5e/3, May 1755. There was no shop bill with the letter so it is not possible to tell whom she recommended or whether it was accepted.
[65] UDL/PG, BB/79/41j/33.

My dear sister . . . am glad you Liked the things. I have not got mrs Mackenzies bill yet, she is a lazy woman. I have asked her for both your's and mine so often I am tired, but she shall have Little Rest till I have it.[66]

Mrs Mackenzie must have been a skilled mantua maker to have continued supplying the sisters after displeasing them. Two other suppliers, Eliza Howard and Elizabeth Beauvais, were less fortunate. Howard wrote to Mrs Baker in 1774 requesting payment of bills sent in May 1771, 'afraid she has offended by not having any commands', which seems to have been the case because there are no more receipts from her and the account was not settled until May 1776.[67] Elizabeth Beauvais probably first met Judith in 1768 during her trip to London and Bath with George, when she bought two caps from Beauvais. However, Beauvais' bill for £4 16s 6d in 1773 was ignored until 1776, when Judith Baker disputed what had been sent and one 'not pleasing return'd it'. She only agreed to pay £3 4s 6d and there is no record of any further purchases from Beauvais.[68]

Mrs Baker's network of female suppliers in London depended on her sister, but during her own stays there she apparently patronised relatively few identifiable women in business.[69] A comparison with her stay in Bath suggests one possible reason for this. In 1768, having been in London since March, the Bakers travelled to Bath on 10 May and stayed until 7 June. The receipts from their stay in the city show that there was a degree of mutual recommendation and co-operation between the female traders there which seems to have been lacking during their London stay. London may have lacked the local community networks of the county town: but it was probably also significant that the Bakers took a house in London for themselves while their lodgings in Bath were run by a local woman, Mrs Catherine Clements, who presumably knew the local traders.[70] It is therefore perhaps not surprising to find that a female butcher called Jane Matthews supplied their meat. She provided beef, lamb, mutton and veal on a daily basis for which she charged about £2 per week.[71] All the Bakers' china, glass and cutlery were hired from a female grocer and chandler, who also provided them with dry goods throughout their stay. The Baker papers included an advertisement, cut from a newspaper, which stated that:

[66] UDL/PG, BB/81/44/94.
[67] UDL/PG, BB/80/43e/19.
[68] UDL/PG, BB/78/36c/13 and 14 April 1768; BB/80/43e/20.
[69] The lack of tradeswomen's cards is more than partly due to the practice of using only an initial on a printed bill which made it impossible to distinguish female traders. The numerous laundry bills with no name or signature were very probably from women.
[70] UDL/PG, BB/78/36e/7, 78/36g/5–7.
[71] UDL/PG, BB/78/36e/9, 78/36g/2–4.

Widow Ross, GROCER
Next Door to the CHRISTOPHER in the MARKET PLACE,
Makes it her Business to FURNISH FAMILIES
WITH ALL SORTS OF
TABLE and TEA CHINA, GLASSES, DUTCH and COPPER
TEA-KETTLES, COFFEE
and CHOCOLATE-POTS, &c.
LIKEWISE SELLS ALL SORTS OF
Grocery and Chandlery Goods

Among the other goods mentioned in this advertisement was 'the best flour mustard from Durham' and 'Fine Newcastle Salmon'. Since Mrs Baker was a keen collector of recipes and had written a list of women's names on the back, she probably meant to pass this information on to her friends, which would also have benefited the widow Ross.[72]

On the first day of the Bakers' stay, Betty Ross hired out a complete set of knives, forks, wineglasses and tumblers, dishes and breakfast plates, kettles, water jugs, teapots, sugar dishes, butter dishes and a cream pot for £1 1s 10d. She also supplied them with vinegar, salt, caster sugar, paper, mustard, tea, candles, moulds, a memorandum book, soap and butter for £1 1s 3½d, and a further 15 shillings of groceries at the end of May 1768. Mrs Ross therefore made a comfortable profit out of the Bakers (she would have made more but Judith sent 11½d of sugar back when they left) which was almost certainly due to a recommendation from Mrs Clements.[73] If, as seems likely, Mrs Clements had regular visitors, then both Betty Ross and Jane Matthews benefited substantially from the association. Indirectly, other local traders also benefited from the Bakers' stay. In just four weeks, the mantua maker, Sarah Hennagan,[74] made no less than four gowns for Judith Baker and she purchased two caps from Catherine Trunel, a milliner.[75]

Although women in trade could benefit from associations with other local women in business, this is not to suggest that they formed exclusively female networks. Businesswomen still needed the services of other male and female traders and family members to facilitate their trading activities, particularly over long distances. Correspondence between Mrs Baker and her hosier Ann Stokell reveals the existence of a complicated and extensive network of trade and family contacts that created social and economic ties between the two families for more than thirty years.[76]

---

[72] UDL/PG, BB/78/36e/15.
[73] UDL/PG, BB/78/36f/2; 78/36e/5.
[74] UDL/PG, BB/78/36e/17.
[75] UDL/PG, BB/78/36f/8 and 36g/15.
[76] UDL/PG, BB/75/5c/2 (1754), was the earliest receipt found for Ann Stokell, although it implied an already existing relationship, and BB/85/50c/36 (1783) was the last.

Mrs Stokell lived with her husband Ralph in Richmond, where Mrs Baker's father Cuthbert Routh kept a house. This was probably where the family connection began, and it was further strengthened because Mrs Baker's son George stayed at Richmond and also used Mrs Stokell's services for himself and his friends.[77] Mrs Stokell herself also had family living in Durham and they too were connected to the Bakers through ties of patronage. Ann Stokell's sister, Elizabeth Arrowsmith, lived with her husband William and their children in Elvet Street, where they appear to have run a public house, which was probably owned by the Bakers. Mrs Baker certainly visited to inspect the 'Cled'ing [sic] of the House'.[78] The Stokells also seem to have been financially involved with the Arrowsmiths' business which, Mrs Stokell complained in 1780, 'have hurt us much as it maks us greatly scarce in cash wich is a great want in trade, and what we never wanted tel we was incumbered with them'.[79] Neither the Stokells nor the Arrowsmiths were financially secure and both families relied on Mrs Baker's patronage. She found Elizabeth Arrowsmith a position with a local gentlewoman until Arrowsmith returned home to 'Bake something in the pastery way'.[80] In 1783, Mrs Stokell wrote to Mrs Baker explaining that she had been unable to redeem her deceased sister's clothes because they had been left with another woman. Mrs Baker's response was to send extra money.[81] In the same letter, Stokell also asked Mrs Baker to exert her influence on another matter because 'I know it will be in vain to write on my own account [but] that he certainly will be afraid of Disoblidging you'.[82] Despite the obvious inequality of the 'friendship', Mrs Stokell's letters to Mrs Baker were as full of family news as those sent from her higher ranking friends; the bill, as so often, was just part of the text or added as a postscript at the end.

Mrs Stokell's business not only relied on her family contacts and the Bakers' patronage, but also on a network of non-related contacts. Her sister provided the most profitable link with Mrs Baker even though Arrowsmith's ill-health and financial problems were a drain. Mrs Stokell sent parcels of hose to Arrowsmith, who forwarded them to the Bakers at Elemore with a letter about future orders. Mrs Arrowsmith's letter of 1779 gives an indication of how several orders from the Bakers and their friends could be received at the same time. She wrote:

K. Wrightson and D. Levine, *The Making of an Industrial Society: Wickham, 1560–1765* (Oxford, 1991), p. 358, found that 'multigenerational involvement' between the gentry and employees was not uncommon.

[77] UDL/PG, BB/82/46l/24; BB/82/46l/25.
[78] UDL/PG, BB/82/46l/25.
[79] UDL/PG, BB/83/47f/26.
[80] Ibid.
[81] UDL/PG, BB/85/50c/36.
[82] Ibid. The letter was torn, obscuring the reason for this request.

Honrd Madm

this day I recved a letter with 4 pr of Hose for mr Baker and the other six pr will be don as soon as possible – and she disiers hir Duty and is much oblidgd to you for sending for the silk stoking but at presant have none that will sute but order in the Spring and should be glad of a pattern stoking from his Friends in Febry when hir Tradesman will be at Richmond and will take the pattern and make them exact.[83]

Mrs Stokell also relied on Mrs Baker herself to generate more orders and to distribute her goods. In 1780 Stokell wrote thanking her for 'diposing of the 6 pr of gray ribbd Stockings', and promising to provide more for George Baker and Mr Liddell.[84] Mrs Baker not only distributed stockings to friends of her own social rank, such as Miss Whitley and the Liddells, but also to Mrs Liddell's maid and her own son's servant Matthew. Matthew's bill was part of a postscript to a bill in May 1781 for eighteen pairs of stockings sent in a letter to Mrs Baker giving news of the Arrowsmiths' bad health.[85]

If the sale and distribution of goods was facilitated by a network of friends, so too was the method of payment. The shortage of ready money and lack of a comprehensive national banking system meant that remitting money over long distances was a complex task.[86] On this occasion, as on several others since 1780, Mrs Stokell arranged for payment to be made through Thomas Pickering, who lived at Darlington but dealt 'at Durham with the Butchers'.[87] Mrs Stokell's husband Ralph eventually received the money from Pickering. On another occasion in 1783, Mrs Baker paid Stokell by an order made out to Thomas Chipchase, her Durham haberdasher, which was received on Stokell's behalf by Katherine Broad.[88] To send and to receive money over long distances, therefore, women in business had to be part of an extensive network of reliable contacts and fellow traders of both sexes, whose assistance almost certainly depended on the maintenance of their own commercial credibility.

Mrs Baker was equally reliant upon the services of friends to convey money and goods, thus producing a mutually beneficial system for vendor and purchaser oiled by the conventions of politeness. For example, Jane Robinson was Mrs Baker's cloth dealer in Darlington for at least nineteen years from 1763 to 1782. She used a network of social and trading contacts to bring orders and to return goods to Mrs Baker, who used a similar network to pay for them. In July 1763 Robinson sent a bill for £4 14s 9d for huggaback, with 'thanks for your favours'. She added that 'Mr Philips brought your letter and Chose the above goods and Mr and Mrs Philips both desires thare Compliments to you'.

[83] UDL/PG, BB/82/46l/25.
[84] UDL/PG, BB/83/47f26: the Liddells were a powerful local coal-owning gentry family.
[85] Ibid.; UDL/PG, BB/82/46l/24; UDL/PG, BB/84/48f/29.
[86] Earle, *Making of the Middle Class*, pp. 135–7.
[87] UDL/PG, BB/83/47/f26. Butchers and graziers played an important role in the remittance business, Earle, *Making of the Middle Class*, p. 136.
[88] UDL/PG, BB/85/50c/35.

The letter was addressed to Mrs Baker at Elemore 'with a Parsel to be left at Mr Waugh's shop in the Market plase Durham'.[89] Over the whole period, business between Robinson and Mrs Baker was conducted through a variety of her friends. These included the Philips family, William Robson and other male agents, Mr and Mrs Tunstall, and John and Mrs Potts. In October 1782, Jane Robinson was paid £3 8s 0d by Mrs Tunstall, who was in turn reimbursed by Mrs Potts, whom Mrs Baker finally paid on 20 November.[90]

Local networks: Durham

Tradeswomen who lived in Durham itself had less need of such networks because they could deal personally with customers and suppliers, usually using the system of periodic settling of accounts. Yet, as seen in the Chancery cases involving businesswomen,[91] there still seems to have been a degree of local co-operation, which could not have existed unless those women were fully integrated members of Durham's trading community. Unlike the Chancery records however, the Durham evidence gives little insight into how co-operation could dissolve into conflict, producing a slightly over-harmonious picture of local trading practice.

Both men and women received money for each other's businesses, some of which seem to have been conducted from shared premises. In the case of apparently unrelated people, this may have been because part of a building had been sublet to a tenant with another trade.[92] But, even if members of the same family were involved, receipts always made clear for whom the money was intended and the recipient always stated that it was being received 'on behalf of' the owner regardless of sex. Mrs Baker, on the other hand, did not necessarily make such distinctions. She regularly paid Elizabeth Goodrick, her local mantua maker, for dresses, negligees, silk and ribbons, but she also sometimes labelled bills from William Goodrick, a furniture maker, 'Mrs Goodrick's'.[93] Mrs Goodrick also received the money for furniture on William's behalf, possibly because Mrs Baker was her regular client. It is not possible to tell whether the Goodricks were married or mother and son, but both were making separate contributions to their 'household economy'. On 12 October 1782, however, Mrs Baker paid Mrs Goodrick 13 shillings for making and trimming two gowns, but on the same day she also gave her 1s 6d due to John Richardson for making picture frames.[94] Richardson was thus either a tenant

---

[89] UDL/PG, BB/75/8/2.
[90] UDL/PG, BB/85/50k/24.
[91] See above, pp. 82–6.
[92] See below, p. 163, for insurance policies showing shared trading/living arrangements.
[93] UDL/PG, BB/81/45j/17.
[94] UDL/PG, BB/85/49j/13 and 14.

or neighbour who Mrs Goodrick was temporarily assisting, although the receipt of money would seem to indicate a high level of trust.

The widow and ironmonger Mercy Ashworth seems to have had a similar but more regular arrangement with Mrs Baker's local hatter, George Carr. Unlike Mrs Goodrick, Mercy Ashworth never received money for her business herself. She had taken over the business in 1776 after the death of her husband, but retained his foreman William Wharton. Nevertheless she ran the business for at least eight years until 1784. It is also possible that Mrs Ashworth or her daughter became a silversmith, as a Mercy Ashworth was listed as a silversmith in Durham from 1785 to 1807.[95] Mrs Baker was a regular customer, buying nails, screws, hinges, locks, knives and forks, scales and weights, inkstands, candlesticks, bellows, brushes and even 'temple specktickles', at least once or twice a month. Her payments were usually received by the foreman William Wharton but on many occasions it was the hatter George Carr who took the money. On 3 March 1784 Carr receipted £1 16s from Mrs Baker for four servants' hats and 6s 11½d for nails, a lock and screws for Mrs Ashworth. Mrs Baker always labelled Ashworth's bills 'Mrs Ashworth's' but in February 1784 she also addressed an account for hats and goods bought from Carr since July 1782 as 'at Mrs Ashworths Mr Carr Bill' so it is likely that the two shared a premises, and that he was a tenant.[96] Mrs Ashworth may not have run a large business but she was part of a chain of credit that linked Mrs Baker with a Chester foundry. In January 1784 the foundry asked Mrs Baker to settle an account with them by a 'bill payable to Mr Wm Wharton Foreman to Mrs Mercy Ashworth in Durham'.[97]

As with Ann Stokell, family ties linked many of the Durham tradeswomen, whether as widows carrying on a husband's trade to support children, or as wives running their own business with children occasionally helping out, as daughters taking over from or helping fathers, or as sisters in business together. Most seem to have possessed high standards of literacy, the exceptions being Mrs Baker's regular spinner Jane Lamb and the moneylenders Grace Bates and Elizabeth Pickering, who were unable to sign their names. Most also seem to have been surprisingly numerate and able to produce accounts, despite the fact that double-entry bookkeeping had only become common among the trading classes in the later seventeenth century.[98] An anonymous female author of an advice manual for women in 1678 declared accounting to be 'an Art so useful for all sorts, sexes and degrees of persons' but she admitted that women risked being 'bid meddle with our distaff' instead.[99] Hunt argues that

[95] A silver spoon with her mark is displayed in the Durham City Museum.

[96] UDL/PG, BB/86/51b/32;51c/23; 51h/21.

[97] UDL/PG, BB/86/51a/7.

[98] Margaret Hunt, 'Time Management, Writing and Accounting in the Eighteenth-century English Trading Family: A Bourgeois Enlightenment', *Business and Economic History*, 2 ser., 18 (1989), pp. 150–9.

[99] Anon., *Advice to the Women and Maidens of London* (1678), p. 1.

accounting skills became 'an important badge of belonging' for women of the middling sort but suggests that they would not normally expect to have access to the capital necessary for its use in business except in unusual circumstances.[100] However, even in the nineteenth century many male small shopkeepers and craftsmen remained indifferent bookkeepers, relying upon memory to recall incoming and outgoing money.[101] What all male and female traders did share was a dependency on networks of credit and the difficulty of regulating customer credit effectively.[102]

Major customers tended to expect and to receive long-term credit,[103] and the Bakers were no exception, but this could cause problems for their suppliers. Mrs Jane Robson was Mrs Baker's wine merchant for at least ten years after the death of her husband in February 1755. From that date, she headed the family company known as Jane Robson & Co, working with her son John who sometimes received money 'for my mother Jane Robson'. Mrs Robson imported large quantities of wine, port, brandy and rum by sea and was owed hundreds of pounds by the Bakers. Of all their suppliers she was the least personal, and maintained a formal, if submissive, tone in her correspondence. This included a fully balanced credit and debit account for 1755 to 1756 showing the interest accruing on their debt, which in July 1756 stood at a little over £120. Underneath the account she wrote a formal letter explaining that she was:

> sory to give you the trouble of your Bill but having wine upon the Sea which I expect in very soon and the Duty betwixt four and five Hundred Pounds hopes you'l be so good as excuse this freedom. If you want any thing in our way will take care you shall have the Best and your Orders punctually observed.[104]

By August 1759 the Bakers owed 4.5 years' interest and had spent over £300 with Mrs Robson, of which only £150 had been paid. The payment of regular sums on account was common practice and from October 1760 the Bakers made four payments of £20 to £50. However, by November 1764 Mrs Robson found the company's financial commitments too pressing to continue with this method. She retreated behind even greater formality and sent a letter explaining that:

---

[100] Hunt, *Middling Sort*, p. 89, also notes that, unlike literacy, it is impossible to quantify the spread of accountancy skills among women.

[101] Kent, 'Small Businessmen', pp. 60–1.

[102] Ibid., p. 51; Julian Hoppit, 'The Use and Abuse of Credit in Eighteenth-century England', in *Business Life and Public Policy*, ed. N. McKendrick and R.B. Outhwaite (Cambridge, 1986), pp. 64–78.

[103] Kent, 'Small Businessmen', p. 53.

[104] UDL/PG, BB/75/6/3.

We having a large Sum to pay this afternoon, it will be a very particular favour if in your power to assist us. . . . With the remainder of the old account or as much as may be convenient which will at this time be for great Service. We hope you'll excuse this Liberty which we shou'd not have taken, could we have made up our paymt without.[105]

The letter was written in a different hand from the first, suggesting that she probably employed a scribe. The unusual formality of Robson's letters may have been because of the size of the debt, the size of the firm, or because of the masculine nature of the trade. The lack of payment was almost certainly not due to her sex. Slow payment was common, particularly among the gentry and aristocracy, who usually settled bills only once a year and Mrs Baker's efforts at economy meant that she frequently pushed this practice to its limits. Slow payment could be at least partially offset by charging interest on the account but, if non-payment continued, some pressure became necessary.[106] As Wiskin has argued with regard to trade credit transactions, 'differences in the treatment of men and women related to their status as business people, determined by whether they were good or bad players and the size of the enterprise'.[107]

However, two groups of female suppliers do not seem to have suffered from this pattern of long-term credit, offset by part payments. Those who lived in Durham and supplied Mrs Baker regularly with small quantities of goods, such as her ironmonger, her stationer and her milliners and dressmakers, were paid frequently, as were those with whom she had a reciprocal arrangement, in which the estate provided some of the raw materials, such as her spinner and tallow chandler. Small businesses, particularly in rural areas, could become very reliant on the extensive custom of a few wealthy patrons,[108] and Mrs Baker may have felt more responsible towards local people than to larger urban suppliers.

Mrs Baker's local newsagent, stationer and bookbinder, Ann Clifton, falls into the category of local traders paid on a regular basis. Mrs Clifton supplied Judith Baker for at least eleven years (1773–84) and sent her more than sixty bills, most of which were either settled on the day or within four to six weeks. Yet although Mrs Baker bought goods from Clifton on an almost weekly basis her average annual spend was just £4 to £5, which suggests that smaller sums were also a factor influencing prompt payment. However, there were some exceptions. Every January Mrs Clifton billed Mrs Baker for the previous year's supply of the *Courant*, the *York Chronicle* and the *Gentleman's Magazine*, plus a charge for binding the magazines into volumes and an annual supply of almanacs, calendars and pocket-books. She also charged for binding books on

[105] UDL/PG, BB/75/6/13.
[106] Earle, *Making of the Middle Class*, pp. 116–17.
[107] Wiskin, 'Women, Finance and Credit', p. 243.
[108] Kent, 'Small Businessmen', p. 53.

an annual basis, but she did not supply the London newspapers, which were sent via the local Durham post office. Periodically Mrs Clifton supplied cash-books, ledgers, copybooks and prayer-books, along with serialised journals on medicine and farriery, and she occasionally placed a special order for a particular book for Mrs Baker. But far more frequently (at least every month), she supplied the Bakers with reams and reams of different types of paper, sealing wax and wafers. From 1783 Mrs Baker's payments were more often received 'for Mother A Clifton', suggesting that Clifton had a child to take over the business and was perhaps suffering from old age or ill-health.

The other local female traders, whom Judith Baker used as regularly as Ann Clifton, were her dressmakers and milliners. Her mantua maker for at least ten years from 1754 to 1764 was Susanna Burton but her accounts appear only to have been sent annually, covering the making of seven or eight gowns, sacks and negligees for Mrs Baker and her daughter, which only cost around £2.[109] In 1764 Mrs Baker was using the Durham milliners M. Johnson & Co, to supply ribbons, net, muslin, pins, gauze, frills, gloves and so on, totalling £12 1s 0½d. This was one of the largest amounts Mrs Baker spent with any one tradeswoman in a year, but she paid all ten bills with surprising alacrity, sometimes on the day but always within a month, which perhaps indicates the importance she attached to her millinery.[110] Mary Johnson was in business with her two sisters Ann and Jane, who both receipted money from Judith, which meant the business was a family affair. The Johnsons' successor in 1780 was Hannah Smith, whose business was also run on a family basis. Some of Smith's bills were received by John Smith, which suggests that she was married because, as in the case of Ann Clifton and Jane Robson, children wrote that they received money 'for mother'. As well as supplying copious amounts of millinery, Smith also washed aprons, ruffles and handkerchiefs. Such specialised washing and dressing was considered a skilled operation for which even members of the professional and landed classes would train.[111] Mrs Baker visited Hannah Smith more frequently than the Johnsons and sometimes even weekly. Smith sent individual notes with each purchase three or four times a month and then an account after four months. Between January and April 1780, for example, Judith Baker made twelve visits and ran up a bill of just over £2.[112] Her annual expenditure, however, was less than with the Johnsons at just over £6, although she still paid promptly within three weeks of receiving the bill.

The second group of local suppliers, who were regularly paid, involved some form of reciprocal exchange. This may be seen in the accounts of Mrs Baker's tallow chandler, Mrs Isabell Taylor. Mrs Taylor supplied candles to Elemore

---

[109] UDL/PG, BB75/5j/16; BB/75/9c/14 .
[110] UDL/PG, BB/75/9a/2; 9b/3; 9c/3; 9c/15; 9g/3; 9g/6; 9h/12; 9h/7; 9h/13; 9j/4.
[111] UDL/PG, BB86/51g/6; and see Sanderson, *Women and Work*, p. 89, on how even gentlewomen were prepared to learn specialised washing and dressing as a trade in itself.
[112] UDL/PG, BB/83/47d/33.

which, particularly during the winter months, could bring in reasonable sums of money. From October to December she charged Judith £6 to £9 for supplying candles, moulds and rush lights and as much again from January to April.[113] Mrs Baker did not always pay in full. In 1776 she paid by £2 instalments each month, but a full debit and credit account which Taylor sent in 1774 reveals that Mrs Baker also sent tallow from Elemore sheep to be credited against her bill.[114] Thus there was a degree of mutual support in trading relations and goods could be part paid for in kind. Mrs Baker sent wool from Elemore sheep to her spinner, Jane Lamb, who was employed on a long-term regular basis. Lamb had spun wool for Judith from at least 1763, when she was in partnership with Ann Walker, until 1783, by which time she had been working alone for many years. In those twenty years, she regularly spun 10 to 15 pounds of wool for which Mrs Baker paid 6s to 8s four to six times a year.[115] Even though Jane Lamb was illiterate, it does not seem to have affected the regularity of payment.

Conclusion

There was less written communication between Judith and her local suppliers to show how the network of buying and selling worked, but sometimes familiar names, such as Mrs Potts, appear on their receipts and Judith made very regular purchases over long periods of time which signified a strong trading relationship. Within the community, male and female traders shared resources and premises, and family links were common, but women's trading networks could also stretch much further than the local community. There does not seem to have been any one model of 'family economy', and children were often involved in the business of receiving money. Women were also engaging in business at every stage of their life and marital cycle. Although it is commonly argued that women's work was intermittent or that their enterprises were short-lived, many of Mrs Baker's female suppliers seem to have remained in trade for extremely long periods, despite changes in their family circumstances. There were very few big businesses among them, but they could all boast the added status of having the Bakers as regular customers. Although most of the 'masculine' trades were carried on by widows, the majority were carrying on businesses involving high degrees of literacy and numeracy, whatever the size of business. The tallow chandler Isabell Taylor's double entry bookkeeping was as neatly presented as that from the large wine merchant Jane Robson. Ann Clifton wrote an immaculate hand, and if Ann Stokell's was considerably less so, she made up for it in interpersonal skills, negotiating a large network of family and 'friends' to assist with delivering and distributing orders and payments.

---

[113] UDL/PG, BB/79/41d/36; 80/43f/33.
[114] UDL/PG, BB/80/43f/33; BB/79/40d/13.
[115] UDL/PG, BB/84/48 A/18; 48 D/13; 48 J/57; 48 L/14.

Judith Baker was herself a businesswoman for thirteen years running the family lead and alum mines, and she used her family and friends as agents for acquiring goods and money in an equally businesslike way. In the eighteenth century both higher and lower ranks seem to have conducted their business, in the widest sense, exchanging goods, services, money and personal affairs, without making any distinctions between them. The conventions of politeness oiled the process of trade, and the possibility of maintaining socially unequal friendships further facilitated both local and long-distance business trans-actions, whether exclusively between women or involving male kin and acquaintances. In short, within the cycle of supply and demand 'the friendship of the world' was vital to both consumers and vendors, whether setting up in business, buying and selling goods, organising payments, or negotiating loans and credit.

6

Women and the business of insurance, 1735 to 1845

'I soon made myself acquainted with Mrs Buchanan . . . [who] I found very active
and as attentive to the Business as a Female can possibly be expected to be.'
Report to the Management Committee on the state of
Sun Fire Insurance Agencies in Scotland (1807)[1]

Debates about women's economic opportunities are commonly linked to
assumptions about the speed and impact of changes attributed to industrialisation and/or capitalism.[2] Regardless of whether these competing narratives
have emphasised the continuity of women's work from 1700 to 1850, or stressed
their increasing exclusion from the marketplace, very few have differentiated
the experience of women in business from that of employed workers, or stepped
outside the familiar framework of a linear trajectory in order to discuss that
experience.[3] Were businesswomen subject to the same narrow (or increasingly
restricted) patterns of occupational segregation as labouring women, who
were concentrated chiefly in the needle trades, personal services and food and
drink preparation? To what extent could the possession of business capital or
family and 'friends' with connections in trade alter women's experience of
economic change? Indeed, was gender the most significant factor in determining the type, scale and size of business in which women were involved?
One way of engaging with these debates is to examine the role of women in
business from the perspective of an industry whose very existence depended
on society's perception of the value of material possessions and the perceived
risk to them, posed by increasing urbanisation and industrialisation. Insurance
was a new business that was not only a product of an increasingly commercial
and industrial age, but also provided key underpinning for manufacturing,

---

[1] GL, Ms., 11935A, Vol. 1, p. 32.
[2] For a detailed discussion of these debates, see above, pp. 4–6.
[3] Notable exceptions being Hunt, *Middling Sort*, pp. 125–46, Wiskin, 'Women, Finance
and Credit', esp. pp. 44–5; both focus specifically on businesswomen, and highlight factors
of continuity *and* change. Sharpe, *Adapting to Capitalism*, esp. pp. 149–51, focuses on
labouring women but also points to uneven economic developments and argues that
capitalism per se did not necessarily bring about a decline in women's work opportunities;
it could even have the opposite effect.

transport and urban expansion.[4] The Sun Fire Insurance office was established in 1710, and it was the first company to insure household goods and trade merchandise as well as buildings from loss by fire.[5] It remained the market leader in insurance for most of the eighteenth century. This chapter and the one that follows will therefore examine the economic activities of business-women who bought and sold insurance policies from the Sun Fire Office between 1735 and 1845. But in this chapter the emphasis is on discussing what type of businesswomen bought and sold insurance, what trades they were in and what their marital status or family connections were.

The market for insurance certainly underwent a remarkable growth during the eighteenth and early nineteenth centuries, but even so policies were still taken out by only a relatively small percentage of the population. In 1801, the market for *potential* insurance has been estimated at only 6 per cent of the total population that year,[6] and by the 1850s still no more than half of the potentially insurable property in Britain was actually insured.[7] A survey of insurance in Surrey, conducted by the Royal Exchange in 1728, found that 'many which would insure do not know how to get it done and many that are insured drop them not knowing how to pay their money to the office'.[8] For women, this time-consuming and expensive undertaking required a degree of agency and financial knowledge not often attributed to their sex at this time. To insure her business a woman would have had to calculate the replacement value of her property and to send a proposal to the insurance company's head office. If it was accepted, the money for the premium (and after 1782 tax as well) would have to be taken to the nearest Fire Office which, particularly in the early years, was likely to have been some distance away. Obtaining a certificate of insurance often meant queuing for long periods and the process had to be repeated annually to pay the premiums within fifteen days of the Quarter day on which they fell due.[9] Those women engaged in actually selling

---

[4] Clive Trebilcock, *Phoenix Insurance and the Development of British Insurance, 1782–1879* (Cambridge, 1985), Vol. 1, pp. 1–3.

[5] P.G.M. Dickson, *The Sun Insurance Office, 1710–1960: The History of Two and a Half Centuries of British Insurance* (Oxford, 1960), p. 26.

[6] L.D. Schwarz and L.J. Jones, 'Wealth, Occupations, and Insurance in the Late Eighteenth Century: The Policy Registers of the Sun Fire Office', *Economic History Review*, 2 ser., 36 (1983), p. 366, based this calculation on the assumption that insurance was predominantly bought by upper/middle-class men or their widows, who formed an estimated 20 per cent of the adult population in 1801.

[7] Trebilcock, *Phoenix Insurance*, p. 11.

[8] Cited in H.A.L. Cockerell and Edwin Green, *The British Insurance Business: A Guide to its History and Records* (London, 1976), p. 29.

[9] In 1793 the secretary of the Sun Fire office reported that it became 'so crowded' when premiums fell due that clients had to wait a 'considerable time' to be seen. As a result the company divided its policy department in two. See Dickson, *The Sun Insurance Office*, p. 58.

insurance would have had to possess an even higher degree of financial understanding and local business knowledge.

The habit of insurance[10] was much stronger in some areas than in others,
and nowhere more so than in London where more than 10 per cent of the
estimated target population took out new policies in 1780.[11] By 1783 the Sun
Fire office had cornered 53.4 per cent of this London market while its nearest
rival, the Hand in Hand, had less than 16 per cent.[12] However, the Sun Fire
office suffered a decline in business towards the end of the eighteenth century,
which continued into the early decades of the nineteenth century as its position was increasingly challenged by a growing number of newcomers.[13] Profits
also fell, as higher risks increased losses and the government imposed a stamp
duty on insured property, which was raised dramatically between 1782 and
1815, thus discouraging smaller insurers.[14] In 1810 the separate enterprise of
Sun Life Insurance was established to restore the company's fortunes, and by
the 1830s they were on the increase once more. As a source for studying insured
women in business, the Sun Fire's policy registers are increasingly representative, particularly of the London insurance market, up until 1780s. After
that, despite an increasing number of potential insurers, the Sun's share of the
market declined, so its clients increasingly came to represent only the tip
of an iceberg. Nevertheless, insurance policy registers provide one of the few
sources of roughly comparable quantitative data for women in business over a
long period of time.

This chapter and the following are based on a case study of the policy
registers of the Sun Fire Insurance Company between 1735 and 1845. Studied
in conjunction with documents relating to the appointment and accounts
of provincial insurance agents, this material shows that significant numbers of
women in a wide range of types and sizes of business actively participated in
this relatively new, elite and apparently masculine culture of insurance.
Although this material relates to a relatively small minority of reasonably
wealthy women in business and not to the employment prospects of working
women in general, it does challenge some strongly held assumptions about
women's economic opportunities during this period. In particular, this chapter
seeks to move the debate beyond the limits of discussing the merits of one

---

[10] On the social and cultural growth of the practice of insurance, see Geoffrey Clark, *Betting
on Lives: The Culture of Life Insurance in England, 1695–1775* (Manchester, 1999), esp.
pp. 1–4.

[11] Schwarz and Jones, 'Wealth, Occupations, and Insurance', p. 367, and see above,
p. 121, n. 6.

[12] Trebilcock, *Phoenix Insurance*, p. 6.

[13] Dickson, *Sun Insurance Office*, p. 104.

[14] D.T. Jenkins, 'The Practice of Insurance against Fire, 1750–1840, and Historical
Research', *The Historian and the Business of Insurance*, ed. Oliver M. Westall (Manchester,
1984), p. 16, and n. 32. In some cases the tax equalled or even exceeded the premiums
payable.

linear narrative of women's continuously limited enterprise over another detailing their increasing marginalisation. In doing so, it is argued that, while women could be seen to be engaged in broadly continuous sectors of trade, this apparent continuity masked both an increasing degree of specialisation in the occupations followed by women and fluctuations in the fortunes of individual trades, which cannot be attributed solely to gender. Moreover, while family ties and marital status remained important, neither can be seen as an overriding factor in determining the economic choices of women in business.

Female insurance agents

Women were involved indirectly with the business of insurance from its earliest days and, as the century progressed and the habit of insurance spread beyond London, women also became agents, selling policies for the Sun Fire office. When Sun Fire opened its first policy register on 11 April 1710, policy no.10 was taken out by Mrs Catherine Hill, a grocer in Portugall Street.[15] In 1711, the Sun Fire office was being run from two rooms beside the Royal Exchange, which were owned by the enterprising Mrs Alice Garraway.[16] Initially, policies were sold by 'walkers' or 'collectors' and in 1712 there were just ten trying to raise business in London. Then, in 1720, in a bid to increase business, the management committee resolved to appoint 'Persons of Reputation, and Substance in the Chief Towns, and Cities to Distribute Policies and receive all Quarterages, and to Allow to such Persons One Shilling in the Pound as an Equivalent for their Trouble'.[17] The first provincial agent was appointed in 1721, and by 1740 Sun Fire had fifty-one agents; by the 1780s this number had more than doubled and women were included among them.[18]

However unlikely it was that Sun Fire initially considered women to be among those 'Persons of Reputation and Substance' suitable to act as company agents, women were certainly involved in selling insurance at least by 1772.[19]

---

[15] GL, Ms. 11936, 1/10.

[16] Dickson, *Sun Insurance Office*, p. 53. Mrs Garraway was also involved with Garraway's Coffee-house and was probably also selling the infamous anodyne necklace as a medicinal cure. See Francis Doherty, *A Study in Eighteenth-century Advertising Methods: The Anodyne Necklace* (Lampeter, 1992), pp. 32–49.

[17] From a report by the management committee, cited in Dickson, *The Sun Insurance Office*, p. 67.

[18] Ibid., and see also Jenkins, 'Practice of Insurance', p. 16.

[19] The paucity of evidence makes it difficult to estimate exactly when women became involved in selling insurance, so there may have been earlier examples in provincial agencies. The earliest entry is 1772 for a Sun Fire female agent in GL, Ms. 14386, 'Alphabetical List of Cities and Towns in Great Britain with the Names of the Agents and Sureties to the Sun Fire Office at Michaelmas 1786', also known as the 'Agents Bond Book'. (See Table 6.1 for female insurance agents listed here.)

An agents' account book for the year 1786 lists 118 agencies, of which five were run by women and another five in which women acted as financial guarantors for a male agent.[20] A much larger list of towns with the names of agents and their sureties, also dated 1786 but continuing up to 1841, contains 480 entries, of which twenty-eight detailed female agents, although, since many entries were renewals, the actual number of individual female agents was twenty. Each agent had to provide a financial guarantee or bond, usually related to the size of the agency, which required at least two other guarantors besides the agent, and a further thirty-seven entries listed women acting as financial guarantors.[21] Indeed, the number of female guarantors for insurance agents doubled after 1800 and an additional list of eighty Sun Fire clerks and collectors shows that eleven of them also had their securities guaranteed by women.[22] It is not possible to speculate how many women were involved in Sun Fire Insurance after 1841, but from the end of the eighteenth century, just when women were apparently disappearing from masculine financial and business institutions, a small number were evidently either making a living from or providing the financial backing for the insurance market.

As was the case with many of Mrs Baker's female suppliers, a significant proportion of female insurance agents also appear to have remained in the business for a considerable length of time. It is difficult to calculate the exact length of time these female agents remained in business, because dates entered in the agents' bond book did not always run consecutively. Nevertheless, it is possible to offer a good estimate by counting the years between when the agent was appointed or from when the bond was given, until the date of the next agent's appointment or the return of a bond. Using these calculations, Table 6.1 shows that eight women ran agencies for fifteen years or longer and seven ran agencies for five to ten years. For example, Elizabeth Dagnell was appointed agent for Aylesbury in September 1784 and the bond was only transferred upon her death in 1817 to her executrix Mrs Muddiford.[23] Even more notably, the Wolverhampton agency may have remained under female supervision for more than forty years. Mary Stubbs, a mercer, took over the agency in 1772, and she was still sending balanced accounts up to head office in 1786.[24] Sarah Davenhill, a shopkeeper, took over the agency in 1799. Davenhill's two guarantors, a grazier and a farmer, were noted 'alive' in 1809, and it is quite possible, given the laxity of surveillance, that she remained in charge until 1814 when bookseller Philip Darman was inducted. Only three women ran agencies for

[20] GL, Ms. 18856, 'Sun Fire Agents' Accounts' (1786) recorded each agent's annual income of premiums and duty, and whether this income was duly returned and balanced with the company's records.
[21] GL, Ms. 14386.
[22] Ibid.
[23] Ibid., p. 8.
[24] Ibid. p. 120; and see GL, Ms. 18856, 'Sun Fire Agents' Accounts' (1786).

Table 6.1 Female insurance agents for the Sun Fire office, 1786 to 1835, ranked by value of security lodged

Agent	Status/ occupation	Family link	Place	Security	Date
Catherine Buchanan	Widow	Y	Glasgow, Scotland	£1,500	1806–21
Elizabeth Biggin	Widow	N	Ware, Herts	£1,000	1784–89
Elizabeth Plant	Spinster	Y	Manchester	£800	1792–96
Mary Davies	?	N	Oxford	£800	1793–1801
Elizabeth King	Widow	Y	Lynn Regis, Norfolk	£800	1805–15
Sarah Mickley	Widow	Y	Buntingford, Herts	£800	1825–?
Anna Maria Norton	Widow	Y	Uxbridge, Middx	£500	1794–1803
Mary Smith	Widow	Y	Newcastle, Staffs	£500	1814–19
Elizabeth Dagnell	Spinster	N	Aylesbury, Bucks	£300	1784–1817
Ann Stuchberry[a]	Grocer	Y	Buckingham, Bucks	£400	1818–22
Sarah Davenhill	Shopkeeper	N	Wolverhampton, Staffs	£400	1799–1814
Mary Bassano[b]	Grocer	Y	Derby	£400	1815–34
Elizabeth Boore	Widow	N	Shrewsbury, Salop	£300	1783–1808
Elizabeth Rowe	?	N	Totnes, Devon	£300	1793–99
Frances Mitchell	Widow	Y	Lymington, Hants	£300	1802–20
Mary King	Widow	Y	Yeovil, Somerset	£300	1802–19
Elizabeth Pearson	Saddler	Y	Wirksworth, Derby	£300	1819–?
Ann Melhuish[c]	Widow	N	Crediton, Devon	£300	1827–34
Mary Stubbs	Mercer	N	Wolverhampton, Staffs	£200	1772–99
Mary Oxenham	Daughter	Y	Dartmouth, Devon	£200	Not appointed

Notes
[a] Ann Stuchberry ran the Buckingham agency in partnership with Benjamin Stuchberry.
[b] Mary Bassano ran the Derby agency from 1829–34 with Henry Bakewell Bassano.
[c] Ann Melhuish continued to act as a financial guarantor for the new agent, Robert Medland, after 1834.
NB: Dates are approximate because calculated from the date of appointment (or bond given if no appointment date) until the succession of the following agent where this was noted.

Source: GL, Ms. 14386, Agents' Bond Book

less than five years. Of these, one, Mary Oxenham, had inherited her father's agency in Dartmouth but would not or could not return a bond and so was refused the appointment.[25] In 1792 Elizabeth Plant took over the Manchester office from James Plant (probably her father), but only ran it until 1796 when she married Robert Duck. He officially took over the agency, although he no doubt appreciated his wife's experience in the business, and the family connection continued for several more years. Olive Plant, who had acted as

[25] GL, Ms. 14386, p. 35. William Oxenham had last returned a bond for £200 in 1777; beneath this Mary Oxenham's entry read: 'Succeeded her father – but won't give bond.'

guarantor for Elizabeth and James Plant before her, also guaranteed Robert Duck until 1819 when he was unable to provide any more sureties.[26]

Insurance agencies were frequently passed on through families, sometimes down through generations. The lack of formal training or qualifications for this relatively new enterprise – most agents merely received printed instructions from head office – meant that experience in the industry became a family asset.[27] A family connection was thus often a strong motivating force. Some 60 per cent of the agencies run by women appear to be businesses inherited from a male relative. Of the twelve women who had a family connection with the previous agent, half were designated as widows and most were therefore presumably carrying on their deceased husbands' business, but three did not share the previous agent's surname and so had either remarried and continued in trade separately, or had entered the business on their own account. Of those widows who do appear to have inherited the business from their husbands, five also used family members to provide sureties for them. Three female agents were also carrying on a trade, but this does not preclude the possibility that they too were widows or daughters, particularly since one, Mary Bassano, was joined by a male relative (possibly her son) for her last five years in the agency. Two were spinsters and may have been daughters succeeding their fathers as Mary Oxenham had done. Ann and Benjamin Stuchberry were grocers and may have been brother and sister or husband and wife. They jointly ran the Buckingham agency, which they had taken over from Thomas Stuchberry, a grocer and probably Benjamin Stuchberry's father, in 1818. The family connection was further strengthened because their sureties were provided by William Stuchberry, a maltster, and a local baker who was replaced by James Stuchberry, also a maltster, in January 1822.[28] Of the forty-two women listed who acted as guarantors for insurance agents, 67 per cent were apparently related to the agent they were financially backing, and most were also local. In terms of marital status, 49 per cent were widows but 21 per cent were spinsters. However, the gender of an agent did not determine the sex of his or her backers as much as did family links, since only two female agents also had female guarantors. Thus family networks remained an important, if not the sole, route for women to become involved in the masculine world of insurance well into the nineteenth century.

In the early days of insurance, agents were chiefly recruited from among the ranks of local shopkeepers, small traders, clerks and skilled artisans. After 1786 a much wider group of people became involved.[29] It is difficult to judge women's social status because those who were not given an occupational label

[26] Ibid., p. 74. Duck was able to return sureties again in 1831 but Olive Plant had been replaced by Elizabeth Walsh, a widow from Knaresborough.
[27] Jenkins, 'Practice of Insurance', p. 24.
[28] GL, Ms. 18856, p. 19.
[29] Dickson, *Sun Insurance Office*, p. 70; Jenkins, 'Practice of Insurance', p. 24.

were usually only accorded marital status. However, among the female agents listed in the 1786 agents' bond book, there were two grocers, a mercer, a saddler and a shopkeeper. Women who followed male relatives into the business came from a wider variety of backgrounds, succeeding men described as anything from 'chapman' to 'gentleman', or as traders such as grocer, bookseller and saddler. Of the women who stood as guarantors for insurance agents, 17 per cent were also in trade: two grocers, a wine merchant, two milliners, a mercer and a farmer, but five had no recorded marital or occupational status. Geographically, the agencies were wide spread across the country – there were agencies in Scotland and the North by the 1730s – but the majority were to be found in southern England. The female agents from 1786 to about 1835 followed a similar pattern of distribution. There was a female agent in Glasgow, but most (six) were in the Home Counties of Oxfordshire, Buckinghamshire, Hertfordshire and Hampshire. Four more were in the southwest and four in the Midlands.

To be chosen as insurance agents, women needed to have a good local reputation, suitable business connections and financial sense.[30] Agents were usually recommended to the position by a manager, or occasionally by a valued client. All agents had to be officially approved by the Sun's Management Committee before being appointed. By the nineteenth century, a confidential report was also sometimes required. Once appointed, agents were expected to 'exert every proper influence in your power to extend its connexion, and procure insurances'.[31] A new agent advertised her presence by erecting a sign, paid for by head office, with her name and the words 'Agent to the Sun Fire and Life Offices in London'.[32] It was also common practice to insert a standard advertisement in the local newspapers.[33] In July 1798, Mrs Elizabeth Tawney took over from her deceased husband to become an agent for the Royal Exchange Assurance Office in Oxford. She advertised her change of circumstances in Jackson's Oxford Journal and announced that she was now 'ready to receive proposals for insurance and yearly premiums on policy'.[34] Agents were responsible for receiving and checking new proposals, sending them to head office, and then issuing approved clients with policies. Fees were remitted to London by bill of exchange, along with the money from annual renewals. In many cases, agents were expected to supervise the local fire brigade and attend any fires to protect the agency's interests. Agents were also

---

[30] Ibid.

[31] Anon., Instructions for the Agents of the Sun Fire-Office (1848), p. 3.

[32] Ibid. p. 61. This wording was used after 1810 when the Sun had added its Life Insurance department.

[33] Dickson, Sun Insurance Office, p. 71.

[34] Jackson's Oxford Journal, 14 July 1798. I would like to thank Susan Skedd for this reference.

responsible for investigating any suspected fraudulent claims.[35] In sum, the management of an agency required women to display a knowledge of local business practice that historians once considered necessary only for the construction of middle-class male economic competence.[36]

Some female agents employed male assistants, presumably not least because they needed male help when attending fires, but this did not negate their overall management of the business. Mrs Catherine Buchanan had a male assistant but her local business knowledge was still widely respected. She ran the Sun's Glasgow agency[37] for fifteen years assisted (in 1807 at least) by Mr Aichison, 'a bustling young man, giving up a great part of his Time to the Agency tho' he has some business of his own'.[38] Members of the Buchanan family had run the Glasgow agency since its inception in 1760, and Catherine Buchanan had taken over from her husband in 1806. In 1815, her son John Gabriel Buchanan joined her and he eventually took over completely in 1821, thus continuing the family connection. Glasgow was a large agency requiring a surety of £1,500, an increase of £700 on her husband's bond, which suggests that Mrs Buchanan had successfully increased the size of the business. Mrs Buchanan was backed by her husband's former guarantor, a writer named John McEwan and a local merchant. When she renewed her bond in July 1810, because the merchant had died, he was replaced by John Flynn, paymaster for the Western District of North Britain. In fact, Mrs Buchanan's good connections were probably at least part of the reason for the 'general satisfaction' the head office felt about her conduct of the agency, particularly since it was noted that her male assistant lacked such influence.

Mrs Buchanan's opinions carried some weight with Sun Fire's head office, and they heeded her advice during a drive to create more agencies in Scotland. Sun Fire representative Philip Bewick drew up a list of suitable towns but, realising that several were near Glasgow where 'it might be presumed Mrs Buchanan had already Deputies', he visited her to discuss the matter in 1807.[39] Mrs Buchanan agreed that more agents should be appointed, but hoped that head office would not deprive her of 'the sub-Agency of Paisley it being so near & the person she employed there, being so respectable, she thought that the Office could not do more by a new Agent'.[40] She suggested Greenock and Kilmarnock as alternatives and she was authorised to conduct sensitive

---

[35] Anon., Instructions for the Agents, pp. 63–4. See also Jenkins, 'Practice of Insurance', p. 25.

[36] Davidoff and Hall, Family Fortunes, pp. 214–15, argue that the insurance business was one of the experiences through which men built up a 'personal competence in business affairs which was part of a masculine persona', formulated in direct contrast to the 'homemaking' of women.

[37] GL, Ms. 14386, p. 48.

[38] GL, Ms. 11935A, Vol. 1, p. 31.

[39] For Bewick's opinion of Mrs Buchanan, see above quotation, p. 120.

[40] GL, Ms. 11935A, Vol. 1, p. 31.

negotiations with other local agents, to obtain their agreement. Her own sub-agency in Paisley seems to have remained unchallenged, as she wished, and a new agency was eventually set up in Greenock.[41]

In terms of income, few agents made large amounts of money out of the business.[42] Hence many ran insurance agencies as a secondary business to their main occupation, or were of a high enough social status not to have to rely on selling insurance for their main income. The size of the bond required as security can give a rough indication of the amount of premium income an agent could expect to make. Agents received a commission of 5 per cent on premiums plus 6d (raised to 3s for good agents) for each new policy sold and, in the later period, 1s in the pound on duty as well. Most of the female agents identified here[43] ran agencies requiring bonds of between £300 and £800. Elizabeth Biggin, a widow who ran the agency in Ware, Hertfordshire from 1784 to 1789, was an exception. She had a bond of £1,500 and returned the largest premium income for a woman in 1786 of £1,550. This was less than half the highest premium income that year (£2,850 from the Exeter agent), but much greater than the lowest premium income (Cranbrook returned just £8 8s). Mrs Biggin's minimum projected earnings would therefore be in the region of £103 (plus new policy payments). But the other four female agents listed in the Agents Accounts for 1786 all returned premiums of £300 or less, which meant that their projected minimum earnings would have been around £20 or less per annum.[44] However, as in the case of Catherine Buchanan, it was possible for insurance agents to boost their income by running sub-agencies.

If female insurance agents could not expect to make vast profits, they also very rarely failed in the business. Agents who failed to display the required level of competence, particularly those who 'defaulted' by failing to remit the correct sums or to provide adequate sureties, could be dismissed by Sun Fire's Management Committee. In 1804 the Committee recorded that approximately one-third of their agents were 'defaulters',[45] but only one out of the twenty women listed in the period 1786 to 1841 was dismissed. She was Elizabeth Boore,[46] a widow who had returned a surety of £300 in 1783, backed by local spinster Margaret Donnes and ironmonger John Edwards. In 1786 Boore had sent and balanced her accounts with head office, returning an annual income

---

[41] GL, Ms. 14386, does not record any entry for Paisley, but an office in Greenock was returning a bond by 1833.

[42] GL, Ms. 18856, 'Sun Fire Agents Accounts' (1786). Only 9 per cent of the 118 agents listed here returned premium incomes over £1,000, 25 per cent returned £500 or more, while 35 per cent returned a premium income of £100 to £299.

[43] 16 of the 20 listed in Table 6.1, above, p. 125.

[44] There is no record of the number of new policies sold by each agent so it is only possible to make a rough estimate of *minimum* projected earnings. See Pullin, 'Business is Just Life', p. 133, Table 6.2.

[45] GL, Ms. 11935A, Vol. 1, p. 7.

[46] GL, Ms. 14386, p. 100.

of £209 on premiums plus £100 duty.[47] This meant that Mrs Boore would not have made very much money but she continued to run the agency as a business for twenty-five years before her eventual dismissal in 1808, which suggests that age or infirmity, rather than incompetence, may have been the cause of her removal. Thus, in general, the new world of insurance provided stable economic opportunities for a number of women of respectable commercial status. They were often, but not invariably, supported by family links, and could expect to make reasonable if not great profits; but perhaps most significantly, they appear to have been accepted in their own right as publicly recognised financial brokers.

Classifying insured women in business

If relatively small numbers of women were involved in the business of selling insurance, far greater numbers were actively purchasing insurance to protect their businesses. Insurance policy registers contain a wealth of detail about the property and stock used for trade purposes as well as about tradeswomen's personal goods and dwelling houses. One of the main aims of this research was to ascertain how many and what sorts of businesses were followed by women buying insurance and how these businesses varied over time, but to do this required the adoption of a flexible system of classification. This was because there are a number of issues which specifically impact on ways of classifying insured businesswomen's occupations, as opposed to men's or employed women's, that need to be considered when discussing long-term economic change.

These issues can generally be linked to gendered assumptions about women's life cycles, marital status and association with domestic tasks. First, for many historians, a woman's marital status and life-cycle stage has been seen as crucial in determining her economic choices.[48] For example, it has often been assumed that spinsters were restricted to genteel feminine trades such as millinery and dressmaking, and that only widows could enter more masculine trades by taking over their husbands' business. It has also been argued that, in the early nineteenth century, a new definition of genteel femininity opposed women appearing to act publicly as independent economic agents, which meant that 'their marital status always pre-empted their economic personality'.[49] Yet,

---

[47] GL, Ms. 18856, n.p.

[48] For example, Olwen Hufton, *The Prospect Before Her: A History of Women in Western Europe, Vol. I: 1500–1800* (London, 1995; rep. 1997), and Hill, *Women, Work and Sexual Politics*, structure women's economic activities around their roles as wives, spinsters and widows. Earle, 'Female Labour Market', p. 337, and idem, *Making of the Middle Class*, p. 169, divides employed and business women in the same way.

[49] Davidoff and Hall, *Family Fortunes*, p. 315.

unlike censuses, the information required to evaluate property for insurance meant that women's occupations were less likely to be obscured behind a declaration of marital status. In fact, insurance clerks were not consistent in recording either marital status or occupations for women.[50] Marital status was not recorded in 70 per cent of businesswomen's policies taken out in 1735 and this figure had risen to 94 per cent by 1845.[51] This strikingly high percentage suggests that, far from erasing their occupational identity for insurance purposes, women in business were increasingly unlikely to be described by their marital status in the nineteenth century.

Another issue to impact upon the classification of women's trades is the ascription of typically gendered values to certain occupations. Hence, by the 1830s, for example, it has been argued that women had become concentrated in traditionally 'feminine' trades and thus marginalised within low-paid and low-status occupations.[52] Yet often the very categorisation of women's occupations serves only to stress links with low-status domestic tasks such as sewing, food preparation and childcare still further, while minimising any elements of skill and business management.[53] Any system of classification minimises differences, but aggregation can be particularly pernicious in the case of women if it is based on assumptions which are ascribed to them solely as a sex rather than as any other class or group. Categorisation in this way minimises any cross-gender similarities between trades but also status (and financial) differences between employer and employee. It also tends to obscure many specialised occupations, the possibility that 'feminine' trades could also be profitable ones and the fact that women could follow multiple occupations which did not fit neatly into gendered descriptive categories of their economic activities. Specialisation, profitability and similarities between trades will be discussed in greater detail below, so just two examples of multiple occupations will suffice here. Ann Porter of Boston in Lincoln was a grocer, ironmonger and silversmith. In 1780 she insured £400 of her stock as a silversmith in her house but another £600 of her stock as an ironmonger and grocer, kept in her adjoining shop and warehouse.[54] As a grocer she engaged in the typically feminine enterprise of retailing food and household supplies, but this obscures her extensive business as a silversmith and the fact that she was engaging in what were

---

[50] Earle, *Making of the Middle Class*, p. 169, similarly found that, in 1726 to 1797, 70 per cent of policies did not record marital status.

[51] In this sample n = 156 in 1735 and 259 in 1845.

[52] Hall, 'Gender Divisions and Class Formation', p. 99; Alexander, *Women's Work*, p. 49.

[53] For example, Alexander, *Women's Work*, p. 21, divides women's work into four main categories: domestic/household; childcare/training; distribution/retail of food and other articles of regular consumption; and lastly specific skills in manufacture, i.e. chiefly needlework. Earle, *City Full of People*, p. 148, divides occupations of businesswomen into five main categories: food and drink; textiles and clothing; pawnbroking; other retailing; and miscellaneous trades.

[54] GL, Ms. 11936, 284/432125 (1780).

traditionally viewed as both 'masculine' and 'feminine' trades at the same time. Similarly, Jane Knight of Upper Holloway took out two policies in 1845.[55] The first was as a grocer, cheesemonger and printer in which she insured her household goods and £80 of 'stock, utensils and fixtures viz as a Grocer and Cheesemonger'. The second policy, in the name of Jane Knight & Son 'Printers & Booksellers', jointly insured another £1,400 of stock, utensils and fixtures, kept in her house and adjoining printing office. Jane Knight was therefore in business on her own in apparently 'feminine' trades but also in partnership in a 'masculine' trade with her son. This is not to argue that the marketplace was not gendered or that most trades were not culturally encoded in gendered ways, but it is important to note that the assumptions behind labelling certain occupations typically 'masculine' or 'feminine' can be misleading. Indeed, gender distinctions were far from impermeable and even the insurance clerks sometimes became confused when writing up policies for women in masculine occupations. For example, in 1780 Anne Cooke, a cooper, apparently took out insurance on 'his' household goods in 'her' dwelling house; and in 1845 Jane Tyler was described as an 'oil and colourman'.[56] By way of contrast, one male Westminster voter conformed to occupational gender expectations by declaring his occupation to be that of 'laundress'.[57]

Categorising women's businesses in ways which overemphasise some essentially feminine characteristics also tends to reinforce the appearance of long-term continuities, i.e. that women have always (or increasingly) worked in 'domestic' trades. Yet there is another problem to be considered when categorising women's trades over long periods of time, and that is the issue of temporal and spatial changes in occupational terminology which can impact upon our understanding of exactly what work was being carried out. Over the 110-year period studied here, the language used to describe similar trades in the policy registers changed subtly.[58] For example, the female 'oculist' of 1780 has become an 'optician' by 1845, which touches on issues of professionalisation and changing technology. Similarly, the 'coachmaster' of 1780 has been joined (or superseded) by the 'omnibus proprietor' in 1845. In some cases there are both minor distinctions between trades as well as spatial and temporal changes, but these are frequently obscured by gendered assumptions. This was the case with victuallers, innholders and hotel-keepers. Victualling was one of the most common and profitable insured trades for women in London policies but less so in the counties where 'innholders' were more common. As

---

[55] GL, Ms. 11936, 603/1480601 and 1480602 (1845).

[56] GL, Ms. 11936, 286/68317 (1780); 605/1492896 (1845).

[57] Charles Harvey, Edmund Green and Penelope Corfield, *The Westminster Historical Database: Voters, Social Structure and Electoral Behaviour* (Bristol, 1998), p. 475.

[58] On the complexities of chronologies of occupational description, see Penelope J. Corfield, 'Defining Urban Work', ed. idem, and D. Keene, *Work in Towns, 1850–1850* (Leicester, 1990), pp. 207–30.

Wiskin points out, 'historians have no problems describing victuallers as businessmen', but where women are concerned the trade is usually linked to their domestic role, and innkeeping is similarly seen as an 'extension of women's caring functions'.[59] After 1780 'hotel-keepers' appear in the registers for the first time. Yet, in the early nineteenth century, the famous coach proprietor, Ann Nelson, who also ran a high-class hotel business from the 'Bull Inn' in Aldgate, refused to let her premises be known as a hotel, because she regarded it as a 'new-fangled' word.[60] Mrs Nelson's chief female rival in the coaching business was Sarah Ann Mountain, who in 1822 gave her occupation as 'innholder', which although it conforms to contemporary gendered expectations in a way that 'coachmaster' would not, again obscures the size and masculine nature of her business. Mrs Mountain's insured business capital that year totalled £8,650 and covered not only the inn but also a coach building and transport business, which included stock kept at seven other inns.[61] 'Shopkeeping' could be a similarly misleading occupational label, one that was almost never used to describe any of London's female specialist retailers but easily the most commonly insured business in county policies. Yet not all shopkeepers can be characterised as small country general dealers (although many were), because others, such as Ann Holmes in Sheerness in 1780, could afford to take out an insurance policy for £1,000.[62]

For these reasons every effort was made to adopt a system of classification that was both flexible enough to take account of the minor differences between individual trades, but could also be used to show long-term trends at the broader sectoral level, while at the same time minimising any gendered assumptions about women's trading activities. Thus the classification system adopted here was an adaptation of the Booth/Armstrong classification used by Harvey, Green and Corfield to categorise the occupations of the entirely male electorate of eighteenth-century Westminster.[63] The occupations of London and provincial businesswomen could therefore be coded using exactly the same criteria as

[59] Wiskin, 'Women, Credit and Finance', p. 115; Davidoff and Hall, *Family Fortunes*, p. 299, do also concede that 'the lines between private home . . . and inn were difficult to draw' and that inns were not only valuable resources but centres of several subsidiary activities.

[60] Charles G. Harper, *Stage Coach and Mail in Days of Yore: A Picturesque History of the Coaching Age* (London, 1903), Vol. 2, p. 232, and see below, pp. 254–5.

[61] Ibid. p. 236; Mrs Mountain not only built her own coaches, she also charged passengers extra to travel in them. GL, Ms. 11936, 491/995205, 995206, 995207 (1822), shows that she insured £4,800 of fixed capital, £3,850 of working capital and £400 of personal goods. See also GL, Ms. 11936, 479/960567 (1819): an earlier policy taken out with her husband before he died, in which the total business capital insured came to only £2,750 and she still insured £300 of her personal goods separately in her own name.

[62] GL, Ms. 11936, 283/427522 (1780).

[63] Harvey et al., *Westminster Historical Database*, pp. 87–117, gives a detailed explanation of the adapted coding system, and see below, Appendix II, pp. 268–71.

those used for tradesmen in Westminster, while retaining the flexibility to analyse different levels of occupational specification. Information on women in business from both the London and provincial agencies was extracted from Sun Fire policy registers for the years 1735, 1755 and 1780,[64] and, from the London series only for the years 1809 and 1845.[65] When entered into a database it was therefore possible to compare data from both London and the provinces from 1735 to 1780 and solely for the capital for the entire period.

Businesswomen insured by Sun Fire, 1735 to 1845

Using data entered from the insurance policy registers, it is possible to make some comparisons with evidence of businesswomen's family and trading activities found in legal records, Mrs Baker's Durham accounts and the insurance agents' bond books discussed earlier. Although the overall incidence of women's marital status recorded in insurance policies was very low,[66] broader family ties are still evident. The handful of recorded spinsters were predominantly engaged in traditional 'feminine' trades of dress, hosiery, lace and artificial flower making, but others were dealing in liquor, tobacco, jewellery and silversmithing. It was certainly not unknown for fathers to insure their businesses in trust for daughters as well as for sons,[67] and numerous trade advertisements testify to both married and single daughters following their fathers into trades. Some of these businesses, such as the print dealership taken over by Thomas Dodd's daughter Eleanor and the oyster business continued by the Freeman sisters after the death of their father Edward in 1765, presented little challenge to contemporary gender stereotypes.[68] However, other businesses were of a much more masculine and dirty or public nature. In the 1750s Mary Burnet continued her father's night soil and rubbish-carting business, and in the early nineteenth century Mrs Jones advertised herself as successor to her father's position as 'Artist in Fireworks' and 'Pyrotechnic' to the Royal family and the Corporation of London.[69] Spinsters insuring masculine or craft-based businesses, such as the jeweller and silversmith Tamary Parker whose

---

[64] The aim was to study the registers at twenty-year intervals between 1735 and 1850, but missing and damaged volumes meant adjustments had to be made to find complete series for each sample year.

[65] After 1793 Sun Fire divided its policy registers into Town and County series to cope with the massive increase in the volume of business, and it was only possible to enter data from one set of registers.

[66] Just 5 per cent of policies recorded widows, 1 per cent wives and 0.9 per cent spinsters.

[67] GL, Ms. 11936, 43/67120 (1735).

[68] GL., Trade Cards, Box 9, n.d.; London *Daily Advertiser*, 19 January 1765.

[69] GL., Trade Cards, Box 26, 695: see Robert Stone's original trade card (1742) and his daughter's alteration to it (1755); Box 13, c. 1803, Mrs Jones also made fireworks and rockets for ships at her manufactory in Lambeth.

business was valued at £1,000 in 1845, had very probably followed the same route.[70] However, the high percentage of related women in partnerships suggests that sisters and mothers and daughters often went into business together. As Table 6.2 shows, partnerships accounted for 16 per cent of all policies in the database and half of those were female-only partnerships. A typical example was two to five women engaged in the same business, as was the case with Mary Mackenzie and Co, Mrs Baker's London dressmakers, or her Durham milliners Mary, Ann and Jane Johnson.[71] In no less than 64 per cent of recorded female partnerships, the members were apparently related to each other. Although there were obvious advantages to female family support, there were, as we have seen, also legal advantages to married sisters being in trade together.[72] There is also evidence that female family members did insure businesses for each other. Spinsters insured in trust for their sisters,[73] and widows insured on behalf of single and married daughters. In 1845, the widow Mary Ann Winton jointly with Esther Wainwright and Jane Winton insured ten barges and their contents for £750. As three of the boats were named *Mary Ann, Esther* and *Jane*, the women were almost certainly from the same family.[74]

Although it is strikingly evident that the majority of female partnerships conform to gender expectations in that they were in traditionally 'feminine' trades, with milliners and dressmakers being the most common, this was only half the picture. The other 50 per cent of all recorded partnerships concerned women in trade with one or more men. Such partnerships were more common in the early eighteenth-century samples but even in the nineteenth century they remained just above the number of female-only partnerships. Indeed, partnerships with men were even more diverse and could also involve family members. Husbands and wives, mothers and sons and sons-in-law all insured together. However, Table 6.2 suggests that family relationships were slightly less common, since only 41 per cent of mixed-sex partnerships were with men to whom the women were apparently related. However, since relationships could only be assumed where surnames matched, it is quite possible or even likely that widows in business with sons-in-law or with children from previous marriages could partially account for this. Defoe suggested that the ideal tradesman's widow should eventually make her eldest apprentice a partner in

[70] GL, Ms. 11936, 611/1498725 (1845).

[71] See above, pp. 108, 117. See also Pamela Sharpe, 'Dealing with Love: The Ambiguous Independence of the Single Woman in Early Modern England', *Gender & History*, 11 (1999), pp. 209–32, on Hester Pinney and her four sisters' role in running a shop in London for their family's lace-dealing business.

[72] Because sisters could own property as jointenants, which meant it could not be divided by a husband or his creditors, see above p. 32.

[73] GL, Ms. 11936, 43/67125 (1735), Mary Pattison insured her inn for herself and in trust for her sisters.

[74] GL, Ms. 11936, 609/1482372 (1845).

Table 6.2 Insured women in business partnerships

All partnerships	1735	1755	1780	1809	1845	Total
Total	17	50	81	40	55	243
As % of all policies	11	18	16	16	19	16
n =	155	272	520	248	295	1490
Women-only partnerships						
No. women-only partnerships	5	24	48	19	26	122
As % all partnerships	29	48	59	48	47	50
No. apparently related	3	14	29	15	17	78
As % women-only partnerships	60	58	60	79	65	64
Mixed-sex partnerships						
No. mixed-sex partnerships	12	26	33	21	29	121
As % all partnerships	71	52	41	53	53	50
No. apparently related	6	15	11	5	13	50
As % mixed-sex partnerships	50	58	33	24	45	41

Source: Sun Fire Insurance database

one-fourth of the business until her son came of age, when she should give both men a one-third share each and marry the apprentice to her daughter, keeping one-third for herself. 'Thus the whole trade is preserv'd, the son and son-in-law grow rich in it, and the widow, who soon grows skilful in the business, advances the fortunes of all the rest of her children very considerably.'[75] As we have seen, this harmonious picture could often be shattered by intergenerational disputes over the trade.[76] However, the widow and son-in-law partnership may be one explanation for why women like Mary Pomeroy insured the Star and Cross with her son-in-law as a victualling business 'in right of his wife', her daughter, in 1755.[77] Nevertheless, a significant number of women also seem to have followed the course taken by Mary Jevon when she joined the mercers Edward Bee and Thomas Bond,[78] and gone into business with men with whom they had no family relationship at all.

If insurance policy registers only provide tantalising glimpses of family relationships, they do yield much clearer evidence of the types of trades insured businesswomen were active in. Yet interpreting this evidence to provide a picture of long-term changes in women's economic position is a far more complex task. As we have seen, linear narratives of decline or continuity clearly

[75] Defoe, *Complete English Tradesman*, pp. 291–2.
[76] See above, pp. 74–9.
[77] GL, Ms. 11936, 111/147032 (1755).
[78] See above, pp. 88–90.

do not provide satisfactory descriptions of women's economic experience.[79] Recently, a number of historians have stressed the need to take multiple factors into account. While remaining neutral on the question of whether middling women retreated from trade in the eighteenth century, Margaret Hunt has highlighted the opportunities for businesswomen provided by the 'consumer revolution', the growth of literacy and service industries, and the breakdown of guild controls in corporate towns. But she has also stressed the negative effects of increased costs in setting up shops with glass windows and smart fixtures, the growth of large-scale factory production and the increasing availability of safer investment opportunities for women less willing to embark on risky ventures in trade.[80] Christine Wiskin has also pointed out the need to examine positive and negative factors influencing continuity and change at the same time. She found continuities in women's access to trade on the basis of family circumstances and that, since most women's enterprises mirrored those of small producer capitalists, access to increased finance was unnecessary. Forces for change include the negative effects of new ideals of femininity but also opportunities in the sale of luxury goods, demand for which could account for higher female participation rates in towns that were also regional centres of polite sociability.[81] Pam Sharpe has emphasised 'expanding niches of economic opportunity' for women in the fashion and service trades (particularly in London) and even in some areas of agriculture in Essex, but at the same time showed how cheaper production methods in the cloth trades, in the context of urban overpopulation and underemployment, caused difficulties for women in many towns. She has also argued that although work is gender specific there are 'no binding generalities across geographical areas'.[82]

Data from the Sun Fire policy registers certainly suggest regional and particularly urban and rural differences, as well as providing evidence that female retailers did try to keep up with innovations in retailing by increasingly including shop fittings and glass windows in their insurance. However, while designing the database to mirror the insurance policy registers as a source provided a wealth of additional information discussed in Chapter 7, it did restrict the size and frequency of sampling. Thus although the methodology adopted for this research means that the database may be regarded as an excellent source for studying the wide variety and changing nature of women's businesses, greater caution is required when using it to address purely numerical long-term trends. The use of widely spaced sample years rather than a series and the fact that Sun Fire's share of the insurance market was increasingly eroded from 1790s mean that the overall number of policies taken out by

---

[79] See above, pp. 8–9, 120 n. 3.
[80] Hunt, *Middling Sort*, pp. 145–6.
[81] Wiskin, 'Women, Finance and Credit', esp. pp. 44–5, 105. Centres of polite sociability included Worcester and Colchester, but also Bath, Durham and London.
[82] Sharpe, *Adapting to Capitalism*, pp. 149–51.

Table 6.3 Number of policies taken out by women in business with Sun Fire Insurance

Date	London	Outside London	Total
1735	86	69	155
1755	138	134	272
1780	310	210	520
1809	248[a]	–	248
1845	295[b]	–	295
Total	1077	413	1490

Notes
[a] Only the Town series was consulted after 1780. In 1809 'London' included parts of Surrey and Middlesex.
[b] In 1845 'London' included parts of Kent and Essex as well as Surrey and Middlesex.

Source: Sun Fire Insurance database

women in business each year should be regarded more as a series of snapshots than signs of a continuous trend. Nevertheless, it is difficult to trace any sign of absolute decline or continuity. Instead, the figures seem chiefly to reflect the company's fluctuating fortunes. Table 6.3 shows that the total number of new policies issued to women in business in 1780 was more than treble that of 1735. In the nineteenth century the number of London policies was lower, but by then, competition for insurance was fierce. In 1845, for example, the *London Post Office Directory* listed 1,040 milliners, but only eight of them took out insurance with the Sun Fire Office that year. It is also noticeable that the number of new policies taken out by businesswomen dipped in 1809, a year in which the percentage of higher policy values was greater than in any other and the numbers insuring property under £500 were at their lowest. This suggests that economic factors such as high inflation and the dramatic increase in stamp duty, rather than exclusion from the market on solely gendered grounds, caused women in smaller businesses not to purchase insurance.[83] Furthermore if, as Beverly Lemire has argued, the drop in numbers of women purchasing insurance policies was indicative of a more general shift towards their participation in ever smaller informal petty enterprises, it seems unlikely that there would be a corresponding rise in the percentage of high-value policies taken out.[84]

[83] See discussion below, p. 140, and Table 7.2, p. 154. Stamp duty was raised 1782–1815 until it equalled or even exceeded some premiums thus discouraging small insurers, see p. 122 and n. 14.
[84] Lemire, *Culture and Commerce*, pp. 106–7, based her argument on the model proposed by Eric Richards, 'Women in the British Economy', pp. 337–57, who traced this decline of women's enterprise in general from around 1700. But see below, p. 143, Table 6.6(a); although this research challenges the broader argument, it does appear to support Lemire's more specific conclusions about declining numbers of female pawnbrokers and saleswomen.

Some degree of comparison can be gained from other surveys of business-women's insurance. Peter Earle surveyed 3,531 Sun Fire policies between 1726 and 1729, and found that 317 or 9 per cent were taken out by women, but of these only 188 (5 per cent) were by women assumed to be in business.[85] David Barnett's much larger study of five major London insurance companies shows that the businesses insured by London women (either alone or in partnership with men) rose from about 2,600 in the 1770s to 4,000 in the 1820s. However, as a proportion of all insured businesses, Barnett found those with female proprietors dropped very slightly from 8.8 per cent to 8.1 per cent.[86] The most that can be said is that the numbers of women insuring businesses fluctuated and that, even if there seems to have been an overall increase in female propri-etors, it was at a lower rate of increase than that shown by male proprietors buying insurance. However, the geographical distribution of businesswomen insured by Sun Fire in the eighteenth century was surprisingly wide. Even though their concentration in any one area was never high, there were policies for women from 278 towns and villages located in thirty-seven counties, the Isle of Wight, Scotland and Wales. The county with the highest number of policies (forty-six) was Kent, possibly because it included some metropolitan areas such as Chatham and Greenwich, but more than half of the counties returned fewer than ten policies in the three sample years. Table 6.4 shows that the highest concentrations of insurance (with notable exceptions) were generally in the south, but overall coverage of the country was extensive. The distribution of female policy holders thus followed a similar pattern to that found by Schwarz and Jones' for upper- and middle-class male Sun Fire policy holders,[87] suggesting that the spread of the habit of insurance and the efforts of local Sun Fire agents influenced a businesswoman's decision to purchase insurance as much as, if not more than, her gender.

Nevertheless, the distribution of policies is also important because analysis of the occupations of insured women in business reveals quite marked dif-ferences between the occupations of those with London policies compared with those outside the capital. This variation further serves to warn against broad generalisations about women's work, and supports the more recent emphasis on regional variations. Both London and provincial policies record an increase in the range of insured businesswomen's occupations but, even allowing for the variations in size and the period covered by each sample, there were significant differences. Table 6.5(a) shows that the number of distinct

---

[85] Earle, *Making of the English Middle Class*, pp. 168–9, based his calculations on whether 'stock in trade' was insured in order to distinguish women in business from those who were not. But see Pullin, 'Business is Just Life', pp. 135–7 on why this was liable to exclude a proportion of businesswomen who did not insure stock.

[86] Barnett, *London, Hub of the Industrial Revolution*, p. 208, also used a narrower definition of women in business and excluded all schoolmistresses, regardless of whether they insured capital or not.

[87] Schwarz and Jones, 'Wealth, Occupations, and Insurance', pp. 366–7.

Table 6.4 Distribution of policies by county (excluding London), 1735 to 1780

Highest concentration (More than 20 policies)		Medium concentration (10–20 policies)		Lower concentration (Fewer than 10 policies)[a]
1	Kent	6	Hampshire	12	Surrey
2	Devon	7	Dorset; Wiltshire	13	Middlesex; Oxfordshire
3	Buckinghamshire	8	Cambridgeshire; Hertfordshire	14	Liverpool; Newcastle; Suffolk; Sussex
4	Norfolk	9	Scotland	15	Gloucestershire; Bedfordshire
5	Essex	10	Northamptonshire; Somerset	16	Birmingham; Leicester; Staffordshire
		11	Berkshire; Lincolnshire; Yorkshire	17	Cheshire; Lancashire

Note:
[a] Counties with fewer than three policies not included

Source: Sun Fire Insurance Database

occupations recorded for the capital in 1780 was more than double that of 1735, but the county policies recorded fewer occupations than London policies in 1735 and a less dramatic increase in 1780. This could be explained partially by the smaller number of policies in the county sample. Yet even in 1755, when there were similar numbers of policies issued in both capital and provinces, London policies recorded nearly twice as many occupations. Indeed, in London, even when the number of new policies taken was lower, as in 1809, there was no corresponding contraction in the range of occupations businesswomen engaged in. Moreover, the range increased again, beyond its eighteenth-century peak, in 1845 when only slightly more policies were issued. Thus regardless of the numbers of businesswomen taking out new policies, the range of their individual trades, far from contracting, actually increased in nineteenth-century London.

Even where the range of women's occupations is not thought to have decreased, historians have still argued that in general women were confined to a relatively narrow band of occupations in the eighteenth century and remained so in the nineteenth.[88] In terms of insured trades, the range of occupations pursued by women in business, even in London, was still much narrower than that followed by men,[89] but it was expanding at both the level of individual specialist trades and at sub-sectoral level. Since diachronic comparisons of occupations can be complicated by changing terminology,[90]

[88] See e.g. Earle, 'London Female Labour Market', pp. 341–2; Schwarz, *London in the Age of Industrialisation*, p. 22.
[89] Barnett, *London Hub of the Industrial Revolution*, p. 28, found that insurance registers recorded 754 separate trades in 1776.
[90] See discussion above, p. 132, and Corfield, 'Defining Urban Work', p. 221.

Table 6.5(a) Number of distinct trades practised by insured businesswomen

Year	London		Counties	
	New policies	No. occupations	New policies	No. occupations
1735	86	48	69	30
1755	138	71	134	40
1780	310	103	210	56
1809	248	103	–	–
1845	295	125	–	–

Note: Based on data from OCLV 4: distinct occupations as recorded in Sun Fire policy registers.

Source: Insurance database

Table 6.5(b) Count of trade sub-sectors in which businesswomen were found

Year	London Trade sub-sectors	Counties Trade sub-sectors
1735	26	20
1755	32	24
1780	38	31
1809	38	–
1845	43	–

Note: Based on data from OCLV 2: sub-sectors of the economy.

Source: Sun Fire Insurance database

particularly at the level of self-ascribed description recorded in the policy registers, a similar exercise was conducted to analyse the range of sub-sectors of the economy in which insured women traded. Table 6.5(b) shows that a similar but less dramatic pattern of widening participation was repeated. Again these changes were greater in London, but until similar research has been conducted on other major cities it is difficult to know to what extent the capital should be considered a special case where women's trading activities are concerned.

It is only at the sectoral level that broad continuities can be seen, with the majority of businesswomen occupied in dealing and manufacturing. Yet this pattern does not seem to have differed greatly from that of men, except in scale. Studies of London's economy between around 1700 and 1850 have stressed broad structural continuities, despite the enormous diversity of specialist trades and seasonal fluctuations.[91] The continuous, if seasonal, presence of the

[91] Ibid., pp. 4–6; Charles Harvey, Edmund M. Green and Penelope J. Corfield, 'Continuity, Change and Specialization within Metropolitan London: the Economy Westminster, 1750–1820', pp. 469–72; David Green, *From Artisans to Paupers: Economic Change and*

fashionable elite and a wealthier, more numerous 'middle class' contributed to the structure of London's multifarious luxury trades,[92] and a considerable section of the capital's economy was based around conspicuous consumption. Harvey, Green and Corfield found that in Westminster between 1749 and 1818, more than 60 per cent of male voters were engaged in the often over-lapping activities of making and dealing.[93] In the 1820s, nearly half of all London's insured businesses were involved in retail distribution.[94] Yet, as we have seen, the retail and manufacture of clothing and new luxury goods for the home such as china, glass and earthenware has also been shown to provide important economic opportunities for women. Thus it is hardly surprising that 52 per cent of insured London businesswomen in each sector were in dealing and 35 per cent were in manufacture. This may have reflected a gendered division of work but it also reflected the capital's consumer-oriented economy.

Even though the majority of policy holders were engaged in retailing and manufacture the numbers in each sector did not remain steady across the whole period; nor did the numbers engaged in individual trades. Table 6.6(a) focuses on the twenty-three trades in which the most insured people could be found and it also demonstrates that while some trades became more popular, others became less so or experienced only minor fluctuations. Moreover, although businesswomen were most numerous in trades that could be labelled 'feminine', Table 6.6(a) illustrates that their presence was also detectable within many 'new' and more specialised trades in London.

Numbers in this sample are small but again some comparisons are possible with other studies. Wiskin's research into tradeswomen's advertisements in Birmingham and Wolverhampton between 1780 and 1825 revealed a similar pattern of fluctuation both within and between trades. In terms of an overall pattern, in Birmingham, for example, the numbers advertising food and drink provision and metalware and other craft trades diminished, but those advertising education and clothing rose.[95] John Styles has shown that although women have long been associated with needlework, millinery and mantua making were new trades that only became feminised during the eighteenth century when male tailors lost control of the production of women's outer garments.[96] This change is reflected in the dramatic rise of insured milliners and mantua makers both in London and provincial policies until 1780. After

Poverty in London, 1790–1870 (Aldershot, 1995), pp. 43–58, 176, argues for a greater degree of change among some trades, but found that London's broad economic mix still conferred a degree of stability.

[92] Ibid., pp. 16–17.

[93] Harvey *et al.*, 'Continuity, Change and Specialization', p. 473.

[94] Barnett, *London, Hub of the Industrial Revolution*, p. 127.

[95] Wiskin, 'Women, Finance and Credit', pp. 120–2.

[96] John Styles, 'Clothing the North: The Supply of Non-elite Clothing in the Eighteenth-century North of England', *Textile History*, 25 (1994), pp. 139–66.

Table 6.6(a) Insured trades with the highest concentration of women in London policies

Trade	1735	1755	1780	1809	1845	Total in trade
Milliner	7	18	41	11	27	104
Mantua/dressmaker	0	9	36	29	15	89
Victualler	7	11	36	16	12	82
Chandler	1	4	22	22	15	64
Haberdasher	6	9	11	15	4	45
Schoolmistress	0	1	10	14	18	43
Grocer/greengrocer	0	1	10	8	12	31
Laundress	0	3	10	6	10	29
Baker	2	6	3	9	7	27
Bookseller	0	1	5	7	11	24
Linen draper/seller	8	4	4	4	3	23
Dealer in china/glass	2	0	8	4	7	21
Butcher/poulterer	2	1	8	6	2	19
Pawnbroker	4	9	4	1	1	19
Tea/coffee-woman	1	3	9	2	1	16
Dealer in stationery	1	2	0	3	9	15
Tobacconist	2	1	2	1	8	14
Broker	1	5	4	2	2	14
Saleswoman	0	2	8	3	0	13
Seamstress	0	0	6	6	1	13
Coffee-house keeper	0	0	1	2	9	12
Cheesemonger	0	1	7	0	4	12
Merchant	2	3	4	3	0	12
Total	46	94	249	174	178	741
% London insured	45	56	66	58	49	57[97]

Note: Based on trades in which more than ten people were insured.

Source: Sun Fire Insurance database

that, the number in the London sample falls, which was probably due to Sun Fire's falling share of the insurance market. As noted above, only a tiny percentage of the milliners listed in an 1845 London directory took out insurance with Sun Fire that year.[98] Although Schwarz also found a drop in the percentage of women in millinery trades when comparing eighteenth-century insurance records with the 1851 census, he noted that it was more than counteracted by a rise in the percentage of women in other trades.[99]

[97] N = 1,306 in total: 1735 = 102; 1755 = 167; 1780 = 376; 1809 = 299; 1845 = 362. And see Appendix II, p. 267; 9 per cent of the database sample were men (but all were either in business with a woman or excluded altogether if they had no occupation). Some men may therefore be included in tables of individuals in specific occupations.
[98] See above, p. 138.
[99] Schwarz, London in the Age of Industrialisation, pp. 21–2.

However, the most marked late eighteenth-century increase of women's insured businesses was that of schoolmistresses. This finding supports both Susan Skedd's research into the expansion of private commercial schools for girls and Wiskin's findings about the growth of educational advertising in Birmingham and Wolverhampton.[100] The number of women insuring retail food businesses such as grocers, bakers, and butchers show only minor fluctuations; but specialist retailers in books, stationery, china and glass increased. Numbers of insured London saleswomen and pawnbrokers were never high but, as Lemire has argued, in the capital they do seem to have declined over the period, although for Birmingham Wiskin found an overall increase in pawnbrokers' advertisements.[101]

In terms of women's propensity to be concentrated within feminine trades, there does seem to have been a degree of clustering in London trades, in that 56 per cent of insured individuals in London policies were concentrated in the top 17 per cent trades. Yet even if all the individual women in London's 'feminine' trades associated with food and drink, dress and education are discounted, more than 40 per cent of insured businesswomen remain spread, albeit thinly, over a wide variety of other trades. Indeed, as specialisation tended to minimise the numbers in any one trade, so it also expanded the number of sub-specialisms. Consequently, the dealer in pictures and curiosities did not compete directly with the dealer in articles of vertu,[102] nor the fancy dressmaker with the dress and stay maker. If individuals in all recorded trades are considered, the numbers were actually more concentrated in 1780, when 376 individuals were recorded in 103 trades (one occupation per 3.65 women) than in 1845. At that date, a smaller total of 362 women were found in a wider number of occupations (125, or one occupation per 2.90 women). Again, this ratio of women to occupations would suggest that at the level of individual trades, insured women's businesses in the capital became increasingly diverse in the later period.

Unfortunately, it is possible to make a comparison between London and county occupations only in the broadest terms because there were no nineteenth-century samples and large towns were not proportionately well represented. Provincial businesswomen were engaged in general shopkeeping, rather than in millinery or specific retail outlets, although numbers of both increased. The presence of farmers, brewers and maltsters also indicates a more rural component to the provincial economy. Table 6.6(b) shows that overall more women – 67 per cent of those insured in county policies – were concentrated into fewer trades, just 7 per cent of all occupations listed. Indeed, in 1780 the county policies recorded a total of 252 people in fifty-six different

---

[100] Skedd, 'Women Teachers and the Expansion of Girls' Schooling', pp. 101, 104–5.
[101] Lemire, *Culture and Commerce*, pp. 106–7; Wiskin, 'Women, Finance and Credit', p. 121.
[102] Upmarket, imported antique furniture, paintings, statuary, and clocks.

Table 6.6(b) Insured trades with the highest concentration of women in county policies

Trade	1735	1755	1780	Total in trade
Shopkeeper	8	36	42	86
Innholder	13	16	12	41
Milliner	5	9	23	37
Victualler	5	12	19	36
Linen draper	2	15	11	28
Farmer	2	5	17	24
Grocer	4	9	7	20
Baker	2	6	12	20
Maltster	2	8	9	19
Brewer	0	8	4	12
Mercer	4	4	4	12
Total	47	128	160	335
% county insured	59	75	63	67[103]

Note: Based on trades in which more than ten people were insured.

Source: Insurance database

trades (one occupation per 4.5 women). Again, these figures promote the argument that London was a special case for women in business, but it must also be remembered that the habit of insurance was not as strong outside the capital and that Sun Fire's coverage of that market was at best patchy.

Conclusion

Women were involved in the masculine culture of buying and selling insurance in small but significant numbers virtually from the inception of this new business. Female insurance agents acted as publicly recognised financial brokers, possessed a command of local business knowledge and were backed financially by people of both sexes who only rarely appear to have been relatives. For both vendors and purchasers of insurance, family ties in the broadest sense remained an important but not overriding factor in women's business enterprises. Widowhood was one, but certainly not the only, route into 'masculine' businesses including the sale of insurance. A significant proportion of insured businesswomen were engaged in 'feminine' trades, particularly those in single-sex female partnerships, but many were also in a wide range of more masculine trades, and mixed-sex partnerships were equally common. Yet feminine trades, including dressmaking, millinery, education and newer luxury retail trades, were all growth areas for women, even though numbers in some other trades seem to have declined. Nevertheless, far from

[103] N = 501 in total: 1735 = 79; 1755 = 170; 1780 = 252.

becoming increasingly restricted, the range of insured women's trades, most markedly in London, became increasingly diverse and specialised. Thus, despite gendered cultural expectations, businesswomen were engaged in a wider range of occupations than has been commonly thought. However, it is true to say that there were broad continuities at the sectoral level, with the majority being engaged in dealing and manufacture, but particularly in London this reflected the wider pattern of insured businesses as much as a gendered division of labour.

7

A risky business

Businesswomen, property and insurance
strategies, 1735 to 1845

We consider that commerce is not a game of chance but a science, in which
those who are best skilled bid the fairest for success.

William Watson (1794)[1]

Insurance has been described as an 'invention expressly designed to tame the
future',[2] a crucial tool in the management of risk and a sign of the belief that
enlightened humanity could exercise rational control over the vagaries of
nature and misfortune. Insurance has also been seen as part of a specifically
middle-class male drive to quantify and to rationalise business practice, which
contributed to the construction of increasingly gendered separate spheres of
action.[3] Yet, as Chapter 6 has shown, the rational exercise of risk management
through insurance was a far from alien concept for women in business. Indeed,
insurance could provide a measure of security that facilitated women's continued involvement in speculative economic enterprises. In this chapter,
different strategies of risk management are examined in order to address two
issues relating to perceptions of women's success, or the lack of it, in business.
Since success is generally measured by size, the first relates to the amount and
type of business capital acquired by women. The second relates to women's
ability to own and control their own property rather than to merely function
as transmitters of property and capital within a patriarchal society.[4] As we have
seen,[5] women's alleged lack of control over property as capital has been viewed
as one of the problems limiting their economic opportunities. Women's
businesses have generally been characterised as largely unprofitable and under-
capitalised. Increases in the scale of production and the costs of setting up, as
well as technical advances, are believed to have further marginalised women's

---

[1] William Watson, *A Treatise on the Law of Partnership* (1794), p. 148.
[2] Clark, *Betting on Lives*, p. 3.
[3] Davidoff and Hall, *Family Fortunes*, pp. 205, 214–15.
[4] For this argument, see Staves, *Married Women's Separate Property*, p. 4; and Davidoff and
Hall, *Family Fortunes*, p. 314, for the argument that therefore, women's 'decision to enter
the market depended on their control over family property'.
[5] See above, p. 11.

small enterprises.[6] David Barnett has argued that London women's overall share of insured business capital fell, from 50 per cent in the 1770s to 30 per cent in the 1820s.[7] It has also been argued that women were very seldom regarded as full partners in business enterprises and that their contribution to family enterprises lay chiefly in providing small capital sums, unpaid skills and networking with business contacts.[8] Yet insurance policies show that while economic changes certainly impacted upon women's businesses, many of which were and remained small, this picture of diminishing capital and 'hidden investment' is too bleak. It obscures both the scale and diversity of women's enterprises and the extent of their control of property.

The argument that separate spheres ideology was largely responsible for women's retreat from business or their increasing concentration in under-capitalised feminine trades places heavy emphasis on gender as the over-whelming factor determining women's economic experience. Yet in previous chapters we have seen how women were embedded in mixed-sex credit networks, that gender was not the sole factor determining the type of trade businesswomen were engaged in, and that they received financial backing from and entered into partnerships with members of both sexes. This chapter begins with a discussion of gendered definitions of business capital and the problems of treating women in trade as a homogeneous group. It continues with an analysis of two different strategies of risk management. First, the insurance of different types of fixed and working capital highlights the great variety of businesswomen's living and working arrangements, and confirms their inte-gration within the trading community. It also suggests that security through diversity rather than via maximum business capitalisation may have been busi-nesswomen's primary concern. Second, it will be argued that the insurance of property in mixed- and same-sex business partnerships shows not only that wives could circumvent legal restrictions on property ownership, but that, somewhat paradoxically, women were more likely to retain control of their individual property in mixed-sex partnerships than in those with other women.

Women and business capital

At first glance, defining business capital may seem to be a relatively simple task. It can, for example, be divided into working capital (which in insurance policies relates to goods described as 'stock', 'utensils', or goods 'in trust' or 'on commission'); and fixed capital (which relates to buildings serving an obviously commercial purpose such as 'warehouses', 'workshops' or 'manufactories').[9] Yet

---

[6] Hunt, *Middling Sort*, p. 145; Davidoff and Hall, *Family Fortunes*, pp. 302, 304.
[7] Barnett, *London, Hub of the Industrial Revolution*, p. 209.
[8] Davidoff and Hall, *Family Fortunes*, pp. 201, 279–89.
[9] Barnett, *London, Hub of the Industrial Revolution*, and 'The Structure of Industry in London'

such a clear demarcation between personal and commercial goods and property is problematic, and in many cases even more so for women in business. Many women, particularly in the earlier period, did not distinguish between household goods and stock, and tended to insure both in one lump sum. In 1735 and 1755 this joint category accounted for 56 per cent of women's insured goods in the sample.[10] Some 'feminine' businesses, such as schools, had no need to insure separate stock as such, and in the case of others, for example, small general shopkeepers and dressmakers, stock could be hidden among household goods. Fixed capital was also difficult to separate, again partly because some insured buildings were used for both private and commercial purposes, but also because 'dwelling houses' remained the prime site of business for women throughout the period. Moreover, particularly in London, the numbers of women actually insuring the property in which they conducted their business remained very low, for reasons which are discussed below.

In addition, the limits to insurance itself partly dictated the amounts of property insured, and this factor affects historians' valuations of businesses run by both sexes. The question of the reliability or otherwise of insurance valuations has resulted in a great deal of heated debate as to whether property was routinely under- or over-insured.[11] For the women in business studied here, a number of points need to be noted before considering the sums insured as an unproblematic indication of wealth or success. First, the Sun set maximum limits for risk insurance, which altered throughout the period according to the assessment of the severity of the perceived risk. For property designated as requiring 'Common Insurance' (usually brick or stone buildings not used for hazardous goods or trades), the limit was £3,000 in 1727 but had risen to £10,000 by 1808. If property was used for hazardous trades,[12] the limit was £6,000 in 1808, and it was lowered to just £3,000 for trades considered 'doubly hazardous' because they were carried out in a timber and plaster building.[13] In this sample, women were numerous in several hazardous trades including those trading as brewers, bakers, tallow and ship's chandlers, and there were some women insured in almost all the occupations designated as hazardous. As the maximum policy value found in the sample rose from £3,000 in 1735 to £10,000 in 1809, risk limits, as well as the growth of business size and the rate of inflation, should be taken into account when considering any growth trends.

(unpub. Ph.D. thesis, University of Nottingham, 1996), pp. 11–13, adopted this approach and only considered sums of commercial fixed and working capital.

[10] N = £159,864. In later sample years, the percentage of jointly insured stock and household goods was minimal: see below, p. 156.

[11] For a summary of the debate, see Barnett, *London, Hub of the Industrial Revolution*, pp. 6–8.

[12] Dickson, *Sun Insurance Office*, p. 83, lists sixteen 'hazardous' trades: apothecaries, bread bakers, brewers, chemists, colourmen, distillers, dyers, flax and hemp warehousemen, oilmen, pastry cooks, roasting cooks, ship's chandlers, soap boilers, sugar bakers and tallow chandlers.

[13] Cockerell and Green, *British Insurance Business*, p. 48.

Second, some businesswomen's policies did not necessarily reflect the full value of their business. Insurance offices habitually expected clients to shoulder part of the risk, and in 1797 a Sun Fire employee estimated that merchants only insured stock at one-quarter or even one-fifth of actual value.[14] Moreover, farmers, merchants, dealers and others storing goods in public warehouses, wharfs or yards could take out 'short insurances' for just three to six months.[15] In these cases, only small amounts of goods were insured at any one time. In this sample, female merchants and dealers took out policies only insuring stock more often than women in other trades, and frequently took out more than one policy. For example, in May 1780 Amelia Stewart, a salt merchant living in Bloomsbury, insured £2,700 of stock kept in two warehouses in East Smithfield, and in June insured another £500 of stock kept in a warehouse in St Catherine's Court.[16] Mary Lawrence, in a partnership described variously as '& Co', '& Son' or '& Sons', dealt in ropes, sails and provisions in Shadwell. She took out five policies in January, April, June, July and August 1809.[17] The first covered £1,100 of stock and the next four were for smaller amounts of £300 to £600. Each was due to expire after a few months, which suggests that she was only insuring stock which she hoped to sell on quickly.

Businesswomen took out partial insurance for a number of other reasons too. Initially, Sun Fire voided any policies where the policy holder was found to have insured with another company but this was changed so that companies could share the risk, which meant that any policy might be only a part valuation of a risk insured with one or more fire offices. In 1809 Sarah Hopkins, a dyer in Spitalfields, insured £1,000 of stock, £500 of private and commercial property and £250 of household goods with Sun Fire. She also held another policy with the Phoenix Fire office for a further £2,400.[18] Since the sums insured were quite large and as dyers were classified as being in a hazardous trade, this was almost certainly an attempt to spread the risk. In addition, it was not unusual for goods held in trust not to be insured.[19] This was a common form of stock held by mantua makers, for example, who often used materials brought by clients to make up dresses. It is also likely that valuations of stock often only covered the replacement of tools and other movable utensils, so that in many cases raw materials were excluded.[20] In this sample 17 per cent

[14] Ibid., p. 49.
[15] *Instructions for the Agents* (1807), p. 20.
[16] GL, Ms. 11936, 282/428539, 284/429333.
[17] GL, Ms. 11936, 443/832297, 832809, 446/825399, 830239, 834290.
[18] GL, Ms. 11936, 443/825754.
[19] Cockerell and Green, *British Insurance Business*, p. 49.
[20] S.D. Chapman, 'Fixed Capital Formation in the British Cotton Manufacturing Industry', in *Aspects of Capital Investment in Great Britain, 1750–1850* ed. J.P.P. Higgins and S. Pollard (London, 1971), p. 91, argues that 'stock and utensils' are the most difficult item of insurance to interpret and that even large factories rarely insured amounts large enough to have covered raw materials, work in progress or finished products.

of all policies taken out by businesswomen insured no stock at all. Retailers of perishable foods such as butchers, bakers, grocers and cheesemongers, were dominant in this category, but schoolmistresses and speculative builders often insured considerable amounts of property and/or household goods but no stock. In 1809 the builder Ann Pool insured just £50 of household goods in Bloomsbury and no stock, but she also insured thirty-three untenanted properties in the Mount Pleasant area for £2,950.[21] In the same year a school-mistress, Hannah Davis in Stoke Newington, insured household goods, clothes and books, both for herself and 'in trust', presumably for her pupils, for £1,000.[22] Schoolmistresses also often insured musical instruments separately for up to £200, but while buildings could be classed as fixed capital, musical instruments hardly constituted stock-in-trade.[23] As Susan Skedd has shown, proprietors of commercial boarding-schools could earn a comfortable living from the business, even though some of the most successful, such as the Stephenson sisters in Queen's Square, had little need of the extra income.[24] The Stephensons did not insure their two adjoining properties but their household goods, clothing, china and glass and musical instruments were valued at £3,200 in 1780.[25] Sophie von La Roche attributed the sisters' success to their being 'persons of merit' and describes their home as 'their own', even though it was not insured. She estimated that the Stephensons were educating 220 girls at more than 100 guineas per pupil.

On some policies, Sun Fire offered an 'average clause' under which the sum payable for fire damage depended on the relation of the sum insured to that of the whole property. As many women were in the brewing trade, it is significant that after 1793 Sun Fire offered a lower premium to brewers accepting this clause and after 1803 refused to insure brewhouses without it.[26] Finally, perhaps one of the more important reasons for partial insurance was the high cost of the government duty after 1782 which was not abolished until 1869. This probably hit women in smaller businesses particularly hard and may have prevented many from purchasing insurance at all, or caused them to buy only partial cover. For example, Elsey Asher, a general dealer in Spitalfields, insured her house for £200 plus £50 of household goods in 1845, but did not cover any stock. A note attached to the policy stated that 'No Goods nor other

---

[21] GL, Ms. 11936, 444/836295. See also Barnett, London Hub of the Industrial Revolution, p. 118, for female speculative builders with substantial insurance policies.

[22] GL, Ms. 11936, 443/825628.

[23] Although schoolmistresses often insured musical instruments, it was not possible to tell if they were for private use or to instruct pupils, and as other businesswomen also insured instruments in their homes these items were coded as 'household'.

[24] Skedd, 'Women Teachers and the Expansion of Girl's Schooling', pp. 113–14, and see Sophie von la Roche's description of the sisters and their school in Sophie in London 1786: Being the Diary of Sophie v. la Roche, trans. Clare Williams (London, 1933), pp. 92–3.

[25] GL. Ms. 11936, 286/434007.

[26] Jenkins, Practice of Insurance, p. 33.

articles paid for which may be lost or stolen at or in consequence of a fire or at an alarm of fire', which meant that the company was well aware that she had goods which she was not insuring.[27]

In addition to problems that relate specifically to insurance policies as a source for ascertaining women's business capital, there are also dangers in viewing women as a unitary entity. As a few historians have begun to note, reducing women to a single homogeneous group obscures crucial differences between different sectors and industries.[28] In fact, even where women were grouped in 'feminine' trades, policy values and strategies of insurance were determined largely by the different trades that women followed and not by their gender alone. A comparison of the types of property insured by London women in two 'feminine' sectors of trade serves to make the point. Figure 7.1 shows that, while women in both catering and clothing trades[29] insured in aggregate fairly similar sums of household goods or joint stock and household goods, those in the clothing trades insured nearly twice as much stock in trade as did those in catering trades. However, those in the catering trades insured more than three times the amount (in value) of buildings than did those in the clothing trades. Many victuallers, inn and tavern keepers owned their premises, but a significant proportion of milliners and dressmakers operated

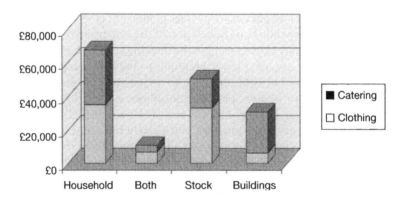

Figure 7.1 Aggregate values of women's insured property in the London catering and clothing trades in sample years, 1735 to 1845

Note: 'Both' = jointly insured stock and household goods.
Source: Sun Fire Insurance database

[27] GL, Ms. 11936, 602/1475713.
[28] Yeager, 'Making a Difference', p. 14; Maxine Berg, 'Women's Property and the Industrial Revolution', *Journal of Interdisciplinary History*, 24 (1993), p. 249; Barker, 'Women, Work and the Industrial Revolution', p. 100.
[29] Here only those in dressmaking, mantua making and millinery were included in the 'clothing' trades; victuallers, inn and tavern keepers as 'catering' trades.

Table 7.1 London trades undertaken by insured women, with maximum policy value exceeding £3,000

Trade		Min. value £	Max. value £
1	Milliners	100	10,000
2	Dressmakers	100	10,000
3	Innkeepers/victuallers/publicans	100	9,400
4	Coopers	200	8,950
5	Packers	1,600	8,000
6	Dealers in tools/marine stores	300	7,800
7	Mattress makers	100	7,800
8	Brewers	100	7,000
9	Coffee-house keepers	100	7,000
10	Mercers	500	5,000
11	Printers	500	5,000
12	Merchants	300	5,000
13	Farmers	100	5,000
14	Rope makers	100	4,700
15	Tea/coffee dealers	200	4,000
16	China dealers	150	4,000
17	Builders	100	3,700
18	Schoolmistresses	100	3,200
19	Grocers	100	3,150
20	Cheesemongers	100	3,150

Note: Grouped trades based on OCLV 3.

Source: Sun Fire Insurance database

from rented premises.[30] Hence broad generalisations about women's propensity as a sex to insure one kind of property over another are likely to be erroneous.

Although different trades did determine the type of property insured and also to a degree the maximum probable capital accumulation, there were still very great variations between the sizes of businesses in each trade. Table 7.1 shows that the clothing and catering trades may have been the most suitably 'feminine' trades for women but, more importantly, they were also the businesses with the biggest potential for capital accumulation. However, the range of policy values was huge and the majority of businesses remained at the lower end of the scale. Looking specifically at London milliners' policy values, for example, the smallest businesses continued to take out the minimum insurance for £100 in each of the sample years but it was not until 1809 that the largest reached £10,000, and in aggregate over the whole period 70 per cent were insured for £500 or less. Schwarz found that from 1776 to 1785 in London, between two-thirds and three-quarters of the members of any one insured trade were concentrated in the lower range of policy values, and London milliners

---

[30] See below, p. 162.

Table 7.2 London businesswomen's policy values, 1735 to 1845

Date	No. all policies	£100– £500	% all policies	£501– £1000	% all policies	£1,001– £3,000	% all policies	£3,001 +	% all policies
1735	86	72	83.7	11	12.8	3	3.5	–	–
1755	138	109	79	20	14.5	9	6.5	–	–
1780	310	237	76.4	48	15.5	21	6.8	4	1.2
1809	248	130	52.4	51	20.5	58	23.4	9	3.6
1845	295	194	65.8	59	20	35	11.8	7	2.4

Source: Sun Fire Insurance database

issued new policies in 1780 followed the same pattern.[31] Indeed, Barnett found that in the 1770s nearly three-quarters of all London firms insured business capital of £500 or less.[32] Since the range of different sizes of business run by women within individual London trades is strikingly similar to that of all London trades, gender cannot have been the most significant factor in determining this pattern of predominantly smaller businesses.

There do, however, seem to have been some gendered differences in the scale of businesses run by men and women. Despite important variations between trades, it is possible to make some general comparisons which suggest that while the overall size of women's businesses did not decline over the period, there was no great increase in scale at the top of the range. Table 7.2 shows that the proportion of London businesswomen taking out policies for £500 or less fell over the period but, even allowing for inflation,[33] in every sample year the majority of policy values remained within this low range. In the nineteenth-century samples, the percentage of insured businesswomen who took out policies in the mid-range of values did rise, but those insuring over £3,000 remained few. The year 1809 stands out as having the highest proportion of high-value policies, even though the total number of policies issued to London businesswomen was lower than in 1780 and 1845. As we have seen, the most probable explanation is that the impact of the Napoleonic wars, increased government duty and high levels of inflation in 1809 meant that only women in larger businesses or those with additional real property took out insurance that year. Conversely, low inflation may have encouraged

[31] Schwarz, *London in the Age of Industrialisation*, pp. 66–7. Of forty new policies issued to London milliners in 1780, 72 per cent were in the lower range of policy values. However, this pattern may have been subject to some variations within individual trades. Lemire, *Dress, Culture and Commerce*, p. 107, found that 10 per cent fewer male than female pawnbrokers from 1777 to 1796 held policies for £600 or less.

[32] Barnett, *London, Hub of the Industrial Revolution*, p. 36. The majority of insured businesses in Birmingham also did not exceed this sum: Wiskin, 'Women, Finance and Credit', p. 194.

[33] See price indices in Phyllis Deane and B.R. Mitchell, *Abstract of British Historical Statistics* (Cambridge, 1971), pp. 468–70.

more women with smaller businesses to insure in 1845.[34] Nevertheless, by way of comparison, Barnett found that while all businesses insuring over £1,000 increased from 13 per cent of the total in the 1770s to 23 per cent in the 1820s, the 4 per cent of female-owned businesses in this category increased to just 5 per cent in the 1820s.[35] Part of the explanation for women's apparently smaller share of insured business capital therefore seems to be a less dramatic growth in larger businesses owned by women rather than an overall decline, but it may be equally important that businesswomen's risk management strategies also meant that business capital often formed a relatively small part of their overall insurance portfolio.

Risk management: property

It has been argued that, during the late eighteenth and early nineteenth centuries, women were increasingly not expected to act as economic agents or to manage property. It is often assumed that, while men inherited land and stock in trade, women were left movable personal possessions or money in trusts.[36] In cases where women did acquire property, the assumption has been that such assets would be used to provide a rentier income with which to aspire to gentility and to retire from economic endeavour.[37] Conversely, it has also been argued that women let property because they were increasingly excluded from trade.[38] However, all these views are disputed. Penelope Lane has queried whether the existence of safer investments meant that women were less likely to continue in business, concluding that inheritance practices in East Midland towns did as much to encourage women's economic activities as to exclude them.[39] Similarly, Maxine Berg found that husbands and fathers left more land and shops to daughters and wives than they did to male kin in eighteenth-century Birmingham, and only slightly fewer bequests than to male kin in Sheffield.[40] Indeed, Berg argues that lack of property and women's ownership of more personal possessions cannot be linked to a rise in 'domestic ideology', since women in these two industrial towns owned and disposed of both realty and personal possessions.

Insured businesswomen certainly owned significant amounts of stock and real property as well as personal goods. In this sample of London and provincial

---

[34] Ibid. shows that prices were particularly high in 1809 but had fallen in 1845. Table 7.4(a) shows the surge of insured rental property in 1809.
[35] Barnett, *London, Hub of the Industrial Revolution*, p. 209.
[36] See e.g., Davidoff and Hall, *Family Fortunes*, p. 209.
[37] Earle, *City Full of People*, p. 150.
[38] David Green, 'Independent Women, Wealth and Wills in Nineteenth-Century London', *Urban Fortunes*, ed. Stobart and Owens, p. 213.
[39] Lane, 'Women, Property and Inheritance', pp. 172–94.
[40] Berg, 'Women's Property', pp. 244–5.

Table 7.3 Total sums of property insured in five sample years, 1735 to 1845

Year	Property £	Stock £	Household £	Both[a] £	Annual Total £
1735	16,635	15,025	2,530	32,605	66,795
1755	27,385	43,265	10,085	56,354	137,089
1780	54,231	142,500	76,004	180	272,915
1809[b]	65,100	112,615	66,895	250	244,860
1845[b]	53,545	79,570	60,619	1,155	194,889
Total	216,896	392,975	216,133	90,544	916,548

Notes
[a] Both = Jointly insured stock and household goods.
[b] London policies only.

Source: Sun Fire Insurance database

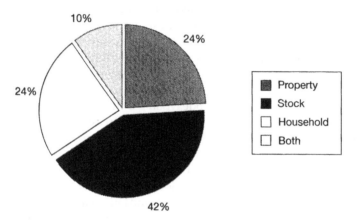

Figure 7.2 Aggregate sums of property insured in five sample years, 1735 to 1845

Note: 'Both' = jointly insured stock and household goods.

Source: Sun Fire Insurance database

policy holders the largest sum (42 per cent of the total sum insured)[41] was laid out to protect stock in trade. However, as Table 7.3 and the pie chart in Figure 7.2 show, if the amount of jointly insured stock and household goods is disregarded, businesswomen insured almost equal sums of real property and household goods. Although the greatest sum was spent insuring stock, businesswomen also owned large amounts of personal goods. These included books, clothing, pictures, jewellery and musical instruments, as well as glass, china, linen and other household wares. As Figure 7.1 shows, those in the 'feminine' trades, particularly in clothing, insured more household goods than property or stock. Indeed, many women in these trades insured personal goods that

[41] N = £916,548. See Table 7.3.

suggested a much higher standard of living than their insured business capital would indicate. Nevertheless, since buildings were relatively more expensive than household goods, the chart suggests that businesswomen insured comparatively less property than stock or personal possessions. The reasons for this are partly to do with the often 'informal' ways in which the majority of women conducted their business and partly because of the different patterns of property holding between the provinces and London.

The incidence of property insurance was much higher in provincial policies than in London. Tables 7.4(a) and (b) show that, in the eighteenth-century samples, provincial policy holders insured more than three times the sums of property insured by metropolitan policy holders. Much of the property in which women lived and conducted business described in the policy registers was not insured at all, but despite the fact that all the major insurance companies were based in London and the culture of insurance was strongest there, Londoners were less likely to insure their property than were provincial businesswomen. For example, in eighteenth-century provincial policies dwelling houses were insured in 47 per cent of the policies in which they were listed, but the corresponding figure for London was just 6 per cent (Table 7.4(b)). The extent of this difference varied according to the type of property being insured, but since insurance was usually taken out by the property owner it would appear that fewer London businesswomen owned their property, particularly since other historians have also found correspondingly lower rates of property ownership in London than in provincial towns.[42] Although the rates of insuring buildings increased in the two nineteenth-century London samples, they remained low: just 22 per cent for private dwellings and 33 per cent for joint commercial and private use, but 50 per cent for separate commercial property.[43] One of the most likely reasons for the lower incidence of insurance in London is that much London property was owned by large aristocratic estates and therefore houses in particular could only be held by leasehold.[44] In such cases it is very likely that insurance, if purchased at all on that scale, may have been taken out in the owner's name rather than in that of the leaseholder. The low incidence of

---

[42] Green, 'Independent Women', p. 210, found that 19.4 per cent of women's wills in his 1830 London sample bequeathed property. However, Berg, 'Women's Property', p. 241, found that 48 per cent of female Birmingham and Sheffield testators owned property. Lane, 'Women, Property and Inheritance', p. 186, found that 23.7 per cent of female testators in Ashby-de-la-Zouche and 38 per cent in Hinckley (1750–1835) left real estate.

[43] See Table 7.4(a). For 1809 and 1845 buildings coded P: n = 475; coded B: n = 51; coded C: n = 50, the exception being the 76 per cent (N = 30) rate of insuring agricultural buildings, but the sums involved here were very small. See Pullin, 'Business is just Life', p. 140, on an apparent nineteenth-century increase in women insuring 'urban'-style agriculture (e.g. cow keepers, florists, market gardeners and even 'farmers').

[44] Green, 'Independent Women', p. 198; Dorothy George, *London Life in the Eighteenth Century* (1925; rep. New York 1965); much property in London was also church or corporate property, pp. 75–6.

Table 7.4(a) Types and sums of property insured by London businesswomen in sample years, 1735 to 1845

Year	No. of policies with type of building	No. of policies with insured buildings	Sum of insured buildings
A. Agricultural buildings			
1735	1	0	–
1755	1	0	–
1780	7	5	£590
1809	11	10	£2,130
1845	19	13	£2,260
Total	39	28 (72%)[a]	£4,980
B. Both commercial and private usage			
1735	7	0	–
1755	8	3	£505
1780	14	3	£3,760
1809	20	9	£6,950
1845	31	8	£5,560
Total	80	23 (29%)	£16,775
C. Separate commercial property			
1735	14	2	£650
1755	20	1	£40
1780	32	7	£1,780
1809	21	10	£5,935
1845	29	15	£5,380
Total	116	35 (30%)	£13,785
L. Let property			
1735	5	4	£1,300
1755	3	1	£1,360
1780	10	10	£4,830
1809	28	27	£14,040
1845	12	12	£4,825
Total	58	54 (93%)	£26,355
P. Private dwellings			
1735	74	5	£1,600
1755	127	9	£2,505
1780	282	16	£4,590
1809	217	55	£36,045
1845	258	51	£35,520
Total	958	136 (14%)	£80,260
Total sum of property insured in all categories			£142,155

Note:
[a] Figs in () = % of policies in which type of building listed was actually insured.

Source: Sun Fire Insurance database

Table 7.4(b) Comparison of types and sums of property insured by provincial businesswomen in sample years, 1735 to 1780

Year	No. of policies with type of building	No. of policies with insured buildings		Sum of insured buildings
A. Agricultural buildings				
1735	17	16		£955
1755	21	15		£1,330
1780	44	24		£3,305
Total	82	55	(65%)[a]	£5,590
London total				
Insured to 1780	9	5	(62%)	£590
B. Both commercial and private use				
1735	23	14		£2,895
1755	42	27		£4,700
1780	53	34		£6,545
Total	118	75	(63%)	£14,140
London total				
Insured to 1780	29	6	(20%)	£4,265
C. Separate commercial property				
1735	15	11		£725
1755	30	15		£4,115
1780	50	23		£2,781
Total	95	49	(51%)	£7,621
London total				
Insured to 1780	66	10	(15%)	£2,470
L. Let property				
1735	17	17		£3,250
1755	35	35		£5,970
1780	50	49		£13,710
Total	102	101	(99%)	£22,930
London total				
Insured to 1780	18	15	(83%)	£7,490
P. Private dwellings				
1735	37	27		£5,260
1755	75	37		£6,860
1780	135	53		£12,340
Total	247	117	(47%)	£24,460
London total				
Insured to 1780	483	30	(6%)	£8,695
Provincial total sum of property insured in all categories				£74,741
London total sum of property insured in all categories to 1780				£23,510

Note:
[a] Figs in () = % of policies in which type of building listed was actually insured.

Source: Sun Fire Insurance database

property insurance in London therefore tends to paint a picture of women in business insuring smaller amounts of property than may have been the case if a larger sample of provincial policies had been obtained.

The value of real property, however, meant that ownership was still an important source of wealth and, even more importantly, dwelling houses remained the main site of business for the majority of insured women in this sample throughout the period. Table 7.4(a) shows that the value of insured private dwellings in London had soared to more than £35,000 in both 1809 and 1845, compared with just £4,590 in 1780 and £12,340 in provincial policies for the same year. In the nineteenth century, London women were more likely to insure such residential property. In aggregate, well over 50 per cent of the value of London businesswomen's insured properties was accounted for by private dwellings, but this figure tends to obscure both the amount of business being conducted by women but also the extent of their business capital which cannot be separated from their personal capital.

For women in business property ownership, whether for personal or business use, or for rental income, could function as a manifest sign of creditworthiness and provide an opportunity to diversify their investments as part of a risk management strategy. But let property[45] has become a significant issue for historians, many of whom see its ownership either as a sign of middle-class women's increasing exclusion or their desire to retire from business. In this sample, 10 per cent of all policies insured let property and the total sum insured was in excess of £49,000, making it the second largest sum of insured property after private dwellings. Table 7.4(b) shows that, again, the aggregate sums insured were much higher in provincial policies (£22,930) than London policies (£7,490) in the eighteenth century, although in both cases this represented just over 30 per cent[46] of the total sum of insured buildings. This corresponds with Earle's finding that approximately one-third of all assets listed in early eighteenth-century middle-class London inventories took the form of investments, although only half of Earle's sample invested in leasehold property.[47] From 1735 to 1780, 23 to 26 per cent of all provincial policies in the sample contained some form of let property. For London, fewer than 5 per cent of all policies insured let property each year, except in 1809 when it rose to nearly 11 per cent with a similarly dramatic rise of the sums insured.[48] Since the levels

---

[45] Let property was the one category of buildings that was almost only ever listed in policies if it was to be insured, so it is not possible to compare rates of insurance with other building types.

[46] Table 7.4(b) above shows that for provincial policies n = £74,741, for London policies n = £23,510.

[47] Earle, *Making of the English Middle Class*, pp. 143 and 147, Table 5.4, but this sample of 375 inventories was not limited to businessmen.

[48] See Table 7.3: n = £118,645. Despite this surge the total sum of let property insured in London policies in 1809 and 1845 fell to just 16 per cent of the value of all insured buildings in those years.

of let property peaked in the very year that the fewest policies were issued, it seems likely that insuring more let property was a reaction to difficult economic conditions rather than a sign of women's increasing exclusion from business. Nevertheless, the predominantly lower levels of insured let property in London may have reflected both the generally lower incidence of property ownership and the fact that London women had better access to other investment markets. Research has shown that women formed a small but significant percentage of stock holders and, in joint-stock companies, shareholding also gave women voting rights on the same terms as men.[49]

The wide disparity of sizes of businesses run by women insuring let property suggests that rentier income was both an important supplement to business income and a form of 'portfolio diversification'[50] to spread the risk in hard times. Wiskin argues that many small-scale capitalists in Birmingham calculated that despite lower returns, investment in property was a worthwhile way to prevent overexposure in any one sector.[51] Thus, if investment in rental property was not a specifically gendered activity for smaller scale traders, there seems little reason to suspect that tradeswomen in particular were investing only in order to retire from business. It seems highly improbable that Sarah Branson, for example, a shopkeeper in Towcester in 1755, expected to buy herself a genteel retirement on the income from two houses and a tenement (let to a labourer, a cordwainer and a barber respectively), which she insured for £80.[52] Her only other insured goods were household items valued at just £20. Although it was more common for women who insured property in which they lived and/or worked to insure additional let properties, it was not unusual for those in rented accommodation to do the same. In 1809 Mary Friend was a saleswoman living in rooms in Tower Hill, which she rented from Mr Langford, a gentleman who was not in trade. At that address, she insured £100 of household goods and £50 of stock. However, Friend conducted her business from another salesman's shop in the Clothes Exchange, Rosemary Lane, and she also rented out a house, insured for £150, in Whitechapel.[53] This was a classic case of a diversified portfolio. The components may all have been related to her major occupation as a saleswoman, but the Whitechapel property was not self-evidently so. For all these women in small businesses, rental income would have been crucial but, even at the top end of the scale, women with significant sums of insurance remained in business. In 1780 Elizabeth Aldwin, a grocer and tallow chandler

---

[49] P.G.M. Dickson, *The Financial Revolution in England: A Study in the Development of Public Credit* (London, 1967), p. 298; Susan Staves, 'Investments, Votes, and "Bribes": Women as Shareholders in the Chartered National Companies' in *Women Writers and the Early Modern British Political Tradition*, ed. Hilda Smith (Cambridge, 1998), pp. 259–78.

[50] I would like to thank Edmund Green for suggesting this means of describing women's investment in let property.

[51] Wiskin, 'Women, Credit and Finance,' pp. 86–7.

[52] GL, Ms. 11936, 110/146713.

[53] GL, Ms. 11936, 444/834702.

in Harrow, had a policy valued at £2,300. She did not insure her own dwelling, nor the candlehouse, warehouse, outhouses and stables around it, in which she kept £150 of household goods and £450 of stock. However, she did insure £340 of other agricultural-type buildings and £1,360 of rented properties including four let to other traders and one let to another farmer.[54] In 1809, the London rope and twine maker, Mary Exeter, had a policy for £4,700 to insure her house, commercial buildings and stock, but she still let nine other properties and owned a further six untenanted ones, which accounted for £1,225 of the policy.[55]

The fact that women insured let property in addition to or instead of stock and commercial buildings, even though it was not in itself a specifically gendered practice, could nevertheless be a contributing factor towards their apparently lower levels of business capital. The group most likely to invest in let property were those in the catering trades, especially of victualling, inn- and tavern-keeping. In all these trades, it is very difficult to divide insured property or goods into domestic and commercial capital, but sometimes the nature of women's business and the existence of let property obscured all their business capital. In 1845, for example, the Westminster laundress Pauline Barlow insured just £100 of household goods, but these included her mangle and fixtures. Barlow also insured her 'dwelling rooms', which were situated over her washing, mangling and ironing rooms at 11 Wilton Street for another £100, suggesting a fairly modest income. Yet she also rented out another part of No. 11, and nos 11½, 12 and 13, as well as two other properties in two differ-ent streets for £650. That took her total insurance up to £850,[56] which suggests a rather higher standard of living, but none of her insured property could readily be classified as business capital.

Living in rented accommodation and not insuring any other property could be another factor contributing to businesswomen's low levels of insured business capital. Again, renting premises was unlikely to have been confined to women, but given their lower levels of property ownership generally it may have been more common for women. In addition, probably because of the high cost of real estate, rented premises were more common in London policies than in provincial ones. Women living in rented accommodation took out 11 per cent of all London policies in the database and just 2 per cent of provincial policies. With some notable exceptions, the vast majority of these women were small-scale traders, usually taking out policies to cover only household goods and/or stock for less than £500, and nearly three-quarters were under £250. Most rented accommodation throughout the period was occupied by women in the lower ranges of the millinery and dressmaking trades, but in 1845 a number of West End milliners took out substantial insurance, despite

[54] GL, Ms. 11936, 287/433946.
[55] GL, Ms. 11936, 447/830399.
[56] GL, Ms. 11936, 611/150164.

occupying rented accommodation. For example, in that year, Julie Adele Metayer had rented rooms from a tailor in Conduit Street, in which she insured £1,500 of stock, and the same amount again on household goods, which included £300 of insured jewellery.[57] These policies remain the exception rather than the rule, but in 1845 policies insuring the payment of rent also appear for the first time. Mary Ann Druce, a butcher in Hoxton, held a policy for £1,400. Her house at 6 Pitfield Street had a slaughterhouse connected to it, in which she insured £100 of stock and livestock, £135 of household goods, and 'twelve months rent thereon' for £65. Druce stored an additional £50 of stock in a nearby stable in Park Street, but she also insured three other adjoining houses, a warehouse and a workshop in Islington for £850 on which Sun Fire would 'be liable for the payment of rent' during any period the properties became 'untenantable'.[58] However, since the number of insured London women living in rented accommodation did not increase over the period, these changes were probably connected with changes in the perception and practice of insurance.

Most of the businesswomen who rented rooms did so from people in other trades such as perfumers, hatters, engravers, tailors, glovers, booksellers, gold-smiths, carvers, tobacconists, oilmen and smiths. Letting furnished rooms was a bye-industry for many London shopkeepers, but it also reflects the degree of women's integration within the trading community.[59] Occasionally, 'private' persons or gentlemen supplied the rooms, and at least one policy appears to indicate a 'company let' from a firm of fancy marble dealers. In 1845 Wyatt and Parker let 96 New Bond Street to milliners Henrietta Henrie and Christine Taylor, who had a substantial policy for £1,000 including lace stock, business fixtures, pictures and prints.[60] The majority of landlords, where sex was described, were men, but there was occasional evidence of possible 'spinster clustering'.[61] In 1780 Elizabeth Baddeford, a tobacconist in Totnes, Devon, insured £200 of stock in her own dwelling house, but also insured a house, stable and cellar for £300, which she let to Hannah Bagwell, a tallow chandler.[62] Bagwell also had insurance for £200 of stock and £100 of utensils at that address but she described herself as a 'milliner' and tallow chandler.[63]

---

[57] GL, Ms. 11936, 610/1475890.

[58] GL, Ms. 11936, 604/1480807.

[59] George, *London Life*, p. 92; and see Sharpe, 'Dealing with Love', p. 211 on how lace dealer Hester Pinney lodged with professionals, over taverns and coffeehouses, and with customers. Sharpe argues that this residency pattern was 'evidence of her professional commitment'.

[60] GL, Ms. 11936, 607/1475523.

[61] Olwen Hufton, 'Women without Men: Widows and Spinsters in Britain and France in the Eighteenth Century', *Journal of Family History*, winter, (1984), pp. 355–67, found some evidence for groups of two to four working women sharing accommodation and costs.

[62] GL, Ms. 11936, 280/424927.

[63] GL, Ms. 11936, 280/424491.

In 1845 Sarah Collyer, a laundress in Stoke Newington, insured her own house, outbuildings and goods in trust, but no let property. However, at the same time Frances Kennard, a woollen draper, was insuring her stock and household goods at the same address, which was described as the 'dwelling of a laundress', so she may have been sharing the house informally.[64] It seems likely that most insured women in business had high enough incomes not to need to share costs in the same way as female employees in rented accommodation. Business-women were more likely to reside at the same address because they were in partnership together than because of lack of funds, and properties used or inhabited by partnerships were rarely rented.

Other insurance- and capital-reducing measures practised by women in business included storing stock in separate commercial buildings that they did not own. In these cases the buildings or the space were usually rented, either from commercial companies or from other local traders, but both prac-tices required co-operation from dealers of both sexes. Women living outside London were more likely to use commercial premises to store and/or distribute stock in the capital. In 1755, Mary Packer, a clothier living in Gloucester, stored £3,000 of stock in warehouses owned by Mr Brice in London's Blackwell Hall.[65] Similarly, in 1780 Mary Caunter, a sergemaker from Ashburton in Devon, insured £2,600 of stock kept in Spencer's Malt Lofts at London's Hayes Wharf and in another warehouse in Little Winchester Street, London Wall, owned by Green & Co. Several other male sergemakers from Ashburton (one of whom may have been related to Caunter) also kept their stock at the same premises,[66] which suggests that there may have been a degree of local co-operation over the transport and storage of goods at long distances. Such arrangements also meant that it was unnecessary to insure commercial storage space. The majority of businesswomen, however, kept their stock in commer-cial or private property either adjacent to or in the neighbourhood of their main residence, although in many cases this also required the co-operation of other local traders. In 1755 Sarah Goodwin, a victualler in Southwark, insured £300 of household goods, clothes and stock at The Ship Inn, where she lived, but she also insured another £100 of stock kept in a cellar belonging to Mary Wise, a pawnbroker who lived next door.[67] In 1780 Sarah Moscropp, another victualler in Smithfield, insured only £200 of stock that she kept in a salesman's cellar in Rosemary Lane.[68] Cellars may have been the resort of many small dealers of both sexes,[69] but even large businesses kept stock there rather than

[64] GL, Ms. 11936, 609/1480795, 1480796.

[65] GL, Ms. 11936, 109/145306.

[66] GL, Ms. 11936, 283/426305 for Mary Caunter. See also ibid., 426304 (John Caunter); 426301, 302 (George and John Winsor); 426306 (Henry Callard); and 426303 (Richard Prideaux from Tavistock).

[67] GL, Ms. 11936, 113/149566.

[68] GL, Ms. 11936, 289/436933.

[69] See George, London Life, pp. 89–90, on how cellars were the natural resort of small dealers

in purpose-built commercial property. Another policy, also in 1780, reveals that Mary Brittnor was a partner with five men in a large brewery business, which insured £7,000 of stock kept in fourteen different cellars under private and public houses all over London.[70] All these informal arrangements meant that, although stock was insured, storage space very often was not.

Indeed, businesswomen very rarely insured any large-scale separate commercial property. Only one policy described a 'manufactory', and 59 per cent of all insured separate commercial buildings listed in the sample were valued at £100 or less, with 26 per cent valued at £101 to £500.[71] Property used for joint commercial and private purposes, which included inns, taverns, and houses with workshops and warehouses attached, was insured for higher sums. More than 55 per cent of all buildings in this category were valued at £101 to £500, and 10 per cent at £501 to £3,000.[72] However, the total sums of separate and joint commercial property together only come to half the total sums of insured private dwellings, even though a higher percentage of policy holders were insuring commercial buildings. Once again there were significant differences between the insurance of both joint and separate commercial property in London and provincial policies. Table 7.4(b) shows that in the eighteenth century, 51 per cent of provincial policies listing separate commercial buildings and 63 per cent of policies listing joint private and commercial buildings insured that property, whereas for London the respective proportions were 15 per cent and 20 per cent, with correspondingly lower total sums insured in both categories. It is not particularly surprising that women in London insured comparatively small amounts of large-scale commercial property, as there were comparatively few large-scale works or factories in the capital, where high overheads and the need for flexible short production runs, to meet sudden changes in fashion, meant that small-scale specialised domestic production remained the norm.[73] But women were not insuring large-scale commercial property in other eighteenth-century towns either. The higher levels of property insurance in provincial policies was mostly due to the prevalence of insured brew and malthouses and the greater propensity to insure shops and warehouses. Although warehouses were by far the most common form of separate commercial property used by women in London, only about one-third were insured, and none of London's shops, which were the second most frequently listed type of businesswomen's property, were insured.[74] In addition, the London pattern of storing stock in cellars, none of which were insured,

---

whose customers needed access from the street, but they could also range from the meanest storage place to occupied business premises.

[70] GL, Ms. 11936, 284/430347.

[71] N = 157 buildings coded C, but a further 139 were not insured.

[72] N = 106 buildings coded B, but a further 104 were not insured.

[73] Schwarz, *London in the Age of Industrialisation*, pp. 31–3.

[74] The term 'warehouse' could also apply to a form of discount 'shop', so there may be some overlapping of categories.

rarely occurred in provincial policies. Workshops, usually situated behind the main house, were the exception. London may have been the centre of work-shop manufacture,[75] but workshops were equally commonly insured by women in both London and provincial policies, although only for small sums. Thus, for a number of reasons, not all of which were solely to do with gender, women in business were more likely to insure smaller sums of business capital, and in particular smaller sums of fixed capital, than seems to have been the case for men, according to current research.

Risk management: gendered division of property

Since insured businesswomen did own both stock and real property, it is important to consider the gendered division of that property, not least because 'property forms indicate relationships between people mediated by the dis-position and control of things'.[76] Women's role in these relationships has been conceived of as subordinate because of their apparent lack of control over their own property. It has been argued that the common law fiction of coverture upon marriage, combined with more restrictive inheritance practices, and the intervention of male kin controlling 'passive' sources of income such as trusts and annuities, reduced women's ability to control their own property.[77] However, as we have seen, inheritance practices have now been shown to be less restrictive than previously thought, and coverture can no longer be viewed as an impervious barrier to businesswomen's control of their own property. Here, the joint and separate insurance of goods and property by married women and those in mixed- or same-sex partnerships can give a good indication of the means and extent to which women sought to protect or to reduce the risk to their own property.

The very low incidence of recorded marital status means that it is impossible to estimate the exact numbers of married women in trade who insured with Sun Fire. In fact, more wives (eighteen) were recorded in comparison with those listed as spinsters (fifteen), but the common law doctrine of coverture did make it very difficult for wives to insure property solely in their own name. However, this does not mean that wives could not insure their business capital at all, and the few examples of named wives in this survey indicate some of the ways it was possible for them to do so.

---

[75] Green, *From Artisans to Paupers*, p. 26.

[76] Davidoff and Hall, *Family Fortunes*, p. 275, base this argument on the 'social character of property' stressed by Ann Whitehead, 'Kinship and Property: Women and Men, Some Generalisations', in *Women and Property – Women as Property*, ed. R Hirschon (London and New York, 1984), pp. 176–92.

[77] Ibid., p. 277.

First, wives trading within the city of London could claim *feme sole* status and could thus insure property under their own name as if they were single. This was no doubt the case for women like Elizabeth Gosling, a milliner and wife of George Gosling of St James parish, who in 1735 insured £500 of stock that she kept at the Pall Mall house of Aaron Lamb, a broker.[78] Wives who traded on the basis of equitable separate property also appear to have been able to insure it and any additional real property that was designated separate.[79] In 1780 Elizabeth Macpherson, a seamstress married to Duncan Macpherson and living in Westminster, insured £200 of *her* stock and goods in trust, and £100 of *her* clothing. As all this property was designated as being kept in *her* dwelling house, it seems likely the couple were either living in her separate property, or in accommodation paid for out of the profits from her business.[80] In the same year, Alice Trip, wife of Thomas Trip, a grocer and cooper in Lowestoft, insured £600 of shops, a warehouse, cellars and fish houses in one policy, while her husband insured £900 of stock kept in those houses in another policy.[81] As the occupational label was applied to Thomas and not to Alice, it is possible she had been widowed and Thomas had married into the business, but in either case she retained and insured her separate property in the trade.

In addition, it was of course possible for wives to carry on a separate business simply with a husband's stated agreement.[82] There are a few cases in the sample where a wife appears to have been carrying on a separate business, presumably with her husband's agreement, as the policy was in his name; but her assets remain hidden. In 1809 Hippolite Martin, a dancing master in Oxford Street, took out a policy for himself and his unamed wife, a milliner, in which he insured £1,085 of *his* household goods, china and musical instruments kept in *his* dwelling house, but also another £115 of 'stock therein'. Given his profession as a pedagogue and his wife's business as a milliner, the stock-in-trade was very unlikely to have been his.[83] In other cases, the wife appears to have been the dominant partner, even if she was not named and the stock was not specifically designated hers. For example, in 1845 François Fortune Amboise Bailly, of no given occupation and living in Portman Square, took out a policy for himself and his unamed wife, 'a milliner and dressmaker', for £1,250. All the household goods, jewellery, pictures and china were *his* and kept in *his* dwelling but the stock and trade fixtures 'therein', amounting to £798, were

---

[78] GL, Ms. 11936, 43/67897.
[79] Although the policy registers clearly described these women as wives and recorded separate use and insurance of their property, there was no record of it being held 'in trust' for them, which might have been expected under strict legal terms. Either this separate property had been created informally, rather than by an equitable trust, or Sun Fire did not feel it necessary to ascribe strict legal ownership to it.
[80] GL, Ms. 11936, 285/432303.
[81] GL, Ms. 11936, 287/433311 and 433312.
[82] See above, p. 42.
[83] GL, Ms. 11936, 448/828080.

all related to lace.[84] This arrangement uncannily paralleled the stock figures of fun in nineteenth-century novels about milliners, which often depicted the pseudo-French proprietress of a top millinery establishment and her non-working husband or lover.[85] Perhaps the most notable was Dickens' Madame Mantalini in *Nicholas Nickleby* (1838). She was married to a man who had previously subsisted in 'a genteel manner' and then, having been persuaded by his wife to change his name from Muntle to Mantalini, confined 'his share of the labours in the business . . . to spending the money'.[86]

It was not uncommon for women to 'hide' their own trades behind that of their husband, as did the energetic Elizabeth Raffald, cook, proprietor of a confectioner's shop and compiler of *The Manchester Directory for the Year 1772*. Thus the sole entry referring to her business in that directory read 'John Raffald, Seedsman and Confectioner'.[87] Something of this nature may explain the case of Mary Bagley, a 'gardener' in Fulham in 1809 and wife of Richard Bagley.[88] She insured her house and various buildings, including a packing house, warehouse and brewhouse, for £690 plus £450 of household goods and £160 of stock, none of which bore much relation to gardening. Occasionally, however, married couples seem to have had a very egalitarian partnership in trade. John and Mary Pool, married butchers and shopkeepers in Devon, jointly insured everything in 1755, namely, *their* dwelling for £50 and *their* household goods and stock for £150.[89] Thomas Masters, a corn chandler, and his unamed wife, a milliner, had a joint policy for £900 in 1780. He insured £200 of *his* household goods in *his* dwelling house in David Street, London, but they jointly insured £100 of clothes and a further £600 of joint stock-in-trade.[90] On this evidence, it seems that women were contributing far more than just loan capital and business contacts to the family enterprise. The difficulty is in establishing how frequently this occurred, given the rarity with which marital status was recorded. There were probably many more wives in business whose marital status remains hidden. For example, almost half of the 121 mixed-sex partnerships in the sample were with men to whom the women involved were apparently related and it seems reasonable to assume that a fair proportion of these women may also have been married. Moreover, since a husband could not seize the assets of a wife in business with her sister,[91] and 64 per cent of the 122 female-only partnerships were composed of women who were apparently related, it seems likely that a proportion of those same-sex partnerships may also have contained wives whose marital status was unrecorded.

[84] GL, Ms. 11936, 611/1496272.
[85] See below, pp. 239, 245, n. 61.
[86] Charles Dickens, *Nicholas Nickleby* (London, 1838, rep. 1995), pp. 116–17.
[87] Hunt, *Middling Sort*, p. 130 and p. 267, n. 10.
[88] GL, Ms. 11936,448/830150.
[89] GL, Ms. 11936, 111/147036.
[90] GL, Ms. 11936, 287/432942.
[91] See above, pp. 32–3.

In fact it is the different strategies of risk management employed by women in partnerships that provide the strongest evidence of insured businesswomen's ability to retain control of their separate property. Such evidence in partnerships is all the more remarkable given the fact that all partners were considered 'joint-tenants in all the stock and partnership effects'.[92] Under common law, partners had no action against each other in respect of partnership property, but one partner could singly dispose of all partnership property, receive and release debts, and bind all co-partners by contract. Moreover, since there was no limit to liability, all partners were liable to the full extent of their property for all partnership debts.[93] Although equity could mitigate this to some extent,[94] women in business partnerships remained vulnerable to their partners' actions as well as to fluctuating economic fortunes.

The legal position of partners is reflected in the fact that stock-in-trade was almost invariably insured jointly in both same- and mixed-sex partnerships. There were, however, significantly different patterns of separately insured personal goods and buildings between these two different categories of partnership. In same-sex partnerships, 91 per cent of all the 122 policies insured everything jointly, whether or not stock was included.[95] However, in the 121 mixed-sex partnership policies, thirty-six (or 30 per cent) insured separate goods and/or buildings for the man and the woman either within the same policy or by taking out separate policies. Of these thirty-six partnerships, 39 per cent were between men and women who were apparently related. This meant that women retained control of their separate property even within family-based partnerships. Moreover, although most real property was described as joint (whether insured or not), in the 40 per cent of mixed-sex partnerships where it was insured, the buildings were either jointly owned or belonged to the female partner. There were no cases, in these policies, of men insuring sole property. By contrast, only 12 per cent of female same-sex partnerships insured real property at all, which probably reflected the high incidence of such partnerships in the dressmaking and millinery trades, compared to the comparative rarity of such partnerships in the catering trades.

One reason for separate insurance in mixed-sex partnerships was because, in partnerships between mothers and sons or mothers and sons-in-law, widows

---

[92] Watson, *Treatise on the Law of Partnership*, pp. 1–2, stated that this rule applied whether both partners contributed labour and money or each contributed one or the other, but, if the shares were unequal, then each partner's contribution to profit or loss should be adjusted proportionately.

[93] R.R. Formoy, *The Historical Foundations of Modern Company Law* (London, 1923), pp. 32–3.

[94] Ibid. Equity could give partners the right of account against co-partners, and relief against fraud and embezzlement.

[95] Eight per cent of these policies were for schoolmistresses in which no stock was involved. Occasionally partnerships of laundresses, dressmakers and inn-holders also chose not to insure stock.

were likely to retain ownership of the property. In 1735 Ann Corkey, a brasier in Totnes, was in business with her son William and several other unnamed children. She insured her dwelling house for £100 and jointly insured their stock for a further £200.[96] Alternatively some women, particularly if they were in business with a man to whom they were apparently not related, insured separate let property. Frances Kentish and Samuel Haynes were goldsmiths and toy dealers in Cornhill in 1780. They shared a dwelling in which they jointly insured £1,200 of stock and £200 of china and glass, but Haynes separately insured £50 of clothes and Kentish £550 of household goods and clothes. Yet Frances Kentish also had a totally separate policy in her own name, insuring ten let properties for £1,100, which would have provided her with a substantial additional income, or a safety net if the partnership did not flourish.[97]

In mixed-sex partnerships, household goods were the category most likely to be separately insured by business partners whether or not they lived in the same house. Again, one of the reasons for separate insurance of this kind may have been because a significant proportion (59 per cent of women in mixed-sex partnerships) were in business with men (see Table 6.7) to whom they were not obviously related. Mary Hewett and Richard Halford were grocers and dealers in wine, food and oil in Spitalfields in 1780 but they lived apart. Their joint stock worth £700 was kept at his house in Lamb Street, where he also insured £300 of household goods and clothes, but they also jointly insured another £1,000 of stock, kept in a cellar under the premises of Greaves and Hacters, silkweavers in Browns Lane. Mary Hewett lived near Halford's house in Red Lion Street, in apartments which she rented from a gentleman. In her house, she insured £200 of household goods and clothes, which was slightly less than the equivalent insured by Halford.[98] Other partners cohabited but still insured personal possessions separately or remained semi-autonomous by living separately but in adjoining houses. Ann Peters and John Dore were dyers living at nos 42 and 43 Brick Lane, London. In 1809 they took out a joint policy for £3,000. They jointly insured their dwelling house, 'being two houses with dye house & lofts all communicating', for £410, plus another drying room and £1,850 of stock kept there. However, they apparently lived separately within this arrangement, because Ann Peters insured £100 of personal goods in No. 42, and John Dore insured £200 of personal goods in No. 43. Yet, despite this evidence of autonomy, both partners also jointly insured two more adjoining houses that were let out to tenants.[99]

In 1845, there seems to have been a change in the nature of many of the mixed-sex partnerships with separate insurance, in comparison with earlier years. Forty-one per cent of the twenty-nine mixed-sex partnership insurance

[96] GL, Ms. 11936, 42/66425.
[97] GL, Ms. 11936, 284/430735.
[98] GL, Ms. 11936, 287/435503.
[99] GL, Ms. 11936, 446/825927.

policies in 1845 were for women in a named trade, insuring real property with a man or men, usually of the rank of gentleman, or Esq., but not in any form of trade. These men may have been simply landlords or they may also have been effectively acting as 'sleeping partners'. They do not appear to have had any financial interest in the business, and the businesswomen concerned often took out separate policies to insure their own stock and/or household goods, or had it described as their 'sole property' within the policy. For example, Mary Stone, a grocer and cheesemonger in Holborn, jointly insured her dwelling house with Samuel Page for £1,500, but she took out a separate policy to insure her stock for £1,250 and £400 of household goods.[100] The existence of 'dormant partners' who invested in businesses but did not perform any other trading function and whose names did not appear as co-partners was acknowledged in the eighteenth century, but such sleeping partners still remained fully liable if discovered.[101] Since most tenanted property insured by the owner in this sample listed only the occupations and/or surnames of the tenants in a single policy, it is quite possible that this form of separate insurance in joint names meant that some property owners 'helped' their commercial tenants pay insurance premiums. If the owner expected some hidden share of the profits in return, any business stock would have had to be insured separately or not at all in order to avoid liability for the business' debts. Regardless of whether they were 'sleeping partners' or merely landlords, female property owners could also act in the same way for both male and female traders. Elizabeth Eichoff jointly insured a £1,000 dwelling house, with a communicating warehouse and stable, with Ann Moss, a tallow chandler, and 'oil and colour man' [sic]. Moss also took out a separate policy to insure her £900 of stock and £100 of household goods.[102] These policies, which were never for less than £500 on a property and frequently for more, provide one example of how women could get around the rising costs of owning and/or insuring expensive London real estate and another instance of mixed-sex economic co-operation.

Conclusion

To treat women in business as a homogeneous group is in itself a risky business, as is an unproblematic acceptance of policy values as an accurate representation of their business capital. This capital was frequently obscured by the

[100] GL., Ms. 11936, 603/1492146.
[101] Watson, *Treatise of the Law of Partnership*, pp. 61–2, 73–4. John Saville, 'Sleeping Partnership and Limited Liability, 1850–6', *Economic History Review*, 2 ser., 8 (1956), pp. 418–33, notes that there were attempts to introduce the French style of sleeping partnerships (en commandite) in the early nineteenth century, but these failed, so there was no legal protection for investors until the Limited Liability Act of 1855.
[102] GL, Ms. 11936, 606/1489115, 1489116; and see GL, Ms. 11936, 612/1496696 in which Penelope Lindsey and Elizabeth Moore insured a tavern in Hoxton for two male victuallers.

nature of their economic activity, by patterns of property ownership and usage, by marital status, and by the different strategies of risk management. However, Sun Fire policy registers do show that women owned and insured significant amounts of stock and real property as well as personal goods, and that the trades in which female policy holders were engaged were at least as important in determining their strategies of insurance as their gender. Women's dominance in 'feminine' or 'domestic trades' did not mean that those businesses were conducted in the same way, as the comparison of catering and clothing trades revealed; nor were 'feminine' trades necessarily undercapitalised or insignificant. There was great variation in the size of businesses in any one trade and, in fact, although the majority remained small, it was these 'feminine' trades that provided the greatest potential for capital accumulation. Nevertheless, although there was no decline in the size of women's insured businesses, there was also not the same expansion in the higher levels of trade, and women did not insure any large-scale commercial property. For businesswomen there was very little separation of home and work during the period, particularly since their dwelling houses remained the prime site of business.

At the same time, these policies confirm the earlier picture that women were well integrated into the trading community and seem to have remained so even in the nineteenth century. The ownership of let property was almost certainly a form of portfolio diversification and hence an effective risk management strategy for women in both small and larger scale businesses, rather than a means to retire from the marketplace. Businesswomen often lived and worked in premises rented from other tradesmen and stored stock in other traders' houses and cellars or shared the cost of warehouse storage. Men and women co-operated in business partnerships and both sexes effectively 'invested' in women's businesses as landlords or sleeping partners. However, although the majority of partnerships of both sexes shared joint insurance for all their stock and effects, women in mixed-sex partnerships were more likely than those in same-sex partnerships to maintain control of their own property by insuring it separately, even where family relationships apparently existed.

Part III

Representation

8

'The Bonaparte of her day'?

Gender, trade and nationalism

Madame Lanchester. Certainly she well understood her business, was tolerably handsome, unlike a French Woman, and possessed *em bon point* – also unlike the French; but . . . all conspired to pronounce her *Madame Lanshestre*; and so she lived, and published and dictated several years; and so she died, commercially. She was the Bonaparte of her day in dress, as he in dressing his ranks: none stood before her undismayed for years.

The Complete Book of Trades (1837)[1]

In the preceding chapters we have seen that, despite legal and institutional impediments, significant numbers of women at every stage of their lifecycle were in business in a wide variety of different trades. Moreover, many of these women conducted their business as well-integrated members of local trading communities. Nevertheless, one of the strongest arguments against the possibility of women trading in this way has been the existence of a huge body of didactic literature prescribing domestic felicity as the pinnacle of female ambition. In addition to the great weight historians have placed on the impact of such literature,[2] considerable emphasis has also been placed on the hostile and often overtly misogynous nature of literature in which representations of women in business do exist.[3] In apparently gender-neutral studies of changing literary perceptions of trade and commerce, businesswomen are conspicuous only by their absence.[4] Women's discursive displacement has

---

[1] N. Whittock *et al.*, *The Complete Book of Trades, or the Parent's Guide and Youth's Instructor Forming a Popular Encyclopaedia of Trades, Manufactures and Commerce . . .* (London, 1837), p. 310.
[2] See above, p. 10, n. 48.
[3] Elizabeth Kowaleski-Wallace, *Consuming Subjects: Women, Shopping, and Business in the Eighteenth Century* (New York, 1997), pp. 111–28; J.G. Turner, '"News from the New Exchange" Commodity, Erotic Fantasy, and the Female Entrepreneur', in *The Consumption of Culture, 1600–1800* (1995), ed. Ann Bermingham and John Brewer, pp. 419–39; Laura Mandell, *Misogynous Economies: The Business of Literature in Eighteenth-century Britain* (Lexington, 1999), pp. 64–86.
[4] James Raven, *Judging New Wealth: Popular Publishing and Responses to Commerce in England, 1750–1800* (Oxford, 1992); John McVeagh, *Tradeful Merchants: The Portrayal of the Capitalist in Literature* (London, 1981).

175

thus been tied to their actual displacement from the world of commerce in narratives describing the formation of gendered separate spheres.[5] Yet this direct association is clearly problematic and the extent to which didactic literature could actually impact upon women's daily lives has now begun to be questioned.[6] Thus the chief aim of this chapter and the two that follow is to widen the debate about representations of women's role in business beyond the limits imposed by the exclusive use of the public/private dichotomy as an analytical tool.

The preoccupation with the language of separate spheres may, as Amanda Vickery has argued, have obscured other languages in use.[7] Indeed, in *Family Fortunes*, Davidoff and Hall pointed out that their study of the role of domestic ideology in class formation highlighted just '*one* set of voices from the men and women who struggled to shape and define the ongoing question of relations between the classes and the sexes'.[8] Since contemporaries continued to use the language of 'public' and 'private' in both the eighteenth and nineteenth centuries, the intention here is not to abandon the concept altogether but to stress its contingency and, more importantly, to consider other voices and other languages used to discuss women and trade. Thus the focus is on how gender operated in conjunction with or in opposition to other categories of economic, racial or class-based difference. All three were present in many different and often competing discourses in the eighteenth century which, as John Bonell has argued, was characterised by 'the hybridity of the discursive formations . . . and the mobility with which different discourses and interests seem to change partners'.[9] However, as we shall see in Chapter 10, this kind of discursive fluidity was equally evident in the nineteenth century.

In the eighteenth century, complex contemporary anxieties about effeminacy, luxury, profit, foreign competition and social mobility all impacted upon representations of women in business; and ambivalence towards businesswomen in luxury trades was particularly common. By studying the representation of women in contemporary literature and satirical prints, including gendered articulations of trade disputes, pamphlets, advertisements, letters, autobiographies and the proceedings of patriotic societies, the analysis in this chapter focuses on three main areas. First, it examines concepts of gender and class in trade disputes concerning women, foreign imports and luxury goods. Second, a case study of milliners and coffee-women forms the basis for a discussion about misogynistic sexualised images of women in 'feminine' trades. This highlights the social and economic anxieties surrounding social mobility, profit and the consumption of luxury goods. Finally, new evidence shows that during the eighteenth century there was also a language of praise available for women

[5] Kowaleski-Wallace, *Consuming Subjects*, p. 113.
[6] Shoemaker, *Gender in English Society*, pp. 57–8; Hunt, *Middling Sort*, p. 94.
[7] Vickery, 'Golden Age to Separate Spheres', p. 401.
[8] Davidoff and Hall, *Family Fortunes*, p. 454 (emphasis added).
[9] John Bonell, *The Birth of Pandora and the Division of Knowledge* (1992), p. xvi.

in business within patriotic discourses, through which even women themselves could express pride in their 'commercial' achievements. Paradoxically, therefore, nationalism could be seen as both supportive of female enterprise and its scourge: women in business could be Britannia's allies or Bonaparte's secret agents.

Gender in dispute

This section begins by examining disputes over the position of women in the most genteel of feminine trades, millinery and mantua making. In these debates issues of class and those of economic necessity remained in tension with one another, but in many cases discussion was framed within the context of French commercial competition. The eighteenth century has been characterised as a period during which a distinctively British sense of national identity was actively forged.[10] In particular, this emerging national identity was formed by and through the construction of an alien 'other', which, although broad enough to include all foreigners, was most specifically defined as French. Hostility between England and France was engendered by lengthy wars and colonial/ trade rivalry between 1689 and 1815. Moreover, the English aristocracy in particular displayed a passion for French imported luxury goods, manners and language, which meant that elements of class antagonism were also built into this mutually fascinated but hostile relationship. Numerous contemporary authors therefore feared that the influence of French culture and luxurious fashions could only lead to cultural disintegration, the emasculation of English men and the degeneration of national character and virtue.[11] Much discussion about luxury trades, and millinery in particular, was therefore framed within the context of French commercial competition and the need to keep the British army supplied with fit men.

Despite the long-term association of women with needlework, the dressmaking trades were not originally in female hands, and the movement of women into the previously male preserve of tailoring caused a great deal of hostility. During the sixteenth and most of the seventeenth century, outer garments for men and women of all ranks had been made by male tailors who were regulated by guilds. As the fashion for structured clothing changed towards the looser-fitting, unstructured mantua dress for women, male 'seamsters' began to be replaced by female 'mantua makers'.[12] The guilds fought

---

[10] Linda Colley, *Britons: Forging the Nation, 1707–1837* (London, 1992); Gerald Newman, *The Rise of English Nationalism, 1740–1830* (London, 1987).

[11] Ibid., pp. 67–73; Colley, *Britons*, p. 88.

[12] Madelaine Ginsburg, 'The Tailoring and Dressmaking Trades, 1700–1850', *Costume*, 6 (1972), p. 64; Prior, 'Women and the Urban Economy', p. 111; Styles, 'Clothing the North', pp. 152–3.

hard to prevent women from entering these trades and were prosecuting 'pretended milliners' in Oxford from as early as 1668. In 1702 they pressed other towns for support to move for an Act of Parliament to suppress female mantua makers. Similar pressure was exerted by northern guilds in York, Ripon, Wakefield, Hull, Newcastle and Pontefract in the 1690s. All these efforts were unsuccessful. The York merchant tailors began accepting women in 1704 and Styles notes that female mantua makers were widespread even in rural areas by the 1780s. Prior argues that guild hostility in Oxford continued longer, into the 1770s and 1780s.[13] However, by 1760, in London at least, the traditional position was reversed, and public opinion began to be overtly hostile towards men in what were now regarded as properly 'feminine' trades.

In the capital, this change of opinion is perhaps first evident in the *London Courant's* announcement of April 1760, that the Female Parliament of the University of Rational Amusement, a debating society, was discussing 'Male encroachments on Female Occupations . . . which ought to be remedied by a restrictive law'.[14] In the 1780s it became a more popular topic for debating societies. In 1781 La Belle Assemblee proposed taxing all male milliners and male mantua makers, as well as 'French Dancers, French Frizeurs, French Cooks, French Milliners and French Fashion Mongers'.[15] In 1786, another group, the New Westminster Forum, discussed taxes on male milliners and debated 'Which is the most ridiculous Character, A Man Milliner or a Military Fop?'[16] By the 1780s, then, the feminisation of the trade was so complete that men working in it were seen as effeminate and contaminated by French mannerisms. In 1787 *The Times* linked the issue of female underemployment with the issue of 'unmanly delicacy' and suggested that the solution to both was military recruitment. The paper declared that it would have been 'a most acceptable service to the public' if only 'the press gangs had swept away all the men-milliners, men-mantua-makers, and men-stay-makers, (not forgetting a considerable number of nominal hair-dressers) and put them on board his Majesty's ships'.[17] Male milliners continued to work in the trade, despite these attacks, but the making of female clothes, which had previously belonged within the male preserve of tailoring, had been reconstructed as ideally feminine.

---

[13] Ibid., p. 152; Prior, 'Women and the Urban Economy', pp. 111–13. But see Vanessa Harding, 'Reformation and Culture, 1540–1700', ed. Peter Clark, *The Cambridge Urban History of Britain, Vol. 2: 1540–1840* (Cambridge, 2000), p. 284, on how guilds gradually lost control of urban economic life.

[14] *London Courant*, 28 April 1760, cited in Donna T. Andrew, *London Debating Societies, 1776–99* (London, 1994), p. 95. I am grateful to Hannah Greig for drawing my attention to these debating society references.

[15] *Morning Herald*, 9 March 1781, cited in ibid., p. 133.

[16] *Morning Herald*, 10 April and 6 March 1786, cited in ibid., pp. 179, 182.

[17] *The Times*, 25 October 1787, p. 2, col. D.

Constructing certain trades as newly feminine also necessitated redefining acceptable forms of masculinity, particularly since a love of French style and the desire for imported luxury goods were believed to be damaging the nation's economic and military strength. Michele Cohen argues that effeminacy became a dominant metaphor for signifying 'problematic gender boundaries for men' in the eighteenth century, and that it was either 'conflated with luxury or viewed as its inevitable consequence'.[18] 'Luxury' was a protean term used to critique many perceived social ills.[19] In much eighteenth-century literature, luxury was also one of several 'potentially emasculating allegorical female figures of disorder' which highlighted the subordination of increasingly feminised economic man to his desires.[20] But luxury and effeminacy commonly denoted an individual and national moral degeneracy, which sapped masculine strength and martial valour and thus patriotic virtue. Manly virtue was thus undermined both by submission to female charms and by the desire for conspicuous consumption.[21] As we shall see,[22] eighteenth-century representations of female milliners most commonly show them using sexual charms to sell luxury goods to fashionably elite males. Moreover, it was French styles that attracted their most lucrative customers. London milliners often advertised their return from Paris with the latest goods. For example, in 1755 Ann Perrin advertised herself as a 'French Milliner' and advised customers of both her Bath and London shops that she had recently returned from Paris with the latest fashions.[23] The larger establishments kept agents in Paris and many proprietors changed their names to sound more French. The famous dressmaker, Madam Lanchester, cited above,[24] had been plain Mrs John Lancaster from Salford, until her return from Paris in 1807. French-speaking shop assistants were additionally desirable.[25] Indeed, hostility towards *faux* French milliners was still evident in the mid-nineteenth century.[26]

---

[18] Cohen, *Fashioning Masculinity*, p. 5.

[19] John Sekora, *Luxury: The Concept in Western Thought, Eden to Smollet* (London, 1977), pp. 2–9, 74.

[20] See Catherine Ingrassia, *Authorship, Commerce, and Gender in Early Eighteenth-century England: A Culture of Paper Credit* (Cambridge, 1998), pp. 3, 24–7. Other 'iconographic female figures associated with the financial revolution, pleasure and business included Credit, Fortune, Oceana and the Lady of the South Sea', all of which, as Ingrassia points out, 'derive pleasure from their sexual and economic seduction of men desirous of their physical and financial charms'.

[21] Bonell, *The Birth of Pandora*, p. 65.

[22] See below, pp. 188–91.

[23] Ann Perrin advertised regularly in the London *Daily Advertiser* in April and May 1755 and in the *Bath Advertiser* on at least one occasion on 18 October 1755. For Perrin's Bath connection, see Peter Borsay, 'The London Connection: Cultural Diffusion and the Eighteenth-century Provincial Town', *London Journal*, 19 (1994), pp. 28–9.

[24] See above, p. 175; and *Complete Book of Trades*, p. 310.

[25] London *Daily Advertiser*, 3 July 1755: a millinery business sought 'a Woman that can speak French well'.

[26] See p. 239.

Figure 8.1 Louis Philippe Boitard, *The Imports of Great Britain from France* (1757)

Source: Courtesy of the Guildhall Library, Corporation of London

Selling fashionable merchandise in the French style thus raised profits for milliners but it caused great anxiety about the effects of foreign luxury goods. There was also concern about the economic effects of importing French millinery. In 1757 a satirical print, 'The Imports of Great Britain from France' (Figure 8.1), pictured ships disgorging French goods including millinery wares, and landing 'swarms of Milliners, Taylors, Mantua Makers, Frisers, Tutors for Boarding Schools . . . &c.'. The print was addressed to the patriotic societies, who promoted 'British' women's manufactures.[27] In 1786 debate was sharpened by negotiations over the Anglo–French commercial treaty. A *Times* editorial complained that millinery goods were to be admitted at just 12 per cent duty, which would 'undoubtedly deprive a number of unfortunate females of the means of existence'.[28] French millinery goods or 'modes' were one of the most hotly contested areas of negotiation because of their popularity in London.[29] The British feared that a general admission of silk modes would

[27] See pp. 195–201.
[28] *The Times*, 2 November 1786, p. 2, col. A. With thanks to John Styles for these references.
[29] Marie Donaghay, 'Textiles and the Anglo French Commercial Treaty of 1786', *Textile History*, 13 (1982), pp. 205–24.

provoke popular protests and annihilate British production, but the French threat to exclude British silk gauze and to raise the duty on cotton and wool led to an eventual compromise.[30]

The Times suggested that the best way to preserve the millinery trade for 'English' women would be to exclude men from the trade or to allow them to practise only under a heavy licence. In a prefiguring of nineteenth-century anxieties, the paper argued that failure to do this would result in increased prostitution, and suggested that one answer would be for aristocratic women to refuse to be served by men.[31] Aristocratic women were also attacked for patronising 'French' milliners and dressmakers, and thus depriving honest 'English' women of an income. For example, in *The English Lady's Catechism*, Lady Vanity was questioned about her beliefs:

Who were your Godfathers and Godmothers?
The Mercer, Laceman, Sempstress and the Milliner.

Who confirm'd you?
Mademoiselle the French Mantuamaker. . . .

Why will you give a French woman three guineas, when an English woman will
   do it full as well if not better?
Only for the name of having it made by another Lady of Quality, who made my
   Mantua? I say in the French tone, Mademoiselle the French Mantuamaker.[32]

There was thus a degree of ambiguity within debates about milliners. On the one hand, it was acknowledged to be a lucrative trade and, if carried out by proper 'English' women, it could also be seen as a source of national pride that the French had been beaten at their own game. In 1837 *The Complete Book of Trades* may have lampooned Mrs Lancaster's wholesale adoption of a French identity to promote her business, but it also celebrated the fact that England now had 'fashion, and taste and whim enough of our own' plus 'a little to spare for exportation to those immense transatlantic possessions'.[33] Indeed, the manual claimed that English dressmakers, lace makers and drapers provided 'further proof of our having supplanted our rivals in trade'. On the other hand, since successful 'English' milliners often spoke French, adopted French names and sold French fashions to effeminate aristocrats, milliners and their customers were equally guilty of propagating the French disease of luxury. French women were constructed as the antithesis of the proper English lady, and were seen as dangerously eloquent and seductive with an appetite for admiration that

[30] Ibid., pp. 210–14.
[31] *The Times*, 2 November 1786, p. 2, col. A; 15 November 1788, p. 2, col. C.
[32] Anon., *The English Lady's Catechism, Shewing The Pride and Vanity of the English Nobility As Are Notorious for Relieving Foreigners, Before their own Country Folks* (n.d., 17..?).
[33] Whittock, *Complete Book of Trades*, pp. 308–9, and see above, p. 175.

Sal Dab giving, Monsieur a Reciept in full.

Figure 8.2 *Sal Dab Giving Monsieur a Receipt in Full* (1776)

Source: Courtesy of the Trustees of the British Museum

remained unchecked in their native country. Hence Cohen argues that 'the construction of French women as other can be said to have served the same purpose and have been as much of a fiction as French politeness and effeminated French men: it forged and emphasized national difference.'[34] In graphic satire the British antithesis to French effeminacy was often a Billingsgate fishwoman (Figure 8.2),[35] a female trader to whom no connotations of luxury were attached. To highlight French male weakness, the fishwoman was depicted displaying masculine aggression, but the sign above the alehouse suggested that she was still a 'Good Woman'. For the satirical images of the fishwoman and milliner to succeed, their presence must have been ubiquitous, and hostility towards the latter's adoption of French manners to sell their goods is also evidence of the success of such efforts. Indeed, the proprietors of girls' boarding-schools suffered not dissimilar hostility, but as Mrs Frances Broadhurst remarked in 1826:

> Much has been written against ladies' schools, and nothing, as far as I am aware has been said in reply to such accusations: because, in spite of all the invective, they continue to flourish.[36]

Discourses around the sale and consumption of luxury French goods linked hostility to foreign competition with fears of male effeminacy and the loss of suitable occupations for genteel women. For women raised to become 'proper ladies' to be able to work in feminine trades, men and the masculine were constructed as alien to those trades. In 1739 an anonymous 'Lady' wrote to the *Gentleman's Magazine* lamenting that the daughters of most gentlemen and tradesmen (of the more prosperous ranks) were poorly educated for real life.[37] Daughters whose parents could leave them only less than £1,000 a year should be apprenticed to 'genteel and easy Trades, such as Linnen or Woollen Drapers, Haberdashers of small Wares, Mercers, Glovers, Perfumers, Grocers, Confectioners, Retailers of Gold and Silver Lace, Buttons etc.'. In fact, most of these were trades that women in London did pursue (as the insurance registers show). Yet in the 1730s, as the 'Lady' argued, many commentators did not think these occupations were 'as creditable trades for the Daughters of Gentlemen as they are for their sons'. Hence she declared that it was 'ridiculous to see a Parcel of Young Fellows, dish'd out in their Tie Wigs and Ruffles . . . busied in Professions so much below the Honour and Dignity of their Sex'.[38] By the 1780s *The Times* was suggesting that the repeal of the shop tax should

---

[34] Cohen, *Fashioning Masculinity*, p. 77.

[35] See also e.g. *Billingsgate Triumphant: Or, Poll Dab No Match for the Frenchman* (n.d., 17..?).

[36] Frances Broadhurst, *A Word in Favor of Female Schools: Addressed to Parents, Guardians, and the Public at Large* (1826), cited in Skedd, 'Women Teachers and the Expansion of Girls' Schooling', p. 125.

[37] *Gentleman's Magazine* (1739), Vol. 9, pp. 525–6.

[38] Ibid., p. 525.

be replaced by a tax 'on all Men Milliners, Men Mercers, or Men Perfumers' in order to open those occupations solely to 'virtuous and deserving young women'.[39] There was therefore considerable pressure to open up more occupations to women, even if these were only of a type now characterised as exclusively feminine because of their associations with luxury goods.

A study of one polemical woman writer on the subject shows that male competition may have been a factor in the difficulties some women found when looking for employment, but that rank or class could be an even more important factor than gender inequality. Women, of 'genteel education or delicate constitutions', were the subject of Mary Ann Radcliffe's work, *The Female Advocate; Or, An Attempt to Recover the Rights of Women from Male Usurpation* (1799). Radcliffe claimed to have actually written the work seven years earlier, and many of her arguments were very similar to those proclaimed by *The Times* in the 1780s. Radcliffe's work has been seen as a proto-feminist cry for the rights of women to work, but it was specifically written on behalf of the 'unfortunate woman who has seen better days', rather than aimed at the sex as a whole.[40] It was also a plea for a return to a more traditional gender order, when men could hold the 'honourable title of MAN', at a time when 'manufactures and commerce were not so extensive' and thus shared the anxiety of many contemporaries about the emasculating effects of commercial expansion.

Although Radcliffe was concerned about economic expansion and female vulnerability, her 1810 autobiography strongly suggests that *The Female Advocate* also drew upon personal experience. Radcliffe had enjoyed a leisured lifestyle, living with her mother in lodgings in Grosvenor Square, before making an unwise marriage to a man whose business failed. When their money ran out, a friend gave her an introduction to a millinery establishment:

> saying her recommendation would give great weight, and she knew a superintendent was wanted, and in time no doubt I might have a share in the business. Accordingly, elated with high expectations, I applied; but Mrs —— finding I had not been regularly taught the business, informed me I could not possibly be admitted to superintend. I then offered myself as an assistant in the making up department . . . but was informed by the lady that she always took apprentices for that part of the business. I then asked her if I could not fill a place behind the counter; but was quite shocked to learn, *they were filled by men!*[41]

Mrs Radcliffe's problem was thus not that she was a woman unable to work, but that her genteel upbringing had not trained her for business. The female

---

[39] *The Times*, 7 April 1789, p. 3, col. C; see also ibid., 7 July 1789, p. 3, col. B.
[40] Mary Ann Radcliffe, *The Female Advocate; Or, An Attempt to Recover the Rights of Women from Male Usurpation* (London, 1799), pp. 32, 76.
[41] Radcliffe, *The Memoirs of Mrs Mary Ann Radcliffe, In Familiar Letters to her Female Friend* (Edinburgh, 1810).

owner of the millinery business, however, obviously employed both men and women and favoured experience over rank or gender. After several years as a governess and then running a boarding-house, Radcliffe was again obliged to seek other employment but once more found her position in society an obstacle. She could not mix with those of her original rank because of her 'contracted circumstances', and could not conceive of mixing with the lower orders at all. Even worse, for 'the middle ranks, such as respectable trades people, from my not having any connections in trade, I was either considered too high, or too useless for their society'.[42] Yet from this experience she concluded that *all* unprotected females were the most pitiful objects on Earth, rather than just those of her own rank.

Even allowing for a degree of self-promotion in her memoirs, Mrs Radcliffe eventually proved far from helpless. She set up a shop selling patent medicines with her children and, when that failed, returned to governessing for a Quaker family, who later employed her in their shoe warehouse in Oxford Street. This shoe shop was run in partnership, and initially the partner's son expressed an 'utter aversion to being under female government', but 'good breeding' and the intervention of his sister led to a more civil relationship, which eventually 'grew to real friendship'.[43] Mrs Radcliffe ran the business until one partner left and the Quakers went bankrupt, whereupon she made a deal with the assignees, who gave her the lease of the shop as an expression of their confidence in her abilities. As sole proprietor, she dismissed her male employee in favour of a female friend and the two women continued in business together. Thus, the failure to set up in business as a milliner may have caused Mrs Radcliffe a great deal of hardship but it certainly did not reduce her to prostitution, which was the only alternative presented in most debates about lack of economic opportunities for women. Moreover, it was not the employment of men in feminine trades that had first prevented her from entering business. Indeed, the male hostility she encountered appears to have been minimal. Both her business partners were male and she was offered the job as manager above one of the partner's sons, who later overcame his understandable jealousy to become a friend. The assignees who expressed confidence in her abilities would also almost certainly have been male. Mrs Radcliffe's biggest disadvantage was her initial lack of business experience due to her social rank. Yet her social position conferred the means and education to raise awareness of her situation, which she presented as generic to all women.

As we have seen, gender could become a central theme around which debates about the proper practice of certain trades were organised. Yet it was also not uncommon for women to combine with men in the same trade to protest during trade disputes, but these women were almost certainly not of the genteel and delicate kind. From August to November 1745 the 'Journeymen

---

[42] Ibid., p. 188.
[43] Ibid., pp. 370–1.

and Women Tobacco-pipe makers of the Cities of London and Westminster' advertised repeatedly to get the support of masters of taverns, alehouses, coffee-houses and the public in a dispute over a new type of 'mark'd pipe'. Their chief grievance was that 'a great many Women are in Want of Business that were always brought up in it', because there was less work involved to make 'that Sort of Pipes'.[44] Meetings were held each Wednesday in Southwark and, as the campaign showed signs of success, they continued to meet and to advertise regularly. Perhaps the chief difference between these women and the milliners was that the pipe makers stated that they were 'always brought up in' the trade and came from a network of trading families. In the late seventeenth century, fan makers of both sexes had similarly played the 'family' card when their trade was threatened by imported fans from the East Indies, and numerous women signed the agreement to get the trade incorporated, again in an attempt at solidarity against foreign imports.[45]

Thus although traditional guilds undoubtedly practised gender exclusion, cross-gender alliances were also important to the practice and language of disputes. When women were included, it was not then made a matter of surprise or comment but a matter of course. In such battles, gendered, racial and class-based hierarchies of difference were constructed and deployed – sometimes in partnership and sometimes in conflict with each other. The articulation of businesswomen's interests sometimes required a display of gender solidarity in the face of foreign competition but at others rested on the expulsion of the masculine from newly feminised trades. Yet, as we shall see, it has been far more commonly argued that the construction of a masculine sphere of business necessitated the wholesale expulsion of the feminine.

Desire and profit

A number of historians have argued that the figure of the whore was one of the most common representations of women in business, and this is usually taken as an expression of hostility towards women's sexuality and their presence in business. Yet a closer examination of many texts reveals a deep ambivalence towards women's commercial activities, which conflated and confused desire for luxury goods with desire for the women that sold them; and anxieties about social mobility with the pursuit of profit. Even where businesswomen were portrayed as whores, these were often accompanied by detailed descriptions of their means of acquiring considerable profits. Moreover, sexualised images

---

[44] London *Daily Advertiser*, 19 August 1745, repeated 24 August.

[45] Anon., *The Fann-Makers Grievance, by the Importation of Fanns from the East Indies* (n.d., 1690s?). An equity case over attempts to get the trade incorporated to prevent the importation of 'foreign wrought fans' started in 1713. PRO C6/410/4 names sixty-eight women who had signed the incorporation agreement.

of women could often be found contrasted with those of idealised femininity within the same trade. This practice of contrasting an ideal form with an abject 'other' was a common rhetorical device used to expel undesirable elements without necessarily condemning the whole.

Late seventeenth-century female traders in the New Exchange, selling luxury goods such as millinery, jewellery, china, embroidered silks and books, were satirised and eroticised in libertine pamphlets such as *The Ape-Gentlewoman, or Character of an Exchange-wench* (1675).[46] There were also sexually subversive representations of coffee-women, particularly in the 'whore's biographies' of Moll King (1747) and Ann Rochford, the notorious *Velvet Coffee-woman* (1728).[47] Kowaleski-Wallace has further argued that women in business were reduced to bawds in the early eighteenth-century works of Bernard Mandeville, the playwright George Lillo, and even Robert Campbell, author of *The London Tradesman* (1747).[48] She maintains that 'in the shift to industrial capitalism this perception of women as the body was crucial to the creation of what is commonly called the separate spheres'.[49] Sexual, often misogynistic representations of women in business were the darker side of the idealised proper lady, but both images were, according to this argument, aimed at removing women from the public sphere of business. However, tying discursive and economic agency too closely together is problematic for a number of reasons, not least because of the nature of the sources used. First, popular literature of any kind was itself a commodity which sold all the more readily with the addition of sexual innuendo. Moreover, even trade manuals merged and colluded with the texts of scandalous pamphlets, so that citing either as evidence of 'non-phantasmic reality' is highly problematic.[50] Second, misogynous representations can serve a variety of functions, none of which are necessarily directly linked to their real world referents. Indeed, as Laura Mandell has argued, such representations were frequently not about women per se but 'rather about society: representations that inspire hatred of and disgust with the female body provide a place for people to work out passionate feelings about changes in economic and social structure.'[51]

Contrasting an ideal form with an abject 'other' was not a specifically gendered way to condemn undesirable elements of commerce. Particularly in

---

[46] Turner, 'News from the New Exchange', p. 422. See also numerous contemporary references to the flirtatious, sexualised nature of women selling luxury goods in the Exchanges and Burlington Arcade cited by Alison Adburgham, *Shopping in Style: London from the Restoration to Edwardian Elegance* (London, 1979), pp. 15, 18, 21, 10.

[47] Markman Ellis, 'The Coffee-women, *The Spectator* and the Public Sphere in the Early Eighteenth Century', in *Women and the Public Sphere*, ed. E. Eger and C. Grant (Cambridge, 2001), pp. 27–52.

[48] Kowaleski-Wallace, *Consuming Subjects*, pp. 111–28.

[49] Ibid., p. 148.

[50] Turner, 'News from the New Exchange', p. 428.

[51] Mandell, *Misogynous Economies*, p. 1.

the later eighteenth century, male merchants were equally subject to satirical attacks. Mandell has argued that the early idealisation of male traders necessitated the abjection of the feminine from the world of business in order to expel all that threatened its ideal status.[52] Certainly, many of the texts cited by those historians, who emphasise negative images of women in business, were written in the first half of the century.[53] However, after about 1750 the earlier representations of heroic male merchant figures, by authors such as Defoe and Lillo, gave way to 'an army of caricatures' from vulgar petty traders to *nouveaux riches* merchants and, later, northern manufacturers.[54] Indeed, some of their fiercest critics were female authors. For example, Anna Gommershall of Leeds (1750–1835) was one of about fifty women who condemned avaricious parvenu tradesmen, usually by creating an ideal gentleman merchant in whom inbred class refinement was combined with a strong ethical business sense.[55] Hence good breeding, rather than the expulsion of the feminine, could mitigate the possible evils caused by the unregulated pursuit of profit in such narratives.

Anxieties about issues of class and social mobility were particularly evident in literature concerning the millinery business. Selling millinery enabled attractive girls from the ranks of the lower middling sort to dress in fashionable clothes and to mix with aristocratic men, so for many it was thus an aspirational ideal. In Eliza Heywood's *History of Betsy Thoughtless* (1751), Betsy's orphaned god-daughter is looked after by the poor but honest Mrs Bushman. She dreams of putting her charge 'prentice to a mantua-maker or a milliner, or some such pretty trade', so that one day 'some great gentleman or other may fall in love with my little Betsy, and I may live to see her ride in her coach'.[56] However, liaisons with men of higher rank far more frequently spelled pregnancy and ruin for these girls. Hence in Fanny Burney's *The Wanderer* (1814), the 16-year-old apprentice Flora Pierson is convinced that a 'Knight Baronight' is courting her. Flora dreams of becoming a lady and her workmates refuse to warn her of the danger because 'each aspiring damsel, too, has some similar secret, or correspondent hope of her own'.[57] Millinery was thus a dangerously seductive trade, but it was also the only 'pretty trade' considered suitable for

---

[52] Ibid., pp. 2–4, 157.

[53] For example, Anon., *Character of an Exchange Wench* (1675), Mandeville's *Modest Defence of Public Stews* (1724), Lillo's *London Merchant* (1731), and the coffee-women's whore biographies (1728 and 1747).

[54] Raven, *Judging New Wealth*, pp. 1–7. See also McVeagh, *Tradefull Merchants*, pp. 83–100, who charts the 'Merchant as Hero, 1700–50', followed by a period of 'Disillusionment, 1750–90'. For caricatures of city merchants see Diana Donald, '"Mr Deputy Dumpling and Family": Satirical Images of the City Merchant in Eighteenth-century England', *Burlington Magazine*, 131 (1989), pp. 755–63.

[55] Raven, *Judging New Wealth*, pp. 112–37.

[56] Eliza Haywood, *The History of Miss Betsy Thoughtless* (1751; rep. Oxford, 1997), pp. 244–5.

[57] Ibid., p. 434.

gentlewomen, for whom commerce was, by definition, demeaning. In *The Wanderer*, Burney's sympathies lie with the pain and embarrassment felt by the heroine, Juliet, as an impoverished gentlewoman forced to work for a milliner. Juliet had tried business for herself but soon found that for women of her rank, 'where business is not necessary to subsistence, how little do we know'.[58] Indeed, Juliet becomes increasingly unhappy and demeaned by the immorality of commercial exchange. Burney herself came from a family with close links to trade but social distinctions were a favourite theme in her novels. In *Evelina* (1778), Burney mercilessly satirised the Branghtons, a family of silversmiths, for their vulgarity and social pretensions, yet her own grandmother was the daughter of a fan shop keeper, and two of her aunts, Ann and Rebecca Burney, ran Gregg's Coffee House in Covent Garden.[59]

Seduction was both a metaphor for social mobility and the desire for luxury goods throughout the eighteenth century. The presence of well-dressed women in an essentially 'public' setting with access to wealthy customers sparked a wealth of literature that shaded from the romantic to the almost porno-graphic. Satirical prints, such as Collett's *The Rival Milliners* (1770), often portray milliners selling the accoutrements of 'love' while flirting with male customers (see Figure 8.3). Plays and poems also highlighted the sexuality of milliners, playing with the idea of confusion between the pretty milliner tripping along the street with her bandbox and the prostitute performing the same action to attract customers.[60] In *An Ode to a Pretty Milliner* (1792), Peter Pindar apologised to the object of his desire, explaining:

> That knave, thy bandbox, wak'd my lawless fires,
> Bade me suspect what CHASTITY reveres.[61]

In the libertine imagination, the 'pretty trade' conflated the desire for luxury goods with desire for the attractively attired women who sold them, women whose independence and verbal facility further blurred the line between selling 'commodities' or themselves.[62] In the *Intriguing Milliners and Attornies Clerks* (1738),[63] a satirical romp about mistaken identity and sexual intrigue, the

---

[58] Fanny Burney, *The Wanderer* (1814; rep. 1991), p. 403.
[59] Claire Harman, *Fanny Burney: A Biography*, (London, 2000), pp. 9, 97. Burney's mother was a freeman of the Company of Musicians.
[60] Dorothy George, *Hogarth to Cruikshank: Social Change in Graphic Satire* (London, 1967), p. 82, cites a verse about a prostitute who 'with empty bandbox she delights to range/And feigns a distant errand from the "Change"'.
[61] Peter Pindar, 'An Ode to a Pretty Milliner', in idem, *Lyrics and Odes* (1792), pp. 62–4.
[62] Turner, 'News from the New Exchange', p. 421, notes that 'commodity' was both a modish word for goods and slang for vagina, and as such often occurs in texts about saleswomen.
[63] William Robinson, *The Intriguing Milliners and Attornies Clerks* (London, 1738).

Figure 8.3 J. Collett, *The Rival Milliners* (1770)
Source: Courtesy of the Trustees of the British Museum

author concludes that his meaning is quite clear, 'A Clerk's a Rogue, a Milliner's a Whore.'[64] In the early eighteenth century, Ned Ward's *London Spy* visited the Exchange and observed:

> Beau's, who I imagin'd, were paying a double Price for Linnen, Gloves, or Sword-knots, to the Prettiest of the Women, that they might go from thence and Boast among their Brother Fops, what singular Favours and great Encouragements they had receiv'd from the Fair Lady that sold them.[65]

The men who frequent these shops are thus equally tarnished by their desire for the goods and the women that sell them, a desire that is further symptomatic of the fops' effeminacy.

However, the pretty trade was also a profitable one, and the acquisition of profit generated both admiration and abhorrence. In an earlier visit to the Exchange, Ward encountered a deformed man with rickets who had:

---

[64] Ibid., p. 59.
[65] Ned Ward, *The London Spy* (4th edn, London, 1709), Part 9, p. 213.

the happiness or the curse, I know not whatever, to have a very Handsome Woman to his Wife, whose prevailing Glances have tempted such custom to her shop, that he can afford to spend three or four Hundred pounds a Year in a Tavern . . . which she very generously allows him out of her Gettings.[66]

Similarly, in Francis Coventry's satirical novel *Pompey the Little* (1751), the impoverished daughter of a gentleman, who had lived above his income, lost her husband and then failed in her attempts to become an actress. However, by using the legacy left by a dead lover, she eventually became 'a Milliner of Vogue, and had the Art to raise a considerable fortune from Lace and Ribbands'.[67] Indeed, the combination of sexual innuendo and hard calculation of profits was a common feature of many eighteenth-century texts about women in business. Campbell's *London Tradesman* (1747) described how milliners make 'vast Profits on every Article they deal in' but their desire to please the wealthy male customer meant that they instructed their apprentices 'to answer all his Rudeness with Civility and Compliance'. Although 'far from charging all milliners with the Crime of Connivance at the Ruin of their Apprentices', Campbell was convinced that nine out of ten apprentices ended up as prostitutes and that private or 'Hedge milliners' were nothing but procuresses.[68] Thus, while Campbell advocated millinery as a profitable trade for women, he warned against the risks inherent in the trade with a misogynistic diatribe against the worst kind of milliners. Yet it is worth noting that, in the same year, other trade manuals also confirmed the trade's profitability, but without the addition of sexual innuendo.[69]

Sex sold literature as well as material goods. Many texts combined almost pornographic moments with descriptions of business practice. Biographies of 'infamous' coffee-women contained long passages of sexual innuendo and even misogynistic representations of the decaying body of women at the point of death, but that did not preclude detailed discussion of business profits. Unlike many representations of milliners, these biographies of coffee-women were based on real women, often of low birth. In *The Velvet Coffee-woman* (1728), Ann Rochford's father was a waterman. Mrs Rochford may have been 'without a rival in Great Britain amongst the Professors of Love's mysteries'[70] but she also amassed considerable profits. The pamphlet detailed how she negotiated a deal with her stepmother to gain two public houses, repaired them, and built two others adjoining. After a famous visit to court, which gave rise to at least one satirical poem attributing her success to her enthusiastic espousal of 'the cause of love', she gained royal consent to build 'a house in the Meuse'. Here

---

[66] Ibid., Part 3, p. 72.
[67] Francis Coventry, *The History of Pompey the Little* (1751; rep. Oxford, 1974), pp. 133–7.
[68] R. Campbell, *The London Tradesman . . .* (London, 1747; rep. 1969), p. 209.
[69] Anon., *A General Description of All Trades* (1747), pp. 149–50.
[70] Anon., *The Velvet Coffee-woman: Or, the Life, Gallantries and Amours of the Late Famous Mrs Anne Rochford* (1728), p. 8.

'she soon flourished both in Wealth and Fame, left off retailing Coffee, tea and Chocolate' and sold liquor instead.[71] Mrs Rochford's downfall was another lover, who spent most of her money and forced her to remortgage her properties. According to the pamphlet, she died the way of most literary whores, horribly, through a 'mortification in her bowels'.

The Life and Character of Moll King (1747) was an equally sexually suggestive pamphlet about a well-known Covent Garden coffee-woman. It told how the daughter of a shoemaker and a fruit and fish seller acquired fame and fortune. Despite describing the more salacious aspects of Mrs King's life, it also provided much significant detail about her business. As a young girl she sold fruit from a barrow, but after marriage to Tom King she opened a stall in the market.

> Moll had exceeding good success in her new Business, and in one Season clear'd upwards of 60 *l.* by selling small Nuts only; she having bought up, very cheap, a large Quantity at a Time, when soon after the Price rose surprizingly, of which she took the advantage, and made a fine Market. Her aspiring Genius, was by the good Success at her Stall raised somewhat higher, so she had Thought of taking a little House . . . in Covent Garden Market, to sell Coffee, Tea, &c.[72]

In the pamphlet it is Mrs King who is portrayed as the driving force in the marital business partnership. Their coffee-house grew so quickly that the couple had to take two adjoining houses to accommodate their customers, and Kings' coffee-house soon became a notorious venue for all the town rakes and 'pretty misses'.[73] Yet Mrs King also loaned money on interest, and tried to protect other women in business. In particular, she opposed the owners of coffee-houses who put in female managers and then charged them exorbitant fees for the use of the house and furniture. However, the Kings' story was also one of social climbing. Mr King, 'with the consent of his beloved', committed the ultimate sin of the *nouveaux riches* by buying 'a genteel Country House' in Hampstead to which he could retire. But 'His spouse was quite of another Way of Thinking; she was an utter Enemy to Retirement, getting Money was all she aim'd at.'[74] At her death, Mrs King left considerable profits to her son, who was 'a very hopeful young Fellow, and on whom she bestowed a liberal Education at Eton school'.[75]

Ann Rochford and Moll King were disruptive and sexually subversive figures operating on the disreputable fringes of coffee-house culture, and such representations are usually seen as an attempt to expel the feminine from the masculine world of business. Yet these were not the only representations of

---

[71] Ibid. p. 35.

[72] Anon., *Life and Character of Moll King*, p. 8.

[73] Kings' Coffee-house is featured in Hogarth's 'Morning' picture in *The Four Times of the Day* (1738).

[74] *Life and Character of Moll King*, p. 10.

[75] Ibid., pp. 20, 22.

coffee-women and, as was the case with milliners, there was a division between the ideal and the disreputable side of trade. Attempts to reform the practice of both trades thus produced conflicting images of the women who engaged in the business. At the very least there was, as Markman Ellis points out, a significant gap between the actual heterogeneity of coffee-house culture and the ideal forum for business and political discussion represented in, for example, the pages of the *Spectator*.[76] As Figure 8.4 shows, prints of coffee-houses often depict a rather formal, respectable woman shielded by the bar from her sociably engaged male customers.[77] Hence E.J. Clery has argued that the female coffee-house keeper was actually integral to projects for the reformation of manners in coffee-houses, because she signified the private ideal of the proper lady whose behaviour the male company should aspire to match.[78] This juxtaposition of ideal and disreputable images is clearly evident in the *Spectator*'s campaign to change the discourses around 'the usual stile of buying and selling' from women, to prevent the exchange of 'ingenious Ribaldry'.[79]

In 1711 a correspondent complained that in several city coffee-houses the female proprietors were idols who 'sit and receive all day long the adoration of the youth' so that goods were left unrecorded in the custom house, merchants stayed away from the change and students neglected their study.[80] Although the letter clearly sought to expunge feminine distractions from the world of business, the response came apparently from women who deplored sexual harassment by their male customers. Mr *Spectator* declared that he had received 'innumerable Messages from that Part of the fair sex, whose Lot in Life is to be of any Trade or publick Way of Life'.[81] The messages, whether real or invented, were from coffee-women, milliners and women in the Exchanges. Two letters were printed in full, one allegedly from a coffee-woman, the other from a milliner. The coffee-woman begged Mr *Spectator* to 'perswade Gentlemen that this is out of all decency. Say it is possible a Woman may be modest and keep a public house', because 'the Chearfulness of Life which would arise from the honest Gain I have is utterly lost to me from the endless flat, impertinent Pleasantries which I hear from Morning to Night'.[82] The milliner also complained of sexual harassment and reversed the metaphor of prostitution, to declare that she would 'assign Rates to my kind Glances, or make all pay who come to see me, or I shall be undone by my Admirers for want of Customers'. The *Spectator*'s answer was to ask all men of 'honour and

---

[76] Ellis, 'The Coffee-women', p. 43.
[77] See below, p. 194: *The Coffee-house Politicians* (1772). See also E.J. Clery, 'Women, Publicity and the Coffee-house Myth', *Women: A Cultural Review*, 2 (1991), pp. 168–77, for *The Coffee-house Ideal* (1688); *The Coffee House Satirised* (1710).
[78] Ibid.
[79] D.F. Bond (ed.), *Spectator* (Oxford, 1965), No. 155, 28 August 1711, p. 109.
[80] Ibid., No. 87, 9 June 1711, p. 371.
[81] Ibid., No. 155, p. 107.
[82] *Spectator*, no. 155, p. 108.

The Coffee-house Politicians.

Figure 8.4 *The Coffee-house Politicians* (1772)

Source: Courtesy of the Guildhall Library, Corporation of London

sense' to remember that women were the weaker sex, that they traded out of necessity due to lack of marriage opportunities, and that they should not be 'treated as if they stood there to sell their Persons to Prostitution'.[83] Thus the equivalence of commerce and sex remained inextricably entwined, but the appeal for better manners towards businesswomen was framed around the helpless modesty commonly ascribed to ideal domestic femininity. In this case, the 'proper lady's' presence was posited in the public sphere of trade as a reforming agent for male manners. The Spectator clearly accepted the presence of women in trade as a normal occurrence but, in its attempts to reform the more undesirable elements of commercial transactions with them, it replicated a gendered division of public and private more usually associated with attempts to remove women from trade.

Manufacturing nationalism

As we have seen, anxieties about the impact of foreign imports upon British trade could result in hostility towards women in the luxury trades and particularly those who styled themselves as 'French', but patriotism could also prove beneficial for women's commercial endeavours. During the Jacobite rebellion, 1745–6, newspaper advertisements give some idea of the importance women in business attached to appearing patriotic. In 1745 an advertisement in the London *Daily Advertiser* accused a milliner of displaying an effigy of a Lady Abbess in her shop window, which 'gravely offended 'his Majesty's loyal Protestant Subjects'. The milliner took the charge seriously enough to publish a lengthy refutation, claiming the image was merely a Flanders lace maker.[84] One shopkeeper advertised her patriotism (and her business) by announcing that she was closing her shop in order to visit her mantua maker for a dress in honour of the King's birthday. She did this, the advert explained, 'to shew Her Self (according to her capacity) as loyal a subject as any his Majesty has'.[85] To show oneself a loyal and patriotic citizen had become an important part of maintaining a good image in trade.

In a number of European countries, but particularly in France and Britain, the mid-eighteenth century witnessed extensive discussions about national identities and the launching of initiatives to glorify national culture.[86] One of these initiatives was the founding of patriotic societies, such as the Laudable Association of Anti-Gallicans in 1745, which aimed 'to discourage by precept and example, the importation and consumption of French produce and manufactures, and to encourage . . . the produce and manufactures of Great

---

[83] Ibid., p. 109.
[84] London *Daily Advertiser*, 6 September 1745.
[85] Ibid., 24 October 1745.
[86] Colley, *Britons*, p. 85.

Britain'.[87] It was to these 'Laudable Associations of Anti-Gallicans' that the satirical print attacking the arrival of swarms of French milliners was addressed.[88] Not all these societies were so xenophobic but most had overtly mercantilist and patriotic aims, and all welcomed contributions from people irrespective of class or gender. Hence, as Linda Colley argues, they effectively encouraged a much broader definition of what it was to be a patriot.[89] But patriotic societies could also encourage a broader definition of what it meant for women to engage in manufacturing enterprises.

Among the bodies established around this time was the Society for the Encouragement of Arts, Manufactures and Commerce, founded in 1754. The Society aimed not only to encourage British manufacture and commerce but also to regenerate British culture by raising its arts above those of the French. It gave prizes in six different categories including Agriculture, Mechanics, Chemistry, Manufactures, Colonies and Trade, and the 'Polite Arts', which was the category in which women most frequently won awards.[90] From its earliest days there were female members, but not in any great numbers,[91] and there was a female registrar from 1802 to 1844. Ann Cocking took over the post from her father and on her death the society erected a monument to her in memory of the 'zealous diligence with which she performed the duties of her office'.[92] More importantly, women also applied for the medals and financial rewards given for work and discoveries that seemed likely to benefit the national economy.

The number and value of awards in each category varied from year to year according to the financial position of the Society. Between 1754 and 1776 twenty-eight premiums were awarded to women for manufactures, the prize money for which amounted to just under 10 per cent of the total sum awarded in that category.[93] The majority of awards to women were in the field of textiles, such as making lace, cambric, wool and yarn, but also for making artificial flowers, catgut and chip hats, and the production of raw silk. The Society's awards resulted in many textiles such as brocades, tapestries, ribbons, embroideries, milled caps and crepe bands for hats, all potentially 'feminine' trades, being produced in England for the first time. The manufacture of straw

---

[87] Cited in ibid. p. 89.

[88] See above, Figure 8.1.

[89] Colley, *Britons*, p. 93.

[90] Alicia C. Percival, 'Women and the Society of Arts in its Early Days: Part 2,' *Journal of the Royal Society of Arts*, 125 (1977), pp. 330–3.

[91] Ibid., 'Part 1', pp. 266–9. The majority of members were merchants, tradesmen and craftsmen.

[92] Derek Hudson and Kenneth W. Luckhurst, *The Royal Society of Arts, 1754–1954* (London, 1954), p. 175.

[93] N = £2026 -1s 0d (excluding medals), extracted from The Society for the Encouragement of Arts, Manufacture and Commerce (hereafter RSA), *Register of Premium Awards, 1754–76*. See Pullin, 'Business is Just Life', p. 211, Table 8.1.

hats was a particular success story,[94] and awards for artificial flower making stimulated that industry. In 1837 one trade directory still feared that 'Parisian gentlemen' infinitely excelled 'our native work people of either sex' at making artificial flowers, but it also described how English haberdashers and milliners exported 'great quantities' to the East and West Indies, America and other colonies.[95] Even if some of these awards for 'feminine' trades seem to have been restricted in range, they were nevertheless acknowledged as making a significant contribution to the national and colonial economy.

Premiums were decided by committees, each dealing with one of the six different categories. Occasionally women also won trade-related awards in categories other than manufactures. In 1793 the Colonies and Trade Committee rewarded Mrs Anstey for planting cinnamon trees in Madras.[96] In 1782 Mrs Jane Richards won an award in chemistry for a new method of cleaning feathers with lime water, and in 1797 Mrs Jane Gibbs won a gold medal for inventing a starch made from non-edible materials as part of the Society's drive to find an alternative to costly wheat flour.[97] The Society's protectionist and paternalistic aims[98] meant that manufactures, which not only boosted British industry but also provided work for the poor, were warmly welcomed. The production of silk was intended to rival the French and Italian output, but it was also declared to be a 'most capital object' because it offered employment for women and children.[99]

A form of social engineering was also evident in the offering of awards for textile products, many of which benefited women. Women in workhouses were rewarded for spinning linen and making worsted hose, but the awards for the more genteel cambrick and lace were intended to help impecunious women of middling rank.[100] Well-off gentlewomen were also keen to receive awards for their 'work', and although they conceived of it in terms of a public service, they were often at pains to distance themselves from any commercial overtones. In 1789 one Ann Ives was awarded a silver medal for 'bringing the art of spinning to such a degree of perfection'; and numerous attempts were subsequently made to have her thread commercially produced. Letters printed

---

[94] Hudson and Luckhurst, *Royal Society of Arts*, pp. 133–4.
[95] RSA, *Register of Premium Awards*, 'Flowers'; Whittock, *Complete Book of Trades*, pp. 248–51.
[96] *Transactions of the Society of Arts*, 11 (1795), p. 295.
[97] *Transactions*, 22 (1805), pp. 210–15; 15 (1797), pp. 237–40.
[98] D.G.C. Allen, 'The Society for the Encouragement of Arts, Manufactures and Commerce: Organization, Membership and Objectives in the First Three Decades (1755–84), An Example of Voluntary Economic and Social Policy in the Eighteenth Century' (unpub. Ph.D. thesis, University of London, 1979), p. 126.
[99] Daines Baring in *Transactions*, 2 (1784), p. 172; and see letter fom the Revd Swaines, *Transactions*, 6 (1789), p. 134.
[100] RSA, *Register of Premium Awards*, Manufactures, section on 'Yarn'; Hudson and Luckhurst, *Royal Society*, p. 130.

in the Society's *Transactions*, describing her efforts, insisted that she spun 'only for her amusement', but nevertheless extolled her great skill, which would produce something 'to the advantage of British manufactures'.[101]

It has also been argued that the Society's role in encouraging industry per se was a great deal more modest that its assistance in 'pioneering the development of natural resources'.[102] This was because, as a small voluntary association, it had limited means. Yet its aims remained wholly patriotic. It was these aims which determined what awards were offered and therefore the categories in which women competed. Women's attempts to rear and to spin raw silk, although doomed to failure for largely climatic reasons, were earnestly believed to be of 'much national importance'.[103] Raw silk production was certainly no more hopeless than the Society's attempts to promote the growth of opium, and both were intended to reduce foreign imports. The women who engaged in these 'manufactures' certainly believed they were helping their country. The production of silk had first been attempted by James I and a large plantation had been tried at Chelsea in 1718, but the Society did not offer a prize for it until 1768.[104] In 1778 two women were presented with awards by the manufactures committee; one was for cambric made with homespun thread and the other was to Mrs Ann Williams of Gravesend for breeding and feeding silkworms. Mrs Williams' seven letters on the subject were all printed in the Society's *Transactions* in 1784 and were read avidly by later producers attempting to improve on her methods.[105] Mrs Williams related how several gentlemen who had seen Italian silk farms pronounced her worms and silk the 'finest they ever saw'. On receiving the 20 guineas, reward, she expressed the hope that her efforts 'may be of service to thousands after [my] death' and, in a spirit of patriotism, added 'Exulting thought! That my poor endeavours may one day prove beneficial to my country.'[106]

To put personal ingenuity to the service of one's country was, as Henrietta Rhodes put it, a 'laudable ambition', apparently irrespective of gender. Miss Rhodes, who was another aspiring silk producer, hoped that if she was found 'to have succeeded better than anyone else . . . I flatter myself that I shall not remain undistinguished'. Miss Rhodes received a silver medal in 1778, but others wished for more concrete assistance as well. Miss Jane Niven had raised a 'large family of silkworms', but her father had refused further help and sent her to be a French teacher. She wrote to the Society, asking for the loan of some reels to complete her project.[107] In an overlapping of domestic and

---

[101] *Transactions*, 7 (1789), pp. 151, 154.
[102] Hudson and Luckhurst, *Royal Society of Arts*, p. 101.
[103] *Transactions*, 2 (1784), p. 153.
[104] H.T. Wood, *A History of the Royal Society of Arts* (London, 1913), pp. 265–6.
[105] *Transactions*, 2 (1784), pp. 153–80. In *Transactions*, 4 (1786), p. 161, Henrietta Rhodes, a silver medal winner in 1785, described how she had drawn on Mrs Williams' account.
[106] Ibid., pp. 154, 169, 171.
[107] RSA, PR/MC/102/10/294.

commercial languages, several women referred to their silkworms as 'family' but described their 'business' as being in an 'office' or 'manufactory'. Mary Jones, a doctor's wife, was fired up by the challenge of producing silk. At first she described this task as a 'useful and elegant amusement',[108] but it soon became the answer to far more pressing financial concerns.

Mrs Jones wrote several letters to the Society between March 1788 and December 1791. None of her letters were published in *Transactions* but she intended to write a treatise addressed 'to the Ladies of this Country'. In a memorial to the Society, endorsed by the Lord Mayor of London, she claimed to know 'how to construct manufactories' for silk production. However, 'family matters' forced her to sell her estate and left her with an income 'now barely sufficient to support your memorialist as a Gentlewoman'.[109] She combined the need for personal financial support with a plea for the national good.

> [she] thought fit to represent to your honourable Society her situation hoping through your kind assistance to have some means given her of establishing in this Country on a permanent Basis this invaluable Branch of Foreign Commerce which cannot fail of being of the greatest utility and Consequence to this Nation.[110]

Although the nature of applications to the Society encouraged such displays of patriotism, by no means all women pursued this course. Mrs Jones explained that she was inspired by her late father who had been an engineer, and in November 1791 she wrote to the Society asking to join: 'that I might by Emulation be proved, and approve myself useful to the general good of this my native Country in whatever my genius as a woman may tend to promote.'[111]

Female applicants to the Society were thus aware of pursuing activities deemed suitable to their sex, but they were also self-confident and fiercely competitive. Mrs Jones declared that, although she doubted her skills as a mechanic, she begged to differ with another gentleman on the subject of producing silk and 'could vie with any woman experienced in the art' of spinning silk.[112] Frances Crofts, who, like Mrs Jones, appears not to have been given an award, was constantly requesting the latest editions of Transactions and complained bitterly when she felt she had been unfairly judged. She not only produced and spun silk but designed a silkworm container, sending the society a detailed description and technical drawing. The Society had rewarded the Revd Mr Swayne, a man who Mrs Crofts had earlier assisted, and published his communications. Frances Croft wrote indignantly that she had 'invented the exact stand that Mr Swayne did extremely well' and for less cost.[113] Mrs

---

[108] RSA, PR/MC/102/10/192.
[109] RSA, PR/MC/101/10/1843.
[110] Ibid.
[111] RSA, PR/MC/102/10/31.
[112] RSA, PR/MC/102/10/26.
[113] RSA, PR/MC/102/10/12.

Croft also felt that she was being discriminated against as a Yorkshirewoman. She demanded to know who sat on the committee and declared that 'we in the North think it hard Ladies in the South are favour'd with rewards, who have not produced the quantity & us left out, as our being about 2 degrees further removed from the Sun, rates against us'.[114]

Letters to the Society give the impression that, although women's enterprises were believed to contribute to national production, their immediate commercial viability was somewhat limited. However, some women were engaged in more public and obviously commercial battles. Ann Leslie and her three sisters were 'gentlewomen' who were engaged in setting up a factory in Scotland to make thread from flax grown locally near Hamilton. In 1763 they applied to the Commissioners for Fisheries and Manufactures in Scotland for assistance and were promised a premium of £56 and a 'throw-miln'.[115] The Leslie sisters sent their thread to local lace workers in Hamilton and to 'the most eminent manufacturers' in London, where it was worked into lace of such quality that the King wore a pair of ruffles made from it. However, the sisters ran into opposition among the Board of Commissioners, apparently because of 'insidious allegations and rumours put about by unknown competitors'.

Ann Leslie went to London seeking support and obtained a certificate from the Society for the Encouragement of the Arts, stating that the Leslie sisters made the best thread in the country, and that 'if a manufacture of this fine thread could be established to the profit of the undertakers it would be of great advantage to the kingdom'.[116] She also sought support from numerous merchants and magistrates in Scotland, as well as testimonies from local lace workers in Hamilton. Margaret Watson declared that she had:

> wrought of Miss Leslie's thread, for some years, and am daily taking good quantities of it, and find it better and stronger than foreign; all made of Scots flax and yarn, made into thread by Miss Leslie, superior to any ever came from abroad.[117]

All the local lace workers' testimonials employed the comparison with 'foreign' thread but the main pamphlet raised the matter to one of national importance 'because the people of a great state [Britain] will purchase from foreigners, perhaps their natural enemies, those luxuries which they cannot manufacture at home'.[118] The pamphlet was aimed specifically at the patriotic societies but it was hinted that the legislature should become involved because British production would not only save the country money, but it would also 'employ numbers of hands which are now idle'.[119] This patriotic discourse fostered both

[114] RSA, PR/MC/102/10/127.
[115] Anon., *The Case of Miss Leslie and her Three Sisters, the Manufacturers of Thread for Lace, Equal to Any Foreign* (1767), p. 6.
[116] Ibid., pp. 5–6.
[117] Ibid., p. 12.
[118] Ibid., p. 1.
[119] Ibid., pp. 1–2.

national commercial and paternalistic aims in support of the Leslie sisters who were praised for their 'noble public spirit'. Moreover, they also enjoyed support across class and gender boundaries – from aristocratic subscribers, to merchants, to local women lace workers. Yet the spectre of gender prejudice had obviously been raised, prompting the question:

> Whether it is for the credit, interest, or reputation of Great Britain, that a cabal of persons, either interested or prejudiced against women, whose industry and good intentions alone procured them friends, ought to defeat the laudable, and national purposes of a British Legislature?[120]

The answer, for the patriotic societies at least, seems to have been that 'laudable and national purposes' were quite enough to qualify women for an active public role in British 'manufacturing'.

Conclusion

On the surface, patriotism could subsume differences of class and gender and provide women with a discourse within which they could claim support for commercial enterprises. However, issues of class and gender also played a part. Women of the lower orders were rewarded for spinning in workhouses, but their wealthier sisters experimented with silk production. These genteel women stressed their public service but remained ambivalent as to whether that service could be regarded as commercial. There was no clear line between private enterprise and commercial 'amusements' for the benefit of the national economy. Nevertheless, all these women could and did use patriotic discourses to further their aims.

Just as it is no longer possible to trace a simple linear decline in women's economic activities, it is equally misleading to focus on a single language of separate spheres in debates about those activities. Issues of race, class and gender were constantly changing partners in the service of different interests during debates over trading practices. Businesswomen, including milliners, made use of patriotic discourses when advertising in newspapers, but fears of French competition meant that milliners who chose to capitalise on French style to attract customers were effectively guilty of cultural treason. The trade itself was constructed as proper only for virtuous 'English' gentlewomen in order to thwart foreign competition, prevent mass prostitution and avoid the emasculation of British men. Yet the 'pretty trade' could also be depicted as a den of vice waiting to trap unwary girls into believing they could achieve a degree of social mobility by marrying aristocratic male customers. Contemporaries also frequently conflated sexual desire with the desire for

[120] Ibid., p. 16.

luxury goods and the women who sold them as well as anxieties about the profits they made, which could result in overtly misogynous representations. Yet attempts to reform the manners of the male customers of milliners and coffee-women used gendered concepts of public and private to posit the existence of the ideal woman in the public sphere of trade. The rhetorical expulsion of the whorish milliner or coffee-woman and her replacement with a shining ideal of domestic femininity was indicative of similar attempts to attack undesirable elements of commercial practice without condemning the whole. Indeed, The dictum, defining the prosperous but dictatorial milliner Mrs Lanchester as the 'Bonaparte of her day',[121] shows that condemnation in one context could become praise in another; and the practice of describing successful businesswomen in 'Napoleonic' terms continued into the nineteenth century and beyond.[122]

[121] See above, p. 175.
[122] See below, p. 254.

9

'This publick method'

Women, trade and advertising in eighteenth-century London

> There is a great deal of useful learning sometimes to be met with in Advertisements.
>
> *Mist's Weekly Journal* (22 May 1725)[1]

The previous chapter examined some of the 'other languages' used to talk about eighteenth-century women in business, but this chapter now turns to a consideration of the language of separate spheres itself. As a number of historians have pointed out, the distinction between public and private, and even the use of 'spheres' as an additional spatial metaphor, was common in the eighteenth century. But they have also emphasised the multiple contrasts which could be covered by the dichotomy and the fluid or shifting nature of the boundaries between the two terms.[2] Since 'there is no single "public/private" distinction to which interpretation can confidently secure itself'[3] and the boundaries between categories are both flexible and historically contingent, it is useful to consider how different issues were inscribed within each category and how they were articulated in terms of one another at any given time or place. One way to do this is to examine the advertising strategies pursued by businesswomen in a London daily newspaper, an activity which, for women, could mean an engagement with multiple public/private distinctions. Within feminist historiography the market is most commonly construed as a public sphere of action for women because of its increasing association with masculine, rational economic practice, even though eighteenth-century commerce and commodity exchange have also been aligned with *private* enterprise, in

---

[1] Cited in Jeremy Black, *The English Press In The Eighteenth Century* (London, 1987), p. 51.

[2] Lawrence E. Klein, 'Gender and the Public/Private Distinction in the Eighteenth Century: Some Questions About Evidence and Procedure', *Eighteenth Century Studies*, 29 (1995), pp. 97–109; Brewer, 'This, That and The Other', pp. 1–21; Jane Rendall, 'Women and the Public Sphere', *Gender & History*, 11(1999), pp. 475–88.

[3] Klein, 'Gender and the Public/Private Distinction', p. 99; and see Gobetti, *Private & Public*, p. 1, on how one of the major problems with the dichotomy is the assumption of a widespread 'confidence in the power of shared meanings'.

opposition to the *public* authority of the state.[4] Placing an advertisement also meant engaging with public print culture and, within Habermas' famous formulation of the creation of an eighteenth-century public sphere, the press was an important medium through which the public was able to imagine itself.[5] Finally, it will be argued here that contemporaries perceived advertising to be a very public way of trading, quite distinct from the more private face-to-face commercial exchange based on the personal reputation of the trader, and facilitated by networks of known friends and acquaintances.

In 1745 Mrs Wright, who had just arrived in London from Nottinghamshire, explained that she took 'this Publick Method of making her Apology'[6] to her customers because pressure of business in drawing designs for needlework meant that she was no longer able to wait on them in their own homes, but they could still speak with her at her brother's house. Thomas Harris, a broker and undertaker, wanted it to be known that he had a large assortment of upholstery goods in stock for sale at very reasonable rates, but his 'Motive for this publick Application is, the unhandsome Answers that have been given to Persons who have enquired for me at a shop within a few Doors of mine'.[7] Both advertisers evidently felt that they should provide a more legitimate reason for advertising publicly than the purely commercial one of boosting sales. One explanation is that since eighteenth-century shopkeeping has been characterised as 'a genteel trade catering to the leisure class, of shopkeepers who took pride in their aristocratic patronage and whose mode of conduct conformed to the norms of their clientele', then many such shopkeepers 'disdained vulgar advertising'.[8] Successful businessmen, according to this traditional model, relied solely on their reputation and skill for their trade and adjusted their individual pursuit of profit to the interests of the communities in which they traded.[9] Indeed, for most of the eighteenth century many retailers continued to rely

---

[4] Trade may be characterised as private both because it is an activity conducted by individuals not the state and because it has particular not general aims; see Brewer, 'This, That and The Other', p. 9. For a discussion of the construction of a masculine, individualist, rational economic public sphere and the representation of commodity exchange as 'private' in the work of Adam Smith and Jurgen Habermas, see Davidoff, 'Regarding Some "Old Husbands' Tales"', pp. 237–9, 242–9.

[5] For a clear summary of Jurgen Habermas' model of three separate but overlapping spheres within which both commodity exchange and the family are contained in the private sphere, see Brewer, 'This, That and The Other', pp. 3–6.

[6] London *Daily Advertiser*, 23 January 1745.

[7] *LDA*, 26 February 1765.

[8] Mui and Mui, *Shops and Shopkeeping*, p. 17, describe this traditional model but challenge it as being only partial. On the emergence of a polite shopping culture as a pleasurable activity for elite and middling sorts, particularly in eighteenth-century London, see Helen Berry, 'Polite Consumption: Shopping in Eighteenth-century England', *Transactions of the RHS*, 12 (2002), pp. 375–94.

[9] Alexander, *Retailing in England During the Industrial Revolution* (London, 1970), p. 159.

on traditional methods of promoting goods through personal contacts, hand-bills or trade cards.[10]

There is some disagreement over the timing and speed of change towards more aggressive marketing techniques,[11] but as we have seen, the period was also one of commercial growth, and witnessed the emergence of a vigorous consumer culture in which the middle classes were active as both consumers and producers. For Paul Langford, their involvement meant that a more refined means of regulating manners developed and thus politeness became 'a logical consequence of commerce'.[12] The polite language of most newspaper adver-tisements may certainly be read as an attempt to appeal to the actual or aspirant manners of the middle and higher orders of society.[13] Fielding highlighted this aspect of advertising to good comic effect in *Tom Jones* (1749) when the eponymous hero's landlady 'determined to show him all the respect in her power', because her inn was 'one of those houses where gentlemen, to use the language of advertisements, meet with civil treatment for their money'.[14] Her respect accordingly vanished on discovering that Tom was neither monied nor a real gentleman. However, Lawrence Klein has argued that the competing demands of polite practice and commercial productivity actually resulted in a 'cultural contradiction of commercial society'.[15] Similarly, Stephen Copley has highlighted how, despite campaigns in periodicals to depict trade as a 'legitimate basis for sociality and so as a foundation of politeness', for many, politeness remained best understood as being quite distinct from trade.[16] Hence, both male and female traders had to engage with this apparent con-tradiction when constructing their advertisements, even if those who spurned advertising altogether were an ever decreasing number.

For businesswomen, the need to negotiate between polite and commercial discourses when advertising had to be added to considerations about the degree

---

[10] Claire Walsh, 'The Advertising of Consumer Goods in Eighteenth-century London', in *Advertising and the European City: Historical Perspectives*, ed. C. Wischermann and E. Shore (Aldershot, 2000), p. 84.

[11] The greatest disagreement occurs over the chronology rather than the actuality of changes in sales and marketing techniques. Alexander locates it in the nineteenth century, Berry in the late eighteenth, while the Muis favour an early eighteenth-century genesis, but all agree that one model only gradually replaced the other. See also Roy Porter, *Health for Sale: Quacks and Quackery in England 1660–1850* (Manchester, 1989), pp. 45–6, on a revolution in marketing techniques spearheaded by medical advertisements.

[12] Paul Langford, *A Polite and Commercial People: England 1727–1783* (Oxford, 1989), pp. 4–5.

[13] Walsh, 'Advertising of Consumer Goods', pp. 83–4.

[14] Henry Fielding, *Tom Jones* (1749; this edn, Oxford, 1989), p. 353.

[15] Lawrence Klein, 'Politeness for Plebes: Consumption and Social Identity in Early Eighteenth-century England', in *The Consumption of Culture 1600–1800*, ed. A. Bermingham and J. Brewer, pp. 362–82.

[16] Stephen Copley, 'Commerce, Conversation and Politeness in the Early Eighteenth-Century Periodical', *British Journal for Eighteenth-century Studies*, 18 (1995), pp. 66–7.

to which their personal credit should be represented as resting on their financial and/or sexual probity. Samuel Johnson distinguished between the 'polite' as 'glossy, smooth' and 'elegant of manners' and the concept of 'politeness' to which he added 'gentility, good breeding'.[17] For women in the luxury trades and, as we shall see, milliners in particular, this frequently meant not only including expressions of gentility and morality, but also a disavowal of any desire for financial gain in their advertisements. Perhaps the most useful definition is that adopted by Klein, for whom politeness embodied 'refined yet sociable gentility'.[18] This encompassed the need for outward polish (refinement), social discipline (sociability) and a compatibility with the manners of society's highest orders (gentility). Politeness was not merely an ornamental accomplishment confined to the leisured elite; the possibility of economic and social mobility meant that manuals purveying politeness found a ready market among the 'busy' or 'business' people of the middle orders. Indeed, the adoption of polite manners for business could dissolve the common distinction between the polite and the productive, the ornamental and the useful.[19] Another common antonym of politeness was 'vulgarity' among the definitions of which Johnson included 'publick, commonly bruited' and 'plebeian, suiting to the common people'.[20] Since either or both definitions could apply to the practise of newspaper advertising it is this distinction between vulgar/polite, public/ private that this chapter will highlight. Here 'politeness' has been aligned with the civil, well-mannered, more traditional approach to conducting business, such as that endorsed by Defoe in *The Complete English Tradesman*.[21] By contrast, 'vulgar' has been aligned with a more 'commercial', competitive and innovative approach to marketing such as advertising, price cutting and 'unhandsome' public remarks about fellow traders. Thus, rather than being a gendered space excluding women from the market, the public space occupied by newspaper advertisements could be seen as a vulgar, but nevertheless useful, tool in a competitive market, one which needed negotiating via a polite discourse aimed at both literate, affluent consumers and fellow traders.

This chapter is based on a study of advertisements placed by women in business in the London *Daily Advertiser* between 1731 and 1775.[22] Although it has been argued that in most trades 'any sort of regular or continuous advertisement was unknown',[23] this was certainly far from the case in London

---

[17] Johnson, *Dictionary of the English Language*, s.v. 'polite'; 'politeness'.

[18] Klein, 'Politeness for Plebes', p. 365.

[19] Ibid., pp. 363–6.

[20] Johnson, *Dictionary of the English Language*, s.v. 'vulgar'.

[21] Klein, 'Politeness for Plebes', pp. 372–4, argues that Defoe's work was one of those marketing politeness to plebes because, despite his anxiety about the blurring of social distinctions, he stressed the need for good manners when selling, a degree of display in order to obtain credit and the tendency of traders to imitate their wealthier or more polite customers.

[22] Advertisements were sampled for the years 1735, 1745, 1755, 1765 and 1775.

[23] Pinchbeck, *Women Workers*, p. 286.

newspapers where, while numbers were initially low, both men and women ran repeated advertisements from the 1730s.[24] It must be stressed, however, that the term 'advertising' has been used here in its broadest sense to include notices of positions wanted and announcements, as well as those strictly promoting goods for sale.[25] I begin by looking at the medium of newspaper advertising in order to show how the newspaper served as a form of community information, or noticeboard, for London traders whose business could be as greatly affected by damage to reputation as by insufficient sales. As such, newspaper advertising effectively functioned as an imagined community of trade within which women formed a significant minority of accepted and competitive participants. The next section examines how this imagined community of trade was predicated on a shared language based on the need to create a discourse of legitimacy with which to maintain creditworthiness through personal honour and reputation. I then go on to consider how women in different trades negotiated between polite and commercial imperatives as well as the gendered norms of the age. For all female traders personal honour was closely bound up with moral or sexual honour, but nowhere was this more obvious than with the genteel and feminine, but highly commercial, trade of millinery. By contrast the most commercially aggressive advertisers were the female 'quacks', yet both they and the rather more polite female midwives also publicised their 'professional' credibility.

A community of trade

In common with the insurance business, women had been involved in the sale and production of some of the earliest eighteenth-century daily newspapers. Initially confined mostly to semi-legal hawking of newspapers and pamphlets, by the 1680s female 'mercuries' were buying newspapers wholesale and either distributing them to hawkers or retailing them from their own shops. One mercury, Elizabeth Mallett, started *The Daily Courant*, the first daily English newspaper in 1702.[26] By the 1730s advertisements formed a significant part of

---

[24] In the London *Daily Advertiser* a mere handful of women were advertising in the 1730s, but there were more than 180 in 1755 and over 250 in 1775.
[25] This broad definition has also been adopted in Black, *The English Press*, and R.B Walker, 'Advertising in London Newspapers, 1650–1750', *Business History*, 15 (1973), pp. 112–30.
[26] Hunt, 'Hawkers, Bawlers and Mercuries', pp. 46–8, p. 63, argues that by 1750 women had vanished from printing, publishing and bookselling trade directories, but more recently Barker, 'Women, Work and the Industrial Revolution', pp. 81–100, has shown that women continued in these trades until at least the early nineteenth century. As Table 6.6(a) above (p. 143) shows, booksellers were certainly still taking out insurance in 1845 and two women gave their occupations as newspaper proprietor and editor that year: GL. Ms. 11936, 611/1501588; 1501589.

London newspapers.[27] The London *Daily Advertiser* was launched in February 1731, using high-quality typography and layout, and sold at 1½d, which put it into the 'superior' group of papers intended for the more affluent orders of society.[28] London papers were aimed specifically at the upper and middling orders, including London tradesmen who formed an important element of the readership, although actual readership could have been wider still.[29] As such it reached the audience most likely to follow, or aspire to, the dictates of politeness until its demise in 1795. At least 75 per cent of the paper consisted of advertisements and in later years it even had to turn away advertisers; its success encouraged other papers to add 'Advertiser' to their titles.[30] The Preface to the first issue boldly claimed that it would be posted up in public places and would contain such a comprehensive display of advertisements that readers would no longer need to buy more than one paper.

Papers were widely available and often read in coffee-houses and taverns where commercial business was frequently transacted. Many advertisers directed anyone wishing to do business with them to a named coffee-house rather than to a private address. Women may have been rhetorically expelled from the ideal coffee-house of prescriptive literature but they were no less likely to cite them as a first point of contact or forwarding address in newspaper advertisements. Lace dealer Hester Pinney's success as a businesswoman was greatly helped by her investments in stocks and shares, and her financial dealings were evidently carried out in coffee-houses, where she could also find merchants to convey messages to her brother in business in the West Indies.[31] Despite Defoe's fears that coffee-houses were 'places devoted to scandal, and where the characters of all kinds of persons and professions are handled in the most merciless manner',[32] it seems that even business matters of a more delicate or genteel nature were initiated there. Coffee-houses certainly provided the necessary good address for those who lived in lodgings,[33] although it is quite possible that letters could have been picked up by a third party. Even the most respectable women, including a 'young Lady' seeking millinery work that would not entail 'sitting in a publick shop', cited coffee-houses as a means of contact.[34] However, it was evidently necessary to assure the proprietor of the venture's

---

[27] For a discussion of the growth of advertising in newspapers, see Black, *The English Press*, pp. 51–86, and Walker, *Advertising in London Newspapers* pp. 112–24.

[28] Ibid., pp. 120–1; Walker divides newspapers into those selling for ½d as 'inferior', and those selling for 1½ to 2d as 'superior'.

[29] Michael Harris, *London Newspapers in the Age of Walpole: A Study of the Origins of the Modern English Press* (London, 1987), p. 165; Hannah Barker, *Newspapers, Politics and Public Opinion in Late Eighteenth-century England* (Oxford, 1998), pp. 22–42.

[30] Walker, *Advertising in London Newspapers*, p. 122.

[31] Sharpe, 'Dealing with Love', p. 222.

[32] Defoe, *Complete English Tradesman*, p. 197.

[33] George, *London Life*, p. 95.

[34] LDA, 3 January 1775.

respectability and secure their agreement before placing an advertisement. In 1775 one woman advertised that rooms where ladies 'wanting to lie in privately may be genteely accommodated on reasonable terms' but where 'secrecy may be depended on' could be secured by sending 'a Letter directed to O.S. at Mr Woodhouse's the Temple Coffee-House'. Mr Woodhouse seems not to have been convinced by the propriety of this offer and issued a disclaimer, declaring that the advertisement had been 'inserted without my Knowledge, nor will I receive any Letters on Such Business'.[35] By contrast, for many coffee-house proprietors newspapers could be a marketing device in themselves. Mrs Abell used the fact that her coffee-house took not just 'domestic' but 'Foreign News' as a selling point in her own advertisement.[36] Indeed, her distinction between 'domestic' meaning native or home and 'Foreign' meaning abroad was a common opposition in the eighteenth century.[37]

Whether they were read in public coffee-houses or in private homes, the wide variety of advertisements for real estate, auctions, loans, runaways, lost and found goods, brokerage, bankruptcies, situations wanted and vacant, ships arriving, apologies for slander, books just published and goods for sale formed, as Black argues, 'part of a system of intelligence not isolated curiosities'.[38] Although contemporaries often condemned vulgar advertising and complained that it reduced the amount of real news and entertainment, its usefulness was also acknowledged. In 1736 one journalist explained that he looked 'upon them as pieces of domestic intelligence . . . the advertisements are filled with matters of great importance'.[39] It is this system of 'domestic intelligence' which effectively constituted what could be described as an imagined community of trade.[40] Indeed, in his advice book for English tradesmen Defoe himself imagined 'a settled little society of trading people, who understand business, and are carrying on trade in the same manner', eager to converse with each other and 'hear all the trading news'.[41] As a writer in the *Westminster Gazette* of 1736 declared, 'all mutual intercourse in the ordinary connections of trade [were] maintained and supported very principally by newspapers'.[42] This sense of community was reinforced by newspaper notices which frequently addressed specific professions or trades rather than individuals, thus constructing an

---

[35] *LDA*, 30 September and 2 October 1775.

[36] *LDA*, 1 March, 1734.

[37] See Brewer, 'This, That and The Other', p. 10; Davidoff, 'Regarding Some "Old Husbands' Tales"', p. 228, points out that historically 'domestic', as in the concept of domestic ideology, has no 'other half' since the literal opposite would be wild or foreign.

[38] Black, *The English Press*, p. 60.

[39] *Fogs Weekly Journal*, 14 February 1736, cited in ibid., p. 59.

[40] On the centrality of newspapers to the concept of an 'imagined community' see Benedict Anderson, *Imagined Communities: Reflections on the Origins and Spread of Nationalism* (London, 1983), esp. pp. 33–5.

[41] Defoe, *Complete English Tradesman*, pp. 36, 35.

[42] *Westminster Gazette*, 28 December 1776, cited in Black, *The English Press*, pp. 59–60.

imagined readership of occupational groupings with shared identities and interests. During the political troubles of 1745 John Steele posted a timely reminder to 'the butchers' of the many occasions papists could not eat meat.[43] Women seeking a position in the millinery business would address their advertisement 'To the Milliners' as an occupational group and, as we have seen in the case of the female tobacco-pipe makers, advertisements were a useful way to lobby for support among other members of a trade during disputes.[44] In addition to notices directed at specific trades and displays of public organisation, most businesswomen immediately followed their names with their occupation when inserting any kind of notice in the paper, even for the interception of stolen goods.[45] The latter may also have been a form of opportune marketing, but it nevertheless suggests that women had a higher degree of occupational identity than has previously been assumed.[46]

Women made frequent use of this network of business intelligence for a number of reasons in addition to generating more sales; these included: to raise money for loans, to announce a change of address or type of business, to look for a business partner or to announce that a partnership had been dissolved, to find a business to invest in or a runaway apprentice, or to defend their reputation against malicious rumour. One common reason given for adopting 'this publick method' of advertising was 'want of acquaintance', or in other words, the lack of a personal network of friends and customers. As we have seen, in a provincial town like Durham networking could be done on a face-to-face basis or personal recommendation by letter, but in an expanding consumer society newspaper advertising was an alternative way of making oneself known to unidentified customers and providing a (good) address for contact. One woman who had 'just arriv'd from Paris . . . who, for Want of Acquaintance, takes this Method to acquaint all Ladies and others' of her business, directed that enquiries should be made for her at Myon's coffee-house in Bloomsbury.[47] Indeed, such was the value of important contacts or acquaintances in business terms that it could be transmuted into financial worth, as the following advertisement for a business partner in 1765 demonstrates.

> ANY Lady of polite address, and who has a general Acquaintance among the better
> Sort, willing to assist a Person of Honour in a particular business, may thereby have

---

[43] *LDA*, 4 October 1745.

[44] See above, pp. 185–6.

[45] See e.g. Mrs Carnells, Pawnbroker, *LDA*, 8 February 1734; or Margaret Child, Button Seller, *LDA*, 11 March 1755.

[46] Hunt, *Middling Sort*, p. 128, argues that women lacked the 'occupational identity and trade consciousness' that characterised their husbands' work. Women's lack of occupational identity is often traced back to their low-profile involvement in guilds; see e.g. Natalie Zemon Davies, 'Women and Crafts in Sixteenth-Century Lyon', in *Women and Work in Preindustrial Europe*, ed. B. Hanawalt (Bloomington, 1986), pp. 167–97.

[47] *LDA*, 22 November 1755.

the Opportunity of gaining a very handsome Sum of Money in Hand, besides other Advantages. Her Advice and Assistance in pointing out will be sufficient, without appearing in it, although it is quite reputable, and no Way exceptionable.[48]

Partnership or investment in business is an area that provides a good insight into the contradictions of commercial gentility and public/private distinctions. Here the needs and risks of business in terms of work, finance and skill were set out by and for both those 'regularly bred' to trade and genteel women who found themselves in financial need of a polite income. Particularly in the latter case, private gentility and public commerce had to accommodate each other. For 'gentlewomen' or those who possessed a genteel education, entering 'into partnership with any of her own sex in a reputable Business' could be a useful way to 'live handsomely'.[49] Those seeking such an investment in business usually explained that they had friends willing to provide capital and/or security, or that they possessed a capital sum of their own. Yet there remained a tension between gentlewomen's need of genteel employment or income and the public nature of trade. Some, as we have seen, were unwilling even to sit in a 'publick shop' and many suggested living with a private family while offering needlework or childcare services as an acceptable alternative to a business partnership in their advertisements.

If the genteel but impoverished Mrs Radcliffe found that her class and lack of experience in trade prejudiced her chances of finding actual employment in a millinery shop,[50] businesswomen seeking partners for primarily investment purposes were far keener to attract gentlewomen with even relatively small capital sums. They were quick to stress the genteel nature and geographical location of the business, the lack of financial risk and the minimum amount of actual work required. One advertiser seeking an investment of £250 capital in her haberdashery business declared that she had no objection if the applicant 'don't understand much of the Business', while another opined that the trade would take just one hour to learn.[51] Advertisers who sought partners to actively help run the business had to state clearly that the motive for seeking a partner was 'assistance'. For an investment of as little as £20 to as much as £500,[52] most businesswomen offered gentlewomen of good reputation a 'genteel livelihood' and sometimes accommodation with the family in a manner calculated not to disrupt the tenets of ideal femininity. Particularly for those in the millinery business or running girls' boarding-schools, the acquisition of a young woman with capital and a 'large acquaintance' who could 'claim to esteem herself polite

---

[48] *LDA*, 8 March 1765.
[49] *LDA*, 22 January 1755.
[50] See above, pp. 184–5.
[51] *LDA*, 22 May 1755; 14 May 1765.
[52] Many of the sums required for partners in advertisements were considerably lower than the £400 to £500 needed to set up a genteel millinery business suggested by Collyer, *Parent's and Guardian's Directory*, p. 196.

and well-bred' could significantly advance their commercial interests. Indeed, one advertiser who had gained 'Approbation and universal Applause' for her management of a girls' boarding-school made it clear that any applications for partnership 'coming from any Lady who has not something genteel at her Command' would be 'found fruitless'. Anyone possessing such qualities, however, could expect to 'improve a scanty fortune in the Station of Gentlewoman' rather than 'risk it in trade', and 'little Attention [was] required to the Business of the School'.[53] Such partnerships, where one partner invested money but performed few other duties, were, as we have seen, not uncommon in the eighteenth century and were known as 'dormant partners'. Newspaper advertisements and insurance registers suggest that this style of partnership was not limited to 'gentlemen of large and independent fortunes' but on a smaller scale could be equally common among women.[54] These advertisements also suggest that rather than being faced with a stark choice of needlework, governessing or prostitution, a gentlewoman of scanty fortune could 'throw it into trade' in order to acquire a handsome living. As one woman looking for a partnership in a chandlery business declared, 'A Sober Woman would be glad to be in business'.[55]

The majority of advertisements for partnerships, placed by gentlewomen seeking a genteel income or businesswomen seeking primarily financial assistance, were specifically aimed at other women, and in some cases even stated the age and marital status of the prospective partner. A woman who had been 'settled many Years in an advantageous Trade' specified that she wished to find a middle-aged, 'active industrious woman', with 'no incumberance' like herself, with whom to forge a partnership.[56] By no means all advertisements for partnerships were restricted to one sex, however. Businessmen were also keen to stress the genteel and profitable nature of their business, and although the majority of advertisements placed by men and women for partnerships requested a partner of the same sex, occasionally the request would be for 'a single Man or Woman', or 'any Gentleman or Lady', or the advertiser would state that he had 'no Objection to a woman of good Character'.[57] For those women already in trade, as opposed to those seeking an initial investment, partnership could be a way up the business ladder and public advertising was the best way of taking such a step. In these cases skill and experience were offered, often on a trial basis at first, followed by the promise of capital in exchange for the prospect of becoming a full partner at a later date.

---

[53] *LDA*, 5 August, 1765.

[54] See above, p. 171, n. 101; Watson, *Treatise of the Law of Partnership* (1794), pp. 73–4.

[55] *LDA*, 8 November 1765.

[56] *LDA*, 24 June 1775; only £40 capital was required.

[57] See e.g. *LDA*, 28 June 1765; 20 September 1765. See also 12 July 1765: the proprietor of 'an easy genteel business' sought a single or married man to go into partnership with, but was willing to 'instruct the party if not bred in this branch' of trade.

Alternatively, there was the possibility of joining forces with another woman already 'in good business'.[58] One boarding-school proprietor sought a partner capable of understanding French and teaching girls, but stressed that it would be a greater advantage if she 'should have a small school and be desirous of bringing her scholars with her'.[59]

Women who had been doing business in well-established partnerships used the newspaper to inform other traders and/or customers of any changes in their partnerships and to whom any outstanding debts should be paid. Thus one of the more common situations requiring public notification was the dissolution of a partnership after which one or both partners would continue trading alone.[60] In January 1745 Lucy Earle of the Turk's Head bagnio announced that her partnership with William Jones had ceased at Christmas but that she had refurbished the house and was continuing the business as usual. Ten days later Jones announced that he had moved and taken over the late Mrs Hayward's bagnio in Charles Street.[61] Earle and Jones were not obviously related but many partnership notices were placed due to changes in family circumstances. Marital separation was one such occasion when the division of business and the acknowledgement of who was liable for specific debts had important financial and legal implications. It was common for husbands to place advertisements denying responsibility for their wives' debts after marital separation or desertion,[62] but if trade was to continue it was important for both partners to stress consent and liability. Hence in 1775 Useby Bettel, a cook in Cripplegate, announced that he had 'with the Consent of Ann my Wife, mutually agreed to separate ourselves, and to become separate Dealers in Trade'.[63] The promotion of another member of the family to partnership was also an event worthy of public notification. Widows, such as shoemaker Mary Storer in 1755, would place a series of advertisements announcing that she had taken her son into partnership and that he was now legally authorised to receive debts.[64] As we have seen, partnerships between widows and sons-in-law were not uncommon, but nor were partnerships between fathers and daughters-in-law. On the death of ivory turner Isaac Buckland in 1765, his former partner and daughter-in-law Deborah Buckland announced that she

---

[58] *LDA*, 18 October 1775; a mantua maker sought either a workwoman to assist her, or 'a young woman that has got good business of her own' with whom to go into partnership.

[59] *LDA*, 31 May 1765.

[60] These were often little more than formal notices. See e.g. *LDA*, 18 March 1765, an advertisement announcing that the partnership between Hester Whitrow and John Shepherd, weavers, had been dissolved and that all persons indebted to the partnership should pay Mrs Whitrow who would be continuing the business.

[61] *LDA*, 15 January 1745; 24 January 1745.

[62] Bailey, *Unquiet Lives*, pp. 56–9, points out that many such advertisements were designed specifically to damage a wife's credit and reputation.

[63] *LDA*, 8 November 1775.

[64] *LDA*, 4, 5 and 8 September 1755.

would 'make it her constant study and care' to continue to serve her customers and friends. In 1775 Mrs Robinson respectfully acquainted her friends and customers that she had quit business and had left the lace warehouse to be continued by her former partner and niece Jane Bell.[65] Alternatively, one ageing woman advertised for a young female partner precisely because she had no family to pass the business on to.[66]

For all those in search of employment, loans, investments, business partners, wider networks of friends and customers, increased sales, or a place to make any other kind of public announcement, the newspaper functioned as an imagined community of trade within which businesswomen were a well-integrated minority. But perhaps the most important factor that enabled businesswomen to manoeuvre within this community and engage in commerce with its more genteel readership was the existence of a shared language of trade, a discourse of legitimacy based on the existence of a creditable reputation which was clearly evident in newspaper advertisements placed by both male and female traders.

A creditable reputation

Credit was both a trading necessity, because of the shortage of ready money available and the problems of transferring it, but also a reflection of the highly personal nature of exchange which took place between people who were known to each other.[67] In addition to the need for financial support and/or investment from family and friends, the instability of the eighteenth-century marketplace and lack of personal protection from the potentially disastrous effects of business debts meant that traders had to rely heavily on the creditable reputations of suppliers and customers to guarantee financial transactions.[68] In this period then, although it was impossible to differentiate between business and personal financial liability, it was important to distinguish between the mere trappings of success and the personal probity of the trader. When Defoe criticised the extravagant displays of goods in shops, he argued that this kind of credit was 'of a different kind from the substantial reputation of a tradesman; 'tis rather the credit of the *shop*, than of the *man*; and in a word is no more or

---

[65] *LDA*, 28 June 1765; 5 January 1775.

[66] *LDA*, 31 October 1765.

[67] Julian Hoppit, *Risk and Failure in English Business 1700–1800* (Cambridge, 1987), p. 163.

[68] See Hunt, *Middling Sort*, pp. 29–34, on the nature of business risk and personal credit; Muldrew, *Economy of Obligation*, pp. 4, 146, 148–52, on the sociability of credit and the importance of trusting in other people's reputation for fairness and honesty, decisions about which were usually based on the local knowledge of friends and business associates; Wiskin, *Women, Finance and Credit*, pp. 128–38, on how businesswomen's creditworthiness was measured according to their conduct, lifestyle and moral worth.

less than a net spread to catch fools.'[69] Thus one explanation for why the number of advertisements solely promoting goods for sale was relatively low compared to other types of advertisement[70] was that the reputation of the shopkeeper was often considered more important than the merchandise she sold. Advertisers used a number of strategies to establish their trading credibility; these included: the backing of friends, length of time in business, and emphasising a distinctive trading identity. Yet if personal credit was necessary to underpin business practice, it still had to be adapted to a more competitive consumer-oriented market, an area which – if it was to be negotiated successfully – required the use of varying degrees of sociable gentility.

Personal recommendation was paramount because as one contemporary put it, 'credit . . . is no more than a *well established* confidence between men, in what relates to the fulfilling of their engagements.'[71] Tom Jones' landlady felt compelled to inform his doctor that Jones' gentlemanly appearance was not matched by a full purse because, as she explained, 'people in business oft always to let one another know such things'.[72] Since influential and trusted 'friends' were vital to provide security for loans and to guarantee payments, as well as to help bring in other potential customers, many businesswomen's advertisements (particularly those for luxury trades) were addressed to customers and friends rather than to the 'publick'. Some vendors, like the milliner Mrs Spencer, merely begged 'Leave to acquaint her Friends, that she has opened a commodious shop'[73] without any mention of customers. Influential friends among the gentry, particularly in the more genteel trades, were an even greater advantage. Miss Matson, the milliner in Fanny Burney's *The Wanderer* (1814), was only too keen to be rid of the friendless Gabriella and hire the well-connected Juliet. She saw no reason to keep Gabriella who was 'known to nobody, and is very bad pay, if I can have so genteel a young lady as you, Ma'am that ladies in their own coaches come visiting.'[74] A 'Young Woman, lately come out of the Country' who wanted to work in a milliner's or haberdasher's shop with a view to becoming a partner after a satisfactory trial period assured any prospective employer that 'She has a Friend that will advance her Money for the same and give any Security that is farther requir'd'.[75] Laetitia Pilkington, who corresponded frequently with Samuel

---

[69] Defoe, *Complete English Tradesman*, p. 278.
[70] Walker, 'Advertising in London Newspapers', pp. 124–5, highlights the variety of consumer goods advertised but points out that these still occurred relatively rarely and many types of goods (e.g. common foodstuffs, gin and beer) were advertised by other means. See also Walsh, 'Advertising and Marketing of Consumer Goods', pp. 82–4.
[71] Steuart, *Principals of Political Economy*, vol. II, p. 440, cited in Hoppit, *Risk and Failure*, p. 163.
[72] Fielding, *Tom Jones*, p. 357.
[73] LDA, 8 April 1775.
[74] Fanny Burney, *The Wanderer* (1814; this edn Oxford, 1991), p. 383.
[75] LDA, 2 October 1755.

Richardson, wrote to him asking if he could provide her with a reference because 'I can get a most compleat beautiful shop in the Strand . . . but the gentleman who owns it wants some person of credit to give me a reference'.[76] Pilkington's own character had been ruined by her husband's public repudiation of her. Richardson's response is unknown, but a similar application to the Bishop of London was returned to her torn to pieces.

With characteristically dramatic imagery, Defoe likened refusing to give a character to shooting a man in the head,[77] but stressed that a businessman with credit 'was invulnerable whether he has money or no'.[78] He devoted an entire chapter entitled 'Tradesman's Characters Inviolable' to the subject in which he declared:

'Good name in man or woman,
Is the immediate jewel of our souls.
Who steals my purse, steals trash; 'tis something, nothing; . . .
But he that filches from me my good name,
Robs me of that, which not inriches him,
And makes me poor indeed.[79]

The newspaper provided an opportunity for those who had slandered another's character to retract it by public notice.[80] In October 1775 mantua maker Ursula Minson took the opportunity to 'acquaint the publick' that she had unjustly accused another of stealing, and H. Spark apologised for having 'through heat of passion only, insulted and spoken several unguarded Words, tending to injure the Character of Mrs. Lee'.[81] In the above rhyme, Defoe appears not to have been making a gendered distinction, but the reference to 'good name in . . . woman' could equally have rested on an assumption of sexual probity. Female advertisers were certainly no less anxious to provide a creditable character, not least because loss of personal credit could result in financial disaster through recalled loans. The unfortunate 'wanderer', Juliet, found that when she incurred debts after losing her personal credit and the support of her noble friends, 'her want of credit made immediate payment necessary'.[82] Yet the female advertisers most likely to promote themselves as a 'Person of Character and Reputation' were those for whom public trading meant engaging with the taint of sexual impropriety, such as milliners and mid-wives. Numerous libertine pamphlets linked economic with sexual reputation

[76] Cited in Turner, 'News from the New Exchange', p. 428.
[77] Defoe, Complete English Tradesman, p. 211.
[78] Ibid., p. 353.
[79] Ibid., p. 204.
[80] Donna T. Andrew, 'The Press and Public Apologies in Eighteenth-century London', in Law, Crime and English Society, 1660–1830, ed. N. Landau (Cambridge, 2002), pp. 208–29.
[81] LDA, 5 October 1775.
[82] Burney, The Wanderer p. 305.

so that female traders 'whose sexual "credit" was broken' could find it hard to gain financial credit or employment.[83] Thus 'Character' could function primarily as shorthand for a reference, as in the case of a young gentlewoman who had served her apprenticeship with a milliner and wanted to go into 'Partnership with a person of Credit in that business', for which she herself could provide an 'undeniable character'.[84] But for women, a good reference usually also depended on a degree of sexual probity. Similarly 'reputation' could equally cover acknowledgement of public fame and reliable trading, as well as personal/sexual honour. One midwife who ran her own 'private' lying-in rooms explained that she had a 'long established Reputation for her Honour',[85] not least because contemporary suspicions about the illegitimacy of children born to women using these private facilities meant that midwives had to defend themselves against possible defamation.

A less explicitly gendered strategy to establish a creditable reputation was to specifically link personal identity with that of the business and announce 'her name above the door'. This was an added precaution because the elaborate signs above each premises could be copied and lead to confusion or malpractice, as was the case for Elizabeth and Lucy Hardy, who stressed that:

> ours is the original Crown and Lace Lappets, remov'd from the third door above Tinker's Alley in the same street, where there is put up a copy of our said sign; also that some evil minded persons, for sinister ends, gave and full continue to give out, that we left off Trade, when we remov'd to our present House for the Conveniency of Ladies coming in their Coaches.[86]

A further measure of reputable trading was length of time in established business. In 1745 Hannah Ward went to great lengths to assure customers of her trading reputation while offering to 'perform all manner of brass and silver work that is done to china ware cheaper than anywhere in London'. She added:

> Note, I am no new started up pretender, for to gain business tells the world a pack of bare faced lyes . . . but I am well known by most of the China shops in London to have been proficient in this art near Twenty years.

Ward was apparently successful, for in 1765 she advertised again and had added another premises to her original one with her name under the sign.[87]

---

[83] Turner, 'News from the New Exchange', p. 427.

[84] *LDA*, 1 January 1755.

[85] *LDA*, 8 July 1755.

[86] *LDA*, 23 January 1745.

[87] *LDA*, 8 February 1745, repeated 25 February; a new advertisement was repeated in April and May, and on 30 January 1765 she announced her additional premises, in which she had branched out into new and secondhand clothes, cloth remnants, funeral furnishing, and even a book.

If establishing a creditable reputation was important for business, increasing sales obviously remained a key reason for advertising, and businesswomen were also quite adept at adopting competitive marketing techniques. Historians disagree on a chronology for the adoption of innovative marketing practices such as using brand names, price cutting and marking fixed prices on goods rather than haggling, but most place these occurrences in the late eighteenth or early nineteenth centuries.[88] However, in those advertisements which sold goods directly, women were engaged in competitive marketing techniques from some of the *Advertiser's* earliest issues. On Monday, 5 November 1733 Ann Digsoote seems to have sparked something of a price war by advertising her coffee-house as possessing not only a handsome garden with a fountain and gravel walks for gentlemen to stroll in, but also listing her competitive prices for Batavia Arrack, Jamaica Rum and French Brandy. By the following Monday three coffee-houses were advertising their drinks at the same prices, because, as the (male) proprietor of the Rainbow declared:

> of late several persons have for the advantage of the public, advertised the selling of Punch at the following reasonable rates . . . [I] do give notice that I will sell Punch at the above prices.[89]

If the coffee-house proprietors were engaged in competitive pricing to increase their sales, it was still articulated in terms of the public's advantage rather than their own.

This situation created something of a contradiction. On the one hand was the ideally industrious, sober, reputable businessperson (who nevertheless had to engage with a competitive market); on the other the ornamental focus on style, display and politeness demanded by a consumer society and necessary to enable a trader to maintain an appearance of gentility and creditworthiness. Yet Klein has shown how this apparent opposition between the productive and the polite could be resolved.[90] He suggests that polite and productive could be seen to complement each other, because '"politeness" was a way of setting off one's capacities so that they could operate effectively'.[91] For Klein, advice manuals such as Defoe's were one way of purveying politeness to traders, and a degree of politeness was very necessary for the highly sociable practice of trade. Although she reversed the emphasis, Fanny Burney made a similar point in *The Wanderer* by stressing that for gentlewomen accomplishments

---

[88] Alexander, *Retailing in England*, pp. 11, 234, locates the development of price competition between shops in the 1820s, but Mui and Mui, *Shops and Shopkeeping*, pp. 21–4, locates greater changes in pricing in the 1770s.

[89] *LDA*, 12 November 1733.

[90] Klein, 'Politeness for Plebes', pp. 363–82.

[91] Ibid., p. 366.

could be *'useful* as well as ornamental'.[92] Indeed, for those gentlewomen not 'regularly bred' to trade this could be essential for their economic welfare. Claims to the status of gentlewoman, however, were rather less clear-cut. In the medium of newspaper advertisements, 'gentlewomen' stressed their gentility and the need to find a 'clean', 'genteel' business to learn or invest in, while businesswomen claimed to be 'gentlewomen' of 'business and character'.

In newspaper advertisements traders were effecting sociable transactions both with other traders and to unseen, but nevertheless literate, affluent and polite potential customers. Many were therefore careful to frame their advertisements accordingly. Mary Street, the widow of a sail maker, wanted all merchants, owners and captains of ships to know that she would carry on the business and would 'esteem it the greatest Favour to receive their Commands and Orders'.[93] Some wrote their advertisements as if in letter form, as did Rebecca Till, an innkeeper, when addressing the 'Nobility, Gentry and others', duly signing herself 'their most obedient and obliged humble servant to command'.[94] In this context 'honour' referred to the privilege of serving clients and patrons. Numerous advertisers spoke of being 'honoured' to serve their customers, 'the first Quality' or even 'the Royal family'. Mrs Pignerolle, wanted to inform 'such Gentlemen who do her the Honour to employ her for SWORD-KNOTS, that they may depend upon being elegantly served with all Sorts'.[95] Only very rarely were these conventions ignored completely, as in the case of Mrs Cox: 'Dealer in Ladies Wearing Apparel, buys and sells all Sorts of rich Gold, Silver . . . with Variety of different articles too tedious to mention. Deals for ready Money only.'[96] For Cox, cash sales evidently meant that credit and the guarantees needed to support it were unnecessary, yet even she felt compelled to establish her trading credentials by explaining that she was the 'Daughter and Successor of the late Mrs. Buckoke'. If the maintenance of a creditable reputation was essential for all traders, male and female, there were still gendered assumptions about sexuality and gentility that businesswomen needed to negotiate. The extent of that negotiation, however, varied according to different occupations, and these differences will be examined in the following section.

Milliners, medics and midwives

The most genteel and feminine trade for women to be engaged in, and the one demanding the most rigorous defence of character, was millinery. It was also

---

[92] Burney, *The Wanderer*, p. 289 (emphasis added).
[93] *LDA*, 8 October 1745.
[94] *LDA*, 2 January 1765.
[95] *LDA*, 16 January 1765.
[96] *LDA*, 10 August 1775.

one of the most competitive, profitable and ornamental of luxury trades. It is in these advertisements that women negotiated most carefully between the competing claims to skill, reputation, fashion and price. As one woman, 'of good character in great business', explained, she had acquired her position through 'assiduity, strict attention to fashion, and reasonable terms'.[97] If, as Corfield has argued, 'occupation was a badge of social acknowledgement as well as an economic role',[98] which had connotations for respectability, then the milliner held a unique status in the hierarchy of trade. Dorothy George argues that there were minute distinctions made between traders and trades, and categorises their status from the 'genteels' to the 'dirty genteels', the 'genteelish' to the 'ordinary', and the 'mean' to the 'nasty mean and stinking'.[99] Trades were graded partly on earnings and capitalisation, but also on custom and the dirtiness of the work required.[100] Milliners' advertisements reflected their 'genteel' status. One advertisement for a milliner's apprentice made it clear that the person was 'not required to carry out boxes',[101] others that there would be no outside work or sitting in public premises.[102] In fact it was possible to avoid being in a public shop by working for a 'chamber milliner' who did not keep a shop, although this necessitated an even larger genteel acquaintance, was usually less profitable and the 'privacy' involved sparked further suspicions of sexual impropriety behind closed doors.[103] Nevertheless, Burney's Juliet chose millinery as the most genteel form of employment she could find.[104] Collyer, in his advice to parents on suitable trades for children, stated that milliners 'ought to have a genteel person' and that it was an ideal occupation for 'the daughters of numerous families, where the parents live handsomely, yet have no fortunes to leave their children'.[105]

It was very probably the effort to maintain a veneer of gentility that explains why many of these advertisements display a conflicting attitude towards money. Those who wanted to sell the latest fashions advertised their goods as being both of the 'genteelest and most approv'd taste' and to be had for 'reasonable rates', or, as Joyce Mason declared, she would 'be content with the smallest

---

[97] *LDA*, 18 March 1745.

[98] Corfield, 'Defining Urban Work', p. 217.

[99] George, *London Life in the Eighteenth Century*, p. 163.

[100] Ibid., and for a more detailed discussion of the hierarchy of occupations see Schwarz, *London in the Age of Industrialisation*, p. 57ff.

[101] *LDA*, 3 April 1775.

[102] Collyer, *Parent's and Guardian's Directory*, pp. 194–6.

[103] Campbell, *London Tradesman*, p. 209, and see above, p. 191.

[104] Burney, *The Wanderer*, p. 220. Juliet was the unacknowledged daughter of a peer, whose need to conceal her identity meant that she could not reveal her birth but made it necessary to keep up her station in life.

[105] Collyer, *Parent's and Guardian's Directory*, p. 194. Sanderson, 'Edinburgh Milliners', pp. 18–28, found most came from gentry or professional families, but Shani D'Cruze, 'To Acquaint the Ladies': Women Traders in Colchester c. 1750–1800', *Local Historian*, 17

profit as anyone whatever'.[106] Nevertheless, to set up shop in a genteel fashion required a considerable investment – perhaps £400 to £500[107] – and the best demanded a high or 'genteel premium' with their apprentices. Hence, even though making large profits was vulgar, paying a high price to enter the trade ensured its genteel status. Those seeking positions would offer 'a handsome Apprentice-Fee' or, if they could not, tried to bargain the advantage of coming from a 'reputable' or 'creditable' family and/or the possession of exceptional skill for a lower premium.[108] Many advertisements for apprentices, partners and journeywomen emphasised the need for skill in the trade. They requested a 'good natural genius', or that the applicant should be 'perfect mistress of her profession' and 'perfectly acquainted with the trade'. Yet while substantial capital and a high premium may have helped guarantee the gentility of the trade itself, it was also somewhat at odds with the gentility of some of those wishing to enter it. Fanny Burney explained Juliet's refined distaste at accepting her wages, despite her dire need; thus:

> However respectable reason and justice render pecuniary emolument, where honourably earned; there is a something indefinable which stands between spirit and delicacy, that makes the first reception of money in detail, by those not brought up to it embarrassing and painful.[109]

This ambivalence towards 'pecuniary emolument' is also visible in the advertisements, although as these mostly appear from 1775, it is equally possible that the pressure of numbers applying made offering to work for little money necessary to gain a good position. Nevertheless, the possession of friends willing to provide part of her income meant that a milliner need not bargain over wages. A woman who had completed her apprenticeship in the West End and now sought a position with a chamber milliner in the city explained that 'As she has Friends, she will leave her wages entirely to her employer'.[110] Another, who had been brought up in a reputable shop in the city but wished to live in the country, wanted a position with a creditable milliner but as

---

(1986), pp. 158–61, found that more came from small trading and manufacturing communities, although all could aspire to gentility.

[106] LDA, 24 January 1745. Joyce was a retailer and wholesaler who made 'proper Allowances to Country Shopkeepers, Fairkeepers &c. who sell again', but she also went abroad herself, imported lace from Flanders and exported lace from Bath and Buckinghamshire. She was a regular advertiser.

[107] Collyer, Parent's and Guardian's Directory, p. 196.

[108] LDA, 27 February 1765; an 'established' milliner looking for an apprentice offered 'a Person of reputable parents will be accepted upon moderate terms'. A widowed mother of two girls sought an apprenticeship for one with no money but emphasised her excellent upbringing, her skill with a needle and her ability to do accounts: LDA, 16 October 1765.

[109] Burney, The Wanderer, p. 454.

[110] LDA, 3 February 1775.

she had 'some Allowance from her Relations, she desires no Consideration but her Board, Lodging and genteel Treatment'.[111] Of two women seeking to move from the country to London, one declared that 'Wages will be the least consideration', and the other that 'Money is not the Object, but to gain more Experience, as she has creditable Friends'.[112]

'Ability, Honesty, Sobriety'[113] were the hallmarks of a good milliner, but perhaps the greatest danger to her reputation was that of sexual slander. As we have seen, milliners were commonly linked with sexual impropriety and seduction in the public imagination. Grantham Turner has argued that serious conduct books such as Campbell's *London Tradesman* discussed above (and so by implication Collyer's *Parent's Directory*) merged and colluded with the texts of scandalous pamphlets.[114] Despite the problems of citing such texts as evidence for 'non-phantasmic reality', they and other texts discussed in the previous chapter,[115] clearly provided a dominant discursive frame of which milliners advertising in public newspapers were only too aware. More than any other type of advertisement, the need for an 'undeniable character' which would bear the 'strictest scrutiny' was demanded in millinery. Moreover, when seeking apprentices, even those who were persons of 'good Character in the strictest sense' had to promise 'the utmost care taken of her morals'. One milliner of 'established Business, in a private Situation' who wanted an apprentice with a premium, declared that 'such an opportunity is rarely to be met with, as Instruction in the Business, and Care of her Morals, will be the constant Object of the Advertiser's Attention'.[116] However, such opportunities became less rare from 1765 as an increasing number of advertisements for apprentices included some form of moral guarantee to protect their purity.

A group of advertisers who were considerably less concerned with emphasising their personal morality or gentility, and who were prepared to engage in far more aggressive advertising techniques, were the female 'quacks' and sellers of cosmetics. Female midwives, however – fellow practitioners in the medical marketplace of eighteenth-century London – went to great lengths to maintain an aura of honesty, gentility and politeness. Yet both were equally determined to establish their 'professional' or business credentials as legitimate traders and possessors of the appropriate medical skills and knowledge. There has been considerable discussion about when, and to what extent, medicine could be called a profession and thus, by implication, increasingly exclude women from the knowledge and skills necessary to practise it successfully.[117] Although it is

---

[111] *LDA*, 31 August 1775.
[112] *LDA*, 6 November 1775; 22 April 1775.
[113] *LDA*, 23 August 1765.
[114] Turner, 'News from the New Exchange', p. 428.
[115] See above, pp. 188–91.
[116] *LDA*, 28 March 1765.
[117] See e.g. Clark, *Working Life of Women*, pp. 253–85; Pinchbeck, *Women Workers,*

not possible to use advertisements to contribute to quantitative debates over the decline of women's involvement in medicine and midwifery, it is possible to reassess the terms of debate. The advertising strategies of female quacks and midwives suggest that the sale and practice of medicine should be viewed more as a business or trade than a profession and that multiple concepts of knowledge and skill could and did co-exist in eighteenth-century London.

Margaret Pelling has warned against viewing professionalisation as a continuous linear development and has pointed out that even today (when medicine enjoys an undisputed status as a modern profession) it remains a fragmented field. She has also highlighted a number of aspects that continued to link early modern medicine to other areas of economic life, such as the persistence of notions of 'apprenticeship', close links with the food and drink trades (both also associated with women) and the idea that a cure was 'in many respects bought as an item'.[118] Roy Porter has similarly argued that eighteenth-century medicine should be seen as an 'occupation' rather than a 'profession', in which light 'quacks' are viewed as highly successful businesspeople who adopted an alternative route to prosperity: they traded in the mass market, to anonymous patients with a high degree or risk, as opposed to the private patronage, known clients and structured career of the professional doctor. In this model too, patients were not dupes but active 'customers' to whom self-medication was a difficult but informed choice. Thus for Porter the practice of self-medicating, and buying medicines and medical manuals was all part of the growth of an emerging consumer society.[119] Within this framework female advertisers of medicines may be viewed as businesswomen 'providing types of medicines . . . which the more rigid structures of orthodox medicine could not match'.[120] Similarly, although midwives may not have sold cures in bottles they did regard themselves as having undergone either formal or informal apprenticeship to 'the Midwifery Business' and so had 'not her business to learn'. In addition, these were very much an urban type of midwife and the majority of those advertising were offering some form of 'genteel accommodation' for 'ladies' or 'gentlewomen' to 'lye-in', not just their midwifery skills. Occasionally, midwives did refer to their 'profession', but until the late eighteenth century

---

pp. 300–4; Hill, *Women, Work and Sexual Politics*, pp. 162–4; A.L. Wyman, 'The Surgeoness: The Female Practitioner of Surgery, 1400–1800', *Medical History*, 28 (1984); Corfield, *Power and the Professions*, pp. 137–65; Margaret Pelling, 'Medical Practice in Early Modern England: Trade or Profession?', ed. W. Prest (New York, 1987), pp. 90–128. For midwifery in particular see e.g. J. Donnison, *Midwives and Medical Men: A History of Inter-professional Rivalries and Women's Rights* (London, 1977); B.B. Schnorrenberg, 'Is Childbirth any Place for a Woman? The Decline of Midwifery in Eighteenth-century England', *Studies in Eighteenth-century Culture*, 10 (1981), pp. 393–408; Adrian Wilson, *The Making of Man Midwifery: Childbirth in England, 1660–1770* (London, 1995).
[118] Pelling, 'Medical Practice', pp. 104–8.
[119] Porter, *Health for Sale*, p. 41.
[120] Ibid., p. 85.

the term was more commonly used to describe an individual's main occupation than a specifically learned vocation.[121] Moreover, midwifery could be a profitable business. According to one contemporary, in the 1770s eminent London midwives kept elegant carriages and could earn over £1,000 a year.[122]

Public concerns about medical advertisements placed by both sexes were not uncommon. Anxieties surrounding the (potentially morally dubious) reasons why gentlewomen might prefer to 'lie in private' apartments rather than their own homes meant that many midwives chose to stress not just their discretion and honour, but also to declare bluntly that such arrangements were 'not meant to encourage Intrigues'.[123] Midwives may have been occasionally asked to remove their advertisements because of fears about the morality of their practice,[124] but antipathy towards quacks caused some papers intermittently to exclude their advertisements altogether, although rarely for long because many newspaper proprietors and agents were also distributors of brand medicines. Advertisements for medicines were the earliest and most innovative to appear in newspapers, and they displayed such a variety of sales techniques that many historians view them as the forerunner to modern marketing strategies.[125] Yet contemporary surgeons and physicians argued that the quacks' 'public way of practice' was vulgar and degrading to the medical 'profession'; again the distinction is not gendered but between the genteel and the vulgar.[126] Dr Johnson's damning definition of a 'quack' as a 'vain boastful pretender to physic' included the charge, 'one who proclaims his own Medical abilities in public places'.[127]

Both male and female practitioners countered allegations of vulgarity by declaring public advertising was necessary both for their business and public benefit. Lydia Turner felt 'obliged to give this public notice to the world, there being many that want me, but know not where to find me', but the widows Gorman and Vaughton declared that although the Old Widow's Ear Balsam had been around for a long time, it was only 'now advertised, this being the

---

[121] Corfield, *Power and the Professions*, pp. 19–20, notes that Johnson's *Dictionary* began to refer to the 'learned professions' in the 1755 edition and it was not until the fourth edition of 1773 that the term was linked specifically to medicine, law and the Church. Midwives were still using the term in the 1765 sample but not in 1775.

[122] F. Foster, *Thoughts on the Times, but Chiefly on the Profligacy of our Women, and its Causes* (London, 1779), p. 95.

[123] See e.g. *LDA*, 8 July 1755.

[124] See above, p. 209.

[125] For a discussion of quack adverts see Walker, *Advertising in London Newspapers*, pp. 126–9. See also Porter, *Health for Sale*, pp. 45–6, on innovative marketing techniques.

[126] See Porter, *Health for Sale*, pp. 196–7, on the vulgarity of public practice, and Pelling, 'Medical Practice', pp. 105–6, on the 'delivery of medicine as a public rather than private act'.

[127] Johnson, *Dictionary* (1755), cf. 'Quack'.

first time, for the Good of the Publick'.[128] Alternatively, some attempted to avoid the charges of quackery and courting vulgar publicity altogether. In 1755 one described herself as 'A Gentlewoman who has the secret to cure Deafness, but will not have her Name in the Papers' in order to let people know that she 'may be heard of at Lewis Brunets in Sherrard-Street'.[129] Once again the concept of public businesswoman and private gentlewoman appear interchangeable. The most significant difference between advertisements placed by midwives and those by quacks was the level of politeness evident in the language used. Female quacks were appealing to the widest possible audience of potential medical consumers, whereas London midwives most commonly addressed their advertisements to 'gentlewomen' or 'ladies'. Hence the midwife's house was frequently 'genteel' and a letter of recommendation could be required, as well as a 'genteel price' for their services. Midwives stressed the 'eminent persons' they had served and expressed gratitude for receiving their 'favours' in a manner rarely used by quacks. Only two midwives in the sample, one male and one female, offered to help 'poor pregnant married women' or those in 'low circumstances'.[130]

In advertisements the distinction between 'professional' and 'non-professional' practice of the various branches of medicine was certainly not clear-cut. Both men and women used a variety of means to substantiate their claims to specialist skill and knowledge and, perhaps more importantly, these were supported by 'references' from more orthodox professional male practitioners. Both sexes used the terms 'oculist' and 'operator', but if only male advertisers described themselves as 'surgeons' they too sold remedies for the pox.[131] One man was driven by malicious insinuations which threatened to ruin his 'Character and Practice' to publish a diploma, as proof that he had served a 'regular apprenticeship to Surgery'.[132] Much has been made of the argument that lack of formal training led to female midwives being supplanted by college-trained male midwives, but in London women paid to serve as deputies to experienced midwives.[133] Indeed, 'professed' London midwives trained for up to seven years and thus enjoyed a high status.[134] Advertisements naming the midwife they had been deputy to and appeals to find runaway

[128] LDA, 1 February 1734; 3 October 1765. The ear balsam was most probably a brand medicine and was next advertised by Gorman and the Seymour circulating library.
[129] LDA, 29 March 1755.
[130] LDA, 3 July 1765; 15 January 1775.
[131] LDA, 30 October 1744.
[132] LDA, 21 December 1765.
[133] Donnison, Midwives and Medical Men, pp. 21–8; Wilson, Making of Man-midwifery, pp. 31–2, 36–8, 201–2; D.N. Harley, 'Ignorant Midwives – a Persistent Stereotype', Bulletin of the Society of the Social History of Medicine, 28 (1981), pp. 6–9; A. Wilson, 'Ignorant Midwives, a Rejoinder', ibid., 32 (1983), pp. 46–9; B. and J. Boss, 'Ignorant Midwives: a Further Rejoinder', ibid., 33 (1983), p.71.
[134] Earle, City Full of People, pp. 134–5, notes this training meant London midwives

apprentices testify that advertisers certainly regarded this training as apprenticeship.[135] In their advertisements too, midwives constantly stressed their 'ability', 'skill', 'experience' and many years of successful practice, which reflected a common contemporary argument that 'experience is the best instructor'.[136] In this context skill was a commodity for sale and what gave it monetary value was not necessarily a professional qualification. Nevertheless, for testimony to their abilities, midwives cited the support of 'eminent physicians'. Furthermore, in response to the growing fashion for male midwives, which becomes apparent in advertisements placed in 1765 and 1775, female advertisers cited the assistance of a male midwife as another unique selling point. Hence declaring that a 'Man-Midwife of eminence'[137] could attend if required suggests not only a degree of cross-gender co-operation (as opposed to outright competition) but also, as Wilson points out, that a 'female tradition could absorb the methods of its male rivals'.[138] The rise of male midwifery and consequent decline in female midwives has been explained as a consequence of changes in fashion as giving birth became another site of conspicuous consumption,[139] but London midwives seem to have been concerned to keep abreast of their elite customer's tastes without losing their own business.

Female quacks certainly adopted the advertising strategies of male rivals, and there was very little difference between those placed by male and female practitioners. It was also not unknown for male professionals to support their cause, not least because, as Porter has argued, 'quack' was a term of abuse levelled at unscrupulous practitioners in general but rarely at individuals. Mrs Joanna Stephens was perhaps the most famous example, for whom a 'professional' doctor, David Hartley, lobbied Parliament to pay £5,000 to make public her recipe to cure stones in the bladder. In 1739 Hartley published a report on the effects of Mrs Stephens' medicine in which he argued that the results justified her large fee and proved that she 'will appear to you in a different light from common Pretenders to NOSTRUMS'.[140] The award became something of a feature in medical advertisements, not just for herself

---

were 'most respected' and well paid, but argues that 'unlearned' midwives training novices meant that most remained comparatively ignorant and thus vulnerable to male competition.

[135] See e.g. *LDA*, 31 October 1745, an appeal to find an 11-year-old 'apprentice to Midwife Dorothy Foster, the Cradle and Ring'; *LDA*, 16 February 1765, Elizabeth Brown, 'late deputy' to the deceased Mrs Wood.

[136] See e.g. Foster, *Thoughts on the Times*, p. 105.

[137] *LDA*, 27 May 1775.

[138] Wilson, *Making of Man-midwifery*, p. 202.

[139] Ibid., pp. 3, 191.

[140] David Hartley, *A View of the Present Evidence for and against Mrs. Stephens's Medicines, as a Solvent for the Stone* (London, 1739), cited in Arthur J. Viseltear, 'Joanna Stephens and the Eighteenth-century Lithontriptics; A Misplaced Chapter in the History of Therapeutics', *Bulletin of the History of Medicine*, 42 (1968), pp. 199–220. Viseltear argues that her remedy would have dissolved some varieties of stones and definitely stimulated further research into non-surgical cures for the condition.

but also to sell other medicines based on her recipe.[141] To legitimise their products, quacks of both sexes emphasised the age of the remedy and length of time in business, but women in particular adopted a policy of tracing a line of descent through which the only 'genuine' recipe or medical skill had been passed. Lydia Turner traced an entire family history about how she had acquired the knowledge of curing 'crooked persons' from the widow of the 'famous D. Palmer' with whom she had lived and for whose daughter she had run the business.[142] Mrs Deane, an oculist, claimed somewhat improbably, that she was the 'only survivor' of a family that had been treating eyes on Mondays and Fridays for more than a hundred years. She had been 'brought up in this useful art by the well known Mrs Jones, and practis'd herself for upwards of twenty years past'. In a rare nod to the dictates of gentility she noted that 'People of the greatest Rank and Fashion' were willing to testify to the success of her cures.[143]

There was, however, strong competition between advertisers of both sexes. Patent medicines were big business, and one of the bestsellers that continued into the twentieth century was Daffy's Elixir, which was advertised for sale by men and women in London and provincial papers. Despite being a well-known proprietary brand,[144] between 1755 and 1775 several generations of women purported to be the direct descendants of the original Daffy and only true possessor of the remedy. In 1755 Susannah Daffy claimed to be his grand-daughter, but for several months her advertisements overlapped with those of Elizabeth Chapman who was apparently his widow.[145] Twenty years later Mary Swinton claimed that:

> THE True Original DAFFY'S ELIXIR is made only by me, who am Niece and Executrix of the late Anthony and Mary Daffy, and personal Representative of Dr. Anthony Daffy, the inventor of this Medicine. There being Counterfeits, I have offered a Reward of 100l. for Evidence in the other News Papers where the many Virtues of this Elixir are mentioned.[146]

To claim that the public was in danger of being duped by 'counterfeits' was perhaps the most aggressive strategy adopted by both sexes and one that clearly justified public advertising. One of the earliest retailers of the famous Anodyne

---

[141] LDA, 19 November 1755; 29 October 1744. For Joanna Stephens see also Porter, Health for Sale, p. 83; Pinchbeck, Women Workers, p. 301.

[142] LDA, 1 February 1734.

[143] LDA, 4 December 1744. Testimonies from cured patients were a common advertising strategy, but to cite elite clients was less so.

[144] Walsh, 'Advertising and Marketing of Consumer Goods', pp. 81–2.

[145] For Susannah Daffy see LDA, 6, 8, 11, 25 February; 26 September 1755. For Elizabeth Chapmen see 19, 20 May 1755.

[146] LDA, 6, 13, 30 June 1775, when she stopped offering a reward, and thereafter at least once weekly until December.

Necklace, a remarkable device supposed to prevent teething problems and almost every other illness in children, was Mrs Garway who ran a shop at the south gate of the Royal Exchange. From 1709 to 1711 she declared herself to be 'the only person in or about London so authoriz'd to sell the same by the original Author'.[147] A furious pamphlet and newspaper advertisement war ensued for several years as other sellers claimed the original necklace was theirs alone and was not sold 'at Mrs Garway's at the Royal Exchange Gate or anywhere else'. In 1717 Dr Chamberlen apparently wrote an open letter recognising three outlets for his necklace, including Mrs Garway's shop. But ten years later another pamphlet proclaimed that the necklace had been 'taken away from the Royal Exchange Gate' because the shop had been making its own and counterfeiting the seals for 'Lucre of larger Profit'. In 1733 the *Daily Advertiser* ran an advertisement from yet another (male) seller who cautioned against 'The Woman that imposes her "counterfeits" on the World at the Royal Exchange', whereas if the reader were to but cross the road he could have the 'Right and True Medicines', proof of which would be a free gift of 'the Author's Books along with your things'.[148] The woman imposing counterfeits in 1733 may well have been Mrs Garway's successor. She was one of many London women who were competitive and prolific advertisers and practitioners in a field where a multiplicity of diverse medical practices flourished, some of whom even acquired fame and fortune.

Conclusion

The numerous advertisements in the London *Daily Advertiser* functioned as a form of intelligence network for people in business. Within these advertisements, the need to negotiate between polite and commercial imperatives resulted in the use of a shared language formulated around the concept of personal honour and credit. This shared language was the basis around which an imagined community of trade functioned, within which women in business were enterprising participants. While still significantly fewer in number than male advertisers they were nevertheless actively engaged in innovative and competitive marketing techniques, displayed similar levels of occupational identity, and shared with male traders the need to ensure their business credit through the maintenance of an untarnished personal reputation. In a rapidly expanding consumer market they adopted various strategies to accommodate sound commercial practice with the genteel manners associated with their high-status customers; to combine the useful and the ornamental, through a

[147] For a history of the advertising campaigns around the Anodyne Necklace see Doherty, *A Study in Eighteenth-century Advertising*, esp. pp. 32–51 for Mrs Garway's many appearances in it.
[148] *LDA*, 18 August 1733.

discourse of personal credit to deflect any suspicion of vulgarity associated with public, commercial advertising. Hence rather than a strongly gendered public/ private distinction I have emphasised a number of distinctions, chiefly between polite and vulgar practice. Although these were sometimes gender-related, as when issues of personal credit were associated with sexual probity, they were rarely entirely gender-specific. Indeed, advertisements provide further evidence of cross-gender co-operation as well as competition.

Businesswomen used public advertisements to facilitate their trading activities in every sphere, from employing apprentices to finding business partners or capital, as well as to promote their goods and services. In doing so the lines between the useful and the ornamental became blurred so that in the language of advertisements the gentlewoman, more commonly associated with the private sphere, was often interchangeable with the businesswoman of the public sphere. For women engaged in the genteel trade of millinery, which nevertheless attracted a great deal of anxiety about luxury and sexuality, an unimpeachable character was an overriding necessity, but to succeed in this profitable and competitive field also required the demonstration of skill with fashionable flair. Milliners trod a careful path between an insistence on the financial worth of the business and the use of competitive pricing to maintain a position in the hierarchy of trade, with a disdain for the vulgarity of dealing with ready money that could ensure their identification with the gentility of the higher orders. For female quacks, sexuality and ready money were less acute issues and their intended audience much wider. They shared with male advertisers the need to counter accusations of vulgarity centred on the opposition of commercial public with professional (private) practice. To this end their advertisements stressed the public's right to be informed of their cures, but their sales techniques were among the most innovative of the age. Their 'qualifications' took the form of length of time in practice and, particularly for women, descent from a long line of healers. Midwives also emphasised their professional skills and long-term experience. They were marginally less visible participants in the field of medicine but equally sharp businesswomen, keeping abreast of the dictates of fashion and sharing with milliners a greater stress on the polite language of their clients.

10

'A heavy bill to settle with humanity'?

Nineteenth-century businesswomen in millinery and dressmaking

> When every allowance . . . has been made on this score we fear it will be found
> that many of them have still a heavy bill to settle with humanity, and that they
> do actually overwork their hands in a very cruel manner.
>
> The Times, 25 July 1856

In many narratives the impact of domestic ideology and thus the existence of
separate spheres of action for men and women seems to have reached its apogee
in the mid-nineteenth century. Representations of businesswomen in this
period can certainly be hard to find, but as we have seen, it can be misleading
to link an apparent lack of discursive agency to a lack of economic agency.
The insurance policy registers showed that women continued to run a wide
range of profitable businesses in 1845 and that some of the most successful were
milliners and dressmakers. This chapter shifts the focus from discourses used
by and about eighteenth-century women in business, to a very specific series
of debates about the regulation and work practices of London's principle
millinery and dressmaking establishments in the nineteenth century. Despite
this shift in time and the much narrower focus on just one group of businesswomen operating in London's West End, there are a number of common
themes which link these debates to those about milliners in the eighteenth
century. As in the eighteenth century, gendered, racial, economic and class-
based arguments swapped partners and prominence within a number of
nineteenth-century discourses about the fashion industry and its problems.
The social and economic context had changed considerably but familiar
anxieties, about the acquisition of large profits, social mobility, aristocratic
immorality, the propensity of milliners to succumb to seduction or prostitution
and even the insidious French connection, were still evident. Similarly, the
figure of the private domesticated woman was again deployed to effect public
change in the marketplace. Whereas writers in the *Spectator* had proposed
treating milliners as 'proper ladies' in order to reform commercial manners
in the eighteenth century, Christian reformers writing to *The Times* in
the nineteenth century argued that millinery proprietors should display the
characteristics of a mother in order to defeat the evils of capitalism. Yet, despite

Figure 10.1 Richard Redgrave, *Fashion's Slaves* (1847)

Source: Photograph courtesy of Christopher Wood Gallery

a relatively low profile and the proliferation of texts about women's domestic duties, women in the fashion business were deeply involved in highly political public debates about nineteenth-century economic life.

By the mid-nineteenth century, the image of milliners as seductive sales-women had undergone a radical transformation. The rosy-cheeked milliner tripping down the street with her bandbox or enticing her customers with coy glances had been replaced by a pale, emaciated needlewoman working late at night. To be precise, the proprietress of the millinery shops was rarely depicted at all; it was the image of her apprentices that caught public attention. In 1844 Richard Redgrave's emotive portrait of an exhausted seamstress caused a fellow member of the Royal Academy to declare that 'if any circumstances could make me wage war against the present social arrangements . . . it is the contemplation of this truthful and wonderful picture'.[1] Figure 10.1 shows

---

[1] P.F. Poole, cited in H.E. Roberts, 'Marriage, Redundancy or Sin: The Painter's View of Women in the First Twenty Five Years of Victoria's Reign', in *Suffer and Be Still*, ed. Martha Vicinus (London, 1972), p. 60.

another Redgrave painting, entitled *Fashion's Slaves* (1847), which depicted a fashionable lady lying on a couch berating a poor milliner, who had been working all night, for being late with her order. *The Spectator* described it as 'pain waiting on the breath of exacting caprice',[2] but nevertheless true to life. The pathetic image of the poor little milliner or dressmaker in art, fiction and political rhetoric consistently mobilised such contemporary reactions to the inequities of intensive production and society's apparent inability to prevent the consequences. The powerful 'truth' portrayed in these pictures, and even more frequently in the 'social problem' novels of the 1840s and 1850s, was based largely on evidence collected by select committees and parliamentary commissions of enquiry, whose reports were then published as Blue Books. The 'facts' uncovered by these investigations were widely discussed in newspapers, magazines, pamphlets and letters, and formed the bases for much contemporary fiction.[3] Following the 1842 Children's Employment Commission Report, the plight of milliners' and dressmakers' apprentices, many of whom worked more than eighteen hours a day in cramped conditions with little food and poor ventilation, became a highly visible cause. Much less visible were the employers of these young girls, London's fashionable *modistes*, the successful proprietors of West End millinery and dressmaking establishments. In newspaper and magazine discussions, where the femininity of the apprentices was constantly dramatised, the gender of the proprietors was rarely mentioned. In fiction, where the poor young milliner was the romantic heroine, the shadowy figure of her employer was at best shallow and indifferent, and at worst cruel and avaricious. In 'fact' and in 'fiction', the female milliner in business was frequently portrayed as French, or worse still, pretending to be so.

The 1842 Commission estimated that there were approximately 1,500 proprietors in London and a count of the entries in a London trade directory for 1845 reveals that all but 6 per cent of the 1,040 businesses listed there were run by women.[4] Furthermore, as the Sun Fire insurance policy registers showed, millinery and dressmaking businesses could be highly profitable,[5] yet these businesswomen have remained almost invisible in modern feminist historiography. Some accounts tend to replicate popular contemporary arguments about the reasons for the apprentices' distress, in which case their employers are rarely mentioned.[6] In others, the focus on working-class women

[2] Cited in S.P. Casteras, 'Social Wrongs: The Painted Sermons of Richard Redgrave', in *Richard Redgrave, 1804–88*, ed. Casteras and Ronald Parkinson, (London, 1988), p. 21.

[3] S.M. Smith, 'Blue Books and Victorian Novelists', *Review of English Studies*, 21 (London, 1970), pp. 23–40; Kate Flint, *The Victorian Novelist: Social Problems and Social Change* (London, 1987) pp. 1–13.

[4] *BPP, Children's Employment* (1843),Vol. 14, f. 204: this purported to be based on a hand-count of 900 names in an 1838 London directory, with an allowance for businesses not represented in the directory plus population growth, producing 1,500 in total; *Post Office London Directory* (46th edn) (London, 1845), s.v. 'milliners', pp. 1264–8.

[5] See above, p. 153.

[6] Neff, *Victorian Working Women*, pp. 115–50.

and the politics of their employment excludes examination of their employers.[7] This may, as was discussed in the Introduction, be partly due to the tendency of studies to concentrate exclusively on either the toils of working-class women or the idleness of middle-class women. Or, it may reflect the lack of conceptual space available within Marxist or feminist narratives for wealthy middle-class businesswomen, many of whom apparently exploited their poor young employees.[8] It seems that the image of the poor dressmaker still functions most successfully as a signifier of the limitations of nineteenth-century middle-class women's lives, whose employment options are shown to be needlework, governessing or a descent into prostitution.[9] Yet for a significant number of London women, running a millinery and dressmaking business remained a profitable alternative to domesticity.

Since wealthy female milliners undoubtedly existed, this chapter examines how and why these businesswomen were both less visible and less often subject to gendered assumptions than were their employees. In doing so it also sheds some light on how women in business could effectively be obscured by the terms of debate, leaving the impression that exploitation or domesticity were the only alternatives for women in the nineteenth century. I begin by discussing the increasing awareness and presentation of a social problem within the previously genteel trade of millinery and dressmaking. I then examine four common discursive frameworks found in debates about the causes of distress in the industry. First, class was a dominant theme of social reformers attempting to address 'the condition of England'[10] in general and the fashion industry in particular. Second, within a discourse of political economy, the principals became enmeshed in fierce debates between supporters of *laissez-faire* and interventionist policies. Third, those attacking 'the accursed system' of capitalism used the racial politics of slavery to champion the rights of oppressed apprentices and to demonise their employers. Finally, evangelical concern

---

[7] Helen Rogers, "'The Good are Not Always Powerful, Nor the Powerful Always Good'": The Politics of Women's Needlework in Mid-Victorian London', *Victorian Studies*, 40 (1997), pp. 589–623; Alexander, *Women's Work*, pp. 34–6.

[8] See above, p. 9.

[9] See e.g. George Frederick Watt's painting *The Sempstress* (1844) which adorns the cover of Martha Vicinus' seminal collection of essays on Victorian women, *Suffer and Be Still*. In that collection Roberts, 'Marriage, Redundancy or Sin', p. 62, replicates the same pathos by comparing seamstress paintings with those of women dying alone to argue that this 'grim reality . . . was often the only alternative for many women to the ideal of domesticity'.

[10] Thomas Carlyle coined the phrase in 1843 but it came to stand for many different attempts by novelists, politicians and social investigators to address issues of rural and industrial poverty brought about by increasing urbanisation, industrialisation and capitalism, and could also signify anxieties about increasing spiritual impoverishment. See Flint, *Victorian Novelist*, p. 1; and Mary Poovey, 'Homosociality and the Psychological: Disraeli, Gaskell, and the Condition-of-England Debate', in idem, *Making a Social Body: British Cultural Formation, 1830–64* (1995), p. 133.

about the lack of Christian ethics in a competitive urban environment placed a heavy moral duty of 'motherly' care on the principals. The representation of London's milliners thus frequently depended on whether the causes of the fashion industry's problems were envisaged as social, economic, political or moral.

A problem discovered

One of the difficulties of studying images of nineteenth-century milliners is the high degree of intertextuality between fictional representations and factual reports. Contemporary authors counteracted the dehumanising reports of political economists by individualising distress in fiction; but both formats sought to mobilise public opinion, and both used the same discursive frameworks. Readers were often referred to parliamentary reports to establish the verifiable reality behind these fictional stories,[11] which reproduced events told to the Commissioners. These same events (usually the most dramatic/poignant images) also featured in newspapers and magazine reports that other authors then cited as 'evidence', so that a series of recitations served to concretise the 'reality' of the evil being suffered. Indeed, Beth Harris has argued that the 'myth' and iconography of the seamstress was chiefly generated by the 1842 Commission and a few sensationalised events.[12] *The Times* had even been accused of fabricating a series of sensational incidents of abuse in workhouses, during a similar campaign against the New Poor Law in the 1830s.[13] Thus, although many apprentices undoubtedly worked in appalling conditions, it is still problematic to accept reports of random mistreatment as automatic evidence of systematic abuse and it is not my intention to judge the guilt or innocence of the proprietors. All the texts examined here, whether 'fact' or 'fiction', have been read as specific cultural productions, employing persuasive rhetorical devices to generate knowledge about the subject under investigation.[14]

Contemporary awareness of the existence of a 'problem', as it was formulated by these texts, may be used to construct a chronology for these debates which roughly spans the years 1828 to 1863, but with two high-profile peaks in the

[11] Elizabeth Stone, *The Young Milliner* (1843), p. A, explained that while the 'narrative is Fictitious the Facts are unexaggerated and true', because they are drawn from parliamentary reports.
[12] Harris, 'Works of Women', p. 86. The condition of milliners' and dressmakers' apprentices was often elided with that of slop-workers, and 'the seamstress' signified the plight of both.
[13] Ibid., pp. 60–4; Gertrude Himmelfarb, *The Idea of Poverty: England in the Early Industrial Age* (New York, 1983), pp. 184–5, also notes that *The Times* had not checked its sources, which were later proved inaccurate.
[14] This approach has been informed by that of Rose, *Limited Livelihoods*, esp. pp. 8–9.

1840s and 1850s. In 1825 *The Times* was printing humorous pieces about how the fear of a strike by milliner's operatives caused their mistresses 'utmost timorousness . . . attended with the usual damage to their cuticles and perukes'.[15] The first signs that a problem existed surfaced in 1828 when a correspondent described how London milliners worked for eighteen to twenty hours a day and warned of the necessity to 'crush an evil in its birth'.[16] There was very little correspondence over the next decade, but by 1841 Lord Shaftesbury had pushed for a parliamentary commission of enquiry which resulted in the publication of the Second Children's Employment Commission Report in 1843. The report concluded that 'there is nothing in the accounts of the worst conducted factories to be compared with the accounts of this inquiry . . . they knew of no instance in which the hours of work were so long'.[17] The report also claimed that employers provided inadequate breaks for frequently poor-quality meals, that the workrooms were too small and poorly ventilated, often dangerously so when gaslight was used; that the sleeping accommodation was inadequate and overcrowded; and that the terms of apprentice indentures were frequently breached. Many of the young employees consequently suffered from very poor health. The principals were further charged with preventing their employees from obtaining medical assistance, and failing to promote good religious and moral conduct. The author of the report, F.D. Grainger, wrote that the evidence from all parties proved that:

> there is no class of persons in this country, living by their labour, whose happiness, health, and lives, are so unscrupulously sacrificed as those of the young dressmakers . . . and I should fail in my duty if I did not distinctly state that, as a body, their employers have hitherto taken no steps to remedy the evils and misery which result from the existing system.[18]

Such damning statements were only slightly mitigated by the less publicised fact that there were also 'happily numerous exceptions'. In the same year two novels dramatised the milliners' plight: Elizabeth Stone's *The Young Milliner* and Charlotte Elizabeth Tonna's *The Wrongs of Woman*,[19] both of which made reference to the report.

Also in the same year, Lord Shaftesbury launched the Association for the Aid and Benefit of Dressmakers and Milliners, of which Grainger became Hon. Secretary. The aims of the association were: to reduce the hours of work to twelve and to abolish Sunday working; to promote improved ventilation; to encourage customers to give their orders in more time; to establish a register

---

[15] *The Times*, 17 October 1825, p. 2, col. D.
[16] *Ibid.*, 26 June 1828, p. 4, col. D.
[17] BPP, *Children's Employment*, Vol. 14, f. 30.
[18] Ibid., f. 32.
[19] Published as Charlotte Elizabeth [Tonna], *The Wrongs of Woman* (London, 1843).

of employees which employers could consult in busy periods; to give medical and monetary help to young workers in need; and to form a provident fund. To facilitate these aims, the Association set up committees of both ladies and gentlemen of rank and declared that it had the support of many of the top West End establishments. The Association annually proclaimed its success in abolishing Sunday working and in the numbers using the registration system, as well as in providing medical help and setting up a provident fund in June 1848. Henry Mayhew published his letters on the dressmakers and milliners in 1850, in which he credited the Association with the introduction of day-workers into the business. Yet he blamed establishments' attempts to undersell each other for prompting employers to cut labour costs. This practice was particularly pernicious because all their employees (apart from day-workers) were paid in kind and so received part of their wages in board and lodging, resulting in poorer quality food and accommodation. Labour costs, he claimed, were further reduced by employing fewer hands to work longer hours.[20] Thus, perhaps not surprisingly, a *Times* editorial of 1853 noted that, ten years after the Association's formation, the paper was still 'as clamorously assailed by the complaints and groans of the sufferers as though it had not existed at all'.[21]

In fact, 1853 marked the zenith of *The Times*' coverage of the subject. This was because the problem was apparently rediscovered through the publication of a series of letters from 'A First Hand' about the 'slavery carried on in millinery and dressmaking houses', which provoked hundreds of letters, and editorials.[22] The 'First Hand' explained that she had been in the millinery business for fourteen years but, as her health had failed and she had both experience and patronage, she hoped to go into business by herself. She wanted to prove that it was possible to run a successful business without cruelly over-working her employees, but she was unable to afford the necessary insurance premiums. Within days, numerous letters not only corroborated her accounts of mistreatment but offered her money to set up in business, which she duly did. As a result of all the publicity, however, she claimed that she had incurred the wrath of other principals, who cut off her lines of credit with the wholesale warehouses. A year later, she wrote again, this time using her own name of

---

[20] Henry Mayhew, 'Letter LXXV' and 'Letter LXXVI' (1850), *The Morning Chronicle Survey of Labour and the Poor: The Metropolitan Districts* VI (Horsham, 1982), pp. 125–7, also stated that in the best houses the rooms were usually large and airy and the young staff well treated (p. 116). Mayhew's descriptions of the West End milliners were considerably less dramatic and romanticised than his earlier letters on the slop-workers and needlewomen, but in many texts the fates of both were frequently elided. On Mayhew's romanticisation of needlewomen see Rogers, 'The Good are Not Always Powerful', pp. 597–603.

[21] *The Times*, 11 April 1853, p. 4, col. E.

[22] The letters began in *The Times*, 25 March 1853, p. 5, col. E, and continued through to May that year. A First Hand was usually the most senior employee in a large establishment; it was her job to attend to customers, receive orders, take measurements and hand out work to the other employees.

Jane d. Le Plastrier.[23] She condemned the abolitionist Harriet Beecher Stowe for her lack of support. Le Plastrier's letters had provoked a response from an 'East End' milliner, who related how Mrs Beecher Stowe had sent her dress to be made in one of these 'death-shops', thus initiating what one correspondent termed 'a sort of second "Uncle Tom" agitation'. The publication of more novels in 1853, including Gaskell's *Ruth*, Reynolds' *The Seamstress: Or, the White Slave of England* and a new edition of Rowcroft's 1846 novel, *Fanny, the Little Milliner: Or, the Rich and the Poor*, ensured the continuing topicality and high visibility of the problem. Beecher Stowe's own account of her involvement in *Sunny Memories* (1854), and various anti-abolitionist texts such as her fellow American John Cobden's *The White Slaves of England* (1853), reinforced the perception of a link between apprenticed milliners' wage slavery and negro slavery, which was reflected in many novels' titles.

The rich and the poor

In *Sunny Memories*, Harriet Beecher Stowe commented on the popularity of novels depicting the poor which had supplanted those about aristocratic high life.[24] Even during the 1840s and 1850s, milliners still occasionally featured in tales of patrician romance and Jacobite intrigues;[25] but their adventures invariably occurred in a (frequently idyllicised) eighteenth century, where poverty, competition and the exploitation of labour did not exist. Trade was conducted on a purely genteel basis and never visibly for profit. Elizabeth Gaskell's portrayal of milliners in *Cranford*, an early Victorian country town with an older and fast vanishing social order, was quite different from their portraits in the social problem novels *Ruth* and *Mary Barton*. In *Cranford*, the Miss Barkers were portrayed as kind, ageing, eccentric milliners, who gave food to the poor and were 'self denying, good people. . . . They only aped their betters in having nothing to do with the class immediately below theirs.'[26] It was only in novels specifically addressing nineteenth-century social problems that a degree of demonisation associated with class antagonism became common.

As we saw in Chapter 8, milliners and dressmakers had long been associated with the aristocracy who were their major clients and whose manners they adopted. As in the eighteenth century, it was around this somewhat symbiotic

---

[23] *The Times*, 29 August 1854, p. 4, col. E.

[24] Cited in Sheilah M. Smith, *The Other Nation: The Poor in English Novels of the 1840s and 1850s* (Oxford, 1980), p. 45.

[25] See, Anon., *Recollections of Mrs Hester Taffetas, Court Milliner and Modiste During the Reign of King George the Third . . . : Edited by her Granddaughter* (1858); and Douglas William Jerrold's play, *The White Milliner* (1841).

[26] Elizabeth Gaskell, *Cranford* (1853; rep. 1986), pp. 105–6.

relationship between milliners and their aristocratic customers that tensions arose. Although hostility towards the latter's Francophile tendencies was no longer evident, nineteenth-century aristocrats were increasingly expected to curb their excesses, including the consumption of fashionable clothing. They were also expected to use their social position to improve the lives of the poorer classes. Hence reformers focused their attention chiefly on the first-class establishments situated in the West End of London, rather than those catering predominantly for the middle classes, which were found in the East End. Shaftesbury explained to Harriet Beecher Stowe that his interest lay only in the West End houses,[27] and it was for their reformation that the Association was specifically formed. The high-ranking women on its committees would certainly have had most influence there; and since elite women's unreasonable demands for low-cost luxurious dresses at short notice were considered to be one of the major causes of distress in the industry, this was the area in which they could be expected to make the most difference. In addition, girls from provincial towns who hoped to go into business for themselves were commonly sent to London after their apprenticeship to be employed as 'improvers'. Without the 'prestige of having been trained to the perfect exercise of London taste and skill' it was believed the young woman would have little chance of attaining the 'patronage of neighbouring ladies', which was so necessary for success in the business.[28] This exercise of sending naive country girls into the moral turpitude of London to earn the cachet needed to attract a high-class clientele was a central concern to many authors on the subject. Of equal concern, was the fact that since the aim was 'improvement' rather than 'training', employers were often paid handsome premiums but very rarely provided their improvers with any remuneration beyond board and lodging.[29]

To some extent, the heads of these West End establishments may have become victims of their own success. The first-rate milliners and dressmakers' houses were, as Mayhew put it, 'more like a mansion for a nobleman than a milliner's establishment'. Often they had 'nothing to indicate that they are places of business except a plate on the door with the names of the proprietors engraved thereon'.[30] Many also had huge plate-glass windows, large, expensively furnished showrooms and polished ebony counters. As well as assistants, improvers and apprentices, the larger establishments employed male clerks to do the books, and domestic servants, including a footman to usher ladies into the showroom. Some would despatch a first hand in a carriage with a liveried servant to take measurements at a lady's home. In most novels there was a marked hostility towards these ornate establishments. Country relatives

---

[27] Harriet Beecher Stowe, *Sunny Memories of Foreign Lands* (London, 1854), p. 198.
[28] Mayhew, Letter LXXV, p. 115, also adds that this prestige must be further 'maintained, when in business, by at least one annual visit to London "for the fashions"'.
[29] Ibid.
[30] Ibid., p. 118.

seeking to visit an apprentice or improver in London are overawed by the bustle and the numbers of carriages waiting outside great doors of 'polished mahogany with gilding all about'.[31] Upon entering the premises they could gain admittance only to the humbler parlours. As we have seen from the insurance policies taken out by milliners, many were clearly prosperous and owned substantial amounts of personal goods and jewellery, but the appearance of such wealth on the grounds of property ownership may have been misleading given the numbers that merely rented their premises.

If aristocratic Francophilia was no longer a target, the 'French' pretensions of milliners remained a source of unpopularity. Just thirty-six of the milliners listed in the 1845 London directory appear to have had French names, but the majority of these were in the West End and Mayhew states that all but two or three of the 'very first rate houses' around Hanover Square were kept by French women. In addition, these houses often employed French women as first hands and specialist 'magasinieres' or 'showroom-women' for high wages.[32] Although some hostility was aimed at these French employees, the chief targets of novelists were the wealthy proprietors who adopted pseudo-foreign manners when their origins were considerably more humble. In *The Young Milliner* (1843), Madame Sarina Mineau turns out to be plain Sally Minnow whose sister Bridget ran a cheese and bacon shop. Bridget sends her dead friend's daughter to Sally as an apprentice but, on arrival at the 'large handsome house', the orphan is chided by a liveried footman for knocking on the front door.[33] In *The Seamstress* (1853), Madame Duplessy had an impressive establishment with plate-glass windows in gilt frames and royal arms mounted over the door, but she was actually an Englishwoman called Snuggins. Duplessy had realised that English ladies would 'patronise nothing in the shape of native industry when French competition was in the way' and 'that the appellation of Snuggins was far from being a passport to patrician favour'.[34] Unusually, she was also pretty and sharp-witted, but she had no husband and so lived with her lover, Bill Smith, 'who thrashed her soundly' and passed himself off as Monsieur Duplessy. Despite such unflattering depictions, both the fictitious Madame Mineau and Madame Duplessy are still portrayed as successful businesswomen who have risen to the top of their trade.

In direct contrast to their fictional employers, the poor little apprentice heroines frequently turn out to be the orphaned/illegitimate daughters of the aristocracy, almost invariably so in those novels focusing on what Disraeli termed 'the two nations' or 'the rich and the poor'.[35] One discovered that her

---

[31] J.M. Rymer, *The White Slave of England* (London, 1844), p. 47.

[32] Mayhew, 'Letter LXXV', pp. 116, 118.

[33] Stone, *Young Milliner*, p. 22.

[34] G.W.M. Reynolds, *The Seamstress: Or, the White Slave of England* (1853), p. 8.

[35] Disraeli first coined the phrase in *Sybil: Or, the Two Nations* (1845), the second of his highly political novels on the condition of England known as the 'Young England' trilogy.

dead mother was an aristocrat spurned by her father for marrying a middle-class man,[36] and Fanny was the daughter of Lord Sarum's secret marriage.[37] Illustrations of these poor milliners show them to be almost exact replicas of their aristocratic relatives but more plainly dressed. The contrast between their poverty and wretched accommodation and the gay parties and huge mansions of the rich further heightens the pathos. This plot device enabled the poor little milliner to effect a form of class reconciliation. By being eligible to marry the son of the aristocratic family, or by dying tragically, the poor milliner caused the wealthy family to realise that it was their duty to heal 'the dangerous division which of late years has so much increased between the RICH AND THE POOR'.[38] This dual caste system of social analysis was an essentially Tory political rhetoric, in which the solution to an increasing social divide was seen as a return to a form of paternalism. Lord Dudley Stuart, at the first annual meeting of the Association for the Aid and Benefit of Dressmakers and Milliners, employed the same rhetoric when proposing the formal adoption of its regulations. *The Times* reported that:

> He dwelt upon the tendency of this association to diminish that gulf which absolutely yawned between those who made dresses and those who wore them. The former would feel that they were cared for; the latter would see how usefully they could exert their influence on behalf of their own sex.[39]

The principal milliners and dressmakers did not fit easily within this dualistic discourse, despite the fact that the problem (the poor apprentices) and its solution (aristocratic women's intervention) were gendered as exclusively female. The milliners were on one level implicitly aligned with the rich as prosperous proprietors, but they had not the social authority of those born into the upper classes. They were also, like the rich, charged with failure in a duty of care for their 'poor' employees, but as women did not fit easily within a discourse of *paternalism*. There was also a fear, particularly among evangelicals antipathetic to aristocratic mores, that the milliners were not only in league with the rich but had a degree of power over them which could prevent aristocratic ladies from performing their social duty. A letter to *The Times* in 1853 'set forth the truth in the matter':

> The heads of these establishments may well smile at any such agitation; they know their own power, and can afford to treat any such threat with contempt. . . . Those who the world thinks command the market in which these young lives are sold are just those least likely to move in the matter; they love the bauble – personal

---

[36] Stone, *Young Milliner*.
[37] Charles Rowcroft, *Fanny, the Little Milliner: Or, the Rich and the Poor* (1846).
[38] Ibid., p. 397.
[39] *The Times*, 6 May 1844, p. 8, col. F.

adornment – too much to care to listen to its cost. They are too deeply involved with the manufacturers of it to dare to question the method of manufacture.[40]

From this perspective, the milliners were portrayed as a class of powerful people, but 'class' was always a relative category. Hence, paradoxically, the principals could also sometimes be aligned with the 'poor' as victims of aristocratic extravagance. In *The Young Milliner*, the orphan apprentice did not blame Madame Mineau for the exhausting work hours because she realised that her employer could not afford to refuse work, and that the ladies' demands were unreasonable. This was certainly the reason cited most often by the principal milliners themselves in the Employment Commission's report.

As tradeswomen, the milliners and dressmakers could have been classified as middle class, but within this essentially Tory discourse the middle classes were noticeably absent. In *Fanny*, the only novel even to mention a middle class, one peer expressed surprise 'that the middle classes do not attempt some plan of amelioration. It is a question that affects them more nearly than it does us, seeing as they are exposed to the reverses of fortune from which we are exempt.'[41] But the middle classes played no further part in the narrative. The effective use of the twin images of rich and poor did not leave room for a third party. Since this 'lamentable picture of what may be suffered by one class of people in order to minister to the extravagance of others'[42] was the 'truth' most calculated to make people 'wage war against the present social arrangements', there was little space for the female proprietors to play any significant role in either representations of the problem or its solution.

Legislation or free enterprise

When the fashion industry's problems were reformulated in economic terms the principals did become more visible participants, insofar as their means and motives for acquiring large profits were questioned, but they were frequently demonised as a result. However, during debates over whether to pursue the principle of *laissez faire* or to legislate to protect the exploited, the principals were again largely portrayed according to the solution envisaged. The most positive images came from campaigners supporting the principles of political economy, within which the interests of employer and employee were believed to be identical. However, when protective legislation was believed to be the answer, the gender of the employers was largely erased, while that of their exploited workers was highlighted. This replicated the images of helpless

---

[40] Ibid., 21 April 1853, p. 8, col. B.
[41] Rowcroft, *Fanny, the Little Milliner*, p. 97.
[42] This was the opinion of Dr Hodgkin, whose report into the health of milliners was reprinted in *The Times*, 15 April 1836, p. 3, col. A.

femininity used in campaigns for protective legislation for women and children in factories run by male employers.[43]

In a letter to *The Times* in 1853 the 'First Hand' declared that 'every lady who patronises Bond-street or its immediate neighbourhood, will at once see that the prices they pay for their goods will amply compensate the person whom they employ to remunerate a sufficient number of people to do their work'.[44] However, if that was the case, why were the employees working for fifteen to twenty hours a day? The answer to that was usually constructed in terms of either the employer's greed for profit or the pressures of 'competition'. Both of these causes, while based on economic conditions, were frequently articulated in moral terms, so that the borders of economic and religious discourses frequently shifted and overlapped. In an article for *Fraser's Magazine*, the evangelical author Charlotte Elizabeth Tonna[45] blamed the excessive hours and overcrowded conditions on:

> The great competition in every department of trade and business at the present day, in dress-making and millinery among the rest, and the exertion made to manufacture every article at the lowest price. . . . But this grievance arises as often from the desire of the proprietress of the house to realise a rapid profit, as it does from the deficiency of accommodation. . . . This is an evil very difficult to remedy, while the importance of wealth, so strikingly characteristic of a commercial age and country is so universally recognised.[46]

Tonna proposed that the solution should be legislation to prevent any young person from working more than twelve hours a day and stipulating a minimum of one month's vacation per annum.[47] However, while both milliners and campaigners viewed 'competition' as part of the problem, the principals felt that economic survival, particularly because of the long, slack season, and not personal greed, was the chief factor. The majority of those interviewed by the

---

[43] Robert Grey, 'The Languages of Factory Reform in Britain, c.1830–60', *Historical Meanings of Work*, ed. Joyce, pp. 150–5.

[44] *The Times*, 25 March 1853, p. 5, col. E.

[45] Monica Fryckstedt, *Elizabeth Gaskell's 'Mary Barton' and 'Ruth': A Challenge to Christian England* (Uppsala, 1982), p. 173, identifies Tonna as a pseudonym for a prolific evangelical writer on the political/religious/social condition of England, particularly in *The Christian Lady's Magazine* which she edited from 1834 to 1846.

[46] *Fraser's Magazine for Town and Country*, 33 (1846), p. 313.

[47] Tonna also proposed that a benevolent society should set up a hospital where sick apprentices could be healed, given religious instruction and some light work; Sundays should be sacrosanct, meals more generous, better personal hygiene enforced and ventilation improved. Boyd Hilton, *The Age of Atonement: The Influence of Evangelicalism on Social and Economic Thought, 1795–1865* (Oxford, 1988), pp. 95, 97, notes that both Tonna and Shaftesbury were pre-millenarian evangelicals and supporters of humanitarian paternalism, who believed that the poor were in need of material help as well as moral guidance and therefore campaigned for protective legislation.

Commissioners declared themselves happy to protect the young, *if* it did not interfere with 'business'. Millinery proprietor Ann Olivier explained that she had shortened her employees' work hours, but only at 'some pecuniary sacrifice'. Moreover, in the past year many principals in the trade:

> appearing to be doing a large and prosperous one, have failed, compromised with their creditors, and again commenced, with these depressing circumstances to struggle against in addition to the fatigue and exhaustion. . . . There is un-questionably a great evil somewhere, and it will never be remedied by the means yet resorted to; a general evil was never yet cured by personal insult, and this we know has been heaped on many individuals who would be themselves thankful to see a better state of things.[48]

The 'personal insult' referred not only to accusations of greed but also to the practice of effectively identifying 'bad' employers and calling for the boycott of their establishments. In a similar tactic to that of 'unmasking' tyrannical factory owners during campaigns for factory reform,[49] *The Times* urged its readers to frequent only those establishments named in the Commissioners' Report as using good practices. The paper interpreted one principal's statement that 'there is nothing to render the late hours necessary; it is simply a question of expense, which as a general rule the principals are unwilling to incur' as an admission of greed. It therefore declared that customers should:

> cease to employ those milliners who exact undue profit to themselves . . . If they peruse Mr Grainger's reports, they will find that there are many employers of labour – and those, too, of no mean repute – who have opposed themselves to the inhuman system of their sisters in the trade.[50]

Shaftesbury's Association would only register milliners' establishments that agreed to follow their code of practice, and in Manchester 3,000 ladies signed a petition urging principals to adopt the London Association's rules.[51] In 1851 the Association published a declaration signed by fifty-three West End milliners and dressmakers who 'felt called upon in self defence, to make the following public statement, especially as we have reason to believe that some of the assertions contained in the letters published in the newspapers are not wholly groundless'.[52] The principals declared that for most of the year the 'young people' were required to work for only twelve hours, but from March to July they worked thirteen hours, but never all night and never on Sundays. Moreover, they were given plentiful high-quality food and had roomy sleeping

---

[48] BPP, *Children's Employment*, Vol. 14, f. 218.
[49] Grey, 'Languages of Factory Reform', p. 149.
[50] *The Times*, 21 April 1843, p. 5, col. E.
[51] Stowe, *Sunny Memories*, pp. 202–3, based upon documents sent to Stowe by Shaftesbury.
[52] As reported by Stowe, *Sunny Memories*, p. 202.

accommodation. However, five of those who signed had asterisks by their names to denote that they could not guarantee that such hours might not occasionally be exceeded.

Those principals who believed they were victims of the 'general evil', along with their apprentices, saw themselves as members of a class of oppressed women. Ann Olivier aligned herself with (female) oppressed operatives by invoking gender to create an alternative 'other' of less oppressed male operatives. She argued that 'in no business connected with the supply of goods to milliners and dressmakers, are tradesmen, either principals or assistants engaged anything like the same number of hours. They are also better paid. . . . How is this?'[53] Yet Olivier also undermined this gendered solidarity by suggesting that part of the problem was due to inefficient supervision and also bad practice in the workroom. Thus she transferred some of the 'blame' for the industry's problems to the apprentices themselves in an extremely rare reversal of the 'helpless' picture of apprentices. This may well have been because her proposition for reform was based on the co-operation of the principal milliners themselves, in order to set regular hours and to improve conditions, rather than on the possibility of legislative action which was usually driven by pity for the poor apprentices.[54]

Those who favoured protective legislation constantly emphasised the feminine delicacy of the apprentices, whose work was deemed well beyond that which any man (or animal) could endure.[55] Furthermore, being of genteel upbringing and delicate health, the 'coarse' and 'improper' food provided by employers was inedible, and indigestion was frequently cited by doctors as one of the consequent ailments.[56] The fate of the poor little milliner was rhetorically and conceptually elided with that of the poor little factory child when legislation was the envisaged solution. This was emphasised by Shaftesbury's active championing of both causes.[57] None of the Commissioners, employers, novelists or journalists concerned themselves with the condition of the paid adult journeywomen working in these establishments. The language of reform,

---

[53] *BPP, Children's Employment*, Vol. 14, f. 217.

[54] Ibid. Olivier was the only principal to make detailed proposals for reform from within the trade, echoing Grainger's disappointment at the lack of earlier action. She suggested a ten-point plan to limit work to a twelve-hour day by setting up a society to issue printed cards to each principal on which hours of work, pay and amount of work should be recorded. The principals would endeavour to reduce the work hours and to hire extra hands, to lessen the burden of which the society would initially provide financial assistance raised by subscription. Each year, medals worth 2 to 5 guineas would be awarded to the top three principals, and the top three workwomen.

[55] Ibid., Vol. 14, f. 206, 207, 208.

[56] Ibid., f. 204, 224, 236.

[57] Ibid., f. 233. Dr Hodgkin commended Shaftesbury for 'devoting to the unhappy condition of the oppressed dressmakers a portion of that benevolent and active zeal which he has so laudably employed in the service of the poor little Factory children'.

employed by investigators and campaigners alike, was primarily concerned with 'young persons'. That class in need of protection was defined in the Factory Bill as being aged between 13 and 21 years. *The Times*[58] carefully noted this in an editorial of 1843, suggesting that the Bill did not go far enough precisely because it did not protect the metropolitan milliners and dressmakers. On these grounds, the paper argued that 'milliners should be included in those meant to benefit from the factory bill's humane provisions'.[59]

Ten years later in 1853, the problem again became highly visible following the enormous response to the letters from the 'First Hand'. *The Times* issued another editorial, elucidating some of the principles involved in legislating for protection. It explained that for the past twenty years:

> We have been discussing in some form or other the problem of whether the State has a right . . . to interfere between the employers and the employed. . . . We . . . acqui[esce] in the decision of the Legislature, to assume it as a principle that it is not only the right but the duty of the State to step in between the employers and *certain classes* of the employed – between capital and labour, to a modified degree. This principle is embodied in all our factory bills for the relief of women and children, and may be fairly incorporated as a basis of action in all future arrangements upon similar subjects.[60]

By classing young milliners with those (women) covered by the Factory Bill, their femininity was emphasised, but their employers were consequently discredited with the same abuses of power as the factory owners. Thus the gender of these businesswomen was completely obscured. However, stressing the peculiar female vulnerability of the class of persons involved opened the way to challenging the hegemony of political economy and envisaging the possibility of state involvement in invigilating private enterprise. *The Times* asked:

> Can the inconvenience you apprehend – and which we admit – be accepted as a sufficient reason for the continuance of such an evil as the destruction of so many young women as are annually sacrificed to the purity of economic principles as matters stand at present! We cannot see why Madame MANTALINI should shrink from rendering account of her stewardship a bit more than the flourishing firm of 'MAMMON BROTHERS,' cotton spinners at Manchester and Stockport.[61]

---

[58] *The Times*, 21 April 1843, p. 5, col. E.
[59] Ibid.
[60] *The Times*, 11 April 1853, p. 4 col. D–E (emphasis added).
[61] Ibid., p. 4, col. E. Madame Mantalini is a reference to the dressmaker in Dickens' *Nicholas Nickleby* (1838), pp. 112, 115–19, to whom Kate Nickleby is sent because 'dressmakers in London . . . keep equipages, and become persons of great wealth'. Madam Mantalini (aka Mrs Muntle) shared many of the characteristics of later depictions, including a handsome house and feckless husband, but she was vain and stupid rather than cruel to her employees.

The editorial argued that the 'cruel system' could be dealt with only if forty or fifty leading establishments in London and the provinces were 'vigorously repressed'.

Three years later the paper had reversed its position somewhat. In July 1856, leading members of the Association (including Shaftesbury and Grainger) attended an Early Closing Association meeting called to procure shorter hours and better conditions for milliners and dressmakers 'through the force and intervention of an enlightened public opinion rather than by legislation'.[62] Shaftesbury argued that the exigencies of the case meant that it would be a long time before they could devise a law that would not be violated as soon as it was passed. *The Times* report on the meeting concurred that there were some problems that no laws could address, even if municipal regulations were brought into 'harmony with the laws of economic science'. But it announced: 'Where legislation ends charity begins' and, in a return to a more paternalistic discourse of class conciliation, it eschewed 'the high sentimental ground . . . taken by the regular manufacturers of pathos'. As the social position of these women could not be changed and 'work they must', those with 'more abundant means' should act for their benefit. The employees' suffering was once again articulated as being caused by 'the avarice of the actual employers' and the unreasonable demands of fashionable women, rather than by the more nebulous pressures of a free market economy which might respond to legislative intervention. Thus *The Times* signalled its abandonment of the remedy of reform by ostensibly abandoning the language of pathos.

Slavery and the 'accursed system'

Pathos was also an effective device for writers who believed that the worst evils were those caused by capitalism, otherwise known as that 'pestilence of competition' or 'the accursed system'.[63] In both factual and fictional accounts of the problem, the rhetoric of tyranny and bondage was common, as was the metaphor of slavery. Hence it was as capitalists and middlewomen that the millinery and dressmaking principals were most harshly demonised. At an Early Closing Association meeting, the Bishop of Oxford defined the 'evil', or the reason the young employees were so helpless, as the need for a 'head of an establishment with capital' and a fashionable reputation to market their work. The operatives could be contented with less gain, but they would be ruined without the principals, 'so that the power of those they served over them was absolute, and their bondage complete'.[64]

---

[62] *The Times*, 12 July 1856, p. 12, col. F.
[63] Reynolds, *The Seamstress*, p. 88.
[64] Ibid.

The chartist G.W.M. Reynolds focused on the activities of the middle-women in *The Seamstress* (1853). The heroine, Virginia Mordaunt, cried with disappointment when she discovered that she would receive only 3s 6d for making up a dress that Madame Duplessy eventually sold to the Duchess of Belmont for £42 9s. Virginia's friend, who eventually takes to prostitution as a result of 'the system', explained how:

> Madame Duplessy employs a middle-woman, because it saves trouble in the first instance – and secondly because the result is to keep down the price of the work . . . by thus keeping down the wages of the needlewomen, the great houses – such as Madame Duplessy's – can from time to time reduce the prices paid to the middle-women . . . finally Mrs Jackson says to Virginia Mordaunt or any other young slave who she employs '*My prices are reduced and your wages must therefore be diminished.*' – The result is that your earnings, Virginia, will continue to grow less and less: but I question whether Madame Duplessy will lower her prices towards her aristocratic customers.[65]

This 'diabolical system' frequently results in the death of the heroine, as it does in Virginia's case, and the destruction of the aristocratic family involved. The middlewomen, however, amass 'a large fortune' from 'the ill-paid toil of others,' ride about in carriages and ostentatiously contribute to religious societies.

When the apprentices were portrayed as slaves, the greed of their fictional employers was reflected in the hideous ugliness of their physical features. The ugliness of the middlewoman in *The Seamstress* was matched by that of the milliner Mrs Curricle in *The White Slave* (1844). She was a rude, gin-drinking widow with a face 'much gifted by nature with numerous pimples and a sanguinary aspect'.[66] Mrs Curricle's repulsive features are contrasted with those of a young woman emerging from the shop, whose 'subdued aspect and pale face showed her at once to be one of the White Slaves of London'. On being told by the poor slave that she would do better to throw herself into the river than work there, the heroine reflects that the problem is:

> the old story of unrequited toil – thousands starving so that one may grow rich and arrogant upon what should have made so many comfortable. Well, well, until those who call themselves respectable persons of business have new hearts given them, the poor will be oppressed.[67]

Hard-heartedness was seen as an inevitable result of the system, and 'every employer who adopts it is a screw-down on her drudges'.[68] As Charlotte Elizabeth Tonna explained, it was not possible for those who inflicted wrong

---

[65] Ibid., p. 20.
[66] Rymer, *White Slave*, p. 72.
[67] Ibid.
[68] Tonna, *Wrongs of Woman*, p. 69.

not to harden their consciences and so block their ears to pleas for help. As a result, 'the individuals thus circumstanced, in whatever line of business placed, form a class, the unrelenting scourges of those beneath them'.[69] As Catherine Gallagher has argued, religious reformers like Tonna found it particularly difficult to reconcile their beliefs in individual moral responsibility with the economic determinism that portrayed all as victims of a system that only legislation could solve.[70] Thus, although the principals were shown to be part of a class of evil employers, they were themselves still victims of a corrupt system.

A discourse linking notions of wage and negro slavery demonised mistresses as tyrants, by operating as a plea for the rights of labourers, with whom the apprentices were conceptually linked. Similar use had been made of the slavery metaphor to engage humanitarian sympathy in campaigns for factory reform since 1825.[71] Macdonagh has argued that since slavery was such an emotive issue and considered an absolute anathema, it effectively overrode prudential and economic counter-arguments.[72] The 'First Hand' letters to *The Times* first appeared under the emotive subtitle of 'ENGLISH SLAVERY' and later with a letter about American slaves under 'LETTERS ON SLAVERY'. The *English Review* in 1849 asked if the milliners' position was now approaching 'the reality of Egyptian Bondage? – Talk of slavery abroad, surely we want a Wilberforce at home.'[73] In a call for protective legislation Tonna classed working milliners with poor labourers 'chained to the earth without the power to rise'[74] because of the 'tyranny' of those who fixed wages. Thus instead of being classed as genteel to claim empathy with the middle and upper ranks, the young milliners' status was elided with that of labourers to motivate political reform, a strategy which effectively branded their employers as tyrants.

The rhetoric of slavery also represented a belief that an evil could be righted through pressure of public opinion, which, as in anti-slavery campaigns, could be led by aristocratic women. That these women were often visibly active in campaigning for the emancipation of non-Christian negroes in a foreign land rather than alleviating the 'galling slavery of their countrywomen'[75] could produce more hostility towards the upper classes. Shortly after the publication of Harriet Beecher Stowe's bestselling *Uncle Tom's Cabin* in 1852, a meeting of aristocratic ladies planned an anti-slavery petition. This was regarded as one of the most significant attempts at exerting moral pressure on

---

[69] Ibid., p. 70.
[70] Catherine Gallagher, *The Industrial Reformation of English Fiction: Social Discourse and Narrative Form, 1832–67* (London, 1985), pp. 21–8.
[71] Oliver MacDonagh, *Early Victorian Government, 1830–70* (New York, 1977), pp. 27–8; see also Grey, 'Languages of Factory Reform', pp. 146–9.
[72] MacDonagh, *Early Victorian Government*, p. 28.
[73] *English Review*, 11/21 (1849), pp. 9–10.
[74] *Fraser's Magazine*, 33 (1844), p. 313.
[75] Tonna, *Wrongs of Woman*, p. 96.

the Americans.[76] Yet numerous vituperative attacks were directed at the group, some of whose members were also prominent in the Association for the Aid and Benefit of Dressmakers and Milliners, for ignoring their national duty. One of these attacks asked if it was not slavery that milliners' and dressmakers' apprentices lived, 'year after year dependent on the hard *masters* in many of the most fashionable shops in our metropolis'.[77] Thus, where aristocratic philanthropic power was believed to be the best solution to the problem, the femininity of the principal milliners was often erased altogether.

American anti-abolitionists used the same rhetoric to undermine British criticism and to posit a counter-attack defining 'English Slavery' as a far worse system than that based on racial inferiority. The milliners were once again a prime example of such a system. John Cobden culled medical reports from the Employment Commission and material from the *Times* to prove this point. In addition to tales of tradeswomen who allegedly beat or starved their apprentices to death, Cobden cited a *Times* editorial, which squarely laid the blame on the milliners and dressmakers. These women not only increased their profits 'from the blood and life of the wretched creatures in their employ', but also had 'hold of English society at both ends'. That is, the women who ran millinery establishments ruled through the aristocratic ladies' love of fashion and the seamstresses' desire not to starve.[78] It made a striking, if hostile, tribute to the perceived power of the principal milliners. Yet Harriet Beecher Stowe was far from regarding the milliners' seamstresses as slaves and consequently was less harsh on their employers. Somewhat appalled at being dragged unwittingly into *The Times* debate by having her dress made at an East End establishment, Beecher Stowe protested that she had been waited on by 'a very respectable woman', who had protested her innocence of any overworked hands or dens of 'miserable white slaves'. Stowe claimed that it had never occurred to her that this 'nice pleasant person' was head of an establishment and had assumed she would make the dress herself.[79] Despite pressure from the newspaper and numerous letters urging her to 'take up the conflict immediately', Stowe refused. She argued that *The Times* was pleading their cause far better than she could, and that nothing showed 'the difference between the working class of England and the poor slave'[80] more plainly than this display of intelligence and determination to resist wrong and the existence of abundant means for them to do so.

[76] Clare Midgley, *Women Against Slavery: The British Campaigns, 1780–1870* (London, 1992), pp. 145–9.
[77] 'An Englishwoman', *A Letter to Those Ladies Who Met at Stafford House in Particular and to the Women of England in General on Slavery At Home* (1853), pp. 15–17 (emphasis added).
[78] John Cobden, *The White Slaves of England: Compiled from Official Documents* (Buffalo, 1853), pp. 178–80.
[79] Stowe, *Sunny Memories*, pp. 196–7.
[80] Ibid., p. 197. Stowe also pointed out that plantation slaves were forbidden by law from learning to read and write and so were unable to plead their own cause.

Christian 'maternalism'

For many, the antithesis of the master/slave relationship was that expressed within what could be broadly termed industrial paternalism, which was made possible by the law of political economy that decreed the interests of employer and employee to be essentially identical. In this view, a greater duty of care by the employer would be met by a reciprocal increase in productivity by the employee and would negate the necessity for external legislation. This could sometimes result in more positive representations of employers and hence the millinery and dressmaking principals. The Association's 1851 Annual report stated that:

> Among the heads of establishments . . . more elevated views of the duties and responsibilities, inseparable from employers, have secured to the association the zealous co-operation of numerous and influential principals. . . . Nor have the young persons engaged in the dressmaking and millinery business remained uninfluenced amidst the general improvement. Finding that a strenuous effort was in progress to promote their physical and moral welfare, and that increased industry on their part would be rewarded by diminished hours of work, the assistants have become more attentive, the workrooms are better managed, and both parties, relieved from a system which was oppressive to all and really beneficial to none, have recognised the truth, that in no industrial pursuit is there any real incompatibility between the employer and the employed.[81]

The statement was one of an idealised and somewhat over-optimistic picture given the renewed cries for reform, but similar arguments repeatedly reappeared. They were also implicit within any proposals, like those from Ann Olivier and the 'First Hand', that were based on self-regulation as a solution.

This paternalistic duty of care could be reformulated as a moral obligation within religious discourses. The Bishop of Oxford rejected protective legislation, because he believed that external laws should not be applied to situations which 'ought to depend on the higher and more sensitive principles of moral obligation'.[82] Nevertheless, he stressed that 'the identity and indissolubility of the interests of the employer and the employed was a great eternal truth'.[83] Yet the moral obligations of the millinery and dressmaking principals who owed the duty of care were particularly onerous because of the moral anxieties raised by the nature of their trade. The manufacture of fashionable clothing and luxury items at best aroused fears about the vanity and shallowness of those who made them, and at worst appeared as the first step

---

[81] Cited in ibid., p. 200.
[82] *The Times*, 12 July 1856, p. 12, col. F.
[83] Ibid.

on the road to moral ruin and prostitution. These fears were exacerbated by the fact that such manufacture took place in an urban context with all the attendant anxieties about disorder and alienation,[84] of which London, 'that great charnel-house of withered hopes',[85] was a prime example. Evangelicals like Tonna and Christian Socialists like Elizabeth Gaskell held employers personally responsible for their apprentices and frequently blamed their lack of true Christian charity, more than the apprentices' vanity or lust, for their moral ruin.[86] For many, the moral welfare of the employees was sacrificed to the principals' heedless pursuit of profit.

Since work practices in the trade were thought to be particularly conducive to moral ruin, proprietors of millinery establishments were especially subject to criticism. Expecting their employees to work on Sunday not only contravened the Sabbath but prevented young girls from going to church, where it was even suggested that employers should provide a pew for them. Many principal milliners did not provide a meal or room for relaxation on Sundays when there was no work. This was deemed equally ruinous for their employees. One frequently recited incident depicted a young girl with no friends in town walking the city hungry and alone all day because her employer maintained that her indentures stipulated she only fed employees on work days.[87] It was due to the milliner Mrs Mason's lack of care and provision on Sundays that Gaskell's orphaned apprentice Ruth met her seducer. Milliners were also accused of lack of care if they allowed the reading of 'pot-boilers' rather than instructional texts to the girls while they worked.[88] One milliner was charged with exhibiting 'a disgusting indifference for the morals and health of those by whose toil she is amassing wealth',[89] because her workroom overlooked a brothel. As in the case of female factory workers, outdoor milliners' apprentices were deemed particularly vulnerable to seduction as they walked home, as were those girls sent out 'matching' silks in different shops around the town.

Since the seduction of poor young milliners was a major concern for reformers,[90] as well as an established trope in eighteenth- and nineteenth-century literature, the principals needed to provide evidence of moral protection for their employees. Mrs Watkins told the Parliamentary Commissioners that she was 'very anxious to promote the moral and religious behaviour of

---

[84] See Robert J. Werlin, *The English Novel and the Industrial Revolution: A Study in the Sociology of Literature* (London, 1990), pp. 66–93, on the problems of urbanisation and how they were perceived as harder to solve than those of rural poverty.

[85] Stone, *Young Milliner*, p. 22.

[86] Fryckstedt, *Elizabeth Gaskell's 'Mary Barton'*, p. 182.

[87] See Tonna, *Wrongs of Woman*, p. 76ff., for a fictionalised version.

[88] Ibid., pp. 36–7.

[89] *The Times*, 26 April 1844.

[90] The Association for the Aid and Benefit of Milliners and Dressmakers would pay a cab fare home for any apprentice who told the police she had been accosted: Mayhew, Letter LXXV, p. 123.

apprentices'.[91] She not only encouraged regular church-going but was reluctant to take girls without London parents because she did not want sole charge of them and could not send them home. She feared that letting those without friends go out at weekends was 'most scandalous' and 'likely to lead to vice'. However, while principals were happy to conform to reformers' moral expectations on one level, they were not prepared to let this interfere with business practice. One anonymous employer told the Commissioners that she did indeed provide moral care for her apprentices, ensured that they attended church regularly and agreed that lack of Sunday dinner could lead to vice. However, she argued that restricting their working hours, which, according to the testimonies of some of her employees, were excessively long, would seriously interfere with her business.[92]

The solution was discussed in terms of self-regulation and a duty of maternal care owed by employers to their peculiarly helpless charges.[93] Many apprentices and improvers were believed to be orphans or from rural homes, so employers were implicitly expected to stand in loco parentis. In Ruth, Mrs Gaskell described how Mrs Mason should have 'kept up the character of her girls by tender vigilance and Christian care'.[94] Many of the principals, when interviewed by the Commissioners, mirrored these concerns by confirming that it was their duty to provide proper care on Sundays, and they stressed how the apprentices ate with them as family.[95] Indeed, Tonna described at length how the ideal mistress could 'counteract any mischief arising from close confinement to business'.[96] The employer should not only keep to reasonable hours and conditions of employment, she must always be considerate and 'join in their conversation, enter into their hopes and prospects, sympathise with them in sickness, and endeavour to make herself rather beloved by her kindness to them'.[97] Thus, unlike the paternalism expected from male factory owners, the duty of 'maternal' care proposed for employers in the millinery trade was heavily resonant of aspects of domestic ideology. As Gallagher has argued, social paternalism and domestic ideology often co-existed in the language of industrial reformers, but this resulted in a tension between representations of women as distressed workers to mobilise reform and calls for their return to the home to become ideal mothers.[98] Principal milliners were expected to be maternal in the workplace to protect the morals of their employees, in much the same way as eighteenth-century milliners had been depicted as 'proper ladies' to protect

---

[91] BPP, Children's Employment, Vol. 14, f. 212.
[92] Ibid., Vol. 14, f. 215–17.
[93] Ibid., Vol. 14, f. 32: Grainger described the apprentices as 'in a peculiar degree, unprotected and helpless'.
[94] Gaskell, Ruth, p. 48.
[95] See e.g. BPP, Children's Employment, Vol. 14, f. 211, 219, 221.
[96] Fraser's Magazine, p. 310.
[97] Ibid.
[98] Gallagher, Industrial Reformation, pp. 129–30.

them from the immoral advances of male customers. Some employers did accept a degree of moral responsibility, but the disparity between the language of business used by the principals and the language of domestic morality used by Christian reformers remained.

Conclusion

This examination of the discursive frameworks within which the condition of milliners and dressmakers was debated has shown that London milliners and dressmakers were successful, influential and frequently unscrupulous managers of flourishing business enterprises, whose power over their aristocratic clients and poor employees gave rise to considerable public concern. Nineteenth-century representations of millinery proprietors built on many of the previous century's concerns over the acquisition of profit, sales and sexuality, social mobility, luxury and moral corruption and pseudo foreign influence. But they also reflected more current issues about the impact of capitalism, urbanisation, slavery, waged labour, private enterprise and the role of state legislation. Yet despite the fact that their work practices became the subject of much public and political debate, the principals were never as visible as their oppressed operatives.

In constructing the 'truth' about the causes of distress in the industry, the need to mobilise public opinion to press for the possible solutions envisaged was paramount. This resulted in representations of the problem which, while highlighting the gender and class of the young women in need of help, often suppressed that of their employers. If the problem was formulated as social, the envisaged solution to heal the divide between rich and poor excluded middle-class intervention. If the problem was economic, calls for protective legislation focused on the helpless femininity of those in need of protection. If the problem was a result of the evils of capitalism, the employers' identity was either subsumed as part of the 'system', or demonised by the rhetoric of slavery used to critique it. If the problem was moral, the principals were deemed to have failed in their moral and parental duties towards their young employees with dramatic and well-publicised results.

Only when the solution envisaged was that of self-regulation did more positive images emerge. However, these never managed to attract the attention that was given to the emotive calls for protective legislation, aristocratic intervention, or the pressure of enlightened public opinion to produce change. All of these claims relied heavily on the image of the poor little milliner and cast her employer into the shadows. Nevertheless, principal milliners continued to profit from their trade rather than retreat into domesticity, and apparently managed to avoid settling their 'heavy bill with humanity'.

11

Conclusion

'Business is just life'

> This most energetic of landladies and Napoleonic of coach proprietors developed
> and managed her extensive coaching interests long before her husband died.
> . . . Up to her seventieth year she was the last up at night, scouring the house
> to see that all was safe; and the first up in the morning, looking after the stable
> people and seeing that the horses had their feeds. . . . Inside and outside the
> house, and down the Eastern roads, her influence was despotic and would brook
> no defiance.
>
> An account of Ann Nelson, London coach proprietor, c.1812–58[1]

As a highly successful, 'autocratic and business-like' woman, it is perhaps not
surprising that Ann Nelson shared the dubious honour of being classified
in Napoleonic terms along with a number of equally successful milliners.
Mrs Nelson was apparently one of a number of women in the transport industry
described as 'awesome figures' whose exploits were recorded in nostalgic
reminiscences of the coaching age.[2] Indeed, Dickens used Mrs Nelson's well-
known inn at Aldgate as the site for Mr Pickwick's departure for Ipswich, just
as her rival Sarah Ann Mountain's establishment was the setting for
Mr Squeer's meeting with Ralph and Nicholas Nickleby, although neither
woman is mentioned in the novels. Mrs Nelson's inn had over a hundred beds
and she ran some of the fastest and most famous coaches to twenty-three
different towns.[3] There were also other women operating coaches in London
on a smaller scale. For example, in 1831 Ann Mitchell ran two twelve-seater
coaches several times a day between St Pauls, Kew Bridge and Turnham
Green.[4] Although Mrs Nelson was a driving force in an industry described
as highly speculative and 'cursed with insane competition',[5] the business was
a family concern that had been handed down from her husband's father, and
gave employment to two of her three sons. In every sense, therefore, Mrs

---

[1] Charles G. Harper, *The Norwich Road: An East Anglian Highway* (1901), p. 19.
[2] See ibid., pp. 19–25, 81–2; idem, *Stage-coach and Mail*, Vol. 2, pp. 232, 236, 343, and
Stanley Harris, *The Coaching Age* (1885), pp. 156, 161–2.
[3] GL, Ms. 15,559, part 4, printed bill dated January 1824 in Nelson's name.
[4] Mitchell was one of fifteen London coachmistresses listed in *Robson's London Directory*
(1831), pp. 1–21. My thanks to David Barnett for this reference.
[5] Harper, *Stage-coach and Mail*, p. 194.

Nelson could be said to have conducted her business both 'inside and outside the house'.

Ann Nelson may not have been a typical example of an early nineteenth-century businesswoman, but her enterprise and her reputation illustrate several of the themes discussed in this book. In retrospect her business success earned her a respectful literary notoriety, but in contemporary literature her business was more visible than she was. She was a widow who took over a family business, but she effectively ran the business before her husband's death and continued to do so for many years afterwards before one of her sons took over. She was also operating in a highly competitive masculine trade well into the nineteenth century, when pressure to conform to a domestic ideal of femininity was supposedly at its height. Apparently Mrs Nelson had engaged in a campaign of vicious price-cutting, forcing several of her rivals out of business. She had even found herself in court defending one of her coachmen, who had been charged with 'furious driving' on her instructions.[6] Although she was one of only a handful of female successes in the business, a significant minority of other women were also functioning in a sector of trade more commonly believed to have been exclusively male.[7] In addition to the licensed London coachmistresses mentioned above, newspaper advertisements and insurance policies confirm that women were not uncommon in the coaching trade. Indeed, if female coachmistresses gave their occupation as 'innholder' to the insurance clerks, as Sarah Ann Mountain did, the actual numbers may have been far higher than the four officially recorded in the policies sampled here – a point that reinforces the difficulties involved in classifying women's occupations. Moreover, Mrs Nelson's dwelling house was both a family home and a source of income, there was no separation of work and home but her enterprise could hardly be described as domestic or a hidden investment. As an 'innkeeper', she conformed to feminine expectations but as a coach proprietor, she challenged masculine ones. In short, for Mrs Nelson the business of life and a life of business were inextricably linked.

The central contention of this book has been that the metaphor of separate spheres does not have sufficient analytical purchase to describe the lives of women in business or to provide an explanatory framework for long-term developments in female participation in economic enterprise. It has been argued that, while gender remains a useful analytical tool it needs to be considered in conjunction with other social, economic and racial hierarchies of difference. The gendered dichotomy of masculine/feminine at the heart of the public/private divide tends to highlight areas of conflict and thus to obscure areas of co-operation between men and women, and between family and business life. Indeed, many non-gendered oppositions could be mapped on to

---

[6] Harper, *Norwich Road*, p. 24.
[7] Alexander, *Women's Work*, p. 20, lists transport amongst those sectors in which no women were found.

this ubiquitous dichotomy, particularly in the eighteenth century. In the same way, a narrow focus on relations of patriarchal power obscures the significance of other commercial imperatives and incidents of cross-gender co-operation in pursuit of these. By focusing primarily on relations between husbands and wives, it also ignores the role of wider family members and friends, and the possibility of intergenerational conflict. These themes have been pursued in the preceding pages by examining three factors that have been commonly perceived as increasingly limiting women's economic enterprise: the law; lack of property and exclusion from forms of business organisation; and the impact of domestic ideology.

Part I examined how women in business fared within the legal system. Legal treatises provided a clear example of how the disabling and apparently immutable doctrine of coverture was constantly reinterpreted and somewhat imperfectly adapted to suit changing social and economic conditions. Many authors of treatises (with notable exceptions) also included examples of when borough customs and equitable principles could mitigate the harshness of the common law. Indeed, many of these show that by the mid-eighteenth century women in business could successfully mount an equitable defence of their separate business property, even in a common-law court, long before the Married Women's Property Acts officially ratified such an action. There were therefore legally sanctioned spaces within which married women could continue in trade, even though the right to do so was never openly conferred during this period. Yet even if this were not the case, it would be a mistake to view coverture as wholly damaging for women in business. For many wives trading according to the 'right' of a *feme sole* trader, coverture was the best defence against being made personally bankrupt. The borough custom of *feme sole* trading, however, seems to have been seen primarily as an aid to debt recovery to facilitate commercial practice in the city. Decisions in such cases were usually based on this principle or on how the custom should function in relation to the common law, rather than on upholding a patriarchal norm. Indeed husbands and wives often collaborated in court cases, and it was not uncommon for husbands to support their wives' *feme sole* status to protect themselves from debt or to ensure the continuation of a family business in case of absence, illness or imprisonment. In fact both men and women took full advantage of the pluralistic legal system to pursue their commercial interests. Businesswomen could and did move their cases between different courts of law and could even be involved in related cases in more than one court at the same time. This meant that although there does seem to have been something of a conservative backlash around 1800 in common-law courts, a number of loopholes, which were highlighted in legal treatises on the subject, remained in other courts.

Going to law, however, was usually the last resort for traders of both sexes who relied heavily on the existence of complex and extensive credit networks to facilitate business. Women were well integrated within these networks, and marriage, or in many cases remarriage, did not necessarily interrupt long-standing credit arrangements. It was only when these broke down that marital status became an issue and even then the categories of *feme sole* or covert trader remained relative and highly contingent upon the best method of debt retrieval. The majority of cases for debt involving married businesswomen were initiated by frustrated male creditors, but even though one function of equity was to remedy husbands' 'exorbitant' common law rights, men were not necessarily businesswomen's chief opponents at law. The nature of credit agreements meant the borrower was always servant to the lender, regardless of gender, and the possession of separate property or capital could also ensure contractual equality. Moreover, there was a high incidence of intergenerational conflict, particularly within second marriages where the new wife ran a successful business. It was not uncommon for children – notably daughters who would cite coverture to their own advantage – to sue their stepmothers in order to gain a greater share of what they saw as their father's estate. Marital discord between spouses was also far from unknown, even given the degree of co-dependency common in family businesses and, legally, a husband would have the advantage in such cases. Yet if a husband's bad behaviour towards his wife upset business and credit relations, other family members and traders in the community would act on her behalf to restore these vital trading arrangements. Indeed, friends and neighbours often acted to help secure the business interests of women regardless of their marital status.

Practical daily trading arrangements may therefore be seen to have over-ridden legal prescriptions until or unless credit relations broke down. The practice of buying and selling, particularly over long distances, also required the co-operation of men and women in trading networks that could stretch across the country. Mrs Baker's considerable consumption of goods from Durham, London and Bath required the services of numerous women to provide both the merchandise and the money necessary to support such purchases. A network of family and friends linked Mrs Baker with her suppliers and they in turn relied on the services of male and female kin and fellow traders to convey money and goods over lengthy distances. Many of these women, moreover, continued to do business with Mrs Baker for long periods of time and at every stage of their life and marital cycle. Here again, marriage and its attendant legal disabilities were not the absolute bar to female enterprise that they appeared to be. The Durham evidence also shows that a remarkably high number of women were doing business with just one gentlewoman, even though many of these female traders would have remained invisible within sources officially relating to the city's trading affairs.

Women running businesses of sufficient size to warrant insurance were rather more visible and also present in even more significant numbers. If women had been increasingly confined to a primarily domestic sphere of action, it might be expected that fewer and fewer women in an ever-narrowing range of trades would have taken out insurance between 1735 and 1845. The Sun Fire policy registers clearly show that this was not the case. Although the actual numbers of businesswomen issued policies in each sample year tended to mirror the fluctuating fortunes of the company, the number of different individual trades in which insured women were engaged expanded dramatically in London and more steadily outside the capital. Much of this expansion occurred in the increasingly feminised fashion trades and specialist retailing, but these were also the most potentially profitable trades for women. At the same time, women were found in an increasing number of diverse and specialised occupations in nineteenth-century London, a pattern which, on a smaller scale, broadly mirrored that of the city's male producers and dealers. Thus, within a broad sectoral continuity, micro-changes were evident among the occupational patterns of both men and women in business.

Treating businesswomen as a homogeneous group is at best a hazardous undertaking because it obscures other categories of regional, economic, occupational, social and religious difference. Nevertheless, there were some similarities between businesswomen in the metropolitan economy and those in provincial towns, such as Durham. Women who bought and sold insurance often had strong family ties to their business but again these went far beyond the stereotypical family enterprise between husband and wife. For those selling insurance, respect and strong local business connections were a prerequisite for the job. The pattern of storing goods and stock in neighbouring houses or nearby cellars also suggests that London women had strong local business networks. Similar networks must have been in place to allow women living outside the capital to store and insure their stock in the same London ware-houses, as did other local producers in the same trade. Neither London nor provincial women traders insured large separate commercial premises, with the exception of breweries, and for the majority of businesswomen throughout the period the dwelling house remained the prime site of business. For most insured women in business, there was very little separation of work and home.

Combining home and work, however, did not mean that women were restricted to 'domestic' trades or to a secondary role in the family enterprise. Insured women in business could and did control sometimes quite considerable amounts of property and capital, although much of this could not be classified solely as business capital. For many women in business, and particularly those living outside London, investment in rental property was an important form of risk management and provided a supplementary income. It did not, as has been commonly argued, provide an escape from business to a more genteel existence, since women in both large and small businesses invested in property in this way. Furthermore, far from excluding women, some forms of business organisation, such as insurance itself and particularly partnerships, served to facilitate their business enterprises. Not only were women active economic agents in business partnerships with members of both sexes, but women in partnership with men were more likely to maintain control of their property by insuring it separately than were women in same-sex partnerships. If raising capital through institutional means was difficult for women, it was possible to go into business with a male or female sleeping partner who could also share the cost of insurance. In these cases female traders invariably insured their own goods and stock separately. As in the case of Mary Jevon's partnership with two male London mercers, women could also remove their share of capital to their own advantage on the dissolution of a business partnership. Even married women could insure stock separately if sometimes covertly. While *feme sole* traders could insure separate stock in their own name, married women with informal trading agreements could effectively do the same with the co-operation of their husbands. Women therefore had access to and could retain control of property and capital. With such opportunities, they did actively participate in business organisations other than family enterprises, a finding supported by the number of newspaper advertisements regarding both single and mixed-sex business partnerships. Women may have been largely excluded from corporate organisations but the newspaper also provided a forum for a degree of consolidated trade action, as did the presentation of petitions.

There is therefore strong evidence to show that significant numbers of women could and did remain in business throughout the years from 1700 to 1850, and that even married women could *de facto* and *de jure* continue to trade. Yet, perhaps one of the strongest arguments against their presence in the marketplace was the proliferation of contemporary literature that was either overtly hostile to female traders or, even more frequently, prescribed an ideal of genteel, domesticated femininity to which middle-class women in particular should aspire. Indeed, complaints about the lack of economic opportunities for women were most often penned by women of the upper-middling ranks whose social aspirations led them to regard trade as complete anathema to their position in society. It is misleading, however, to see the boundaries between gentility and trade as set in stone. Historians need to allow for a greater degree of social mobility for women, one that was not necessarily tied to their father's or husband's economic status. Economic necessity could force many a gentlewoman into business, but not necessarily one that they would describe as a trade, as in the case of the school proprietors and silk manufacturers. There was also considerable slippage in the language of class or social description. Within the polite medium of newspaper advertising the term 'gentlewoman' could apply equally to those of genteel birth seeking investment or employment and those businesswomen seeking a partner or elite clients. This mode of description was frequently mirrored in insurance policy registers where women running agricultural enterprises were equally likely to describe themselves as 'gentlewomen'. Although historians have now questioned how effectively didactic literature and domestic ideology could actually limit women's daily lives, there has been little discussion of any alternative representations of femininity concerning women in business. Thus other voices and other languages about women in business were the focus of Part III of this book.

Representations of women in business, no matter how negative or circum-spect, were nevertheless evidence that women did operate in the economic sphere. That their presence there frequently caused anxieties about social and economic change should not obscure the fact of their existence in the marketplace. Misgivings about excessive profits and the desire for luxury goods were mirrored in representations of the alleged sexual lasciviousness of eighteenth-century milliners; abhorrence at the human cost of capitalism often found expression in the hideous features attributed to prosperous nineteenth-century milliners. Paradoxically, representations of ideal femininity and domesticity often occurred during debates about how to reform trading practices. Thus in 1711 the *Spectator* reminded its readers that, as the weaker sex, women in trade were even more deserving of male politeness, when it attempted a reformation of manners in milliners' shops and coffee-houses. In the nineteenth century, evangelicals argued that principal milliners should show more maternal care for their young apprentices. Yet in neither case was the use of such imagery intended to remove these women from trade. Both the *Spectator* in the eighteenth century and *The Times* in the nineteenth were quite clear about the necessity for some women to work for their living. *The Times* had even in the eighteenth century campaigned vigorously to reserve millinery and mantua making for women, despite earlier attempts by guilds to maintain male control of the fashion trades.

The fluid nature of discursive formations meant that articulations of gendered, class and national differences often swapped partners during debates about profit, luxury and national superiority in the eighteenth century, and during nineteenth-century discussions of social reform and protective legislation. National identities were involved in gendered expressions of French and English commercial interests, which could both hinder and encourage women in business enterprises. In nineteenth-century debates about milliners, England itself was divided into 'two nations', and milliners' apprentices were alleged to be more oppressed than were the negro slaves. Such arguments left their employers either invisible or guilty of industrial tyranny. Class, as we have seen in the application of the term 'gentlewoman', was an even more slippery category. Daughters of impoverished gentlemen, desperate to run a genteel business but appalled at the prospect of receiving 'pecuniary emolument' in the eighteenth century, had become a class of wealthy, avaricious employers from low origins, who callously exploited their poor but nobly born apprentices in the nineteenth century. The femininity of eighteenth-century milliners was constantly emphasised with little distinction between employer and employee. The gender of nineteenth-century millinery proprietors was almost invisible, but their apprentices had become excessively feminine and infantilised. The single constant theme was the potential profitability of such businesses and, by implication, the continuing economic success of substantial numbers of women running them.

Positive representations of women in business were undeniably rarer. They were perhaps strongest in eighteenth-century efforts to promote British manufactures above those of the French and this provided a rare opportunity for women to express their own pride in commercial achievements. Some were even awarded prizes for their contribution to the nation's manufactures. Some women also openly expressed that they were 'glad to be in business' within the more gender-neutral forum of the eighteenth-century London *Daily Advertiser*. Within this imagined community of trade women engaged in similarly innovative and competitive marketing techniques both with and against men, and displayed comparable levels of occupational identity. In negotiating between the polite and commercial ideals of the age and promoting their honour, reputation and professional skills, this mode of self-representation resulted in a very public declaration of successful female enterprise. In the nineteenth century, milliners who proposed self-regulation within the industry also found a rare and approved voice with which to express their commercial interests. Too often a lack of easily visible discursive agency has been taken as a sign of lack of economic agency, but this was clearly not the case.

Finally, this book has shown that long-term developments in women's diverse business enterprises were not a linear process that can be easily measured, or explained by simple reference to 'patriarchy', 'capitalism/industrialisation' or 'domestic ideology'. Capitalism cannot be said solely to have marginalised women's economic enterprises, since they responded to changing economic conditions by engaging in increasingly diverse and newly specialised trades, especially in London. Overall, the fortunes of individual trades and the numbers entering them seem to have fluctuated considerably over time. In addition, the impact of patriarchal values was weakened, both by wider family relationships and because commercial imperatives were often more important. Domestic ideology, moreover, was just one of many competing and largely 'politically' determined discourses. Despite the pressure of gendered cultural expectations, financial barriers and legal disabilities, women remained a significant, if not always visible, part of England's expanding economy. A few amassed considerable wealth, some flourished even in traditionally masculine trades, most entered and continued to trade with the help of networks of family and 'friends', and many continued to combine home and business in the same house. For those not 'bred' to business, it was a difficult cultural and economic adjustment, but for many, business was 'just life'.

Appendix I

Judith Baker's trading networks

Family

Judith Baker (1725–1810) m. 1749 George Baker (d. 1774)
Judith Routh – mother, moneylender
Elizabeth Bland – sister, agent (London)
Dorothy Chapeau – sister (London)
Captain William Conyers – related to George Baker's mother's family
Miss Conyers – Captain Conyers' niece, apprenticed to Elizabeth Goodrick, mantua maker

'Friends'

Agents

Mrs Bland (London, sister)
Mrs Chapeau (London, sister)
Mrs Potts (Durham)
Mrs Perrot (Newcastle)
Mrs Tunstall (Darlington)

Moneylenders

Mrs Priscilla Attlee (Newcastle) £500
Grace Baites £60
Dorothy Holmes amount unknown
Eleanor Nelson £100 (sister Mary in Chester social friend)
Mrs Peard (London) £6,500
Elizabeth and Mary Pickering £80 (spinsters, Durham)
Judith Routh (mother) amount unknown
Eliza Todd £360

Main Durham trading network (regular receipts in household accounts 1755–84)

Mrs Mercy Ashworth (widow) – ironmonger
Susannah Burton – mantua maker
Mrs Ann Clifton – newsagent, stationer, bookbinder
Elizabeth Goodrick – mantua maker
Mary Johnson & Co – milliners
Jane Lamb – spinner
Elizabeth Lampson – hoop maker
Ann Mowbray – dealer in candles
Mrs Ann Pearson – hatter
Hannah Smith – milliner, dressmaker, specialised washing and dressing
Ann Stokell (Richmond) – stocking maker, sister of Elizabeth Arrowsmith, Durham
Isabell Taylor – tallow chandler
Miss Susan Todd – perfumer
Jane Robinson – cloth dealer
Mrs Jane Robson (widow) – wine merchant
Dorothy Verty – milliner, dressmaker
Elizabeth Waugh – grocer
Mrs Jane Waugh – copper pan maker

Additional Durham suppliers

Mrs A. Chewe – ladies' boarding-school proprietor
Robert and Isabella Darling – curriers
Ann Emmerson – haberdasher
Jane Potts -corn chandler
Rose Pratt – milliner and lace washer
Mrs E. Raine – milliner
Mrs Rushworth – gardener/tree seller (?)
Isabella Salvin – chimney-sweeper, widow
Susanna Steel – linen draper
Esther Wilson – cloth dealer (?)

Regular London suppliers

Elizabeth Beauvais – milliner
Mrs L. Leach – milliner
Mary Mackenzie & Co – mantua maker
Mary Oliver – French-trimming maker

Additional London suppliers

Catherine Connor – milliner
Barbara Hill – haberdasher
Margret Ross – milliner
Mrs Story – coffee-woman (?)
Ann Willerton – of Willerton & Wall, milliners

The Bath connection

Mrs Catherine Clements – lodging house owner
Jane Matthews – butcher
Betty Ross (widow) – grocer and chandler

Additional Bath suppliers

Sarah Hennagen – mantua maker
Thomas and Elizabeth Paulin – haberdashers and milliners
Catherine Trunel – milliner

Appendix II

Classification and occupational coding of
women in business

Classification

To reflect the diversity of women's business activities it was necessary to match the definition of 'woman in business' discussed in the Introduction[1] with practical criteria for data entry, and then adopt a flexible scheme of classifying occupations. As with any source, there were a number of problems in collecting occupational data from insurance policy registers. Deciding which female policy holders were in business was complicated by the fact that where policy registers recorded an occupation they did not distinguish between whether this meant the policy holder was in business or merely an employee.[2] Thus other historians have taken a relatively restrictive approach. David Barnett adopted the criterion of entering only those policies in which fixed and/or working capital was insured, and Peter Earle took 'stock-in-trade' as an indication that women possessed business capital.[3] However, this type of approach is particularly problematic for women because it is liable to exclude many who were entered in the registers in an ambiguous or inconsistent way, or who had diverse portfolios to insure. Many of the reasons for this were discussed in Chapter 7, where the different insurance strategies pursued by women in business were examined in detail.[4] Nevertheless, there was also a small number of women with policies insuring stock and/or commercial buildings who were not given an occupational label.[5] Furthermore, women who were given occupational labels, even obviously manufacturing ones, did not necessarily insure stock but did insure amounts of property and household goods at levels that were far

---

[1] See above, pp. 2–3.
[2] This is less of a problem for studies of women's work in general which could include both employers and employees, as in Schwarz, *London in the Age of Industrialisation*, pp. 14–22.
[3] David Barnett, *London, Hub of the Industrial Revolution*, pp. 26-7; Earle, *Making of the English Middle Class*, p. 169.
[4] See above, pp. 148–52.
[5] Twelve policies in 1735, two each in 1755 and 1780, one in 1809, none in 1845.

too high for an employee. For example, in 1780 Ann Sawyer from Birmingham was described as a spoon maker; she insured £900 of property but no stock.[6]

In order to take account of these problems the following criteria were adopted for selecting policies to be included in the database of businesswomen:

1   Women with a named occupation and sums insured too high to be an employee, but not necessarily insuring stock.[7]
2   Women with no named occupation but none the less insuring 'stock-in-trade' (or an equivalent phrase) and/or commercial property.[8]

Going directly to the original policies provided a wealth of detail not available simply from the listed indexes. This exercise resulted in a database of 1,490 policies for the five sample years studied, covering the business activities of approximately 1,800 people, 9 per cent of whom were men because they were in partnership with, or married to, women in business. It is difficult to be more accurate about the number of people involved due to the existence of multiple policies ascribed to a single name, which may have belonged to different people with the same name, or to one person either changing insurance amounts or moving address. However, in this study, the problem was considerably lessened due to the great descriptive detail in the policy registers (as opposed to indexes) and the wide spacing of the sample years.

Multiple policies and multiple occupations could cause additional problems of classification. Sometimes multiple policies occurred due to changing occupations, as a result of either upgrading or downsizing. On 27 May 1780 Catherine Laverick was living in apartments in the Sun Tavern, Ludgate Street. She took out a £100 policy, £50 of which was for a billiard table, and her occupation was given as 'billiard table keeper'. Two weeks later she took out another policy for £400, including the same sum on the billiard table, but the Sun Tavern had become her 'dwelling house' and her occupation was given as 'vintner'.[9] However, as discussed in Chapter 7, some merchants and other occupations also took out multiple policies, although again, the detailed

---

[6] GL, Ms. 11936, 286/433063 and 433062.
[7] This involved making a judgement on the amount and type of property insured. For example, in the nineteenth-century samples, schoolmistresses with insurance policies issued of less than £200, where no real property or stock was listed, were assumed to be employees rather than running a school as a business. By contrast, in the case of spoon maker Ann Sawyer, cited above, the possession of £900 of real property was assumed to mean that she was unlikely to have been merely an employee.
[8] The majority of women in this category had no named occupation but did insure 'stock' and (sometimes) additional commercial property. Only one policy involved a woman with no stated occupation who insured only commercial property. She was a widow who let an inn and stables to a Mrs Lawrence, who presumably ran the enterprise, and let the outbuildings to two other women. See GL, Ms. 11936, 43/67841 (1735).
[9] GL, Ms. 11936, 283/429201 and 429603 (1780).

descriptions of types of building included in each entry made it possible to determine those cases where multiple policies belonged to one woman. Similar problems arose when assigning an occupational label to an individual woman with multiple occupations. As a general rule, the first listed occupation only was counted, so Mercy Paterson at the King's Arms in Poole, victualler, grocer, haberdasher, slop-seller, and dealer in china, glass and earthenware, for example, was coded as a victualler.[10] Since she had just £400 of general stock-in-trade, this did not greatly affect any further valuations or calculations except by suppressing the range of her activities. As discussed in Chapter 6, however, this method of coding could still obscure the range of occupations followed by women engaged in both masculine and feminine trades at the same time.[11]

Agricultural activities raised an additional problem, because a significant number of women clearly insuring farm buildings, ricks, corn and livestock were not given an occupational label. Nearly one-third of the thirty-seven agricultural policies in the sample years were taken out by women who were not given an occupational label. All but one of these women were living outside London, but the one exception in 1845 was recorded as a 'gentle-woman', despite the fact that the insurance was clearly described as being 'on her farm'.[12] Possession of land may have accorded a social status that superseded or was preferable to an occupational identity, but farming policies were also a special category of insurance that could be taken out for just six months at a time.[13] This meant that farm stock or produce could be seen as a by-product of landowning rather than an occupation, but it also meant that new widows could briefly insure stock while deciding whether to continue or to abandon the enterprise. Thus 16 per cent of all 'agricultural' policies belonged to women who were described only by this marital label.

The coding system adopted for classifying businesswomen's occupations was an adaptation of the Booth/Armstrong classification used by Harvey, Green and Corfield in the *Westminster Historical Database*.[14] To achieve maximum flexibility each occupation was coded at four levels. Level 1 represents the sector of the economy, such as agriculture, manufacturing, dealing and transport. Level 2 represents the subsectors, so that manufacturing, for example, may be divided into dress, dress sundries, food preparation, baking, drink preparation and so on. Level 3 represents groupings of related trades within each subsector. For example, 'baking' would include groups of biscuit makers

---

[10] GL, Ms. 11936, 286/433059 (1780).

[11] See above, pp. 131–3.

[12] GL, Ms. 11936, 602/1494060 (1845).

[13] GL, Ms. 15671, *Instructions for the Agents* (1807), p. 21.

[14] See Harvey *et al.*, *Westminster Historical Database*, pp. 87-117, for a detailed explanation of the adapted coding system. In origin it goes back to Charles Booth's census classification of 1881, but it contains many more levels of categorisation to allow for exercises of aggregation and disaggregation.

and sweet makers as well as bread bakers. Level 4 represents each distinct occupation as originally recorded in the policy registers.

Coding of occupations

Oclv 1: Sector of the economy

AG Agriculture
BU Building
MF Manufacture
TR Transport
XX Unallocatable
DE Dealing
IS Industrial service
PP Public service/professional
DS Domestic service

Oclv 2: Subsector of the economy (examples)

MF23 Dress
MF24 Dress sundries
MF25 Food preparation
MF26 Baking
MF27 Drink preparation
DE03 Clothing
DE04 Dress
DE05 Food
DE06 Tobacco
DE07 Wines, spirits, hotels

Oclv 3: Grouped trades or occupations (examples)

MF23001 Tailors
MF23002 Breeches makers
MF23003 Milliners, hat makers
MF23004 Shoe/boot makers, cordwainers

Oclv 4: Distinct occupations as recorded in the policy registers (examples)

MF230031 Hat manufacturer
MF230032 Hat presser
MF230033 Straw hat manufacturer
MF230034 Straw bonnet maker
MF230035 Straw plait maker
MF230036 Milliner

Coding of buildings

A = buildings of agricultural type used to house animals and/or coaches, or to store grain, hay and straw for private or commercial purposes. This category includes farm buildings and those attached to inns, taverns and private dwellings (e.g. barns, stables, sties, granaries, coachhouses, greenhouses).

B = buildings that were used for both private and obviously commercial purposes. This category includes private dwellings with commercial buildings attached or close by, which were insured as one unit (e.g. houses with shops, warehouses, offices or adjoining workshops). It also includes inns and other catering establishments that were also the owner's primary dwelling house.

C = separate buildings used solely for commercial purposes or for storing stock (e.g. shops, warehouses, workshops, brewhouses, cellars, yards and sheds).

L = buildings which have been let for commercial or private purposes.

P = buildings that were recorded as 'dwelling houses' and had no obvious additional commercial purpose, regardless of whether or not stock was insured within. However, it should be noted that this method of coding (although respecting the original form of the data) obscures the real extent of women's property used for commercial purposes because many 'dwelling houses' remained the main site of business throughout the period.

Coding of goods insured

Household: included miscellaneous goods recorded in the policy registers as 'household', plus, china, glass, plate, books, furniture, 'household fixtures', musical instruments, printed music, clothes, jewels, watches, trinkets, pictures, prints, servants clothes and boxes.

Stock: included all items where stock or business items were separately recorded (e.g. 'stock and utensils', 'business fixtures', 'goods in pledge', 'goods in trust', 'goods on commission'); also specifically named items of stock (e.g. lace, wine, liquor, straw, hay, corn, carriages, livestock).

Both: included all items where household goods and stock-in-trade were recorded together as one and allocated a single insured value (e.g. 'household goods, utensils and stock'; 'household goods and goods in trust'; 'house and business fixtures'; 'household goods, stock and goods in pledge').

Select bibliography

Unpublished material

Public Record Office
Chancery Pleadings, C6.
The English Reports, 1220–1867, CD-Rom.

Palace Green Section, University of Durham Library
Baker Baker Papers, BB/75–86.

Guildhall Library
Sun Fire Insurance policy registers, Ms. 11936/40–44; /108–13; /280–89; /443–48; /602–17.

RSA Archive
Register of Premium Awards, 1754–76
General Correspondence to the Committee of Manufactures, PR/MC/102/10/ 1–313.

Printed source material

Journals and newspapers

[London] Daily Advertiser (1731–1809).
Edinburgh Review, 109 (1859).
English Review, 11 (1849).
Fraser's Magazine for Town and Country, 33 (1846).
Gentleman's Magazine, IX (1739).
Jackson's Oxford Journal (1798).
Spectator, ed. D. F. Bond (Oxford, 1965).
Transactions of the Society of Arts (1784–1805).

Books

Anon., *The Lawes Resolutions of Womens Rights: Or, the Laws Provisions for Woemen* [sic] (London, 1632).

—— *An Answer to the Character of an Exchange Wench: Or, a Vindication of an Exchange-Woman* (London, 1675).

—— *The Ape Gentlewoman: Or, the Character of an Exchange Wench* (London, 1675).

—— *Advice to the Women and Maidens of London* (London, 1678).

—— *The Fann-Makers Grievance, by the Importation of Fanns from the East Indies* (n.d., 1690s?).

—— *The English Lady's Catechism, Shewing the Pride and Vanity of the English Nobility as are Notorious for Relieving Foreigners before their Own Country Folks* (n.d., 17..?).

—— *Baron and Feme: A Treatise of the Common Law Concerning Husbands and Wives* (London, 1700; reprinted 1719).

—— *The Velvet Coffee-woman: Or, the Life, Gallantries and Amours of the Late Famous Mrs Anne Rochford* (London, 1728).

—— *A Treatise of Feme Coverts: Or, the Lady's Law* (London, 1732).

—— *The Hardships of the English Laws in Relation to Wives* (London, 1735).

—— *A General Description of All Trades . . .* (London, 1747).

—— *The Life and Character of Moll King, Late Mistress of King's Coffee House in Covent Garden* (London, 1747).

—— *The Case of Miss Leslie and her Three Sisters, the Manufacturers of Thread for Lace, Equal to Any Foreign* (London, 1767).

—— *The Laws Respecting Women, As they Regard their Natural Rights or their Connections and Conduct* (London, 1777).

—— *Instructions for the Agents of the Sun Fire-Office* (London, 1807 and 1848).

'An Englishwoman', *A Letter to the Ladies of Stafford House in Particular and to the Women of England in General on Slavery at Home* (London, 1853).

Blackstone, William, *Commentaries on the Laws of England* (London, 1769; reprinted 1809).

Bohun, William, *Privilegia Londini: Or, the Rights, Liberties, Privileges, Laws and Customs of the City of London* (London, 1702; reprinted 1723).

Burney, Fanny, *Evelina* (1778; reprinted Oxford, 1982).

—— *The Wanderer* (London, 1814; reprinted 1991).

Campbell, R., *The London Tradesman* (London, 1747; reprinted 1969).

Cobden, John C., *The White Slaves of England: Compiled From Official Documents* (Buffalo, 1853).

Collyer, Joseph, *The Parent's and Guardian's Directory and Youth's Guide to the Choice of a Profession or Trade* (1761).

Cooke, William, *The Bankrupt Laws* (London, 1785).

Coventry, Francis, *The History of Pompey the Little* (1751; reprinted Oxford, 1974).

Defoe, Daniel, *The Complete English Tradesman* (this edn London, 1738).

Dickens, Charles, *Nicholas Nickleby* (1838; reprinted 1995).

Fielding, Henry, *Tom Jones* (1749; this edn Oxford, 1989).

Foster, F., *Thoughts on the Times, but Chiefly on the Profligacy of our Women, and its Causes* (London, 1779).

Gaskell, Elizabeth, *Mary Barton* (London, 1848).

—— *Cranford* (London, 1853).

—— *Ruth* (London, 1853).

Heywood, Eliza, *The History of Miss Betsy Thoughtless* (1751; reprinted Oxford, 1997).

Jerrold, Douglas William, *The White Milliner* (London, 1841).

Johnson, Samuel, *Dictionary of the English Language* (London, 1768, 1755 edns).

La Roche, Sophie, *Sophie in London 1786: Being the Diary of Sophie v. la Roche*, trans. Clare Williams (London, 1933).

Lush, Montague, *The Law of Husband and Wife within the Jurisdiction of the Queen's Bench and Chancery Divisions* (1884).

Mayhew, Henry, 'Letters 75, 76' (1850), in E. Yeo and E.P. Thompson (eds), *The Unknown Mayhew* (New York, 1972).

Mill, John Stuart, *The Subjection of Women* (London, 1869; reprinted 1974).

Pindar, Peter, 'An Ode to a Pretty Milliner', in idem, *Lyrics and Odes* (London, 1792).

Radcliffe, Mary Ann, *The Female Advocate: Or, an Attempt to Recover the Rights of Women from Male Usurpation* (London, 1799).

—— *The Memoirs of Mrs Mary Ann Radcliffe in Familiar Letters to her Female Friend* (Edinburgh, 1810).

Reynolds, G.W.M., *The Seamstress: Or, the White Slave of England* (London, 1853).

Riley, Henry Thomas (ed.), *Liber Albus: The White Book of the City of London* (London, 1419; reprinted and translated 1861).

Robinson, William, *The Intriguing Milliners and Attornies Clerks* (London, 1738).

Roper, R.S. Donnison, *A Treatise of the Law of Property Arising from the Relation Between Husband and Wife* (London, 1820).

Rowcroft, Charles, *Fanny, the Little Milliner: Or, the Rich and the Poor* (London, 1846; reprinted 1853).

Rymer, J.M., *The White Slave: A Romance for the Nineteenth Century* (London, 1844).

Saxby, Mary, *Memoirs of a Female Vagrant* (London, 1806).

Sterne, Laurence, 'Letter to Achdeacon Sterne' (1751), in L.P. Curtis (ed.), *The Letters of Laurence Sterne* (Oxford, 1935).

Stone, Elizabeth, *The Young Milliner* (London, 1843).

Stowe, Harriet Beecher, *Sunny Memories of Foreign Lands* (London, 1854).

Taffetas, Hester, *Recollections of Mrs Hester Taffetas, Court Milliner and Modiste during the Reign of King George the Third ...: Edited by her Granddaughter* (London, 1858).

[Tonna], Charlotte Elizabeth, *The Wrongs of Woman. Part I: Milliners and Dressmakers* (London, 1843).

Ward, Ned, *The London Spy* (4th edn, London, 1709).

Watson, William, *A Treatise on the Law of Partnership* (London, 1794).

Whittock, N. *et al.*, *The Complete Book of Trades, or the Parent's Guide and*

Youth's Instructor Forming a Popular Encyclopaedia of Trades, Manufactures and Commerce . . . (London, 1837).

Secondary material

Adburgham, Alison, *Shops and Shopping, 1800–1914* (London, 1964; reprinted 1981).

Alexander, David, *Retailing in England during the Industrial Revolution* (London, 1970).

Alexander, Sally, *Women's Work in Nineteenth-century London: A Study of the Years 1820–50* (London, 1976; reprinted 1983).

Anderson, Benedict, *Imagined Communities: Reflections on the Origins and Spread of Nationalism* (London, 1983).

Andrew, Donna T., *London Debating Societies, 1776–99* (London, 1994).

—— 'Noblesse Oblige: Female Charity in an Age of Sentiment', in *Early Modern Conceptions of Property*, ed. J. Brewer and S. Staves (London, 1996), pp. 275–300.

—— 'The Press and Public Apologies in Eighteenth-century London', in *Law, Crime and English Society, 1660–1830*, ed. N. Landau (Cambridge, 2002), pp. 208–29.

Armstrong, Nancy, *Desire and Domestic Fiction: A Political History of the Novel* (London, 1987).

Arthurs, H.W., *'Without the Law': Administrative Justice and Legal Pluralism in Nineteenth-century England* (London, 1985).

Atiyah, P.S. *The Rise and Fall of Freedom of Contract* (Oxford, 1979).

Bailey, Joanne, 'Favoured or Oppressed? Married Women, Property and Coverture in England, 1650–1800', *Continuity and Change*, 17 (2002), pp. 351–72.

—— *Unquiet Lives: Marriage and Marriage Breakdown in England, 1660–1800* (Cambridge, 2003).

Baker, J.H., *An Introduction to English Legal History* (London, 1979; reprinted 1990).

Barker, Hannah, 'Women, Work and the Industrial Revolution: Female Involvement in the English Printing Trades, c.1700–1840', in *Gender in Eighteenth-century England*, pp. 81–100.

—— *Newspapers, Politics and Public Opinion in Late Eighteenth-century England* (Oxford, 1998).

Barker, Hannah and Chalus, Elaine (eds), *Gender in Eighteenth-century England: Roles, Representations and Responsibilities* (London, 1997).

Barnett, David, *London, Hub of the Industrial Revolution: A Revisionary History, 1775–1825* (London, 1998).

Barron, Caroline, 'The Golden Age of Women in Medieval London', *Reading Medieval Studies*, 15 (1989), pp. 35–58.

Bateson, Mary, ed., *Borough Customs* (London, 1904).

Beard, Mary, *Woman as a Force in History: A Study in Traditions and Realities* (New York, 1946).

Bennett, Judith, '"History that Stands Still": Women's Work in the European Past', *Feminist Studies*, 14 (1988), pp. 269–83.

—— 'Medieval Women, Modern Women: Across the Great Divide', in *Culture and History, 1350–1600: Essays on English Communities, Identities and Writing*, ed. David Aers (London, 1992), pp. 147–75.

—— 'Women's History: A Study in Continuity and Change', *Women's History Review*, 2 (1993), pp. 173–84.

Berg, Maxine, 'Women's Work, Mechanisation and the Early Phases of Industrialisation in England', in *The Historical Meanings of Work*, ed. Patrick Joyce (London, 1987), pp. 64–98.

—— 'Women's Property and the Industrial Revolution', *Journal of Interdisciplinary History*, 24 (1993), pp. 233–50.

—— *The Age of Manufactures, 1700–1820: Industry, Innovation and Work in Britain* (London, 1994; reprinted 1996).

Berry, Helen, 'Polite Consumption: Shopping in Eighteenth-century England', *Transactions of the RHS*, 12 (2002), pp. 375–94.

—— 'The Metropolitan Tastes of Judith Baker, Durham Gentlewoman', in *On the Town: Women and Urban Life in Eighteenth-century Britain*, ed. P. Lane and R. Sweet (Aldershot, 2003), pp. 131–55.

Black, Jeremy, *The English Press in the Eighteenth Century* (London and Sydney, 1987).

Bonell, John, *The Birth of Pandora and the Division of Knowledge* (London, 1992).

Borsay, Peter, *The English Urban Renaissance: Culture and Society in the Provincial Town, 1660–1770* (Oxford, 1989; reprinted 1991).

Brewer, John, 'This, That and the Other: Public, Social and Private in the Seventeenth and Eighteenth Centuries', in *Shifting the Boundaries: The Transformation of the Languages of Public and Private in the Eighteenth Century*, ed. D. Castiglione and L. Sharpe (Exeter, 1995), pp. 1–21.

Brodsky, Vivian, 'Widows in Late Elizabethan London: Remarriage, Economic Opportunity and Family Orientations', in *The World We Have Gained: Histories of Population and Social Structure*, ed. Lloyd Bonfield, Richard M. Smith and Keith Wrightson (Oxford, 1986), pp. 122–54.

Buck, Ann, *Dress in Eighteenth-century England* (London, 1979).

Cannadine, David 'British History: Past, Present and Future?', *Past and Present*, 116 (1987), pp. 131–72.

—— *Class in Britain* (London, 1998; reprinted 2000).

Casteras, S.P., 'Social Wrongs: The Painted Sermons of Richard Redgrave', in *Richard Redgrave, 1804–88*, ed. S.P. Casteras and Ronald Parkinson (New Haven, CT, 1988), pp. 9–28.

Chapman, Beatrice and Wallis, Mary, *The Status of Women under the English Law* (London, 1909).

Chapman, S.D., 'Fixed Capital Formation in the British Cotton Manufacturing

Industry', in *Aspects of Capital Investment in Great Britain, 1750–1850: A Preliminary Survey*, ed. J.P.P. Higgins and S. Pollard (London, 1971), pp. 57–107.

Clark, Alice, *The Working Life of Women in the Seventeenth Century* (London and New York, 1919; reprinted 1992).

Clark, Geoffrey, *Betting on Lives: The Culture of Life Insurance in England, 1695–1775* (Manchester, 1999).

Clery, E.J., 'Women, Publicity and the Coffee-house Myth', *Women: A Cultural Review*, 2 (1991), pp. 168–77.

Cockerell, H.A.L. and Green, Edwin, *The British Insurance Business: A Guide to its History and Records* (London, 1976).

Cohen, Michele, *Fashioning Masculinity: National Identity and Language in the Eighteenth Century* (London, 1996).

Colley, Linda, *Britons: Forging the Nation, 1707–1837* (London, 1992).

Copley, Stephen, 'Commerce, Conversation and Politeness in the Early Eighteenth-century Periodical', *British Journal for Eighteenth-Century Studies*, 18 (1995), pp. 66–7.

Corfield, Penelope J. *The Impact of English Towns, 1700–1800* (Oxford, 1982; reprinted 1989).

—— 'Defining Urban Work', in *Work in Towns, 850–1850*, ed. P.J. Corfield and D. Keene (Leicester, 1990), pp. 207–30.

—— 'Class by Name and Number in Eighteenth-century Britain', in idem (ed.), *Language, History and Class* (Oxford, 1991), pp. 101–30.

—— *Power and the Professions in Britain, 1700–1850* (London, 1995).

Cornish, W.R. and Clark, G. de N., *Law and Society in England, 1750–1950* (London, 1989).

Cotterell, Roger, *The Politics of Jurisprudence* (London, 1989).

Cummings, Edith Mae, *Pots, Pans and Millions: A Study of Woman's Right to be in Business* (Washington, 1929).

Davidoff, Leonore, 'Regarding Some "Old Husband's Tales": Public and Private in Feminist History', in idem, *Worlds Between: Historical Perspectives on Gender and Class* (London, 1995), pp. 227–76.

—— and Hall, Catherine, *Family Fortunes: Men and Women of the English Middle Class 1780–1850* (London, 1987).

Davis, Dorothy, *A History of Shopping* (London, 1966).

D'Cruze, Shani, '"To Acquaint the Ladies": Women Traders in Colchester, c.1750–c.1800', *Local Historian*, 17 (1986), pp. 158–61.

Deane, Phyllis and Mitchell, B.R., *Abstract of British Historical Statistics* (Cambridge, 1971).

Dicey, A.V., *Lectures on the Relation Between Law and Public Opinion in the Nineteenth Century* (London, 1905; reprinted 1917).

Dickson, P.G.M., *The Sun Insurance Office, 1710–1960: The History of Two and a Half Centuries of British Insurance* (Oxford, 1960).

—— *The Financial Revolution in England: A Study in the Development of Public Credit* (London, 1967).

Doggett, Maeve E., *Marriage, Wife-beating and the Law in Victorian England* (London, 1992).

Doherty, Francis, *A Study in Eighteenth-century Advertising Methods: The Anodyne Necklace* (Lampeter, 1992).

Donaghay, Marie, 'Textiles and the Anglo–French Commercial Treaty of 1786', *Textile History*, 13 (1982), pp. 205–24.

Donald, Diana, '"Mr Deputy Dumpling and Family": Satirical Images of the City Merchant in Eighteenth-century England', *Burlington Magazine*, 131 (1989), pp. 755–63.

Donnison, J. *Midwives and Medical Men: A History of Inter-professional Rivalries and Women's Rights* (London, 1977).

Drury, Linda J., 'The Baker Baker Portfolio of Prints: Its Content and Acquisition', *Durham County Local History Society Bulletin*, 56 (1996), pp. 3–20.

Earle, Peter, *The Making of the English Middle Class: Business, Society and Family Life in London, 1660–1730* (London, 1989).

—— 'The Female Labour Market in London in the Late Seventeenth and Early Eighteenth Centuries', *Economic History Review*, 2 ser., 42 (1989), pp. 328–53.

—— *A City Full of People: Men and Women of London, 1650–1750* (London, 1994).

Ellis, Markman, 'The Coffee-women, The *Spectator* and the Public Sphere in the Early Eighteenth Century', in *Women and the Public Sphere*, ed. E. Eger and C. Grant (Cambridge, 2001), pp. 27–52.

Erickson, Amy Louise, *Women and Property in Early Modern England* (London, 1993; reprinted 1995).

Finn, Margot, 'Debt and Credit in Bath's Court of Requests, 1829–39', *Urban History*, 21 (1994), pp. 211–36.

—— 'Women, Consumption and Coverture in England, c. 1760–1860', *The Historical Journal*, 3 (1996), pp. 703–22.

Flint, Kate, *The Victorian Novelist: Social Problems and Social Change* (London, 1987).

Folland, Angel Kwolek, *Incorporating Women: A History of Women and Business in the United States* (New York, 1998).

Formoy, R.R., *The Historical Foundations of Modern Company Law* (London, 1923).

Fryckstedt, Monica, *Elizabeth Gaskell's 'Mary Barton' and 'Ruth': A Challenge to Christian England* (Uppsala, 1982).

Gallagher, Catherine, *The Industrial Reformation of English Fiction: Social Discourse and Narrative Form, 1832–67* (London, 1985).

Gavigan, Shelley A.M., 'Law, Gender and Ideology', in *Legal Theory Meets Legal Practice*, ed. Anne F. Bayefsky (Edmonton, 1988), pp. 283–95.

George, Dorothy, *London Life in the Eighteenth Century* (1925; reprinted New York, 1965).

—— *Hogarth to Cruikshank: Social Change in Graphic Satire* (London, 1967).

Ginsburg, Madelaine, 'The Tailoring and Dressmaking Trades, 1700–1850', *Costume*, 6 (1972), pp. 64–71.

Gobetti, Daniela, *Private and Public: Individuals, Households and the Body Politic in Locke and Hutcheson* (London, 1991).

Goodman, Dena, 'Public Sphere and Private Life: Toward a Synthesis of Current Historiographical Approaches to the Old Regime', *History and Theory*, 31 (1992), pp. 1–20.

Green, David, *From Artisans to Paupers: Economic Change and Poverty in London, 1790–1870* (Aldershot, 1995).

—— 'Independent Women, Wealth and Wills in Nineteenth-century London', in *Urban Fortunes: Property and Inheritance in the Town, 1700–1900*, ed. John Stobart and Alistair Owens (Burlington, 2000), pp. 195–222.

Greenberg, Janelle, 'The Legal Status of the English Woman in Early Eighteenth-century Common Law and Equity', *Studies in Eighteenth-Century Culture*, 4 (1975), pp. 171–81.

Grey, Robert, 'The Languages of Factory Reform in Britain, c.1830–60', in *Historical Meanings of Work*, ed. Joyce, pp. 143–293.

Hall, Catherine, *White, Male and Middle Class: Explorations in Feminism and History* (Cambridge, 1992; reprinted 1995).

Harding, Vanessa, 'Reformation and Culture, 1540–1700', in *The Cambridge Urban History of Britain, Vol. 2: 1540–1840*, ed. Peter Clark (Cambridge, 2000), pp. 263–88.

Harley, D.N., 'Ignorant Midwives – a Persistent Stereotype', *Bulletin of the Society of the Social History of Medicine*, 28 (1981), pp. 6–9.

Harman, Claire, *Fanny Burney: A Biography* (London, 2000).

Harper, Charles G., *The Norwich Road: An East Anglian Highway* (London, 1901).

—— *Stage Coach and Mail in Days of Yore: A Picturesque History of the Coaching Age* (London, 1903).

Harris, Michael, *London Newspapers in the Age of Walpole: A Study of the Origins of the Modern English Press* (London, 1987).

Hart, Walter G., 'The Origin of Restraint upon Anticipation', *Law Quarterly Review*, 15 (1924), pp. 221–6.

Harvey, Charles, Green, Edmund and Corfield, Penelope J., *The Westminster Historical Database: Voters, Social Structure and Electoral Behaviour* (Bristol, 1998).

—— 'Continuity, Change, and Specialization within Metropolitan London: The Economy of Westminster, 1750–1820', *Economic History Review*, 52 (1999), pp. 469–93.

Hay, Douglas, 'The State and the Market in 1800: Lord Kenyon and Mr Waddington', *Past and Present*, 162 (1999), pp. 101–63.

Hill, Bridget, *Women, Work and Sexual Politics in Eighteenth-century England* (London, 1989; reprinted 1994).

—— 'Women's History: A Study in Change, Continuity or Standing Still?', *Women's History Review*, 2 (1993), pp. 5–19.

Himmelfarb, Gertrude, *The Idea of Poverty in the Early Industrial Age* (New York, 1983).

Holcombe, Lee, *Wives and Property: Reform of the Married Women's Property Law in Nineteenth-century England* (Toronto, 1983).

Holderness, B.A., 'Credit in a Rural Community, 1660–1800', *Midland History*, 3 (1975), pp. 94–115.

Holdsworth, William, *A History of the English Law* (London, 1903; reprinted 1923).

—— *Sources and Literature of English Law* (Oxford, 1925).

—— *Some Makers of the English Law* (Cambridge, 1958).

Honeyman, Katrina, *Women, Gender and Industrialisation in England, 1700–1870* (Basingstoke and London, 2000).

—— and Goodman, Jordan, 'Women's Work, Gender Conflict, and Labour Markets in Europe, 1500–1900', *Economic History Review*, 44 (1991), pp. 608–28.

Hoppit, Julian, 'The Use and Abuse of Credit in Eighteenth-century England', in *Business Life and Public Policy*, ed. N. McKendrick and R.B. Outhwaite (Cambridge, 1986), pp. 64–78.

—— *Risk and Failure in English Business, 1700–1850* (Cambridge, 1987).

Horwitz, Henry, *A Guide to Chancery Equity Records and Proceedings, 1600–1800* (London, 1995; reprinted 1998).

Howell, Martha C., 'Women, the Family Economy, and the Structures of Market Production in Cities of Northern Europe during the Late Middle Ages', in *Women and Work in Preindustrial Europe*, ed. Barbara Hanawalt (Bloomington, 1986), pp. 198–222.

Howell, Sarah and Humphries, Jane, 'Women's Labour Force Participation and the Transition to the Male Breadwinner Family', *Economic History Review*, 48 (1995), pp. 89–117.

Hudson, Derek and Luckhurst, K.W., *The Royal Society of Arts, 1754–1954* (London, 1954).

Hudson, Pat, *The Industrial Revolution* (London, 1992).

Hufton, Olwen, 'Women Without Men: Widows and Spinsters in Britain and France in the Eighteenth Century', *Journal of Family History*, 9 (1984), pp. 355–67.

—— *The Prospect Before Her: A History of Women in Western Europe 1500–1800* (London, 1995; reprinted 1997).

Hunt, Margaret, 'Hawkers, Bawlers, and Mercuries: Women and the London Press in the Early Enlightenment', in *Women and the Enlightenment*, ed. M. Hunt (New York, 1984).

—— 'Time Management, Writing and Accounting in the Eighteenth-century English Trading Family: A Bourgeois Enlightenment', *Business and Economic History*, 2 ser., 18 (1989), pp. 150–9.

—— 'Wife Beating, Domesticity and Women's Independence in Eighteenth-century London', *Gender and History*, 4 (1992), pp. 10–33.

—— *The Middling Sort: Commerce, Gender and the Family in England 1680–1780* (Berkeley and London, 1996).

Jenkins, D.T., 'The Practice of Insurance Against Fire, 1750–1840, and Historical Research', in *The Historian and the Business of Insurance*, ed. O.M. Westall (Manchester, 1984), pp. 9–38.

Jones, Vivien, *Women in the Eighteenth Century* (London, 1990).

Kent, David A., 'Small Businessmen and their Credit Transactions in Early Nineteenth-century Britain', *Business History*, 36 (1994), pp. 47–64.

Kerber, Linda, 'Separate Spheres, Female Worlds, Woman's Place: The Rhetoric of Women's History', *Journal of American History*, 75 (1988), pp. 9–39.

—— *et al.*, 'Beyond Roles, Beyond Spheres: Thinking about Gender in the Early Republic', *William and Mary Quarterly*, 46 (1989), pp. 565–85.

Klein, Lawrence, 'Politeness for Plebes: Consumption and Social Identity in Early Eighteenth-century England', in *The Consumption of Culture 1600–1800: Image, Object, Text*, ed. A. Bermingham and J. Brewer (London, 1995), pp. 362–82.

—— 'Gender and the Public/Private Distinction in the Eighteenth Century: Some Questions About Evidence and Procedure', *Eighteenth Century Studies*, 29 (1995), pp. 97–109.

Kowaleski, Maryanne, 'Women's Work in a Market Town: Exeter in the Late Fourteenth Century', in *Women and Work in Preindustrial Europe*, ed. B. Hanawalt, pp. 145–64.

Kowaleski-Wallace, Elizabeth, *Consuming Subjects: Women, Shopping and Business in the Eighteenth Century* (New York, 1997).

Lacey, Kay E., 'Women and Work in Fourteenth- and Fifteenth-Century London', in *Women and Work in Pre-Industrial England*, ed. L. Charles and L. Duffin (London, 1985), pp. 24–82.

Lane, Penelope, 'An Industrialising Town: Social and Business Networks in Hinckley, Leicestershire, c.1750–1839', in *Industrial Change in the Midlands, 1700–1840*, ed. P. Lane and J. Stobart (Leicester, 2000), pp. 139–66.

—— 'Women, Property and Inheritance: Wealth Creation and Income Generation in Small English Towns, 1750–1835', in *Urban Fortunes*, ed. J. Stobart and A. Owens (Aldershot, 2000), pp. 172–94.

Langford, Paul, *A Polite and Commercial People: England 1727–83* (Oxford, 1989).

—— *Public Life and the Propertied Englishman, 1689–1798* (Oxford, 1991).

Lemire, Beverly, *Dress, Culture and Commerce: The English Clothing Trade before the Factory, 1660–1800* (Basingstoke, 1997).

Liddington, Jill, *Female Fortune: Land, Gender and Authority. The Anne Lister Diaries and Other Writings, 1833–6* (London, 1998).

Lieberman, David, *The Province of Legislation Determined: Legal Theory in Eighteenth-century Britain* (Cambridge, 1989).

Lown, Judy, *Women and Industrialisation: Gender at Work in Nineteenth-century England* (Oxford, 1990).

MacDonagh, Oliver, *Early Victorian Government, 1830–70* (New York, 1977).

McKendrick, Neil, 'Home Demand and Economic Growth: A New View of Women and Children in the Industrial Revolution', in idem (ed.), *Historical Perspectives: Studies in English Thought and Society* (London, 1974), pp. 152–210.

—— Brewer, John and Plumb, J.H., *The Birth of a Consumer Society: The Commercialisation of Eighteenth-century England* (London, 1982).

McVeagh, John, *Tradeful Merchants: The Portrayal of the Capitalist in Literature* (London, 1981).

Mandell, Laura, *Misogynous Economies: The Business of Literature in Eighteenth-century Britain* (Lexington, 1999).

Mercer, Alex, *Disease, Mortality and Population in Transition* (London, 1990).

Midgley, Claire, *Women Against Slavery: The British Campaigns, 1780–1870* (London, 1992).

Mui, H.C. and Mui, L.H., *Shops and Shopkeeping in Eighteenth-century England* (London, 1989).

Muldrew, Craig, *The Economy of Obligation: The Culture of Credit and Social Relations in Early Modern England* (Basingstoke, 1998).

Neff, W.F., *Victorian Working Women: An Historical and Literary Study of Women in British Industries and Professions, 1832–1850* (New York, 1929).

Newman, Gerald, *The Rise of English Nationalism, 1740–1830* (London, 1987).

Ogden, C.K., *Bentham's Theory of Fictions* (London, 1932).

Okin, Susan Moller, 'Feminism, the Individual and Contract Theory', *Ethics*, 100 (1990), pp. 658–99.

Oldham, James, *The Mansfield Manuscripts and the Growth of English Law in the Eighteenth Century* (London, 1992).

Olivier, Pierre J.J., *Legal Fictions in Practice and Legal Science* (Rotterdam, 1975).

Pateman, Carol, *The Sexual Contract* (Oxford, 1988; reprinted 1989).

Pelling, Margaret, 'Medical Practice in Early Modern England: Trade or Profession?', ed. W. Prest (New York, 1987), pp. 90–128.

Percival, Alicia C., 'Women and the Society of Arts in its Early Days', *Journal of the Royal Society of Arts*, 125 (1977), Part 1, pp. 266–9; Part 2, pp. 330–3.

Peterson, M. Jeanne, 'No Angels in the House: The Victorian Myth and the Paget Women', *American Historical Review*, 89 (1984), pp. 677–708.

Pinchbeck, Ivy, *Women Workers and The Industrial Revolution, 1750–1850* (1930; reprinted London, 1981).

Poovey, Mary, *The Proper Lady and the Woman Writer: Ideology as Style in the Works of Mary Woollstonecraft, Mary Shelley and Jane Austen* (London, 1984).

—— *Uneven Developments: The Ideological Work of Gender in Mid-Victorian Britain* (London, 1988).

—— *Making a Social Body: British Cultural Formation, 1830–1864* (London, 1995).

Porter, Roy, *Health for Sale: Quacks and Quackery in England 1660–1850* (Manchester, 1989).

Prest, W.R., 'Law and Women's Rights in Early Modern England', *Seventeenth Century*, 6 (1991), pp. 169–87.

Prior, Mary, 'Women and the Urban Economy: Oxford, 1500–1800', in *Women in English Society, 1500–1800*, ed. M. Prior (1985), pp. 93–117.

Raven, James, *Judging New Wealth: Popular Publishing and Responses to Commerce in England, 1750–1800* (Oxford, 1992).

Rendall, Jane, *Women in an Industrializing Society: England, 1750–1880* (Oxford, 1990).

—— 'Women and the Public Sphere', *Gender and History*, 2 (1999), pp. 475–88.

Richards, Eric, 'Women in the British Economy since about 1700: An Interpretation', *History*, 59 (1974), pp. 337–57.

Roberts, H.E., 'Marriage, Redundancy or Sin: The Painter's View of Women in the First Twenty Five Years of Victoria's Reign', in *Suffer and Be Still*, ed. Martha Vicinus (1972), pp. 45–76.

Rogers, Helen, '"The Good are Not Always Powerful, Nor the Powerful Always Good": The Politics of Women's Needlework in Mid-Victorian London', *Victorian Studies*, 40 (1997), pp. 589–623.

Rose, Sonya O., *Limited Livelihoods: Gender and Class in Nineteenth-century England* (Berkeley, 1992).

Sanderson, Elizabeth C., 'The Edinburgh Milliners, 1720–1820', *Costume*, 20 (1986), pp. 18–28.

—— *Women and Work in Eighteenth-century Edinburgh* (New York, 1996).

Saville, John, 'Sleeping Partnership and Limited Liability, 1850–56', *Economic History Review*, 2 ser., 8 (1956), pp. 418–33.

Schwarz, L.D., *London in the Age of Industrialisation: Entrepreneurs, Labour Force and Living Conditions, 1700–1850* (Cambridge, 1992).

—— 'Residential Leisure Towns in England towards the End of the Eighteenth-century', *Urban History*, 27 (2000), pp. 51–61.

—— and Jones, L.J., 'Wealth, Occupations, and Insurance in the Late Eighteenth Century: The Policy Registers of the Sun Fire Office', *Economic History Review*, 36 (1983), pp. 365–73.

Schnorrenberg, B.B., 'Is Childbirth any Place for a Woman? The Decline of Midwifery in Eighteenth-century England', *Studies in Eighteenth-Century Culture*, 10 (London, 1981), pp. 393–408.

Scott, Joan, *Gender and the Politics of History* (New York, 1988).

Sekora, John, *Luxury: The Concept in Western Thought, Eden to Smollet* (London, 1977).

Sharpe, Pamela, 'Continuity and Change: Women's History and Economic History in Britain', *Economic History Review*, 48 (1995), pp. 353–69.

—— *Adapting to Capitalism: Working Women in the English Economy, 1700–1850* (London, 1996).

Shepard, Alexandra, 'Manhood, Credit and Patriarchy in Early Modern England c. 1580–1640', *Past & Present*, 167 (2000), pp. 75–106.

Shevelow, Kathryn, *Women and Print Culture: The Construction of Femininity in the Early Periodical* (London, 1989).

Shoemaker, Robert, *Gender in English Society, 1650–1850: The Emergence of Separate Spheres?* (London, 1998).

Simonton, Deborah, *A History of European Women's Work, 1700 to the Present* (London and New York, 1998).

Skedd, Susan, 'Women Teachers and the Expansion of Girl's Schooling in England, 1760–1820', in *Gender in Eighteenth-Century England*, ed. H. Barker and E. Chalus, pp. 101–25.

Smith, Sheilah M., 'Blue Books and Victorian Novelists', *Review of English Studies*, 21 (1970).

—— *The Other Nation: The Poor in English Novels of the 1840s and 1850s* (Oxford, 1980).

Staves, Susan, *Married Women's Separate Property in England, 1660–1833* (London, 1990).

—— 'Investments, Votes and "Bribes": Women as Shareholders in the Chartered National Companies', in *Women Writers and the Early Modern British Political Tradition*, ed. Hilda Smith (Cambridge, 1998), pp. 259–78.

Stopes, Charlotte Carmichael, *British Freewomen* (London, 1907).

Stretton, Tim, *Women Waging Law in Elizabethan England* (Cambridge, 1998).

Styles, John, 'Clothing the North: The Supply of Non-elite Clothing in the Eighteenth-century North of England', *Textile History*, 25 (1994), pp. 139–66.

Swan, Beth, *Fictions of the Law: An Investigation of the Law in Eighteenth-century English Fiction* (Frankfurt, 1997).

Tadmor, Naomi, '"Family" and "Friend" in *Pamela*: A Case-study in the History of Family in Eighteenth-century England', *Social History*, 14 (1989), pp. 289–306.

—— *Family & Friends in Eighteenth-century England: Household, Kinship and Patronage* (Cambridge, 2001).

Tague, Ingrid, *Women of Quality: Accepting and Contesting Ideals of Femininity in England, 1690–1760* (Woodbridge, 2002).

Thomas, Janet, 'Women and Capitalism: Oppression or Emancipation? A Review Article', *Comparative Studies in Society and History*, 30 (1990), pp. 535–49.

Tilly, Louise A. and Scott, Joan W., *Women, Work and Family* (London, 1978; reprinted 1987).

Todd, Barbara, '"To Be Some Body": Married Women and the *Hardships of the English Laws*', in *Women Writers*, ed. H. Smith, pp. 343–61.

Tosh, John, *A Man's Place: Masculinity and the Middle-class Home in Victorian England* (London, 1999).

Trebilcock, Clive, *Phoenix Insurance and the Development of British Insurance, 1782–1879* (Cambridge, 1985).

Turner, J.G., '"News From the New Exchange": Commodity, Erotic Fantasy and the Female Entrepreneur', in *The Consumption of Culture, 1600–1800*, ed. Ann Bermingham and John Brewer (London, 1995), pp. 419–39.

Valenze, Deborah, *The First Industrial Woman* (Oxford, 1995).

Vickery, Amanda, 'Golden Age to Separate Spheres? A Review of the Categories and Chronology of English Women's History', *Historical Journal*, 36 (1993), pp. 383–414.

—— *The Gentleman's Daughter: Women's Lives in Georgian England* (New Haven and London, 1998).

Viseltear, Arthur J., 'Joanna Stephens and the Eighteenth Century Lithontriptics: A Misplaced Chapter in the History of Therapeutics', *Bulletin of the History of Medicine*, 42 (1968), pp. 199–220.

Wahrman, Dror, *Imagining the Middle Class: The Political Representation of Class in Britain, c.1780–1840* (Cambridge, 1995).

Walby, Sylvia, *Patriarchy at Work: Patriarchal and Capitalist Relations in Employment* (Minneapolis, 1986).

Walker, R.B. 'Advertising in London Newspapers, 1650–1750', *Business History*, 15 (1973), pp. 112–30.

Walsh, Claire, 'The Advertising of Consumer Goods in Eighteenth-century London', in *Advertising and the European City: Historical Perspectives*, ed. C. Wischermann and E. Shore (Aldershot, 2000).

Weatherill, Lorna, 'A Possession of One's Own: Women and Consumer Behaviour in England, 1660–1740', *Journal of British Studies*, 25 (1986), pp. 131–56.

Wilson, Adrian, 'Ignorant Midwives, a Rejoinder', *Bulletin of the Society of the Social History of Medicine*, 32 (1983), pp. 46–9.

—— *The Making of Man Midwifery: Childbirth in England, 1660–1770* (London, 1995).

Wood, Henry Truman, *A History of the Royal Society of Arts* (London, 1913).

Wright, Susan, 'Holding Up Half the Sky: Women and their Occupations in Eighteenth-century Ludlow', *Midland History*, 14 (1989), pp. 53–74.

Wrightson, K. and Levine, D., *The Making of an Industrial Society: Wickham, 1560–1765* (Oxford, 1991).

Wyman, A.L., 'The Surgeoness: The Female Practitioner of Surgery, 1400–1800', *Medical History*, 28 (1984).

Yeager, Mary A., 'Review of Angel Kwolek-Folland, *Incorporating Women: A History of Women and Business in the United States*', H-Business, H-Net Reviews, April, 1999. URL: http://www.h-net.msu.edu/reviews/showrev.cgi?path=30313927576847.

Zemon Davies, Natalie, 'Women and Crafts in Sixteenth-century Lyon', in *Women and Work in Preindustrial Europe*, ed. B. Hanawalt (Bloomington, 1986), pp 167–97.

Unpublished papers, theses and dissertations

Allen, D.G.C., 'The Society for the Encouragement of Arts, Manufactures and Commerce: Organisation, Membership and Objectives in the First Three Decades, 1755–84. An Example of Voluntary Economic and Social Policy in the Eighteenth Century' (unpub. Ph.D. thesis, University of London, 1979).

Barnett, David, 'The Structure of Industry in London' (unpub. Ph.D. thesis, University of Nottingham, 1996).

Harris, Beth, '"The Works of Women are Symbolical": The Victorian Seamstress in the 1840s' (unpub. Ph.D. thesis, City University of New York, 1997).

Hunt, Margaret, 'Women and Money: Female Litigants in Equity in Eighteenth-century England' (unpub. paper presented at the PRO, 1999).

Pullin (Phillips), Nicola, '"This Publick Method": Women, Advertising and the Discourse of Legitimacy in Eighteenth-century London Trade' (unpub. MA thesis, Royal Holloway, University of London, 1997).

—— '"Business is Just Life": The Practice, Prescripton and Legal Position of Women in Business, 1700–1850' (Ph.D. thesis, Royal Holloway, University of London, 2001).

Wiskin, Christine, 'Women, Finance and Credit in England, c. 1780–1826' (unpub. Ph.D. thesis, University of Warwick, 2000).

Index

Printed and bound by CPI Group (UK) Ltd, Croydon, CR0 4YY

23/04/2025

14661041-0005